A Social History of Sexual Relations in Iran

Willem Floor

MAGE
PUBLISHERS

Library of Congress Cataloging-in-Publication Data

Floor, Willem M.
A social history of sexual relations in Iran / Willem Floor.
p. cm.
Includes bibliographical references and index.
ISBN 978-1-933823-33-1 (pbk. : alk. paper)
1. Sex--Iran--History. 2. Sex customs--Iran--History. I. Title.
HQ18.I7F66 2009
306.70955--dc22

2008030903

ISBN
1-933823-33-X
978-1-933823-33-1

Printed and Manufactured in the United States

Mage books are available at bookstores,
through the internet, or directly from the publisher:
Mage Publishers, 1032 29th Street, NW, Washington, DC 20007
202-342-1642 • as@mage.com • 800-962-0922
visit Mage Publishers online at
www.mage.com

CONTENTS

FIGURES

TABLES

Selfishness is not living as one wishes to live.
It is asking others to live as one wishes to live.
OSCAR WILDE

There is as much difference between us and
ourselves as between us and others.
MONTAIGNE

PREFACE

When in July 2007, I went to pick up my latest printed book from Mage Publishers and handed in the CD with the text of a new book, Mohammad Batmanglij jokingly said to me: 'Why don't you write something more sexy so we can have a bestseller?' I equally jokingly replied: 'sure, I will (note: not can) try and do that. What about a book on sexual relations in Iran; wouldn't that be of interest to a larger public?' As he thought that this might be a good subject for my next book (he's not so sure now), I decided to do so, especially, since, at that time, I knew little about the subject, which is usually a good reason for me to undertake the necessary research, learn something new and write a new book or article. Moreover, I was surprised, when trying to collect information about this subject that relatively very little had been written about it. Given that sex, after eating and drinking, is humankind's most powerful urge, as well as the fact that discussing sexual matters was not a taboo subject in Iran,[1] one would expect that one or more books detailing relations between the sexes over the centuries would already have been written. However, this is

---

1. "Sex is also a constant subject of dreaming, of preoccupation, of conversation. In conversations among men, among women, and even between men and women, it is discussed without shame: jokes, sexual boasting, questioning others' sexuality, fear for one's sexuality, erotic stimulation, utilization with the aim of seduction, and so forth." Paul Vieille, "Iranian Women in Family Alliance and Sexual Politics," in Lois Beck and Nikki Keddie eds. *Women in the Muslim World* (Cambridge, 1978), p. 461; see also J. E. Polak, "Die Prostitution in Persien", *Wiener Medicinische Wochenschrift* 32 (1861), p. 563; Kaveh Safa-Isfahani, "Female-Centered World Views in Iranian Culture: Symbolic Representations of Sexuality in Dramatic Games," *Signs* 6/1 (1980), pp. 33–53. It also formed part of public songs and ditties. D.C. Phillot, "Some Lullabies and Topical Songs Collected in Persia," *Journal of the Asiatic Society of Bengal*, March 1906, pp. 42-53. "I was told by Dr. Mirza Huseyn Khan Persian children are taught such expressions as are unpublishable upon their mother's lap, and made to repeat them in the presence of the father. 'Listen,' the fond mother will say to her husband, 'how prettily the little soul says ...'!" Wilfrid Sparrow, *Persian Children of the Royal Family* (London-New York, 1902), p. 205.

not the case. For although Ravandi devotes a major part of volume seven of his *Social History of Iran* to the subject his treatment remains limited in scope. In addition, fortunately, there are a number of excellent studies dealing with a particular era or topic, but there is no study that covers the full array of sexual relations throughout the ages as this book does.

Although women figure prominently in this book, this is not a study about the status of women, but rather one about the various forms of sexual relationships between men and women and their consequences. Most of the available information concerns the upper classes. Much less is known about the situation between ordinary men and women, i.e. 95 percent of the population, unless it concerns subjects such as temporary marriage and prostitution. In that case the common people, or rather lower class women, were and still are the main *dramatis personae* as they are the service providers. However, such information is not provided by them, but also originates from members of the elite, whether local or foreign. Some of the information applies to all layers of society, of course, such as the formal rules governing marriage, although that information was not always understood by the common people.

Another problem is the male-centered nature of the sources, which therefore reflects the patriarchal, i.e. male dominated nature of society. Hence most information about sexual relations is about men and their needs and problems. When women are mentioned it is almost invariably as the object of male desire and frustration. It is rare that the sexual needs of women are touched upon, let alone expressed, as sources written by female authors are rare and they mostly were upholders of male dominated society. Both these 'defects', i.e. the elite- and male-centered nature of sources makes it difficult to paint a balanced picture of the sexual relationship between men and women and between men and men and women and women in Iran, but one has to work with the bricks that are available.

Some readers understandably would have liked to know whether the situation described in Iran differed much, somewhat or not at all from that in other countries and eras. To have done so would have made this book a very bulky one and, therefore, let it suffice to say that, in my opinion, sexual relations in Iran did not differ that much from those in other culture areas, whether in Asia or Europe. However, this is not a comparative study and, therefore, the reader should not draw the conclusion that I render judgment in one way or another on how sexual relations in Iran were and have developed over time. The sole purpose of this study is to provide the reader with a balanced view of sexual relations in Iran as they present themselves in the sources. These sources, as pointed out above, have their own problems (elite- and male-centered, foreign observers), but I have tried to allow for all these biases and to present a picture that is as close as possible to reality.

A seventeenth century English visitor to Iran, the merchant John Cartwright, correctly characterized the range of options for sexual relations between a man and a woman as follows: "To sensuality they are much inclined, having three sorts of women, as they terme them, *viz.* honest women, halfe honest women and courtesans; and yet they chastise no offence with like extremity as adultery, and that as well in the halfe honest women, as in the honest."[2] There were and are indeed three options for sexual relations between a man and a woman: covenanted marriage or *nikah*, temporary marriage or *mut'ah*, and prostitution or *ruspigari*. Only the first two were and are legal, and only the first and third options were and are widely practiced. All three options are discussed, respectively in chapter one, two and three. In chapter four the prevalence and the nature of homosexual relations are discussed; what religion had to say about it and how society actually behaved. The last chapter deals with the issue of sexually transmitted diseases, which are the result of sexual contacts and which, at one time, were rampant in Iran. Nowadays, AIDS also has made inroads into Iranian society, which like other societies elsewhere in the world has to find the appropriate response to this problem. This chapter has appeared first as "Venereal Disease in Iran (1855-2005): A Public

---

2. John Cartwright, *The Preacher's Travels* (London, 1611), p. 735.

Affair," *Comparative Studies of South Asia, Africa and the Middle East* 26/2 (2006), pages 260–78 and appears here with the permission of the editor of the said Journal.

Although writing is a lonely activity I was fortunate that a few people—Irene Schneider (Göttingen), Ali Gheissari (San Diego), Hannie Meulenbeld (Bedum), Janet Afary (Purdue), and Hasan Javadi (Washington DC)—were willing to cast a critical eye at the final draft of this text so that I might have the benefit of their doubts. I am very grateful to all of them and I hope that they agree with me that the end result is a better product. Last, but most certainly not least, I thank Keith Openshaw for having read the entire text twice and having made the necessary editorial and stylistic changes, which indeed has made this a better work.

CHAPTER ONE

MARRIAGE IN IRAN: A FAMILY AFFAIR

MARRIAGE IN IRAN:
A FAMILY AFFAIR

*There seems to have been and there still are in Persia
two types of marriage, one that was and is a covenanted
marriage and the other a contracted marriage.*

Bassett, *Persia, The Land of the Imams* [1]

In this chapter I discuss the formal rules governing covenanted or permanent marriage and marital relationship, such as those that existed in Imperial Iran and Islamic Iran, as well as the notions about how husband and wife should and did behave towards each other.

IMPERIAL IRAN

ACHAEMENID PERIOD (559–330 BCE)

Since the Persian Empire was large and encompassed many peoples, cultures and religions that practiced their own marriage customs, it is difficult to draw a picture of all the types of marriages that prevailed during that period, leaving aside the fact that there is a dearth of information. Apart from Zoroastrians, the Empire encompassed

---

1. (New York: Charles Scribner's Sons, 1886), p. 288

Christians, Jews, and a large variety of polytheists, each having their own marriage customs. As to the Zoroastrians, the dominant religion in Iran proper, basically they knew two types of marriages: first, the covenanted marriage (*zanih i zan patixshayiha*) and second, marriage by proxy (*sturih*). In case of covenanted marriage the husband acquired the guardianship over his wife. In doing so, she became the mistress of his house. Children born from this union were legitimate. Together they formed a patriarchal agnatic family; that is a kinship that is traceable exclusively through the male line. The wife and her children were entitled to maintenance during his lifetime and to inherit the property after his death. The marriage required the authorization of the father or guardian of the bride, the bride's consent, as well as a marriage contract (*payman i zanih*). It was customary to give the bride a dowry.

The most meritorious type of marriage was the so-called 'next of kin' union (*xwedodah*), described in the *Denkard* as the "union of father and daughter, son and mother, brother and sister." This type of consanguineous (same blood) marriage was originally practiced by the nobility and later allegedly also by commoners. It is doubtful whether the next of kin marriage was much practiced in Iran prior to and even during the Sasanian period as only a few cases are known for the Achaemenid period, although it was practiced by Parthian and Sasanian royalty.[2] The covenanted marriage could be temporary, for a mutually agreed period. Upon termination of the stipulated period, the wife's dowry and private belongings reverted to her, but, if she had died, her property belonged to the husband.

Also, there were a few irregular types of marriages, about whose legality jurists held different opinions. It occurred, for example, when the father did not give his daughter in marriage and she choose to do so herself. In that case she took herself a guardian without the father's sanction and married him. Another irregular type of marriage was

---

2. Herodotus, *History*, III.25-27; Maria Brosius, *Women in Ancient Persia* (Oxford, 1996), pp. 66-67.

when the daughter, upon coming of age, simply rejected the father's candidate, and married a man of her choice.

The second type of recognized Zoroastrian marriage was *sturih*. The 'Letter of Tansar' describes this marriage as follows: "When a man dies without a male issue, his widow, if he has left one, was given in marriage to one of his closest next of kin. If he has no wife, but a daughter, the same was done. If there were neither of these two, they would provide a woman from the dead man's property and give her to his nearest kinsmen, and every son who was born they assigned to the man who had left the legacy." This substitute man or woman is called *stur*. In case of natural (*butak*) *stur*, such as when the man's daughter or his widow was selected as such, they entered into a so-called *chakar* or levirate marriage with one of deceased's agnates. Male issue was indispensable to salvation, for a person without a son was unable to cross the bridge to the next world. *Sturih* marriage was therefore a religious obligation, for it helped Ohrmazd, the Zoroastrian supreme deity, to attain the restoration of the world. In the Sasanian caste system the *stur* and deceased were to be of similar social class, wealth, and standing. Once a son had been born, the *sturih* marriage, though not the guardianship over the woman, could be terminated without divorce. *Sturih* was not limited to a single person, the widow, sister, daughter, or brother of the deceased; rather, both parties to the marriage or even several couples.

Again, there was concubinage, when, for example, a widow [with child] took to herself a bedfellow (*gadar* "fornicator") and cohabited with him under his guardianship. It was specified that the woman seeking such cohabitation should be without a guardian and free from the obligation of *sturih*, but the bedfellow was by duty bound to maintain her and her children until they came of age.

Although in Bactria (Central Asia) polyandry was practiced, the marriage contract reflected the arrangements of Zoroastrian covenanted marriage. However, there were significant differences. For example, women could initiate divorce proceedings, without forfeiting the right to their dowry, which was unthinkable in Sassanid law.[3] In Babylo-nia, marriage was concluded by a contract between the husband and members of the bride's family. The contract stipulated the terms of the dowry and other gifts as well as the husband's pledge that when he decided to take a second wife, he would give the first wife a specified sum of money. Moreover, she had the right to return to her family. In the case of wife's adultery punishment normally was death.[4]

Under the Achaemenid dynasty the kings and male members of the elite had both covenanted wives and concubines. Polygyny was an ancient privilege of the aristocracy and religious leaders. The number of wives was a reflection of wealth and dignity and tended to increase with the person's socio-political standing. According to Herodotus, "Every man has a number of wives (*gynaikes*) and a much greater number of concubines (*pallakai*)."[5] It was and still is, of course, im-possible for every man to have more than one wife given the gender distribution of the population. The reference by Herodotus to "every man," therefore, must refer to important and wealthy men, just like the same logic and reality applied to this situation in later centuries, for polygyny could only be practiced by a limited number of wealthy men. The covenanted wives, who were to bear legitimate off-spring, were first in the line of succession, while the *pallakai* or concubines were to carouse with and for pleasure. Therefore at parties the cov-enanted wives were absent; the only women present were the con-cubines and music-girls.[6] However, according to Herodotus, visiting

---

3. The description of Zoroastrian marriage is based on [http://www.cais-soas.com/CAIS/Law/family_law.htm]; Faraxvmart i Vahraman, *The Book of a Thousand Judgements (A Sasanian Law-Book)*, transcribed and translated from Pahlavi into Russian by Anahit Perikhian; translated into English by Nina Garsoïan (Costa Mesa, 1997); Ilya Yakubovich, "Marriage Contract," *Encyclopedia Iranica*, which also reproduces the texts of various marriage contracts; N. Pigulevskaia, *Les Villes de l'Etat Iranien aux epoques Parthe et Sassanide* (The Hague-Paris, 1963), pp. 138-41; and Christian Bartholomae, *Die Frau im sasanidischen Recht* (Heidelberg, 1924).

4. [http://www.cais-soas.com/CAIS/Women/women_ancient_iran.htm]

5. Herodotus, *Histories*, I.135.

6. Pierre Briant, *From Cyrus to Alexander. A History of the Persian Empire* (Winona Lake, 2002), p. 277.

Persian dignitaries told their Paeonian hosts that "It is our custom in Persia to get our wives and mistresses to come and sit with us in the dining-room." In fact, the women then most likely were the object of the men's amorous attentions, what later Persian poets referred to as *bus va kenar* (kissing and embracing).[7]

As in later centuries, vanquished rulers whose daughters were demanded for the king's women's quarters insisted that these would be accepted as covenanted wives rather than as concubines, as a sign of respect.[8] Such treatment of respect was not given to daughters of the vanquished king's subjects, for most concubines were captives of war, who had been enslaved after the conquest of a town or country. Not all concubines were bedded, for many if not most were put to work as domestic servants at court or in the mansions of the wealthy.[9] Atossa, the daughter of Cyrus the Great and one of the wives of Darius I, allegedly told her husband: "I should like to have Spartan girls, and girls from Argos and Attica and Corinth, to wait upon me."[10]

There were also other methods to provide the king with fresh nubile girls, such as the one related in the Bible, viz. by having a royal commission scour the realm for beautiful girls.

> Let beautiful girls be selected for the king. Let the king appoint commissioners throughout the provinces of this realm to bring all these beautiful young virgins to the citadel of Susa (Esther 2: 2-3).

7. Herodotus, *Histories*, V.17. It is, of course, possible that the Persians made this remark mendaciously to the Paeonians (Macedonians), whose custom it was that men and women were kept separate, to have them change their mind and allow their women to sit after dinner together with the Persians, which was what happened. The Persians, "who were very drunk, began to touch their breasts, and even, in some cases, to try to kiss them." However, if that had been the objective of the Persians then it would have been too good a story for Herodotus to ignore.

8. Briant, *From Cyrus*, pp. 277-78; Herodotus, *Histories*, III.3-4.

9. Herodotus, *Histories*, VI. 19, 32, 76; IX. 76; Briant, *From Cyrus*, p. 279.

10. Herodotus, *Histories*, III.134; for some of his other wives see Ibid., III.88.

This method, as is shown in what follows, would also be used by later kings in the realm of Iran. Similarly, as in later centuries, parents, without being prodded, would send exceptionally beautiful daughters to court in the hope that they be accepted as concubines. A similar method was also used to provide women to the Babylonians, who had risen up against Darius and, to make their food supplies last longer, had strangled all their womenfolk, with the exception of their mothers. After Darius had retaken Babylon, "to prevent the race from dying out, [he] compelled the neighboring peoples each to send a certain stated number of women to Babylon."[11]

The kings' concubines were all selected for their looks and they had both to be virgins and beautiful. What was beauty, according to Achaemenid males? We really do not know, but an inference may be obtained from religious texts such as the Avesta and the Hadoakht Nask, where Anahita and Daine are described as tall and powerful women with prominent breasts, white arms, stylishly dressed, well made up, and bejeweled.[12]

As the Achamaenian kings had many women, allegedly 360, - a figure of magical or symbolical significance, - how did they choose their bed partner? According to Diodorus, "Each night [the concubines] paraded round the couch of the king so that he might select the one with whom he would lie that night."[13] The women came well primed. First they had to be prepared for months before they were presented to the king, having been washed, perfumed, shampooed, and decked out in costly finery and jewels. The women came in the evening and the selected one left in the morning and unless the king asked for her specifically, as happened with Esther, she would have to take part in the rotation again. Briant has rightly questioned whether this elaborate system of rotation is not an invention by Greek authors to allow for the 'management' of the equally invented number of 360 women (one for each day of the year). He convincingly argues that

---

11. Herodotus, *Histories*, III.157.
12. Djalal Khaleghi-Motlagh, "Erotic literature," *Encyclopaedia Iranica*.
13. Briant, *From Cyrus*, p. 282.

there probably were less concubines and that the rotation probably is an embellishment of Herodotus observation that "In Persia a man's wives share his bed in rotation."[14]

It is believed that the king and other members of the elite also had harems, complete with covenanted wives, concubines and eunuchs. There indeed were eunuchs and apartments reserved for the women that were separate from those of the men. It would seem that normally they lived together in one building, because Phaidime, the daughter of Otanes and wife of the false usurper Smerdis (d. 522 BCE), wrote to her father that: "I have no means of speaking to Atossa, nor of seeing any other of the king's wives; for as soon as this man [Smerdis], whoever he may be, came to the throne, he separated us and gave us each a different room."[15] In general, it seems that women lived in separate female quarters, because Herodotus also reported that "before the age of five a boy lives with the women and never sees his father."[16] Whether women all lived a cloistered life as in the harems in Islamic times is questionable, although Greek authors go at great lengths to argue that "the Persians especially, are extremely jealous, severe, and suspicious about their women, not only their wedded wives, but also their bought slaves and concubines, whom they keep so strictly that no one sees them abroad; they spend their lives within doors, and when they take a journey, are carried in closed tents, curtained on all sides, and set upon a wagon."[17] However, even so, it would seem that princesses led a less reclusive life, because they not only participated in public appearances of the king, but they also traveled and had contacts with strangers such as Atossa, who was treated for an abscess on her breast by the Greek physician Democedes.[18] It is quite likely that in the rural areas and among nomadic groups, just as in later centuries, the

---

14. Herodotus, *Histories*, III.69; Briant, *From Cyrus*, p. 283.

15. Herodotus, *Histories*, III.68.

16. Herodotus, *Histories*, I.135; see also Ibid., III.129 ("the eunuchs who conducted him to their [Darius's wives] apartments").

17. Briant, *From Cyrus*, 284.

18. Herodotus, *Histories*, III.134; she and other women had enormous influence. Ibid., VII.3.

women had relatively much freedom and worked alongside their male kinfolk in the pursuance of their agricultural and pastoral activities.

Persians were also interested in romance and some of the love stories that were told, in particular the romance of Zariadres and Odatis, achieved cult status. Chares of Mytilene reported that "The Persians paint this epic in their temples, palaces and houses."[19]

PARTHIAN (227 BCE–224 CE) AND SASANIAN PERIODS (226–651)

Under the Parthians and Sasanids it would seem that familial relations did not change much, as is clear from the observation made by Justinus:

> Each man has several wives, for the sake of gratifying desire with different objects. They punish no crime more severely than adultery, and accordingly they not only exclude their women from entertainments, but forbid them the very sight of men.[20]

Polygyny was permitted, and a wealthy Parthian man, in addition to his chief covenanted wife or wives, could have as many concubines as he desired. The latter could reach the highest status. In 20 BCE, Phraates IV (37–2 BCE) received a slave girl named Musa as a gift from Augustus, whom he later married under the name of 'Goddess Musa'. He appointed her son Phraataces as his successor (the later Phraates V) and she repaid the kind gesture by murdering Phraates IV in 2 BCE.[21] Adultery was severely punished, the reason why wives

---

19. Josef Markquart, *Eranshar nach der Geographie des ps. Moses Xorenacci* (Berlin, 1901), p. 126, §94. For the story of Zariadres and Odatis see [http://ambarts.tripod.com/files/odatis.htm].

20. Marcus Junianus Justinus. *Epitome of the Philippic History of Pompeius Trogus*, translated, with notes, by the Rev. John Selby Watson. (London: Henry G. Bohn, 1853), xli.3.

21. Flavius Josephus, *Judean Antiquities* XVIII, 2, 4 [http://classics.mit.edu/Josephus/j.aj.html].

were never invited to banquets, but divorce for women of the upper-class was very easy; they could obtain it by just having complaints about their husband's treatment of them.[22] However, dissolution of the marriage for commoners was not possible during Parthian times.[23] Noblemen often had a large number of women in their household, but this, of course, was only possible for those who were wealthy. Plutarch reported about Surena, whom he described as the second man in the kingdom, that when he traveled he "had one thousand camels to carry his baggage, two hundred chariots for his concubines and a thousand completely armed men for his lifeguards." Moreover, he was followed by a large rear-guard, "terminating in loose women and castanets, music of the lute, and midnight revellings."[24] As women were available in large numbers they were used as bribes in political intrigues such as when a Parthian governor promised money and 500 women to a pretender to oust the local ruler of Jerusalem, whom he wanted removed.[25]

The Parthian *Vis and Ramin* romance gives some interesting information on marriage customs in Parthia. From the various relationships that are detailed in that romance it is clear that lineage and status were very important and the text makes the point that Shahru, the mother of Vis, was of better birth than her husband, because she was descended from Jamshid and, therefore, her son Viru was also called son of Shahru.[26] Given the importance of lineage it may be assumed that this is one of the criteria for choosing a bride as is clear from the marriage between Ramin and Gol. She told Ramin who her parents were, what the occupation of her brother was and that "she herself was

22. Justinius, *Epitome*, xli.3; Josephus, *Judean Antiquities*, xviii.9 para 6; Clement, *Book of Recognitions*, chapters xxiv, xxv, xxix [http://www.essene.com/Recognitions/Book9.htm].

23. Mansour Shaki, "Divorce," *Encyclopedia Iranica*.

24. Plutarch, *Life of Crassus*, para 21 [on line edition].

25. Josephus, *Wars of the Jews*, Bk I, 12, para 1. [http://www.interhack.net/projects/library/wars-jews/b1c13.html]

26. V. Minorsky, "Vis and Ramin, a *Parthian Romance*," in Ibid., *Iranica. Twenty Articles* (Tehran, 1964), pp. 166, 176.

the Lady of Gurab."[27] The same considerations also held for choosing a husband, but with some regional variations. The Vis and Ramin romance mentions the fact that it was customary for women in Merv to choose their husband from two suitors.[28] What is of further interest is that Ramin was Vis's milk-brother, which, unlike in Islamic times, clearly was no obstacle to their marriage. The text of Vis and Ramin further suggests that the marriage ceremony could be a simple affair of hand fasting. "Shahru herself solemnizes the marriage of her children Viru and Vis by joining their hands, while she declares: 'there is no need of a mobad's seal on the contract, or of the presence of witnesses,' for God alone is a sufficient witness."[29] It was customary, however, to have a wedding party, complete with marriage contract, priest and witnesses.[30]

As in the preceding period, in Parthia the sexes were separated and men and women generally lived apart, and even had their meals apart. Respectable women did not talk to strange men, but only to their relatives and eunuchs. Urban women who went outside their home wore a hooded cloak (*himation*). This is clear from the pose adopted by female figurines recovered at Nineveh. One hand holds the cloak, so that she may adjust it, if need be, while with the other hand she slightly gathers up her skirt at the side of her body to facilitate walking.[31]

However, other customs also prevailed in the Parthian Empire. In the Vis and Ramin romance, king Mobad insists that Vis come to Marv and stay no longer in Mahabad (Media), "where people dallied with women (*zan-baragi*) and were addicted to pleasure."[32] Similarly, according to the Essenes:

---

27. V. Minorsky, "Vis and Ramin," p. 161.

28. V. Minorsky, "Vis and Ramin," p. 156.

29. V. Minorsky, "Vis and Ramin," pp. 156, 177-78.

30. V. Minorsky, "Vis and Ramin," p. 161.

31. For a picture of such a figurine of a Parthian woman, see [parthia.com/nineveh/04.htm]

32. V. Minorsky, "Vis and Ramin," p. 156.

In Susae the women use ointments, and indeed of the
best sort, being decked with ornaments and precious
stones; also they go abroad supported by the aid of their
maidservants, with much greater ambition than the
men. They do not, however, cultivate modesty, but have
intercourse indifferently with whomsoever they please,
with slaves and guests, such liberty being allowed them
by their husbands; and not only are they not blamed for
this, but they also rule over their husbands.[33]

The marriage between Viru and Vis without a priest not only implies that in Parthian times Zoroastrian religion may not have been as
yet all powerful, but that nevertheless the Zoroastrian custom of the
preferential 'next of kin' union was adhered to. The Essenes indeed
confirm that the Parthians practiced 'next of kin' marriage, because
they state that the Persians were "pleased with intercourse with their
mothers, or incestuous marriages with their daughters." They further
emphasized that Babylonian women were not chaste. Fortunately, the
proselytizing Saint Thomas was able to report that those who converted to Christianity abandoned all such vile practices.[34] The alleged
incest, in which Persians were engaged, refers to the practice of endogamy—sexual reproduction between near relatives - and the closer
relationship of consanguinity—sexual reproduction between siblings
and parents - that the Persians not only allowed, but preferred. The
alleged sexual relationship with their mothers probably had to do with
the fact that on the father's death the son, who inherited his father's
estate, also inherited his father's wives. This did not necessarily mean
that he had sexual relationships with his birth mother. The restricted
role of women did not mean that romance did not play a role in Parthia as is clear from the famous Parthian love story of Vis and Ramin,

33. Clement, *Book of Recognitions*, ch. xxiii.
34. Clement, *Book of Recognitions*, chapters xxv, xxix. See also Minorsky, "Vis and Ramin," pp. 176 (Ramin is the brother and child of Mobad), 178. For the same impact of Christianity on sexual mores see Bardesanes (ca. 175 CE) in his *The book of the laws of the countries: dialogue on the date of Bardasein of Edessa translated by H.J.W. Drijvers (Assen, 1954).*

where spiritual and physical love intertwine, and which still set hearts aflame in later centuries.[35]

According to a Roman observer named Ammianus Marcellinus, prostitution and pederasty (sodomy with boys) were less prevalent among the Persians than among the Greeks. The Persians punished pederasty by death. There was allegedly much adultery among the Persians, and while a Persian husband could divorce his wife for infidelity, a wife could not win a divorce from her husband on the same grounds. But she could divorce him for desertion or cruelty. A wife found guilty of adultery could have her nose and ears cut off. And men caught with someone else's wife could be banished.

The situation in the Sasanian period (224–642 CE) did not differ that much from that of their predecessors. The Zoroastrian religious texts show that the rules of marriage during the Sasanian period were complex. In addition to covenanted marriage with full rights (*patix-shay*) you had *sturih* or marriage by proxy, levirate marriage (*chakar*) and forms of marriage *sine manu mariti* (*ba'aspan, xvasrayonih,* and *gat*).[36] Marital relationships now considered incestuous were considered meritorious in pre-Islamic Iran. For example, the Sasanian law book *The Book of a Thousand Judgements* contains laws relating to brother-sister and similar kinds of 'incestuous' marriages.[37] The number of women a man could marry was unlimited. The Greek sources mention cases, where a man had several hundred women in his house.

35. V. Minorsky, "Vis u Ramin, a Parthian Romance," *Bulletin of the School of Oriental and African Studies, University of London* 11/4 (1946), pp. 741-763. For a recent and excellent translation of the entire text see Dick Davis, *Vis and Ramin* (Washington DC: Mage, 2008). See also the comments by 'Obeyd-e Zakani, *Resaleh-ye Delgosha* ed. 'Ali Asghar Halabi (Tehran, 1383/2004), p. 241, who wrote (the definition of) "a cornuto and a cuckold is he whose wife reads Vis and Ramin."

36. Vahraman, *The Book* (see Index). Of *sturih* marriage there were three forms: natural, instituted and appointed. The term *gat* also means: sexual intercourse and adultery.

37. Vahraman, *The Book*, p. 237, section 105, 5-10; p. 281, A18, 7-12; p. 315, A36, 6-12), father-daughter-marriage (p. 33, 3, 11-14; p.121, 44, 13-14; p.235, 104, 12-14) and mother-son marriage (p. 33, 4, 1-4).

Only those men who could afford it had more than one wife, and as before, depending on the nature of the relationship, covenanted wife or concubine, the children born of those unions might or might not inherit depending on whether there were living children from covenanted wives. Noblewomen could obtain a divorce, but this was not possible for women of the lower classes.[38] If Ardashir's *Karnamag* reflects reality, then concubines, or perhaps we should call them hand-maidens, had considerable freedom, because the Parthian king's Arta-ban's favorite handmaiden slept with Ardashir and after a night well spent returned to Artaban's quarters. Although she helps Ardashir es-cape from Artaban's palace and thus gain the throne, she disappears from the story. Ardashir then marries Artaban's daughter, who bears him his successor, Shapur, thus confirming the old rule that only the covenanted wives bore heirs.[39] Adultery was punishable, including in the after life.[40]

The followers of Mazdak (d. ca. 524), the leader of a proto-socialist movement, allegedly practiced the sharing of women and if a man had guests all of them not only would eat his food, but also 'tumble' with his wife. According to later Islamic sources:

> Their custom was that whenever a man went into a room
> to have commerce with a woman, he put his hat on the
> door and then went inside. If another person was seized
> with the same desire, on seeing the hat hanging on the
> door he turned back, knowing that somebody was already
> engaged in that business within.[41]

---

38. Mansour Shaki, "Divorce," *Encyclopedia Iranica*.

39. Frantz Grenet, *La geste d'Ardashir fils de Pabag* (Die, 2003), pp. 64-67.

40. Philippe Gignoux, *Le Livre d'Arda Viraz*, transliteration and transcription of the Pahlavi text. Persian translation by Zhaleh Amouzegar (Paris-Tehran, 1984), pp. 87 (69.5), 88 (para 78.3); Vahraman, *The Book*, pp. 47, 51, 75, 95, 101, 103, 181, 197, 253, 271.

41. Nizam al-Mulk, *The Book of Government or Rules for Kings* translated into English by Herbert Darke (London, 1960), p. 198; see the same story in Narshakhi, *The History of Bukhara* translated into English by Richard Frye (Cambridge, 1954), p. 7.

This may have been a form of polyandry, which was widely practiced before the rise of the Mazdakite movement in Bactria as well as among the Massagetae[42] and the Gelids, rather than the communal sharing of women.

> Amongst the Geli also there is a custom, that women cultivate the fields, build, and do every manly work; and they are also allowed to have intercourse with whom they please, and are not found fault with by their husbands, or called adulteresses: for they have promiscuous intercourse everywhere, and especially with strangers; they do not use ointments; they do not wear dyed garments, nor shoes.[43]

During the Sasanian period wealthy men had many concubines, often slaves. There does not seem to have been some kind of legal relationship between such a man and his concubines, apart from the legal statute concerning slavery.[44] As discussed in chapter two, they either were used as sex toys or as domestics. A case in point is the attitude and behavior of Bahram, as described in the *Shahnameh*, who was raised by an Arab called Monzer and who was as a surrogate father to him: one day the adolescent prince addresses his guardian as follows:

> You are a noble, well-intentioned man, but you hem me
>   in with your excessive care and constant worry.
> Everyone we see has some secret sorrow, that turns his
>   face yellow with grief,
> And a free man's health is revived by pleasure, so allow
>   me this one further pleasure then, the pleasure that
>   cures all pains.
> Whether he's a prince or a warrior, a young man finds
>   comfort and happiness with women.

---

42. Herodotus, *Histories*, I. 214; Ilya Yakubovich, "Marriage Contract," *Encyclopedia Iranica*.

43. Clement, *Book of Recognitions*, ch. xxii (Customs of the Gelones).

44. On the status of slaves in pre-Islamic Iran see M. A. Dandamayev, M. Macuch, "Barda," *Encyclopedia Iranica*.

They are the foundation of our faith, and they guide
   young men toward goodness.
Have five or six beautiful slave girls, as splendid as the
   sun, brought here,
So that I can pick one or two of them. I've been
   thinking too that I should have children.
If I had a child that would bring me some comfort.
The king would be pleased, and men would praise me
   for it.[45]

The slave girls bought by Monzer for Bahram are described as being of Western (Rumi) origin, and they were bought from a broker,
who had a depot where he sold his human merchandise. For Bahram,
women, or rather beautiful women, any other would not do, were
there to give him pleasure, happiness, and children. In a Pahlavi language treatise attributed to the time of Khosrow I (531-78) or Khosrow II (590-628) ideal female beauty is described as follows: "That
woman is the best who in her mind loves her husband and is of great
intelligence, whose stature is middle-sized and whose chest is broad
and whose head, buttocks, and neck are well-formed and whose legs
are short and waist slender and soles of the feet arched and whose
fingers are long and whose limbs are soft, smooth, and fleshy (lit.
filled) and whose breast is quince-like and whose body down to the
toes is snowy-white and whose cheeks are pomegranate-red and whose
eyes are almond-shaped and lips coral-like and eye-brows vaulted and
whose denture is white, fresh, and brilliant and locks black and bright
and long, and who has soothing words in bed for her husband but
does not talk indecently."[46]

45. Dick Davis, "Women in the Shahnameh: exotics and natives, rebellious
   legends and dutiful histories," in Women and Medieval Epic: gender, genre
   and the limits of epic masculinity, ed. Sara S. Poor and Jana K. Schulman (New
   York, 2007), pp. 67-90.
46. Djalal Khaleghi-Motlagh, "Erotic literature," Encyclopaedia Iranica.

ISLAMIC PERIOD (651–TO DATE)

We were with the Prophet while we were young and
had no wealth whatever. So Allah's Apostle said, "O
young people! Whoever among you can marry, should
marry, because it helps him lower his gaze and guard his
modesty (i.e. his private parts from committing illegal
sexual intercourse etc.), and whoever is not able to marry,
should fast, as fasting diminishes his sexual power."[47]

Premarital Sex

Islam recognizes that human beings have a strong sexual drive, but
it insists that all sexual relations can only occur within marriage,[48]
of which Shi'a Islam recognizes two forms: (i) covenanted (*'aqd al-
nikah*) and (ii) temporary marriage (*mut'ah*). Therefore, premarital
and extra-marital sex was and is religiously and socially banned. Not
much is known about the sexual experience of young boys and girls
prior to their marriage, because it is a subject even more taboo than
(marital) sex itself. According to Wills, referring to the situation in
the 1870-80s, "this vice among young women *prior to marriage* is very
unusual; and the Persian woman compared favourably with her European sister in this respect."[49] Girls, of course, had very little opportunity for pre-marital sex, because they were closely guarded due to the
importance of their virginity and thus their family's honor. Therefore,
parents took care to marry off their daughter as soon as possible after

---

47. Bukhari, *Sahih*, 62. 4; see also Muslim, *Sahih*, 8, *3231-3239*. For an
electronic version of these collections of Traditions see [http://www.usc.edu/
dept/MSA/reference/reference.html].

48. See, e.g., Ayatollah Ebrahim Amini, *Entekhab-e Hamsar* (Tehran,
1374/1995), pp. 17-18, 64, 91-92; Ibid., *Ayin-e Hamsardari* (Tehran,
1378/1999) (section *hadaf-e ezdevaj*), [http://www.hawzah.net/Per/K/Ain-
Hams/Index.htm]. The prophet allegedly has said: "Truly, woman is one of the
pleasures and joys [of men]. So, anyone who takes a wife should not spoil this
[pleasure]." Mohammad Ebrahim Avazeh (Razavi), *Qanun-e Qovveh-ye Bah*
(Qom, 1382/2003), p. 22. In general see Ze'ev Maghen, *Virtues of the flesh:
passion and purity in early Islamic jurisprudence* (Leiden, 2005).

49. C.J. Wills, *In the Land of the Lion and the Sun* (London, 1893), p. 316 (italics
in the original).

her first menstruation, if not earlier. It is also quite unlikely that girls, who were nine years old, had any interest in sexual contact, despite the fact that many were married off by that age. The problem was not so much the women, but the men, who were more lustful than the females as well as the fact that the sex drive was very much suppressed before marriage and needed an outlet.

After toddlerhood, children are explicitly discouraged from playing together because of the perceived sexual risk to which they might be exposed.

> Children do not play unsupervised. An invitation to a child to play at the house of a neighbor or a schoolmate always includes the mother. Such invitations are in any case rare, as are all social interactions with nonkin. Children, in general, play with their cousins under the watchful eye of all mothers. Female children are watched very carefully. Access to information on sex-rehearsal play would be severely hampered by cultural taboos on admitting anything detrimental about one's children, especially to nonkin.[50]

Prior to puberty, male children gain knowledge of female anatomy at all stages of the life cycle, and all stages of pregnancy and lactation. Also, being brought in the women's quarter "listening with his sisters to conversations which are quite unfit for children's ears."[51] Children's rhymes also provide sexual information as these include oral, anal and genital themes.[52] Moreover, when their mothers take them to the public baths with them on women's day young boys are

---

50. J. Gulick, *The Middle East: An Anthropological Perspective* (Pacific Palisades, Calif., 1983), p. 208; see also J. Gulick & M. E. Gulick, "The domestic social environment of women and girls in Isfahan, Iran," in Lois Beck & Nikkie Keddie eds. *Women in the Muslim World.* (Cambridge, 1979), pp. 513-14.

51. Dorothy de Warzeé, *Peeps into Persia* (London, 1913), p. 165; Häntzsche, "Haram," p. 429; P. E. Drew, "Iran," in R. T. Francoeur ed. *The International Encyclopedia of Sexuality* (New York, 2004), p. 559.

52. Erika Friedl, *Children of Deh Koh: young life in an Iranian village* (Syracuse, 1997), p. 235.

exposed to the naked bodies of the women present there. "It is up to the bath attendants to decide, based on their own observations, whether a young boy is too old to be present on women's day. Clearly men retain in adulthood images of what they saw in the bathhouse during childhood."[53]

There is little information available about sexual activities of boys and young males before marriage, but pre-marital sex indeed occurred among the young, according to information from the twentieth century. They not only experimented by themselves (masturbation[54]), but also copulated with men and animals, and had relations with girls. Among the Jews, "masturbation is strongly opposed on religious grounds but it is said to be common. Informants claim that when the boy is old enough to ejaculate, he is taken to a Muslim prostitute; in the past he would be married off to avoid the problem."[55] Rich Moslems provided their sons with a temporary wife (see chapter two), while the sons of the poor were engaged in sodomy, both with other boys as well as with animals. This leaves aside the fact that young boys were used by pedophiles and pederasts for sexual purposes (see chapter four).

Papoli-Yazdi, in his fascinating memoir, mentions that in the poor neighborhood of Yazd, where he lived in his youth in the 1950-60s, boys and girls were acquainted with one another through daily contact in the same alley (*kucheh*) and house (where often multiple poor families lived; one family per room) and through attendance at the local *maktab* or Koran school. Also, the entry to the nearby *qanat* or the subterranean water canal that supplied water to his quarter, but not to the street in which he lived, was used by boys to get acquainted with girls from the neighborhood. He does not reveal how far that

---

53. Drew, "Iran," p. 559.

54. Masturbation is forbidden to Moslems; it is considered to be one of the major sins, see e.g., Avazeh, *Qanun-e Qovveh-ye Bah*, pp. 82-86. For an entertaining story about masturbation (*jalq zadan*) see 'Obeyd-e Zakani, *Resaleh-ye Delgosha*, pp. 176-77.

55. Lawrence Loeb, *Outcaste - Jewish Life in Southern Iran* (New York, 1977), pp. 72, 171 (refers to the occurrence of premarital sex).

getting acquainted went, but it could go all the way as is clear from his description of the occurrences at the Koran school. Here boys and girls from the neighborhood for a nominal fee were taught to memorize the Koran and the poems of Iran's most famous poets, in this case by a local woman, who was called *molla baji* as her counterparts elsewhere in Iran also were. She sometimes had to absent herself for one hour or two and left the school in the control of pubescent boys, who were in fact too old for this type of school. Some of these older boys took advantage of one of the girls, whom they took to the basement, where they had sex. Finally, when this became known outside the school, the older boys were all sent away and measures were taken to prevent such things from happening again. The girl concerned was taken out of school and Papoli-Yazdi later learned that she had ended up in one of the brothels of Abadan. A similar occurrence concerned the use of a nine-year old by a 15-year old under similar circumstances. And if it were not the older boys in the Koran school it might be the male relatives of the *molla baji* who took advantage of their position, as is clear from a 1907 letter to the editor.[56]

Older boys also received sexual gratification by 'visiting' willing married women, when they were home alone.[57] Allegedly, this even happened in large villages. Young men in the village of Davarabad in the 1950s, for example, claimed that they visited "well-to-do married women," who welcomed liaisons with young men "for variety and entertainment, or because they find their husbands inadequate." The

---

56. Mohammad Hoseyn Papoli-Yazdi, *Khaterat-e Shahzdah-e Hammam* (Mashhad, 1384/2005), pp. 30, 32, 103. The sexual molestation of school girls by male relatives of the *molla baji* is also mentioned by Janet Afary, *Iranian constitutional revolution, 1906-1911: grassroots democracy, social democracy & the origins of feminism* (New York, 1996), p. 191 quoting a "Letter of one of the women," *Habl al-Matin* nr. 105 (01/09/1907), pp. 4-5, which suggests that the phenomenon was not limited to incidental cases. Mahmud Daneshvar, *Didaniha va Shenidaniha-ye Iran* 2 vols. (Tehran, 1327/1948), vol. 1, p. 249 also intimates that pre-marital sex took place such as in Jahrom.

57. Papoli-Yazdi, *Khaterat*, p. 22; Pierre Ponafidine, *Life in the Moslem East* (New York, 1911), p. 317.

ethnographer who recorded this information rightly stated that "the matter is open to doubt."[58]

It also happened that older girls had sexual, mostly abusive, relations with boys or men of their acquaintance or family members. This constituted incest and is a subject even more taboo than pre-marital sex. Although not much is known about it, as it usually remains in the family, in many if not most instances this occurred in the form of rape, which was not reported, of course, when the perpetrator was a family member. If a rapist, from outside the family, was caught he was punished by the authorities.[59] Von Poser relates such an occurrence in 1622. In Isfahan, four royal soldiers had grabbed a girl, who had left the public bath-house a little late, and they had taken her to their house, where they sexually used her for eight days after which time they strangled her. When the crime and criminals became known, Shah 'Abbas I ordered the soldiers' hands and feet to be cut off.[60] The problem was, of course, what happened to the girl who had been raped? In a case reported from Fars in the 1970s, where a man had tried to rape his former fiancée, the girl, although she was still a virgin, was told that she would have to marry her rapist, because nobody else would have her after this.[61] She probably was 'lucky', because it would seem that a raped girl usually was sent to a brothel.

Although, some pre-marital sex occurred, it was rare that this happened with very young girls. If it occurred, it mostly was of the nature of pedophiliac relations with pre-pubescent girls, in particular, sexual abuse by relatives and old husbands (see also below). Such

---

58. Robert Charles Alberts, *Social Structure and Culture Change in an Iranian Village* 2 vols. (Ph.D. dissertation University of Wisconsin, 1963), vol. 2, p. 654.

59. 'Ali Akbar Sa'idi Sirjani, *Vaqaye'-ye Ettefaqiyeh* (Tehran, 1361/1982), p. 424 (flogging, imprisoned, and castrated); Pietro della Valle, *Les Fameux Voyages* 4 vols. (Paris, 1663-64), vol. 2, p. 609 (castration); Auguste Bricteux, *Au Pays du Lion et du Soleil* (Brussels, 1908), p. 60 (in 1904, or thereabouts, two soldiers were executed for having raped a young girl); Drew, "Iran," p. 563.

60. Heinrich von Poser, *Als Schlesischer Adliger in Iran und Indien*. ed. Helmhart Kanus-Credé (Allendorf a/d Eder: Antigone, 2003), p. 36.

61. Erika Friedl, *Women of Deh Koh* (Washington, 1989), p. 118 ("They'll beat her up at home until she says yes, just like my folks tried it with me.")

endorsement of what elsewhere is considered to be child abuse, of course, engenders exactly that. Therefore, this has an impact on how children and especially girls are raised and who has custody over them. It also means if such abuse occurs, more often than not it is not reported, because of the dishonor that will fall on the family and rather than punishing the perpetrator the victim is punished.

> Since marriages can be contracted at any point after a girl has reached the age of 9, it is legally feasible for a very little girl to be married to a man of any age, and thus be physically at his mercy. This no doubt constitutes the broadest category of potential sexual abuse of children. One of the strongest arguments made in Iran against the custody of children, particularly girls, being given to the mother, is that on her remarriage, the children will be in danger of sexual abuse from the new husband. Sexual abuse of children, particularly little girls, often occurs at the hands of uncles and cousins staying under the same roof. In such cases, the child's mother is inevitably blamed for leaving her child unguarded, and little outrage is directed at the abuser. Sexual abuse of children in a family setting is not the concern of the police, nor are there any relevant social agencies to which it could be reported. A young servant boy would be withdrawn from the household by his parents if he were the victim of abuse. Only in the case of a young servant girl could the police be implicated, and then only if her virginity had been certified prior to employment.[62]

Moslem girls at the Jewish school in Shiraz regaled their Jewish female classmates with the stories of their sexual adventures in minute detail. These could also have been partly invented stories, because, due to the later age of marriage and no mixed socializing, girls had

---

62. Drew, "Iran," p. 563; J. Gulick and M.E. Gulick, "The domestic social environment of women and girls in Isfahan, Iran," in Lois Beck & Nikki Keddie eds. *Women in the Muslim World*. (Cambridge: Harvard University Press, 1979), pp. 513-14; Djamchid A. Momeni, "The Difficulties of Changing the Age at Marriage in Iran," *Journal of Marriage & Family* 34/3 (1972),p. 547.

"considerable sexual curiosity as well as sexual frustration."[63] This dilemma is quite well expressed by the 1950s comedienne Mahvash:

> A Kashani girl was standing in a field and a boy was passing by. At that moment the nearby girl said to the boy in a thick Kashi dialect:
>
> > Don't look at me, or I will cry out
> > The boy looked. The girl said:
> > Do not come closer, or I will cry out
> > The boy came closer. The girl said:
> > Do not go further, or I will cry out
> > The boy come came further. The girl said:
> > Do not come close to me or I will cry out.
> > The boy came close to her. The girl said:
> > Don't touch me or I will cry out.
> > The boy touched her. The girl said:
> > Do not touch my breasts or I will cry out.
> > The boy put his hands on her breasts. The girl said:
> > Do not kiss me or I will cry out.
> > The boy kissed her. The girl said:
> > Do not put your hand on my navel or I will cry.
> > The boy put his hand on her navel.
> > Don't you dare to go lower or I will cry out.
> > The boy put his hand lower. The girl said:
> > Don't you put it in there or I will cry out.
> > The boy penetrated her. The girl said in a flirting and
> >   amorous way:
> > Oh God, … do not withdraw! Or else I will cry out[64]

Because traditional norms towards premarital sex are still strong and rigid in Iran, modern urban youth, who cannot marry early because of the high cost[65] and having no other outlets such as discos as

---

63. Loeb, *Outcaste*, p. 73.

64. Mahvash, *Asrar-e magu* (Tehran, n.d.), p. 15.

65. On the issue of obstacles to marriage, including the high cost of the dowry,

in the past (1970s), have girls friends and/or organize parties where necking and other forms of foreplay are indulged in, which may finally result in pre-marital sex, usually of the non-penetrative kind so as to preserve the girl's virginity. In this connection these young men seem to heed 'Obeyd-e Zakani advice: "Have anal intercourse with the daughter of your neighbor and do not tamper with her hymen so that you will not have betrayed your neighbor's trust and you will have been a considerate and good Moslem. Thus, on her wedding night she will not be ashamed before the bridegroom and she will be proud among the people."[66] Boys also visit prostitutes to find sexual gratification, a trend that seems to be on the rise during the last two decades. One recent study found that 28 percent of the sample of unmarried adolescent men in Tehran had engaged in sex.[67]

ISLAMIC RULES CONCERNING MARRIAGE

Moslems as well as Christians, Jews and Zoroastrians, however, should only have a sexual relationship within the confines of marriage, which means the union of a man and a woman. Not only does the Koran (24:33) command Moslems to marry: "And marry those among you who are single," which should be a sufficient command by itself, but the prophet Mohammad himself rebuffed 'Othman b. Mazun, when he asked if he could be permitted to live a life of abstinence.[68]

---

see Amini, *Entekhab*, pp. 33-54, who also offers advice to troubled youths.

66. Obeyd-e Zakani, *Ethics of The Aristocrats*, p. 79.

67. Farah Esna-Ashari, "Differences in attitude towards premarital sex: The Impact of Some Demographic and Socio-Economic Factors in a Sample of Shiraz City Youth (Poster Session), 2005." [available via internet]; Mohammad Reza Mohammadi, Kazem Mohammad, Farideh K.A. Farahani, Siamak Alikhani, Mohammad Zare, Fahimeh R. Tehrani, Ali Ramezankhani and Farshid Alaeddini. "Reproductive Knowledge, Attitudes and Behavior Among Adolescent Males in Tehran, Iran," *International Family Planning Perspectives* 32/1 (2006), pp. 35–44; Mohammadreza Hojat, Reza Shapurian, Habib Nayerahmadi, Mitra Farzaneh, Danesh Foroughi, Mohin Parsi, Maryam Azizi. "Premarital Sexual, Child Rearing and Family Attitudes of Iranian Men and Women in the United States and in Iran," *Journal of Psychology* 133 (1999).

68. Bukhari, *Sahih*, 62.12

Therefore, it is not surprising that outside observers concluded that "It is regarded as a cardinal sin not to marry. ... Even lepers, segregated in their wretched villages, feel the pressure of opinion and are obliged to marry in accordance with religion."[69] As a result, an American missionary commented around 1900, "In the course of extensive travels, covering a period of more than twenty years, I have myself met but four spinsters or confirmed old maids.[70] Not having been married was such an oddity that it merited to be mentioned. The calligrapher Mirza Sanglakh Khorasani was considered to be such an oddity, because when he died at the great age of allegedly 110 he had never married.[71] This does not mean that the unmarried men had no sex, for unlike women they had a choice of options, among which marriage was but one. They may well have followed Sana'i (d. 1141) the misogynist twelfth century poet's advice:

> Don't marry! Leave aside women in this spring time:
> No man marries if he is in his right senses.
> If you are a slave of passion, buy a bondsmaid,
> Beautiful, fair-faced, comely and well-shaped
> As long as you wish she will comply with your desires,
> When you don't want her, she will be ready cash.
> It is much better to rise in the morning
> To see the face of your own property than that of a
>   creditor.[72]

---

69. Van Sommer and Zwemer, *Our Moslem Sisters*, p. 221; James Bassett, "Child Life in Persia," *Frank Lesley's Popular Monthly* 36 (August 1893), pp. 167, 170.

70. Annie van Sommer and Samuel Zwemer, *Our Moslem Sisters* (New York, 1907), p. 221; see also J. E. Polak, *Persien. Das Land und seine Bewohner* 2 vols. (Leipzig, 1865), vol. 1, p. 205.

71. Mirza Mohammad Hasan Khan E'temad al-Saltaneh, *Al-Ma'ather va'l- Athar* (Tehran, 1306/1889), p. 216. His contemporary, the poet Jelveh of Ardestan also had remained a lifelong bachelor. Hasan Javadi, *Satire in Persian Literature* (Cranbury, NJ-London, 1988), p. 211; 'Abdollah Mostowfi. *Sharh-e Zendegani-ye Man* 3 vols. (Tehran, n.d.), vol. 1, p. 521. In the Zand period there was the poet Aqa Yadgar Hajat, who likewise remained a lifelong bachelor until his death well into his seventies. Abu'l-Hasan Ghaffari Kashani, *Golshan-e Morad* ed. by Gholamreza Tabataba'i-Majd (Tehran, 1369/1990), p. 404.

72. The English translation of this poem is by Javadi, *Satire*, pp. 207-08.

But as most people marry, first there is a discussion of the do's and don'ts of Islamic marriage, i.e. what were the formal rules that had to be respected for a marriage to be valid and what norms were there to govern the breaking of any of these rules or the voiding of the marriage contract. Second, the execution of those rules is examined; how people did or did not deal with them and how they shirk, skirt and/ or embellish them.

CONTRACT

According to Islamic law, marriage as a legal institution is defined and described in terms of a number of pillars *(arkan)* and statutes *(ahkam)*. The pillars are those essential elements of the marriage contract whose absence nullifies the contract. The statutes are the rules and regulations that govern the contract.[73] Marriage, according to Shi'ite Islamic law, is only valid when there is a contract (*'aqd*), respect the limits in the choice of partners, the agreement on the payment of the dowry (*mahr*), and a proper formula, pronounced by two accepting parties. The Sunnis add one or two other conditions, depending on the theological school. The Arabic term used for marriage, *nikah*, actually means sexual relations, thus underlining that these relations can only lawfully take place by virtue of a lawful marriage contract. The bride declares that she is willing (*ijab*) to marry and the groom declares that he accepts (*qabul*). All schools differ about the exact wording that has to be used, including whether it should be in the perfect or imperfect sense. The words should be spoken in Arabic, but if the persons do not know that language they may do so in their own language.

As to the contract, which must be in Arabic, it must state the terms of what is offered and that this is accepted by both parties.[74]

---

73. This section on the description of marriage, according to Islamic law, is based on Khomeyni, *Tahrir*; Ibid., *Towzih*; Sachiko Murata, *Temporary Marriage in Islamic Law* (MA thesis Tehran University 1974); for the electronic version of this study see [http://www.al-islam.org/al-serat/muta/]); Shahla Haeri, *Law of Desire. Temporary Marriage in Shi'i Iran* (Syracuse, 1989) and J. Schacht, "Nikah," *Encyclopedia of Islam*2.

74. It is not by chance that the marriage contract has the form of a sales

Both are standardized and ritualistic in nature and cannot be changed by either party. Both parties can add provisions, provided they do not contradict Koranic boundaries. For example, a woman cannot insist that her husband should not take a second wife, but she can stipulate that this will be a cause for divorce. If it is the first marriage for the woman (in which case she must be a virgin) her legal guardian (*vali*) needs to give his consent to the marriage, although many olama disagree on this point. From about 1970, girls 18 and older, were allowed to contract their own marriage, if they could show that their father or in his absence the other leading male in the family was being unreasonable about the marriage.

Two witnesses are usually presented, but are not required, provided all legal conditions are met. In case of minors (i.e. for girls below nine years of age and for boys about 14 years) the father, brother or other legal guardian signs. Their signature is binding and the parties when they have reached legal majority, cannot claim that the marriage is void, because the marriage contract was signed without their consent. They can, however, decide to divorce.

When the marriage contract has become valid the woman becomes the owner of the dowry or *mahr*. The dowry must consist of a specified amount of property, cash, or profit. It must be ritually pure and owned by the husband. Payment of the dowry has to take place on consummation of the marriage or death of one of the spouses. The woman can demand payment of the dowry before she consents to sexual intercourse, unless the marriage contract explicitly states that it would be paid later. If she consents to intercourse without payment then thereafter she cannot refuse her husband his conjugal rights. This even holds when he cannot pay the dowry, according to the Shi'ites, but the Sunnis hold that in such a case she may refuse her husband.

---

contract, because popular religious texts explain that the reason that a man does not receive a dowry is because he buys the woman, who sells herself to him; see e.g. Avazeh, *Qanun-e Qovveh-ye Bah*, p. 91. In Azeri Turkish, marriage is therefore referred to as *arwat almaq* or 'the purchase of the bride.'

The bride price is the most important part of the marriage; its payment may be deferred, i.e. the marriage is concluded on credit, reason why the poet Sana'i (see above) called a wife a 'creditor'. It represents the social standing of both families in the community and the value (or esteem) given to the bride. Today, some modern women consider the bride price demeaning, but tradition as well as Koranic injunction (4:4) makes it impossible to do away with the custom. In fact, bride prices in general seem to have risen and are often expressed in an ever increasing number of gold coins to provide security against inflation. This relative high current level of dowries presents a major obstacle for young people, getting married, in particular when unemployment is high, for many young men (or their families) do not have the necessary funds.[75]

Marriage means that the husband has to support his wife, which entails: providing her with food, clothing, shelter, and other necessities, but only if she obeys him. If she does not then he is not obliged to support her. A husband must provide support to a divorced wife during the waiting period; or in the case of an irrevocable divorce only if she is pregnant during the pregnancy.

EQUALITY

This is the first of the statutes of marriage. Apart from the pillars of marriage (contract, formula, dowry) other conditions or statutes have to be respected. A woman may only marry a man who is equal *(kafa)* to her. For the Shi'is the only condition is that he must be a Moslem; for the Sunni schools other factors (lineage, property, profession, slave, etc.) also play a role.[76] In reality, in Iran, whether it was Sunni or Shi'ite, the socio-economic and political/religious position of the families that contracted a marriage were and are still very important.

---

75. Although, from a religious viewpoint, it is very meritorious to ask a very low, if not a symbolic, dowry, very few Moslems are inclined to do so. Avazeh, *Qanun-e Qovveh-ye Bah*, p. 92.

76. Around 1907, an Armenian man who had married a Moslem girl was killed in the street by a mob, while his wife was stoned to death. Ponafidine, *Life*, p. 326.

For men it was important that the wife was of a less influential family than his own, so that he could feel superior. The author of the *Qabus-nameh* advises his son as follows:

> Do not marry a wife of nobler birth than yourself. ...
> Marry a woman of honourable family, because men
> marry in order to have a lady for the house and not to
> indulge in sexual pleasure; to satisfy your desire you can
> buy slave-girls in the bazaar, which involves neither so
> much expense nor so much trouble.[77]

Sometimes it could not be avoided and a marriage took place with a woman of nobler birth, allying the family, e.g., with the royal family or with a political more influential clan. In such cases the man had to show more consideration to his wife as she might complain to her father and/or brothers and uncles.[78] Even in these cases some measure of superiority could be maintained if one ensured that the bride was much younger than her husband.

Marriage between different ethnic groups could be problematical. Although the victories of the Moslem armies following the prophet's death made the Arabs the masters of a large part of the Middle East and North Africa, marriage between Arabs and non-Arabs was actively discouraged since Caliph 'Omar's regulation to that effect. Nevertheless they started to occur. In 783, in Tabaristan there were Arab-Persian unions that were, however, dissolved in case of revolts, when the women would hand over their Arab husbands to the rebels for execution.[79] Often, these were political marriages and in many

---

77. Kai Ka'us b. Iskandar, *A mirror for princes, the Qabus Nama*, translated into English by Reuben Levy (London, 1951), p. 118, Ch. XXVI.

78. James Morier, *A Second Journey through Persia, Armenia, and Asia Minor ... between the years 1810 and 1816* (London, 1818), pp. 57-58. Mirza Abu'l-Hasan Khan's only son had died and his wife was too old to expect another child, "and moreover so jealous, as to oppose a second marriage. She is a lady of superior rank to himself; being the daughter of Hajee Ibrahim, the late Grand Vizier of Persia; and it is said, that if her husband in any manner ill-treated her, she has such powerful relations, that they would soon avenge her."

79. Berthold Spuler, *Iran in Früh-Islamischer Zeit* (Wiesbaden, 1952), p. 378.

cases were seen as a "practical means to prevent wars."[80] The fact that a Moslem could have four wives facilitated such marriages, of course. As a result, there were numerous marriages of this kind.[81] Apart from marriage between Persians and Arabs, later marriages between these two groups and Turks also happened. In all cases one tried to respect the equality in standing and rank of both parties.[82] Sometimes there were complaints, when, e.g., a vanquished ruler (Soltan of Kashgar) had to give his daughter in marriage to the victor (Malek Shah), while he himself had to marry the daughter of a servant or a slave.[83] The religion of the women was not a major obstacle, and usually one insisted that they converted to Islam.[84]

The author of the *Qabus-nameh* advised his son: "also marry not above your rank nor below it, of good lineage."[85] During the Ilkhan period rank and family remained important parameters for a marriage. When the Sarbardar leader Amir Jamal al-Din 'Abdol-Razzaq wanted to marry the daughter of Khvajeh 'Ala' al-Din Hendu she fled. When overtaken by the suitor's brother she told him that it was impossible to marry Jamal al-Din, because "you were my father's servants."[86]

Not only political and military leaders and their family had high standing, but also religious families, in particular those that were descendants of the prophet Mohammad and his nephew 'Ali, who are

The other religious communities also discouraged marriage with Moslems. Jamsheed K. Choksy, "Women during the Transition from Sasanian to Early Islamic Times," in Guity Nashat and Lois Beck eds. *Women in Iran. From the rise of Islam to 1800* (Chicago, 2003), p. 56

80. Ibn al-Athir, *Kamil f'il-Tarikh* 15 vols. ed. C. J. Tornberg (Leiden, 1885), vol. 5, p. 113 (744 Khorasan).

81. Spuler, *Iran*, p. 379, n. 3.

82. Ibn al-Athir, *Kamil fi'l-Tarikh*, vol. 8, p. 158.

83. Spuler, *Iran*, pp. 378-89.

84. W. Barthold, *Zwölf Vorlesungen über die Geschichte der Türken Mittelasiens* (Darmstadt, 1962), p. 88f; Ibid, *Turkestan down to the Mongol Invasion* (Karachi, 1981), p. 286.

85. Kai Ka'us b. Iskandar, *Qabus Nama*, p. 118, Ch. XXVI.

86. Kamal al-Din 'Abdol-Razzaq Samarqandi, *Matla'-ye Sa'deyn va Majma'-ye Bahreyn* 2 vols. ed. 'Abdol-Hoseyn Nava'i (Tehran, 1353/1974), vol. 1, p. 276.

known as sayyed. "To wed a sayed is thought to be a great honor, and she is not slow to assert the rights of her order and family."[87] It was in particular an honor if the ruler selected one of his courtiers to marry one of his female relatives. Shah 'Abbas I was in the habit to divest himself of a surfeit of concubines by giving them in marriage to courtiers, who stated, when asked by the shah later, that they were very happy with the arrangement.[88] When the shah decided to send an important man one of the royal princesses:

> As a wife, a most expensive honour which necessitated a large sum being sent up to the treasury at Tehran. In addition to this the bride, being of royal rank, possessed a good deal of power over her husband. In one case I remember a Persian notable, who had as a youth known the joys of Europe, went off to Paris with all the available cash he could get together. When after a few months of unalloyed, if expensive, pleasure in the night resorts of the gay capital his funds had vanished away, he ruefully returned home. Hardly had he entered his house when his spouse had him taken into the *Anderoon*, or women's quarters, where she forthwith proceeded to supervise a *bastinadoing* on the soles of his feet such as her erring husband was never likely to forget. In doing so she was perfectly within her rights. She was of the royal blood, and under the circumstances was entitled to such reparation as she chose to exact. [89]

---

87. James Bassett, *Persia: Eastern Mission. A Narrative of the founding and the fortunes of the Eastern Persia Mission* (Philadelphia, 1890), p. 60.

88. Valle, *Voyages*, vol. 2, pp. 343-44, 355-56.

89. Ralph Neville, *Unconventional Memories* (New York, 1923), pp. 144-45. See also Warzeé, *Peeps*, pp. 62-63; J.C. Häntzsche, "Haram und Harem," *Zeitschrift für allgemeine Erdkunde* XIII (1862),p. 381; Mirza Khanlar Khan E'tesam al-Molk, *Safarnameh* ed. Manuchehr Mahmudi (Tehran, 1351/1972), pp. 106, 136, 149, 170, 226 who was 'pursued' by letters from his princess-wife, during his journey. 'Abdol-Hoseyn Khan Sepehr, *Mer'at al-Vaqaye'-ye Mozaffari va Yaddahstha-ye Malek al-Mo'arrekhin* 2 vols. in one. ed. 'Abdol-Hoseyn Nava'i (Tehran, 1368/1989), vol. 2, p. 285 reports that Movaqqer al-Saltaneh's wife, the daughter of the shah, told her husband that he could not divorce her. He had to pay a huge sum before she consented to a divorce, a procedure totally

A similar situation still exists when the wife's family is of higher socio-economic standing than that of her husband, in which case it can happen that she refuses to have sex with him, unless he 'pays' for it in one way or the other.[90] Such a situation, of course, has been the subject of one of the many Persian stories that deal with the various aspects of marriage. One well-known example is the following. Sadeq Beyg was married to a beautiful lady called Hoseyni. But, "giving a husband of the condition of Sadik Beg to a lady of Hooseinee's rank was, according to usage in such unequal matches, like giving her a slave. … [People] mourned the fate of so fine and promising young man, now condemned to bear through life all the humours of a proud and capricious woman." However, matters turned out well for Sadeq Beyg, despite his friends' misgivings, and he was very happy with his obedient wife. His friends wanted to know how he had tamed his beautiful headstrong wife. "After the ceremonies of our nuptials were over, I went in my military dress, and with my sword by my side, to the apartment of Hoosseinee. She was sitting in a most dignified posture to receive me, and her looks were anything but inviting. As I entered the room a beautiful cat, evidently a great favourite, came purring up to me. I deliberately drew my sword, struck its head off, and taking that in one hand and the body in the other, threw them out of the window. I then very unconcernedly turned to the lady, who appeared in some alarm; she, however, made no observation, but was in every way kind and submissive, and has continued so ever since."[91] This story was so popular that it also produced a very well-known Persian proverb 'to kill the cat at the bridal chamber's door sill.'

---

contrary to Islamic law and one in which the olama did not want to interfere even when asked by the husband to pronounce and endorse the divorce.

90. Vieille, "Iranian Women," p. 464.

91. Anonymous (John Malcolm), *Sketches of Persia* 2 vols. (London, 1828), vol. 2, pp. 54-56.

Marriage Restrictions
(family, other relationships, and religion)

Equal rank was the second statute of marriage and thus one of the obstacles that might have to be overcome to conclude a marriage. There are also categories of people who one may not marry at all, which is determined by blood relationship (*qaraba*), relationship by marriage (*mushara*), foster relationship (*rida'*), and religion. The Koran (4:22-23) provides the basic rules on marriage impediments based on consanguinity, affinity, and fosterage. A man may not marry his mother, daughter, sister, aunt, niece, foster-mother, foster-sister, mother-in-law, stepmother (or any of his father's wives), stepdaughter, or daughter-in-law, or be married to two sisters at the same time. Such a non-marriageable person is called *mahram* (plur. *maharem*), implying that it is taboo. A milk-relationship establishes exactly, or nearly exactly, the same impediments as blood relationship, so that one may not marry, for instance, the sister of one's foster-mother or a girl suckled by one's own mother or wet-nurse.[92]

Nevertheless, during the first centuries of Islam old habits died hard, for people still performed marriage practices that were contrary to Islamic law. In the remote areas of the Elburz Mountains, at least until the eleventh century, one Deylami tribe continued to practice a kind of endogamy that Moslems considered to be incestuous and any deviance of this rule was punished by death.[93] This was but a continuation of Zoroastrian practice, which favored marriage between close relatives and its suppression, as certain types of these marriage were contrary to Islam, was difficult as shown in the case of Seystan.[94] Even as late as the nineteenth century similar practices were reported to

---

92. Bukhari, *Sahih*, 62, 36-45; Muslim, *Sahih*, 8, 3412-3413, 3268-3277.

93. Muhammad b. Ahmad al-Muqadassi, *Kitab ahsan al-taqasim fi ma'rifat al-taqalim* ed. M.J. de Goeje (Leiden, 1906), p. 368f.

94. Spuler, *Iran*, p. 378.

persist in remote areas. Mirza Mehdi Khan noted that in Baluchestan, among the adherents of Dhakeri sect in the Kuhvand and Kaskur region incestuous marriage relations occurred.[95]

Finally, a third statute is that a Shi'i man may only marry a Moslem woman and not more than two slaves, but a Sunni man may marry Christian, Jewish and Zoroastrian women. If either of the parties becomes an idolater the marriage is automatically dissolved.[96]

SOCIO-ECONOMIC SELECTION CRITERIA
PREFERENCE FOR CONSANGUINEOUS MARRIAGE

Marriage in Iran was and is not a union between individuals, but one between families. For although the bride and the groom agreed to form a lifelong companionship (in principle), so did their two families. In effect, it was standard practice, until modern times that the choice of the partner was made by the parents or older family members, and not by the partners themselves. Endogamy, especially marriage between parallel and cross-cousins, was and still is common in Iran.[97] In the eighteenth century, for example, members of the ruling Zand family usually married their cousins.[98] Polak, based on his experience in Tehran, submits that endogamy was the rule, while Wills, basing himself on his experience in Fars, reports that marriage outside the family was nevertheless a frequent occurrence.[99] An English female physician

---

95. A. Houtum-Schindler, "Notes on Persian Baluchistan. From the Persian of Mirza Mehdi Khan," *JRAS* 1876, pp. 151.

96. The marriage of European women with Moslem Persians did not always have a happy ending. Ponafidine, *Life*, p. 325.

97. Lady Sheil, *Glimpses of Life and Manners in Persia* (London, 1856 [New York: Arno, 1973]), p. 143; Hantzsche, "Haram," p. 431; Jane Dieulafoy, *La Perse, La Chaldee et la Susiane* (Paris, 1887), p. 178; Mostawfi, *Sharh-e Zendegani*, vol. 1, pp. 183-85, 199 with his description of how his extended family lived together and how they inter-married.

98. Mehdi Roschan-Zamir, *Die Zand-Dynastie* (Hamburg, 1970), p. 150 (They also made political marriages, of course, to ensure political stability. In fact, it was customary among the Lurs to marry the wife of the killed enemy, a custom known as *khun-bast*).

99. Polak, *Persien*, vol. 1, p. 200; Wills, *In the Land*, p. 52.

observed that "One great advantage of the cousin-marriages is that the contracting parties know each other and have probably played together as children."[100] She seems to be borne out by the fact that "There is a [Persian] saying, 'Cousin-marriages are made in heaven,' because they are often happier, as the partners have more in common."[101] The fact that the newly weds were cousins and would live in the compound of their extended family reinforced the power and role of the family, of course.[102] According to a 1977 survey, about one quarter of marriages reported in rural areas was endogamous. The rate of such marriages is estimated to be about 50 percent among some ethnic minorities.[103]

This comes as no surprise, given the fact that family played and still plays an essential role in the life of Iranians, and is more important than any other relationship. The constitution of the Islamic Republic underscores the role of the family, which it identifies as the fundamental unit of society and the major center for the growth and advancement of human beings (article10). Even today among modern families, parental approval is almost a *sine qua non* for a marriage to go ahead and paradoxically, despite growing modernization it would seem that there has been a rise in consanguineous marriages over the last 40 years.[104]

---

100. Elizabeth N. MacBean-Ross, *A Lady Doctor in Bakhtiari Land* (London, 1921), p. 67.

101. O. A. Merritt-Hawkes, *Persia – Romance & Reality* (London, 1935), p. 285.

102. Reza Shapurian and Mohammadreza Hojat, "Sexual and Premarital Attitudes of Iranian College Students" *Psychological Reports*, 1985, pp. 67-74.

103. Benjamin P. Givens and Charles Hirschman, "Modernization and Consanguineous Marriage in Iran," *Journal of Marriage and the Family* 56 (1994), pp. 820-34; Loeb, *Outcaste*, pp. 110-14; Vida Nassehi-Behnam, "Change and the Iranian Family," *Current Anthropology*, 26/5 (1985), p. 558 [557-62]. See for a discussion of the pros and cons of cousin marriage as seen by Persians, Fischer, Michael M. J. "On Changing the Concept and Position of Persian Women," in Lois Beck & Nikki Keddie eds. *Women in the Muslim World*. (Cambridge: Harvard University Press, 1979),pp. 198-200; Gulick and Gulick, "Domestic Social Environment," pp. 507-08.

104. Givens and Hirschman, "Modernization and Consanguineous Marriage," pp. 823, 826-34.

VIRGINS ONLY

Girls, who married for the first time, had to be virgins and if "found out that she had not retained the seal of virginity" her life was in danger, for the husband would send her back in disgrace to her parents, who might kill her, because of the dishonor she had brought on her family.[105] For, "virginity has meaning not in the perspective of the young girl but in that of her family and of the honor of the family in social relations; she is the sign of this honor."[106] This despite the fact that Imam 'Ali has allegedly stated that a girl's hymen might have been broken by many normal daily activities, thus by other things than having had sex.[107] To ensure that a girl's hymen remained intact, which was the proof of her virginity, girls were and are restricted in their movements as well as in the kind of games they were engaged in, for not only sexual penetration breaks the hymen. For example, "jumping, climbing, and straying away from home are all discouraged."[108]

---

105. Farid al-Din 'Attar, *The Ilahi-nama or Book of God* translated into English by John Andrew Boyle (Manchester, 1976), p. 170. In some rural areas people counseled the husband not to cause a scandal by sending the girl back to her family, but to acquiesce in the situation, for God will recompense him. Khosro Borhanian, *Die Gemeinde Hamidieh in Khuzistan* (dissertation University of Cologne, 1960), p. 148. It also happened that an impotent man killed his bride, claiming that she had not been a virgin, to hide the fact that he had not been able to perform. Nancy Lindisfarne, "Variant Masculinities, Variant Virginities: Rethinking 'Honour and Shame,' in *Dislocating Masculinity: Comparative Ethnographies*, eds. Andrea Cornwall and Nancy Lindisfarne (London, 1994), p. 92.

106. Paul Vieille, "Iranian Women in Family Alliance and Sexual Politics," in Lois Beck and Nikki Keddie eds. *Women in the Muslim World* (Cambridge, 1978), p. 456.

107. Avazeh, *Qanun-e Qovveh-ye Bah*, pp. 48-49.

108. Behnaz Pakezegi, "Legal and Social Positions of Iranian Women," in Lois Beck and Nikki Keddie eds. *Women in the Muslim World* (Cambridge, 1978), p. 216; Friedl, *Women of Deh Koh*, p. 229. This obsession with virginity and above all not to break your hymen causes many a youth trauma among women, see Fataneh Farahani, "Diasporic Narratives on Virginity," paper read at the Private Lives and Public Spaces in Modern Iran conference held in Oxford (7-10 July 2005).

Given such importance attached to virginity, the author of the *Qabus-nameh* counsels his son to make sure that his daughter is a virgin, and "seek for her a son-in-law who shall be a virgin also; in that way the husband will have an attachment for his wife as great as the wife's for her husband, and he will desire no one else because he will have known no other person."[109] This advice was the expression of the belief that if a girl is a virgin when she marries, "she will be closer in affection" to her husband.[110] This obsession with virginity was food for satirists, the more so, as 'Obeyd-e Zakani's dictum, *Virginity: A name denoting nothing*[111] implies that a virgin was not always a virgin. In fact, some hold the opinion that middle class marriage in Iran begins with the lie that the bride is a virgin.[112] Hence, according to one report from 2007, "In the smaller towns and villages, it is still common to find the degrading practice where the mother and sisters of a bridegroom-to-be inspects the prospective bride to ensure she is a virgin."[113] Given the increase in pre-marital sex a growing number of girls have their hymen repaired, if they have been deflowered and can afford the operation, which in 2006 cost about 250 Euros in Tehran. Such an operation, technically called hymenoplasty, in Iran is appropriately referred to as *bakhiyeh zadan* (stitching) or *gol-duzi* (flower stitching).[114]

---

109. Kai Ka'us b. Iskandar, *Qabus Nama*, p. 125.

110. Abu Hamed Mohammad al-Ghazzali, *On Marriage*. Translated by Muhammad Nur Abdus Salam (Chicago, 2002), p. 20. A similar sentiment also existed among the Armenians in Jolfa ca. 1670, according to Ambrosio Bembo, *The Travels and Journal of Ambrosio Bembo* translated by Clara Bargellini (Berkeley, 2007), p. 359 "the Armenians contract marriages for their daughters when they are seven or eight years old: that also allows more affection to grow between husband and wife."

111. 'Obeyd-e Zakani, *The Ethics*, p. 71.

112. Lindisfarne, "Variant Masculinities,' p. 90. Referring to the 1940–50s, Molly Williams, *The Rich Tapestry of My Persian Years. Memoirs of Maud Hannah (Molly) Wiliams, a missionary nurse, 1937-1974* (Bendigo Victoria, 1994), p. 108, notes that "In more recent times when the veil was discarded, and women and girls socialised more, some men, especially older, wealthy ones, demanded certificates from a doctor to pronounce that the girls were virgins before the marriages took place."

113. [http://www.mianeh.net/en/articles/?aid=99].

114. See, e.g., among many other websites, [http://www.qantara.de/webcom/ show_article.php/_c-478/_nr-414/_p-1/i.html?PHPSESSID=5]

Not everybody in Iran attached the same importance to a girl's virginity. In the Bandar 'Abbas area adherents to a local sect dealt with the notion of virginity in a different way. In that area a prophet arose around 1900, who had quite a few followers among the population. One of the customs that was practiced by this new sect was that girls who married were sent by their parents to the prophet to be 'blessed' by him during their first night of marriage, rather than by their husbands. In the morning, the girl concerned went to her parents with the blood spotted sheet as proof that indeed she had been blessed and found to be a virgin. In this way the prophet aimed to prepare the new wives for their marriage and by 1947 he had already blessed some 1,100 girls in this manner. The prophet at that time had reached the venerable age of 72 and although only his most fanatic followers still sent their daughters on the first night of marriage to be 'blessed' the number of girls that were graced in this way was on the wane, also due to opposition to this particular practice of deflowering.[115]

In the 1940s, in Minab the population was mostly made up of Baluchis, who did not attach any importance whatsoever to the notion of virginity. And thus the showing of the blood-spotted sheet after the consummation of a marriage, a custom elsewhere adhered to in Iran, was totally ignored by them. In fact, parents went so far as to do away with virginity, by breaking the hymen of a girl with her finger after birth. At a later age, usually three to four years old, when the girl was circumcised once again her finger was used to enter the vagina to ensure that the hymen had not healed itself and, if so, to break it again; this was repeated each year until she married. Contrariwise, in the same area, to prevent pre-marital sex, the people of the islands of Qeshm, Larek and Hengam as well as the gypsies, gave their daughters chastity belts when they had reached the age of five to six.[116] In addition to the Baluchis of Minab, other groups in Iran also practiced female circumcision such as the Arabs of Khuzestan and

115. Daneshvar, *Didaniha*, vol. 1, pp. 180-82; Anonymous, "Dar Khuzestan, Banader-e Jonub, Gorgan, Korasan va Baluchestan didam," *Khvandaniha* 8/62 (1326/1947), p. 10.

116. Daneshvar, *Didaniha*, vol. 1, pp. 216-17; Anonymous, "Dar Khuzestan," p. 10.

Kurdestan. Any girl who was uncircumcised was not considered not to be a Moslem among these Sunni groups.[117] Otherwise, the practice of female circumcision is unknown in Iran.

AGE

Age was, of course, another factor in the choice of a wife. The younger she was the more likely that she would be a virgin, while older men generally appeared to prefer young girls. The Koran indicates maturity rather than a specific age limit for marriage. Based on the Traditions and custom, the minimum age for the consummation of a marriage is nine years, according to Islamic law, despite the fact that most girls mature only by the age fourteen.[118] Many religious authorities, therefore, not only favored marriage at such an early age, but also in fact encouraged it. As a result, early marriage for both men and girls was a common practice. The author of the *Qabus-nameh* counsels that a daughter should be married off as soon as possible, taught to be well-behaved and know the religious precepts, but not how to read and write. She should be married quickly, and thus make her somebody else's problem.[119]

---

117. Daneshvar, *Didaniha*, vol. 1, pp. 92, 217.

118. Khomeyni, *Towzih*, p. 506; Avazeh, *Qanun-e Qovveh-ye Bah*, p. 23; A. Querry, *Droit musulman. Receuil des lois concernant les musulmans-schyites* 2 vols. (Paris, 1871-72), vol. 1, p. 644, art. 30; L. Thot, "Das persische Rechssystem," *Zeitschrift für vergleichende Rechtswissenschaft* 22 (1909), p. 390; Ponafidine, *Life*, p. 319; Häntzsche, "Haram," p. 429. According to Imam Baqer, the girl must have completed her ninth year, i.e. she must be ten years. Avazeh, *Qanun-e Qovveh-ye Bah*, pp. 23. A recent study showed that in Mazandaran in the 1980s "the mean (standard deviation) age of menarche was 12.5 (1.1) years." M.A. Delavar and K.O. Hajian-Tilaki, "Age at menarche in girls born from 1985 to 1989 in Mazandaran, Islamic Republic of Iran," *Eastern Mediterranean Health Journal* 14/1 (2008) [http://www.emro.who.int/Publications/EMHJ/1401/article9.htm].

119. Kai Ka'us b. Iskandar, *Qabus Nama*, p. 125. Khomeyni, *Towzih*, p. 514 (no. 2336) states that according to Imam Sadeq it is one of a man's fortunes if his daughter does not menstruate in his house, i.e. that she has been married off prior to that event; Ibid, *Tahrir*, vol. 2, p. 215.

According to Islamic law, marriage of minors is permitted, provided it was contracted on their behalf by the parents or, in the absence of parents, by other suitable guardians. The early marriage age may be attributed to several factors such as an attempt to prevent the temptation of sexual relations before marriage. Both pubescent boys and girls were carnally desirable and thus, the potential object of the desire of adult males. Therefore, religious texts advised women to avoid finding themselves alone in the same room with a member of the opposite sex who is not kin.[120]

In Iran, parents therefore often arranged the betrothal and even marriage of their children at an early age, even before puberty. Consummation would occur at physical maturity only, but sometimes as early as nine years. "Engagements take place as early as three years old, and the bride is sometimes then taken to grow up with the future husband."[121] Among the Bakhtiyari tribe, marriages were often arranged between families long before the actual marriage took place. It was not uncommon that two sisters of the Bibi class [i.e. women from the chieftain class] to agree: " 'If I have a son next year, and you have a daughter three or four years after, they shall be engaged,' and the compact is generally carried out."[122] This custom of betrothing children even before they were born, or still in the cradle, or still very young was known in Iran as sweetmeat-eating (shirini khurdan), "and the given promise is sacredly carried out when the children grow up."[123] However, what was prohibited was the pre-Islamic Arab practice of shighar, which means that a man gives his daughter in marriage on the condition that the other gives his daughter to him in marriage without any dower being paid by either.[124] This early betrothal agree-

---

120. Amini, *Entekhab*, p. 65; al-Ghazzali, *On Marriage*, p. 25.

121. Van Sommer and Zwemer, *Our Moslem Sisters*, p. 220; MacBean, *A Lady Doctor*, p. 70

122. MacBean-Ross, *A Lady Doctor*, p. 66.

123. Ponafidine, *Life*, p. 320.

124. Muslim, *Sahih*, 8, 3295 (also 8-3296-3301). However, sister-exchange marriages were quite common among the Baseri tribe. Fredrik Barth, *Nomads of South Persia. The Baseri tribe of the Khamseh confederacy* (Boston, 1961),

ment could be dissolved without loss of face and honor if both parties agreed. In that case the family of the groom paid the bride's family half of the dowry (*mahr*).[125] Sa'di counseled the suitability of the ages of husband and wife as follows:

> I have heard that in these days a decrepit aged man
> Took the fancy in his old head to get a spouse.
> He married a beauteous little girl, Jewel by name,
> When he had concealed his casket of jewels from the
>   eyes of men
> A spectacle took place as is customary in weddings.
> But in the first onslaught the organ of the sheikh fell
>   asleep.
> He spanned the bow but hit not the target; it being
>   impossible to sew
> A tight coarse robe except with a needle of steel.
> He complained to his friends and showed proofs
> That his furniture had been utterly destroyed by her
>   impudence.
> Such fighting and contention arose between man and
>   wife
> That the affair came before the qazi; and Sa'di said:
> 'After all this reproach and villainy the fault is not the
>   girl's.
> Thou whose hand trembles, how canst thou bore a
>   Jewel?'[126]

---

p. 32.

125. Polak, *Persien*, vol. 1, p. 206; Jane Dieulafoy, *La Perse, la Chaldée et la Susiane* (Paris, 1887), p. 178; Ella Sykes, *Through Persia on a Side-saddle* (London, 1901), p. 171.

126. The story is from *Golestan*, chapter six, story nine in the translation by Richard Burton [http://www.enel.ucalgary.ca/People/far/hobbies/iran/Golestan/].

But in pre-industrial states like Iran it was normal that girls married early, not only among Moslems,[127] but also among Christians and Jews. The Spanish ambassador de Silva y Figueroa, for example, noted in 1619 that many Georgian girls were already married when they were 10 years old and the same held for Jewish girls around 1900.[128] More data are available from the nineteenth century, when it would seem that in some urban areas girls married when they were 12-13 years old. This was certainly the case in Tehran among the middle and upper classes.[129] Among the lower classes in urban Tehran girls were already married when they were 10-11 years old.[130]

Usually the husband waited for his wife to become nine years of age before consummating the marriage, but that did not prevent him from having sexual relations with his minor wife, if he wished to. Polak (the shah's physician during 1851-1860), reports a case of a seven-year old girl, who was not only married, but the marriage had also been consummated, after the husband had bought dispensation from a religious authority.[131]

---

127. For child marriage around 1000 CE see, e.g., Abu Fazl Mohammad b. Hoseyn Beyhaqi,. *Tarikh-e Beyhaqi* eds. Ghani and Fayaz (Tehran, 1324/1945), pp. 525-26.

128. Don Garcia de Silva y Figueroa,. *Comentarios de la embajada que de parte del rey de España Don Felipe III hizo al rey Xa Abas de Persia* 2 vols. (Madrid, 1903), vol. 2, p. 232; Loeb, *Outcaste*, pp. 108-09; Bassett, "Child Life in Persia," p. 170; Joh. Jansz. Strauszens, *Sehr schwere, wiederwärtige, und Denckwürdige Reysen* (Amsterdam, 1678), p. 130 reports that a merchant in Shamakhi bought two Georgian slave-girls of 11 and 12 years old and had intercourse with them.

129. Polak, *Persien*, vol. 1, pp. 200-02; Carla Serena, *Hommes et Choses en Perse* (Paris: G. Charpentier, 1883), p. 100.

130. Polak, *Persien*, vol. 1, p. 199; A. de. Gobineau, *Trois Ans en Asie (de 1855 A 1858)* 2 vols. (Paris, 1923), vol. 2, p. 187.

131. Polak, *Persien*, vol. 1, p. 199; Häntzsche, "Haram," p. 429. At the end of the nineteenth century, it was not exceptional for girls to be married at eight years of age among the Bakhtiyaris. MacBean-Ross, *A Lady Doctor*, p. 75; see also J. B. Feuvrier, *Trois ans à la Cour de Perse* (Paris: F. Juven, 1900), p. 182, where Naser al-Din Shah married his 8-year old daughter to his favorite catamite, 'Aziz al-Soltan.

Apart from the fact that parents wanted girls to marry as quickly as possible, for the poor there was the additional reason that there would be one less dependent, while a payment of a bride-price (*shir-baha*) was welcome as a form of financial infusion, especially in poor families.[132] Other contemporary authors confirm this range of the age of marriage; some favoring 14-15 years, while others submitted that the minimum age was usually 11 years.[133] This also held for the villages, for Hume-Griffith reports in 1900 or thereabouts that in a village around Isfahan it was very rare that a girl of 11 years would not be married.[134] Another missionary writes: "I am credibly informed that in many places it is impossible to find an unmarried girl of thirteen."[135] Bassett after 12 years of having worked in Persia reported that "She may legally wed at nine years of age, and is deemed an unfortunate old maid if not married before the close of her twelfth year."[136] In Azerbayjan it was customary to throw a hat at a girl (see Figure 1.1); if she did not fall down then she was considered to be at a marriageable age.

---

132. Anonymous, "Die moderne Perserin," *Das Ausland* 1880, p. 848; Bassett, "Child Life in Persia," p. 167; Maud von Rosen, *Persian Pilgrimage* (London, 1937), p. 139.

133. R.B.M Binning, *A Journal of Two Years' Travel in Persia, Ceylon, etc.* 2 vols. (London: Wm. H. Allen & Co, 1857), vol. 2, p. 402; John G. Wishard, *Twenty Years in Persia. A Narrative of Life under the Last Three Shahs* (New York: Fleming H. Revell, 1908), p. 244; Ella Sykes, *Through Persia on a Side-Saddle* (London: MacQueen, 1901), p. 187; Warzée, *Peeps into Persia*, p. 75 wrote "the bride was fifteen, quite old for Persia," where the 'normal' marriage age was thirteen (Ibid., p.208).

134. M. E. Hume-Griffith, *Behind the Veil in Persia and Turkish Arabia* (Philadelphia, 1909), p. 101. Around Kerman, brides of 10 and 11, and much younger occurred. Clara C. Rice, *Mary Bird in Persia* (London, 1916), pp. 125-26.

135. Van Sommer and Zwemer, *Our Moslem Sisters*, p. 221.

136. Basset, "Child Life in Persia," p. 170. As to marriage Jewett writes: "From twelve to sixteen is the most acceptable age. From twenty to twenty-five it is considered to be a calamity if she is unmarried." Mary Jewett, *Reminiscences of My Life in Persia* (Cedar Rapids, 1909), p. 109.

Figure 1.1: Hat test to see if a girl is old enough
for marriage (Mulla Nasruddin).

There were exceptions to the early marriage age. In the village of
Dahuk (Kerman), girls married late and were not allowed to marry
before they were about 25-30 years.[137] Among the Bakhtiyaris it was
the rule that the husband was four years older than the wife, although
the older khans, of course, often took young wives from among the
lower class tribeswomen.[138] In general it would seem that boys of
wealthy families married a *sigheh* when they were about fifteen and
they made a covenanted marriage when they were about twenty. It
also happened, "owing to family reasons [that] a youth of fifteen or
sixteen married to a girl much older."[139]

137. Gholam Hoseyn Khan Afzal al-Molk, *Safarnameh-ye Khorasan va Kerman*
Qodratollah Rowshani Za'frananlu ed. (Tehran, n.d.), p. 161.

138. MacBean-Ross, *A Lady Doctor*, p. 66.

139. Ponafidine, *Life*, p. 319; Merritt-Hawkes, *Persia*, p. 282. MeacBean-Ross, *A
Lady Doctor*, p. 67 reported that a 22-year old Bakhtiyari chief wanted to marry
the 15-year older widow of his uncle. It was only when he threatened to kill
himself that he was allowed to do so.

The Azeri poet 'Ali Akbar Saber (1862-1911) described the situation where a fifteen-year old girl was induced to marry a man as old as her father, if not her grandfather, having been told that he was young. When she finally sees him she is taken aback and shocked at the sight and smell of him:

> O Auntie, don't let him come!
> The sight of him is hateful, don't let him come!
> O God, it's as if he is not human,
> His face is not like any man.
> For [the] love of God, he is no husband for a woman.
> He is a devil and a swine, don't let him come!
> The sight of him is hateful, don't let him come!
>
> I was too shy to inquire when betrothed;
> 'He is young and nice,' I was told.
> This could be my husband! Heavens, what a thought!
> O Auntie, don't let him come!
> His doings are hateful, don't let him come!
>
> A chimney-like hat does he wear,
> His eyebrows are bespecked with white hair.
> Though he seems as old as my father fair,
> He is a swindler, don't let him come!
> His doing are hateful, don't let him come! [140]

These marriages of partners who were unequal in age were indeed shocking if not traumatic for little girls. Dr. Wishard reported that such marriages could cause much damage and suffering to these child-wives. "I have seen children brought to the hospital that the mere mention of their husbands' name would cause outbursts of shrieks, lest they might be compelled to return to them."[141]

---

140. The English translation of this poem is by Javadi, *Satire*, p. 211.

141. John G. Wishard, *Twenty Years in Persia. A Narrative of Life under the Last Three Shahs* (New York: Fleming H. Revell, 1908), p. 244; Merritt-Hawkes, *Persia*, p. 286.

جهنم اول كيت ايوه سنك اوبناماق وقالك كجدى ملا عم گوب سكا كاين كسوز

Figure 1.2 Young girl sent off as a bride to her husband's
house *(Mulla Nasruddin)*.

In Isfahan, around 1918, a group of Persian women "tried to form
a league to combat the custom, the mullahs immediately condemned
the league as infringing the law of their prophet." Even the deadly
consequences of the practice did not deter them. "A short while ago,
one of the leading mullahs, who had given his own little daughter in
marriage at a very early age, [observed that] this hateful custom had
brought [her] to the point of death. Anxious and alarmed enough
he was then, but, so hardened was his heart, that, when the child
recovered as by a miracle, he gave an even younger daughter in marriage a few months afterwards."[142] Under the influence of the reform-
ist movement, by 1920 there was a sentiment among parents, mostly
in urban areas, certainly of the middle and upper class, to postpone

142. Emmeline M. Stuart, *Doctors in Persia* (London, n.d. [1921?]), pp. 14-15.
Miss Bird reported about Kerman: "One case is a child of 12 years old. She was
married five years ago, and last year she had a baby boy. For four months she
had been crippled; forty days ago her baby died, and the husband, not wanting
a 'childless, crippled wife,' divorced her. She is only a child, and calls me as
soon as I go into the house to pet her." Rice, *Mary Bird*, p. 122.

their daughters' marriage till they were older.[143] This was also the case among the leading class of the Bakhtiyaris. "The age of marriage is gradually rising. Bibi Sahebdjan, wife of Samsam-os-Saltaneh, told me she was married at the age of eight, her daughter-in-law at the age of fifteen, and her granddaughter will not be married till she attains her seventeenth birthday."[144]

Although women's groups and reformists had been arguing for modernizing the rules governing marriage and divorce since around 1900 it took until 1931 when such an event finally took place. Although modernists, like the group writing the journal '*Alam-e Nesvan*, praised the new Marriage Act of 1931, it barely changed anything regarding polygyny and temporary marriage, both institutions that the journal opposed.[145] The law of 1933 did not state the age at which girls might be married, but it was understood that it was sixteen. Marriage also had to take place in the presence of an officially registered mullah and of an agent of the civil administration.[146]

Rural Iranians continued to betroth children very young, but marriage was often delayed until fourteen (girls) and eighteen (boys) or 12 and 15.[147] This development was due to the fact that the Iranian authorities in 1957 approved a law that required court approval for the marriage of girls below the age of 13 and boys younger than 15.[148]

---

143. MacBean-Ross, *A Lady Doctor*, p. 75; Stuart, *Doctors*, p. 15.

144. MacBean-Ross, *A Lady Doctor*, p. 75. Barth, *Nomads of South Persia*, p. 35 indeed confirms that by the 1950s, if not earlier, that among the Baseri tribe, which held pasturage adjacent to the Bakhtiyaris, girls usually married when they were past 16 years of age.

145. '*Alam-e Nesvan* 1 (Sept 1932), pp. 6-9.

146. Ruth Frances Woodsmall, *Moslem women enter a new world* (New York, 1936), p. 120.

147. Reza Arasteh and Josephine Arasteh, *Man and society in Iran* (Leiden, 1964), p. 156; Angela Petrosian, Kazem Shayan, K.W. Bash, and Bruce Jessup, *The Health and Related Characteristics of Four Selected Villages and Tribal Communities in Fars Ostan* (Shiraz, 1964). Also in urban areas there was pressure to marry daughters at age 15. Gulick and Gulick, "Domestic Social Environment," pp. 507, 511, 516-17.

148. D. A. Momeni, "The Difficulties of Changing the Age at Marriage in Iran,"

Despite the new law, "until recently girls married before pubertal onset,"[149] but this has been delayed since about 1970, partially because of the legal age of marriage for girls was raised.[150] The new law of 1963 fixed the minimum lawful age of marriage at fifteen (girls) and eighteen (boys), although courts sometimes permitted marriage at ages thirteen (g) and fifteen (b) in accordance with article 1041 of the Civil Code.[151] The Marriage Act (art. 1041) raised the age of marriage to 15 (for women) and 18 (for men), and both had to give consent (art. 1963). For her first marriage a women required the permission of her grandfather and father (art. 1042-43). The man remained the head of the household, responsible for the woman's upkeep (art. 1105), while polygyny was allowed as well as temporary marriage (art. 1075-77). Divorce remained the right of the husband (art. 1133), but to be legal the declaration required two male witnesses, without the wife either being present or being aware of it. A wife could only request divorce if the husband did not provide her with maintenance, was insane, impotent, or mistreated her (arts. 1121-32). New was that a wife had the right to refuse intercourse if her husband had a sexually transmitted disease (STD), but this was no cause for divorce (art. 1127). Moreover, a man could only marry a second covenanted wife or a *sigheh* with the permission of the first wife, and the man had to state in writing that he did not have any other wife, when marrying for the first time, or state how many wives he had when he was already married. If he had lied about the number of wives then this constituted grounds for divorce. He also had to give evidence that he was able keep two wives in the same circumstances. The husband, in case of refusal, could of course threaten to divorce his first wife, in which case, for economic

Journal of Marriage & Family 34/3 (1972), pp. 545-51.

149. Erika Friedl, "Parents and children in a village in Iran," in A. Fathi, ed., *Women and the Family in Iran.* (Leiden, 1985), pp. 206, 209.

150. Erika Friedl, "Women and the Division of Labor in an Iranian Village," *MERIP Reports* March/April, 95 (1981), p.17; Borhanian, *Die Gemeinde Hamidieh*, p.145; Loeb, *Outcaste*, pp. 109-110.

151. Reuben Levy, *The Sociology of Islam* (London, 1957), p. XXX

and social reasons, she might capitulate. The identity card of the man still had space for four wives, however.[152]

In 1975, the legal age for marriage was raised to 18 years for girls and 20 years for boys, which exceptions for girls older than 15 years.[153] The new law did not significantly reduce the frequency of child marriages. Girls were permitted "as young as nine, even seven in some cases, to be married if a physician signs a certificate agreeing to their sexual maturity."[154] The doctor was said to consult the family without seeing the girl. Men usually were older than the minimum age at which they were allowed to marry, due to the time it took to mobilize the financial wherewithal required to marry. Thus, it was the father who usually determined the marriage age, as the children depended on his financial assistance. The law required the recording of all major family events such as marriage, birth and death by the civil authorities.

The adjustment of the law indicates that young marriages were still quite common, but that the higher legal age of marriages reflected the upward trend in the actual age of marriage. The higher legal age as well as education had a positive impact on the increase in the actual age of marriage over time. Also, the fact that the law stipulated that those who arranged marriages at lower than the legal age would be punished, if convicted. The fact that marriages had now to be officially registered with the civil authorities rather than with a religious authority, as had been the case for centuries, made parents take heed of the requirements of the law. Of course, these changes took time to take effect and have an impact, because the civil authorities only

---

152. Ali Reza Naqvi, "The Marriage Laws of Iran," *Islamic Studies* 7/2-4 (1968).

153. Pakezegi, "Legal and Social Positions," p. 219.

154. J. Goodwin, *Price of Honor* (Boston, 1994), p. 114; Marie Ladier-Fouladi, "The Fertility Transition in Iran," *Population: An English Selection* 9 (1997), pp. 198-99. [191-213]; Momeni, "The Difficulties," p. 547 ("The law states that exemptions are to be granted for 'proper reasons' but fails to define specifically the 'proper reasons'. Apparently these include cases involving premarital pregnancy and rape, but exemptions are also granted whenever the girl is judged 'physically mature'").

slowly spread their hold over the rural areas. Also, in the absence of birth registration at that time, the age of birth of many a person was guess-work. Even after the law had been promulgated in many cases marriage was concluded without the intermediacy of a religious dignitary, because there was none. This was the situation in the rural areas where marriage was 'solemnized' by a compact between families. In 1946, Mahmud Daneshvar observed that in the Garmsirat it was not unusual that a man and wife, with a few children, if it so happened that they had come to 'town' for another reason, had their marriage formalized or annulled post-factum by a religious official.[155]

Under the Islamic Republic these 1975 and other laws were declared null and void and new laws were written that were considered to be in line with Islamic law. In June 2002, Iranian authorities approved a law increasing the age at which girls can marry without parental consent from 9 to 13. The elected legislature actually had passed the bill in 2000, but the Guardian Council, a 12-man body of conservative clerics, vetoed it as contradicting Islamic law. Iran's clerical establishment insists that the marriage of young girls is a means to combat immorality. The Expediency Council, which arbitrates between the elected parliament and the Guardian Council, passed the measure. The law however does not change the age at which children can get married (nine for girls and 14 for boys), but says that girls below the age of 13 and boys younger than 15 need their parents' permission and the approval of a 'Righteous Court.' However, the law also allows exceptions to this rule, when a case can be made for marriage at an earlier age. Reformists state that the new law does not protect children, since most of those who marry at such a young age are forced to do so. The law also revitalized a pre-existing organization, the *Bonyad-e Ezdevaj* or the Marriage Foundation, and renamed it as *Edareh-ye Ezdevaj* or the Marriage Bureau.[156] The new family law

---

155. Daneshvar, *Didaniha*, vol. 1, pp. 248-49.

156. Ashraf Zahedi, "State ideology and the status of Iranian war widows," *International Feminist Journal of Politics*, June 2006, pp. 267-86. N. Yassari, "Who is a child" in: Rutten ed., *Recht van de Islam* 22 Teksten van het op 18 juni 2004 te Leiden gehouden tweeentwintigste RIMO-symposium (Maastricht,

also placed a ban on coitus with girls below the age of nine, which is accordance with Islamic law. However, there is an interest in such young virgins, because there was and is the belief that "a young girl rejuvenated an old man."[157] Girls of eight to 12-years, therefore, are still 'sold' for 300 to 400 *tumans* in the rural areas of Khorasan, Seystan and Baluchestan and probably elsewhere in Iran as well. If 'sold' to a 60 or 70-year old man they are widows before they are twenty with one or two small children and little chance to remarry and face a life of poverty.[158]

The number of such marriages seems to be on the decrease. A recent study concluded that between "1986 and 1996, the mean age at first marriage rose from 19.8 to 22.4 among females and from 23.6 to 25.6 among males,"[159] which is in line with the sentiments of young people. According to a study carried out among Iranian twelfth graders in Shiraz in 1982, the average intended age of marriage was 21 for females and 23.8 for males; both considerably above the legal age of marriage for the two sexes (13 for females and 15 for males).[160]

WIDOWS MAY ALSO APPLY

It seems odd to include this section in the discussion, but in the tenth century, marriage with widows was forbidden in Deylam,[161] and probably in other areas, although that impediment was slowly

---

2005), pp. 17-30 points out that the Civil Code considers a child of nine to be mature enough to marry, i.e. sign a marriage contract, but not mature enough to sign any other contracts, such as those that are financial in nature.

157. Merritt-Hawkes, *Persia*, p. 286; Bricteux, *Au Pays*, p. 190.

158. Papoli-Yazdi, *Khaterat*, p. 23.

159. A. Aghajanian and A.H. Mehryar, "Fertility transition in the Islamic Republic of Iran, 1976–1996," *Asia-Pacific Population Journal*, 14/1 (1999), pp. 21–42.

160. Abbas Tashakkori, Vaida D. Thompson, and Amir H. Mehryar, "Iranian Adolescents' Intended Age of Marriage and Desired family Size," *Journal of Mariage and the Family* 49 (1989), p. 922. [917-27]; Ayatollah Ebrahim Amini, *Entekhab-e hamshahr*, pp. 30-31 favors that boys do not marry before 18 years and girls not before 15 years.

161. Muqadassi, *Kitab ahsan*, p. 370; Paul Schwarz, *Iran im Mittelalter nach den arabischen Geographen* 7 vols. (Leipzig, 1929), vol. 7, p. 857.

disappearing.[162] Because of the lax divorce rules, marriages, made for political or other reasons, could easily be dissolved. Nevertheless, there still remained a reluctance to marry widows.[163] According to the counsel given in the *Qabus-nameh*, "a woman who has had many husbands is held in no esteem."[164] These attitudes reflected pre-Islamic sentiments, for in Islam there is officially no such lack of esteem for widows and remarriage with them. According to the Koran (2:234),

> If any of you die and leave widows behind, they shall
> wait four months and ten days. When they have fulfilled
> their term, there is no blame on you if they dispose of
> themselves in a just manner.

However, there was the belief among the jurists as well as among the believers in general that divorcees and widows "remain attached to" their former husband.[165] There is already some difference and not only in years between the *Qabus-nameh* and Nezam al-Molk's *Book of Government*, written 150 years later. Nezam al-Molk makes it clear that widows with sufficient wealth could find suitable husbands again.[166] Not only wealth and social standing helped overcome social custom. Also, those widows with other attractive characteristics, such as a large bottom, had a comparative advantage and presumably could even find a younger husband.[167] Widows were often married to their husband's brother, something that, for example, all Timirud princes practiced.[168] Khvandamir relates a case, where a soldier wanted to marry his brother's wife, so that his brother's two sons would have a good home. The wife refused, because she wanted to marry a mercer and

162. Beyhaqi, *Tarikh*, pp. 193, 432, 537; Spuler, *Iran*, p. 380.

163. Adam Mez, *Die Renaissance des Islam* (Hildesheim, 1968), pp. 343-44; Spuler, *Iran*, p. 380.

164. Kai Ka'us b. Eskandar, *Qabus Nama*, p. 107, ch. XXIV.

165. al-Ghazzali, *On Marriage*, p. 20.

166. Nizam al-Mulk, *Book*, p. 84.

167. Nizam al-Mulk, *Book*, p. 126.

168. John E. Woods, *The Timurid Dynasty, Papers on Inner Asia* no. 14 (Bloomington, Indiana 1990), p. 20-21, 29-30.

although Olugh Beyg (r. 1411-1449) had wanted to forbid the wife from marrying the mercer, the olama pointed out that he was wrong and he had to let her to have her way.[169] The mother of Karim Khan Zand, the ruler of most of Iran between 1756 and 1779, married her brother-in-law and bore him children.[170] In the nineteenth century it was customary to marry one's brother's wife [wives] when he died.[171] D'Allemagne depicts a rather positive picture of a widow's prospects for remarriage during the nineteenth century.

> If she has some wealth she may look around and make a better marriage than otherwise, based on her previous experience. Among the common people, widows are in particular sought after and they sometimes get a very nice bride price. This is due to the fact that during their previous marriage they have acquired very useful skills as to management of the household, and that they have become very good at weaving of carpets, making of bread, making of clothes, etc.[172]

Similar sentiments were reported in the 1930s, where a man said that one of his wives was his best wife and rich, because she had been widowed three times. "The first taught her to cook, the second to knot mats, and the third whipped her so often that she is now an ideal wife."[173]

However, not every widow was so lucky. According to Dr. Wishard, referring to the situation around 1900, wrote: "As many

169. Ghiyath al-Din Khvandamir, *Tarikh-e Habib al-Siyar* 4 vols. ed. Mohammad Dabir-Siyaqi (Tehran, 1362/1983), vol. 4, p. 36.

170. Roschan-Zamir, *Zand Dynastie*, p. 150.

171. See, e.g., E'temad al-Saltaneh, *al-Ma'ather*, p. 176; MacBean Ross, *Lady Doctor*, pp. 73-74.

172. H. d'Allemagne, *Du Khorasan au Pays de Bakhtyaris*, 4 vols. (Paris, 1911), vol. 1, p. 216.

173. Von Rosen, *Persian Pilgrimage*, p. 186. Jews practiced levirate marriage as did the Baseri tribe. Loeb, *Outcaste*, p. 116; Barth, *Nomads of South Persia*, p. 32.

of these widows are left without means of support, there is only one road open for them, and that road leadeth to destruction. Most of them are almost compelled to become plural wives, or, what is worse, temporary ones."[174] Being a widow in Yazd of the 1940-50s, in Papoli-Yazdi's experience, who was the son of one and the neighbor of many, was being condemned to be a very poor woman, who had to lead a hard life to make ends meet.[175] A study among widows in Shiraz in the late 1960s showed that widows are less likely to remarry than widowers. This is mainly due to the fact that a widow is expected to stay with her children and not remarry, at least until they reach adulthood. On the other hand, a widower is encouraged to remarry; they generally marry young women, who have never been married before. "In fact, it has been considered undignified for a man-even a widower or one who has divorced his wife- to marry a widow or divorcee."[176]

BEAUTY

Having taken into account the categories of women that a Moslem man could not marry, he, or rather his family would decide which girl or women they would chose for their son. The choice then was between a virgin, a divorcee or a widow. To further refine that choice other parameters would be taken into account such as station, wealth, beauty, and character. When girls were beautiful, family relationship and lineage was disregarded, even though most of these beauties were from the lower classes.[177] Moreover, Islamic law states that "One

174. Wishard, *Twenty*, p. 244.

175. Papoli-Yazdi, *Khaterat*, p. 96.

176. Akbar Aghajanian, "Living Arrangements of Widows in Shiraz, Iran," *Journal of Marriage and the Family* 47/3 (1971), p. 782. In would seem that widows easily remarry in rural areas, for in the village of Ahar widows often remarry, even when they are 50 or 60. In the late 1960s, widows only represented two percent of the women in the village, Ali Akbar Djirsarai, *Das Dorf Ahar (Iran). Die bevölkerungs-, sozial-, und wirtschaftsgeographische Struktur und Entwicklung* (Boon, 1970), p. 35.

177. John Malcolm, *The History of Persia*. 2 vols. (London, 1820 [Tehran, 1976]), vol. 2, p. 591; Lady Sheil, *Glimpses of Life and Manners in Persia* (London, 1856 [New York: Arno, 1973]), p. 143; Polak, *Persien*, vol. 1, p. 200;

should not be content with beauty or riches; it is indeed forbidden to contract a marriage with these points alone in consideration."[178] Even so, not everybody agreed that beauty should be a selection criterion, for that was but a fleeting characteristic, when you should be looking for more lasting ones. The author of the *Qabus-nameh*, for example, counsels his son as follows:

> When you seek a wife do not demand her possessions also; and look well to her character, refusing to be enslaved by beauty of face-for prettiness, man can take a mistress. A wife, to be good, should be chaste and of sound faith, capable in household-management and fond of her husband, modest and God-fearing, brief-tongued, sparing and economical of materials. Men say that a good wife is one who looks to the consequences of every action. Yet even if a woman is affectionate, handsome and well-beloved, do not submit yourself entirely to her control nor be subservient to her command. Someone asked Alexander why he did not marry Darius's daughter, who was very beautiful. He replied: 'It would be an ugly matter if we, who have become the master of all men in the world, should have a woman as master over us.
>
> Your wife must be of sound health, of mature age and intelligent and a person who in her parents' house has seen how the mistress of the house conducts her affairs. If you find a woman of those qualities, do not fail to ask for her in marriage; do your utmost to marry her and endeavour at all costs never to display jealousy in front of her. If you are of a jealous disposition, it is better for you not to marry, because a display of jealousy does nothing but suggest impropriety. Also, it is as well to know that women frequently destroy men because of jealousy, but

---

Wills, *In the Land*, p. 64.

178. S.G.W. Benjamin, *Persia and the Persians* (London, 1887), p. 448. al-Ghazzali, *On Marriage*, p. 20 had argued that other qualities, such as intelligence and piety, was more important than beauty.

will sacrifice their persons only for very few; moreover, they have no fear of jealousy or rage.[179]

These are wise words, but not always heeded by men and sometimes to their loss. In 1335, Malek Ashraf desperately wanted to marry the daughter of the governor of Mardin and to make that happen he sent much property to him. When she finally arrived after one year, he did not find her beautiful enough and apart from the wedding night did not see her anymore.[180] Others were even more disappointed such as a man who had been induced by friends to marry a certain girl, whose face he only saw on his wedding night for the first time. To say that she was a disappointment to behold was not even close to reality; in short she was ugly. After a few days the new wife asked her husband: "My life! As you have many relatives, I wish you would inform me before whom I may unveil. ... 'My soul!' responds the husband, 'if you will but conceal you face from *me*, I care not to whom you show it.'"[181]

Despite these experiences men continue to value beauty, be it that over time the nature of the concept of beauty that enraptured men evolved.[182] Also, the poetic effusions of what beauty constituted was not always reflected in what men appreciated in reality. For example, instead of the cypress-shaped girls of the poets Iranian men liked women who were more solid and hefty.[183] Also, during the nineteenth

---

179. Kai Ka'us b. Iskandar, *Qabus Nama*, p. 117 (ch. XXVI). There are also Traditions expressing the same sentiments, see, e.g., Avazeh, *Qanun-e Qovveh-ye Bah*, pp. 17-19.

180. Samarqandi, *Matla'-ye Sa'deyn*, vol. 1, p. 148.

181. Javadi, *Satire*, p. 207.

182. By the early 1800s, e.g., "When a Persian wishes to give a high idea of a woman's beauty, he says, she is *Missal Frengui*, like a European; and on the other hand, Europeans pay the same compliment to the fair sex of Georgia and Circassia." Morier, *Second*, p. 39.

183. This was perhaps because the Imam 'Ali recommended men to marry a wife who was hefty and short, because she would give higher sexual pleasure. Avazeh, *Qanun-e Qovveh-ye Bah*, p. 19. For a discussion of what constitute the elements of beauty, see Niloufar Jozani, *La Beauté Menacée* (Paris-Tehran:

century to make women more attractive a thin shade of mustache (*khatt*) was penciled above their lips, thus emulating one of the alluring characteristics of a young boy that attracted so many men. This, combined with the boy-like body of a young bride, probably helped men overcome their inability to sexually perform with a woman. However, by the second decade of the twentieth century the painted moustache was depicted as something undesirable.[184]

How to Select a Partner

The fact that parents often chose the wife or husband for their children did not mean that the latter never had a say in the matter. It depended on the family, the ethnic group, the era and other considerations. In the tenth century, in the Caspian Provinces it was customary to award the winner of athletic bouts the choice of wife, subject to the father's permission. The winner would come to the father's house in the evening and made his pitch for the daughter's hand, who was veiled during that occasion. If permission was given then the marriage was concluded and the groom nailed a water bottle, which he had taken with him, to the wall.[185] Elsewhere women were subject to a less restrictive regime during that same period. In Pirrim (Tabaristan), "every fifteen days a market is held there, and from all the region men, girls, and young men come there dressed up, frolic, organize games, play on string instruments, and make friends. The custom of this province is such that each man who loves a girl, beguiles her, carries her away, and for three days does with her as he likes. Then he sends someone to the father of the girl that he should give the girl in marriage."[186] Whereas

---

IFRI, 1994), pp. 53-76.

184. Afsaneh Najmabadi, *Women with Mustaches and Men without Beards. Gender and Sexual Anxieties of Iranian Modernity* (Berkeley, 2005), pp. 232-33; Serena, *Hommes*, p. 260 ("a thin shade of a mustache over my lips"); Warzeé, *Peeps*, p. 73 (the bride "had a heavy black moustache of paint on her upper lip, which is supposed to render a woman beautiful in Persia").

185. al-Muqadassi, *Kitab ahsan*, p. 369f.

186. V. Minorsky, *Hudud al-Alam, 'The Regions of the World': a Persian geography 372 [A.]H.-982 A.D.* (London, 1937), p. 136.

this form of institutionalized 'bride robbery' in the Caspian provinces was a social custom, it was considered to be unlawful that a ruler forcibly took the womenfolk, free or slave, from one of his subjects.[187] These customs clearly were a holdover from a previous era and with the gradual spread of Islam many of these customs were supplanted by (more proper) Islamic customs.

Nevertheless, some groups preserved their old customs. Among the Marsh Arabs of Khuzestan, for example, it was customary that if a girl wanted to marry a particular man she would put a needle on his robe; two days later at the same spot if she would do the same she indicated and confirmed that she indeed would be happy to marry this man. If the man had the same feelings for the girl he would send the needle to the girl's father and the father, who already knew of his daughter's choice, would give his permission and the marriage ceremonies could begin.[188] It also happened in Khorramshahr's surrounding villages that if a man wanted to have a particular woman (even if she was married) he then took her by force and put her in his own house. If the husband wanted his wife back the kidnapper would ask for a ransom. If he did not have the wherewithal or his clan lacked the strength to take to woman back by force the husband would be the looser.[189]

However, this traditional 'courting' and the girl having a say in whom she wanted to marry was the exception to the rule. For in general, the conclusion of a marriage also shows the inequality of the woman, because she really had no formal say in the matter. A girl does her duty, even if she is too young to know exactly what it is and what is in wait for her, because her family told her to do so. This even holds when you know what you are doing and you do not want the old man they have selected for you. But it is rare that you oppose your family, for family is what shelters and protects you. In rare cases

---

187. Ibn al-Athir, *Kamil f'il-Tarikh*, vol. 4, p. 217 (711 in Khvarezm), vol. 8, p. 61 (929/Mardavij).

188. Daneshvar, *Didaniha*, pp. 101-02.

189. Daneshvar, *Didaniha*, pp. 121-22.

a girl would refuse to marry the husband her father had selected for her. In one particular case, in the 1880s, the girl refused, because her father agreed with her.[190] Even in traditional Moslem families, girls sometimes could 'fight' for their choice of husband. Bibi Khanom, the author of 'The Vices of Men' (*Ma'ayeb al-Rejal*), wrote that in her youth she was so impassioned with a young man that she only wanted to marry him, especially because he reciprocated her love. However, her mother's brother, a leading Islamic scholar, considered it most inappropriate and would have nothing of this kind of girl nonsense. However, Bibi Khanom's mother was sympathetic to her feelings and supported her. It took Bibi Khanom five years to wear down the opposition against her choice of husband, but she finally won.[191]

It was not only the girl who could express a preference, which was risky anyway, because it was considered improper and dangerous for her reputation and therefore, the girl had to be married off as quickly as possible. It seems to have been more usual that a boy became enamored of a girl, either because he saw her, which was the usual situation, in villages of tribal areas where veils were not always worn, or because of the description given of the girls by a sister or other female relatives—the usual situation in an urban environment. Through a female relative, or a professional go-between, the man would ask the father's consent to marry her. If he agreed then often the suitor often was given a chance to glance at his future wife's face, and if this did not douse his ardor, the negotiations concerning the conditions of the marriage contract, the amount to be paid to the girl's mother (*shir-baha*) and other matters would follow. If these resulted in an agreement, the marriage date was set.[192]

190. Ensiyeh Sheykh Reza'i, and Shahla Azari, *Gozareshha-ye Nazmiyeh az Mahallat-e Tehran* 2 vols. (Tehran 1377/1998), p. 137.

191. Bibi Khanom, "Ma'ayeb al-Rejal," in Hasan Javadi, Manjeh Mar'ashi and Simin Shakarlu eds. *Ruyaru'i-ye zan va mard dar 'asr-e Qajar. Du Resaleh. Ta'dib al-Nesvan va Ma'ayeb al-Rejal* (Washington DC, 1992), p. 189.

192. Ponafidine, *Life*, pp. 320-21. In Khorramshahr (Khuzestan), the *shir-baha* of girls was expressed in a number of palm trees. Fathers sold their daughters in return for a palm grove with say 10 trees. Daneshvar, *Didaniha*, pp. 121-22.

Although during the ceremony the bride is asked for her permission, this is a formality, because, according to the Traditions, "Silence is enough as permission for a virgin."[193] This is pro-forma involvement of the bride is reinforced by the fact that a father can give his daughter away when she is not yet fully mature.[194] Moreover, the influence of parents over their children is enormous. They can sell them, "which frequently happens among nomadic tribes without being considered disgraceful."[195]

Therefore, for a girl to say 'no' to a marriage that had been arranged by her family was almost unheard of. Everybody would be against her, including the neighbors' wives, who tried to convince her that it was her duty to obey her parents and brothers. Love, they said, was something that might come later and that she should just accept her fate. Nevertheless, it sometimes happened, against all odds. Yazdi-Papoli relates an interesting case where a girl from his alley refused to marry the man chosen by her family. When she still had not given in, after repeated appeals and much pressure by family and friends, she was literally beaten to the marriage carpet and, when those present started ululating, one of the women present said 'Yes' instead of her to the question whether she agreed to the marriage. Everybody knew that the bride had not said 'Yes' including the groom, but nobody cared, except for the bride who continued to say, even after the signing of the marriage contract, that she did not want to marry the groom. She refused to go into the bridal room, but was beaten into it. When the guests were waiting for the groom to come out after having done his duty, he reappeared much earlier than expected and in his underwear, bleeding allover, as his bride had attacked, scratched and bitten him and had refused to submit to him. The bride did not speak or move for more than one year. When the husband once again tried to exercise his conjugal rights he came out of the bedroom even more bloodied than the first time. Her husband then divorced her. She then

---

193. Muslim, *Sahih*, 8, 3302-3308.

194. Muslim, *Sahih*, 8, 3309-3311.

195. Ponafidine, *Life*, p. 320.

came alive and talkative again, which earned her a beating from her uncle, but she finally was allowed to marry her choice of husband with whom she still happily lived in 2005.[196]

Traditionally, the stages of the arrangements leading to the actual marriage differed by urban area, village and tribal group and therefore, descriptions are not provided thereof.[197] Suffice to say that once the two families agree on the marriage, an auspicious day was selected. No marriage can be concluded during Razaman and Moharram, and "no marriage should be consummated while the moon is in the sign of the Scorpion ... nor during an eclipse of the moon; nor on the day of an eclipse of the sun; nor at noon-time; nor towards the end of twilight; nor during the last three days of the months called *el mohak*, during which the moon is below the horizon; nor between dawn and the rising of the sun; nor during the first night of each month, excepting the month of Ramazan; nor during the middle of the night of the month; nor during a journey; ... nor in a tempest, nor during an earthquake."[198]

The groom's family pays for the marriage feast, while the groom also promises to pay a bride-price or *shir-baha* (milk-price) to the bride's family, in addition to a dowry or *mahr*.[199] This could be anything ranging from a girdle in the prophet Mohammad's time to large sums of money and/or landed property soon thereafter, all depending on

---

196. Papoli-Yazdi, *Khaterat*, pp. 192-201.

197. For a description of some local marriage customs see, e.g., Parviz Varjavand, *Sima-ye Tarikh va Farhang-e Qazvin* 3 vols. (Tehran, 1377/1998), vol. 2, pp. 911-21; Baba Safar, *Ardabil dar Godhargah-e Tarikh* 3 vols. (Tehran, 1350-62/1971-83), vol. 2, pp. 154ff.; Henri Massé, *Croyances et Coutumes Persanes* 2 vols. (Paris: Maisonneuve, 1938), pp. 61-94; Daneshvar, *Didaniha*, vol. 1, pp. 29-30, 58-59, 102, 110, 122, 248-49; vol. 2, pp. 22-25, 48-50, 61, 111, 158-59, 203-06, 261-62, 293.

198. Benjamin, *Persia*, p. 448.

199. "The portion paid at the time of marriage is sometimes called *shir baha* (milk price) and theoretically is to pay the mother of the bride for bringing up the girl. In practice the milk price should be an egg nest for the bride or for use in providing the dowry brought by the bride, usually consisting of the furnishings for the house: cooking utensils, carpets, and so on." Fischer, "Persian Women," p. 200.

the wealth, social position and relationship of the families. The bride is entitled to receive this dower at any time after her marriage. However instead of being a source of financial security for married women in case of divorce or widowhood, it is used by the husbands as a leverage to deny their wives a divorce or grant her one without paying her the marriage portion. The bride's family pays for the dower or *jezyeh*, which usually included such items necessary for the newly-weds to set up a household, such as rugs, bedding, cooking pots. Nowadays, payments of the dowry and *jezyeh* have become status symbols and are often inflated in value, which constitute a major obstacle for young people to marry. In fact, without their family's support they find it difficult to do so. On the other hand, among modern urbanized as well as among religious families the high level of the dowry is considered to be a symbol of lack of trust between the future spouses and their families. They, therefore, often agree on a symbolic, but spiritual, dowry (e.g. the Koran).[200] After a party the marriage was consummated and a blood-stained cloth was shown thereafter as evidence of the bride's virginity. In the villages a rifle shot announced the good news to the world at large.[201]

---

200. Shahla Haeri, *Law of Desire. Temporary marriage in Shi'i Islam* (Syracuse, 1989), p. 37; Fischer, "Persian Women," pp. 201-02; Pakizegi, "Legal and Social Positions," p. 221. In rural areas, the young brides did not even know what was written in the marriage contract, and in case of divorce, it was her family, who decided in the matter of payment of the divorce money. Friedl, *Women of Deh Koh*, pp. 187-88.

201. Among the Mamasani tribe, who practiced the custom of 'wife robbing', the blood-stained cloth was not shown, but rather the groom had to emerge from the bridal room with an open collar as a sign that he had been able to 'take' the bride and he had to show himself like that during three days. If he emerged without an open collar as a sign that he had not been able 'to take' the bride then he had to flee from the tribe, because he had shown not be a real man. For not having been able to master the bride, how could he be expected to take a fort? Daneshvar, *Didaniha*, vol. 2, p. 111.

POLYGYNY

According to Islamic law, a man may not have more than four covenanted wives at the same time[202] and, in that case, he cannot marry another wife until a divorced wife has completed her waiting period. Also, a Shi'a man can only make a covenanted marriage with not more than two slave-girls as unmarried concubines.[203] In addition, a man may have an unlimited number of temporary wives or *sigheh*s and an unlimited number of slave girls.[204] The Islamic system was more or less in harmony with actual practice in Sassanid Iran. Polygyny was practiced in Iran before the advent of Islam: there also were two classes of wives (covenanted and temporary married wives), girls were married young, while otherwise the position of the wife within the marriage did not change that much either. Nevertheless, for Persian rulers, there were start-up problems even when they formally had converted to Islam, because they did not limit themselves to four wives. The Ispahabad of Tabarestan had 93 wives in CE 755, each with their own household, while he had built a palace for his favorite wife at the seaside. He had a schedule for visiting each of his wives, which is reminiscent of the practice of Achaemenid kings as well as in harmony with Islamic precepts to treat each wife equally in the same manner.[205] In 1029, Majd al-Dowleh the Buyid governor of Rey had more than 50 freeborn wives, a practice that he defended by saying that it was an ancestral custom.[206] The ruler of Bukhara also had many favorites and slave-girls in the mid-tenth century.[207] Thus, it took some time

---

202. Moslems in Iran were not the only ones to marry more than one wife. "Polygyny is lawful and is practiced among the Jews." Bassett, *Eastern Mission*, p. 67, but they practiced it only and rarely as an alternative to divorce. Loeb, *Outcaste*, p. 119.

203. Querry, *Droit*, vol. 1, p. 672, art. 241.

204. The qualification 'unlimited' in the latter has been challenged by some olama at the end of the twentieth century (Motahhari; Khomeyni). Haeri, *Law*, p. 2.

205. Spuler, *Iran*, p. 377.

206. Ibn al-Athir, *Kamil f'il-Tarikh*, vol. 9, p. 128; Nizam al-Mulk, *Book*, p. 68 (nine wives).

207. Narsakhi, *History*, p. 26.

before rulers in Iran adjusted to the manner in which they satisfied their sensuality, according to Islamic precepts. Some men took this commandment very far. Fath 'Ali Shah (r. 1797-1834) had as many as 158 wives over his lifetime. But the shah was outdone by a merchant in Minab who was 46 years old in 1946, and, allegedly, already had had 568 wives, both covenanted and temporary ones. At the time of reporting he kept five wives, of which one *sigheh*, in his house.[208]

However, despite all the stories about Iranian men with harems filled with women, polygyny was the exception rather than the rule. First, there were not enough women to make polygyny possible and secondly it was too expensive. The cost involved in having more than one wife was one of the reasons that made it so unattractive. According to Sura 4:128, men have to keep separate households for each wife and treat them all equally. A late nineteenth century Russian diplomat noted that "In many former Persian harems this is carried out with pedantic exactness, but with the extravagance of the Persian ladies, such households can only be maintained by the very rich."[209] Late nineteenth century American missionaries noted that "A husband being bound to maintain his wife in comfort, a well-filled *Anderoon*, or harem, was an expensive affair. Princes and wealthy men occasionally indulged in such a luxury."[210] In reality, therefore, men did not treat their wives equally, although they kept them in a separate room or hovel. Papoli-Yazdi writes that he and his mother lived in a poor neighborhood, in a rented room, while his father's other wife lived in a nice house and in luxury.[211] But it was not men of wealth who married more than one wife, although some suggest that this was usu-

---

208. Daneshvar, *Didaniha*, vol. 1, pp. 211.

209. Ponafidine, *Life*, p. 323. al-Ghazzali, *On Marriage*, p. 27 wrote "One should observe equality in gifts and in spending the night with them; however, it is not obligatory in affection and sexual intercourse. ... If a person is fed up with one wife and does not want to embrace her, he must divorce her and not keep her fettered."

210. Neville, *Unconventional Memories*, p. 145.

211. Papoli-Yazdi, *Khaterat*, pp. 59, 96,

ally the case,[212] for more often it was men who could ill-afford to do so, who had more than one wife. "The system takes from her all confidence in the permanency of the affection of her husband. … It fosters feelings of jealousy and occasions intrigue in the household. It should not be thought that poverty is any barrier to the practice of polygyny; the rich men do not commonly have the largest number of wives. The men who are least able to bear the expense are often found to have several wives."[213] For the prevalence of polygyny all depended on the social position of the woman and the financial position of the husband. If she was a simple villager, then a man might be able to provide for more than one wife, given her low level of needs. Of course, the premium a man set on peace and quiet at home also determined how many wives he wanted to have. For a polygynous household was not always a happy one. "The system fosters feelings of jealousy and occasions intrigue in the household."[214] Sometimes, at least according to popular tales, two co-women had the better of their husband and forced him to sleep in the mosque, because they refused to sleep with him, "because he has another wife and need not bother her."[215] Although probably unrelated to these issues, towards the end of the nineteenth century the prevalence of polygyny seems to have fallen.[216]

Although polygyny was and is still allowed, not everyone in Iran knew exactly how many wives one might take. In the 1950s, in Davarabad (Khorasan), "the villagers' understanding of maximum permissible numbers, ranged, from two simultaneously and seven serially. Seven (a prominent 'magical' number throughout Iran) figures

212. Polak, *Persien*, vol. 1, p. 209; Hantzsche, "Haram," p. 416; Ponafidine, *Life*, p. 323.

213. Bassett, *Eastern Mission*, p. 66; Häntzsche, "Haram," pp. 416-17; Bricteux, *Au Pays*, p. 229.

214. Bassett, *Eastern Mission*, p. 66; Häntzsche, "Haram," pp. 416-17.

215. Erika Friedl, "Women in Contemporary Persian Folk Tales," in Lois Beck and Nikki Keddie eds. *Women in the Muslim World* (Cambridge, 1978), p. 640.

216. Sykes, *Through*, p. 189; Wishard, *Twenty Years*, p. 94; Ponafidine, *Life*, p. 323.

most frequently in informants' notions, and some explain that this is due to the fact that Imam Reza … had seven wives."[217] Despite the permissibility of polygyny few men availed themselves of this option for various reasons. Among which figured considerations such as peace and quiet in the house, fairness, effect on children as well as the physical impossibility for each man to have more than one wife. Most importantly, the religious injunction of impartiality to each wife ensured that many traditional villagers prefer monogamy. "The saying, 'One God, one wife,' (*Khoda yeki, zan yeki*), is frequently quoted as if it were somehow a sacred injunction against polygyny, and supported by the maxim that, 'In one heart there is not room for two loves.'"[218] Among the middle class of merchants, shopkeepers and artisans as well as among peasants and nomads it was and is unusual that men had more than one wife.[219]

By the end of the nineteenth century, such sentiments also gave rise to a movement among intellectuals to give women more, if not equal, rights and to limit polygyny. One of them was the poet Jelveh of Ardestan (d. 1896), who remained a lifelong bachelor, addressed the issue of polygyny in a tongue-in-cheek poem:

> One night a girl sweet and fair-shaped,
> Asking a question of her mother said:
> 'Oh mother, I have a problem
> From which my heart is in flame.
> Why has our Prophet wise allowed
> A man several wives to wed

217. Alberts, *Social Structure*, vol. 2, p. 666. This belief that seven wives were allowed was also held at the other side of Iran, in Khuzestan. von Rosen, *Persian Pilgrimage*, p. 199.

218. Alberts, *Social Structure*, vol. 2, p. 668.

219. T.M. Lycklama à Nijeholt, *Voyage en Russie, au Caucase et en Perse* 4 vols. (Paris-Amsterdam, 1872), vol. 2, p. 366; Polak, *Persien*, vol. 1, p. 122, 209; Julien de Rochechouart, *Souvenirs d'un Voyage en Perse* (Paris, 1867), p. 204; Serena, *Hommes*, p. 276; Gobineau, *Trois Ans*, vol. 2, p. 188; F. Houssay, 'La structure de sol et son influence sur la vie des hommes. Etudes sur la Perse méridionale 1885-6,' *Annales de Géographie* 3 (1894), pp. 293-94; Ponafidine, *Life*, p. 323.

> But that most sage and learned one
> Of men for women did not grant but one?'
> A deep sigh heaved the mother
> Which made the daughter even sadder.
> And said, 'Since the Prophet was a man,
> For sure, if the Prophet had been a woman
> Several husbands would be part of the plan.
> O my darling, good women suffer most
> As from womenfolk has never a prophet come forth.[220]

This issue of 'why polygyny and not polyandry?' was not one that really resounded in society, despite the fact that the poetess Qorrat al-'Eyn (1817-1852) allegedly advocated that a woman should marry nine men. It is more likely that this was just an accusation similar to those aimed at other sects in the past (see below) to show that this champion of Babism was but a deranged and corrupted mind rather than an accomplished woman, who advocated the belief in a competing religion.[221]

Based on the census data of 1956 and 1966, Momeni calculated that the prevalence of polygyny was rather limited. In 1956, there were 11 out of 1,000 men who had more than one wife and in 1966 this figure was 10 men out of 1,000. He further found that poylgyny was more common in rural areas than among the urban population.[222] With the enactment of the Family Protection Law of 1967 men could not marry more than one wife, unless he had the permission of the court (art. 14). The latter had to establish the capacity of the man to treat all his wives equally, and seek, if possible, the first wife's opin-

---

220. The English translation of this poem is by Javadi, *Satire*, p. 211.

221. Mohammad Taqi Lesan al-Molk Sepehr, *Nasekh al-Tavarikh-e Qajariyeh* 3 vols. in 2 ed. Jamshid Kiyanpur (Tehran, 1377/1998), p. 997; Mohammad Ebrahim Parizi-Bastani, *Haft Sang* (Tehran, 1346/1967), p. 357, n. 3 even changes the nine men into ninety. This story was also reported by Polak, "Die Prostitution", p. 564, without any comments.

222. Djamchid A. Momeni, "Polygyny in Iran," *Journal of Marriage and Family* May 1975, pp. 453-56.

ion with regard's to this capacity. With the new law of 1975, a man needed the permission of his first wife to marry a second one, unless she could not bear children or was unable to have sexual relations. For the first wife the proposed second wife was allowed as grounds for divorce (art. 16, 17). Although an improvement, the man could force his wife to give the permission by threatening to divorce her. As women fear divorce, which means loss of financial security, separation from her children, social stigma and thus the 'devaluation of her market value' for a second marriage, they usually gave in. With the advent of the Islamic Republic most of the old laws were abolished and the rules of Islamic law were re-instated, although polygyny has not increased.[223] The fear to leave the marital home and lose one's child was and is a major dilemma for many women, which has been evocatively expressed by the poetess Forugh.

> Each bright morning, from behind the bars,
> Before me a child's look laughs with bliss;
> When I start singing a song of joy,
> His lips take wing toward me with a kiss.
>
> If, O sky, I want one day to fly
> From out this silent prison, cold and stern,
> What shall I say to the child's weeping eyes?
> Forget about me, for I'm a captive bird.

Although polygyny is lawful, it is not lawful to share these women with other men, for this constitutes fornication (*zana*). The practicing of the sharing of women was the standard accusation aimed at all and sundry, who represented a religious threat to orthodox Islam. The religious revolt led by al-Muqanna' in the 770s was said to practice communism of women, or group marriage.[224] However al-Muqanna'

---

223. Vieille, "Iranian Women," p. 459; Hamideh Sedghi, *Women and Politics in Iran. Veiling, Unveiling, and Reveiling* (Cambridge, 2007), p. 144. For more information on how divorce is being handled in contemporary Iran see the moving and instructive movie 'Divorce Iranian Style.'

224. Narshakhi, *The History of Bukhara* translated into English by Richard Frye

did not seem to have shared his own women with others, although he had a multitude of them, for many of his adherents had offered their daughters to him as token of devotion, a practice that was followed throughout the centuries in Iran.[225] Similar accusations were also made against all sects such as the Qarmatians. "They used not to hide their privy parts from one another, and did not refrain from mutual commerce; when a man was married, their chief was the first to lay hands upon the woman, afterwards the husband, …, they made free with their mothers and sisters."[226] The same accusation was made against the Khorramdins, who, as well as the other Batinis, which included Shi'ites, were just considered to be the heirs of the Mazdak religion.[227] In more recent times, similar accusations were and are addressed at heterodox religious groups, who were accused of organizing mixed male-female gatherings with so-called light-extinguishing ceremonies (*cheragh-koshan*) as part of their ritual. During this period of lights-out they allegedly were engaged in sexual debauchery, for which accusation, like that of the earlier group marriage, never any piece of evidence was and is offered.[228]

ROYAL PREROGATIVES IN SELECTING WOMEN

So far the discussion has focused on the choice by men, or rather by their families, of a suitable wife. However, kings and powerful governors did not necessarily follow the same rules, for they sometimes took abusive advantage of their position and power. Whether this was a pre-existing condition or the result of the Arab conquests of the Middle East is a moot point. It would appear that the Arabs, who

(Cambridge, 1954), p. 75 (same story as in Nizam al-Mulk].

225. Narshakhi, *History*, pp. 67, 73.

226. Nizam al-Mulk, *Book*, p. 232, see also p. 236 the same accusation against the Sa'idis in Bahrain.

227. Nizam al-Mulk, *Book*, p. 244.

228. Matti Moosa, *Extreme Shiites. The Ghulat Sects* (Syracuse, 1988), pp. 126-27, 136-38. For example, Polak, "Die Prostitution", p. 564, reported that "some religious sects, such as the Dawudi, allegedly, as I was frequently told, would give the lady of the house to guests, being part of the guest right."

until the advent of Islam had practiced a more liberal tradition to-wards woman, then adopted a more restrictive role of women, follow-ing Sura 4.36 and hence made free with female captives.[229] For, it was permissible to have sexual intercourse with a captive woman after she was purified (of menses or delivery). In case she had a husband, her marriage was abrogated after she had become a captive.[230] Tabari men-tions the case of Qutayba's brother, who took the wife of Barmak the priest of Nowbahar. Such an attitude may also have given rise to the attitude of rulers and high officials to grab beautiful wives and daugh-ters of their free subjects.[231] Narshakhi relates the case of an emir who forcibly took two daughters from a man, who then killed the emir and as a result the village was considered to be in revolt and was destroyed and everybody in it was killed.[232] A similar event happened in 1387, when a group of tax collectors acted a little too high-handed towards the people of Isfahan by demanding the use of their women. The peo-ple became very angry, lashed out and killed them. Troops were sent and that same evening a battle was engaged that lasted through the night, during which engagement two high-ranking emirs were killed. After surrender it was ordered that as punishment 70,000 heads had to roll, "like on the day of resurrection," and in total 28 towers made of skulls and mud were erected between the Tawqchi Gate and Taba-rak Castle, or half the length of the wall of Isfahan.[233]

Whereas the above examples were on a more impersonal basis, sometimes personal love or passion also played a role. Soltan Abu Sa'id (r. 1317-1335) was passionately in love with the daughter of Amir Chupan, his regent and the de-facto ruler of his lands in 1325. Since she was already married, Amir Chupan discouraged the Soltan from pursuing the matter, who had wanted to invoke the old Mongol rule established by Chengiz Khan that if the king sees a woman that

---

229. Spuler, *Iran*, p. 382.
230. Muslim, *Sahih*, 8, 3432-3443.
231. Spuler, *Iran*, p. 382; Nizam al-Mulk, *Book*, p. 58.
232. Narshakhi, *History*, p. 44.
233. Samarqandi, *Matla'-ye Sa'deyn*, vol. 1, p. 596.

he likes, the husband has to send her to the king's harem. This refusal was one of the contributing factors that led to the break with Amir Chupan. It also led to Amir Chupan's downfall, which made it possible for Soltan Abu Sa'id to marry his beloved.[234] However, there was a problem, she was still married and he expressed his frustration about this in a poem.

> The love the same, the pain the same, the heart the same
> The grief the same, the story the same, the problem the
>   same…

Fortunately, the problem was resolved after her husband quickly divorced her in 1328. This decision was aided by the Soltan's poem that the mediating Qazi Mobarak Shah recited for the husband.

> Your love is a fact that I cannot express
> It's a secret I cannot hide I confess…

And since it is obligatory to heed the wishes of kings the husband took heed, because, as Sa'di has said:

> In counsel gainst the wish of kings to stand
> Is in a man's own blood to wash his hands
> If he shall call the broadest daytime night
> Say, 'Sire! Moon and planets swing inside…[235]

Other rulers or officials did not even need the excuse of resistance to obey orders or the passion for a beautiful woman. One of the officials of 'Ala al-Dowleh oppressed the population of Larejan so much so that he forced their women to join him in drinking bouts and he divided them up among his *gholams*, who had intercourse with the women while he entered the *gholams* on top, and if they

234. On these events see Charles Melville, *The Fall of Amir Chupan and the Declcine of the Ilkhanate, 1327-37: a decade of discors in Mongol Iran* (Bloomington, 1999).

235. Samarqandi, *Matla'-ye Sa'deyn*, vol. 1, p. 116. The English translation of the second poem is by Edwin Arnold, *Gulistan* (New York, 1899), p. 72.

protested he extinguished candles on their bodies.[236] In 1470, Hasan 'Ali b. Jahanshah brought the women of his emirs and intimates (*inaqs*) together and then he sat among them. He ordered them to dance for him and whichever one he liked he took. If the husband was angered by this he forced him to divorce his wife. He also had the women mount on horses as if on parade and ordered them to do so with their legs bared.[237]

It also seems to have been an accepted tradition that when the king wanted to have his pick of the female crop, orders were given to collect such women. 'Attar, for example, relates the story when the nobles wanted the king to marry, he said to them: "Send a hundred maidens."[238] One cannot shrug this off as just another story by a poet, for it also had happened in Queen Esther's time. That such proceedings actually occurred is also clear from the above and the following in March 1671, Shah Soleyman gave orders "to make a general muster of Girls, from two years of Age upward, out of which the Beauties select were to be chosen out for the King of Persia." Struys further reported that some parents were downcast, because their daughter had not been picked for this honor, for a daughter in the harem was a certain road to financial surety for poor families.[239] A similar event took place in 1700 when Shah Soltan Hoseyn's "first care in the begining of his reign was to cause a general search to be made for all the handsome women in Persia and to order them to be brought to his Haram." This year was remembered as *kizlarun-il* or the Year of the Girls.[240] These events were satirized by Asaf, who wrote:

236. Ravandi, *Tarikh*, p. 419

237. Hasan Rumlu, *Ahsan al-Tavarikh* ed. 'Abdol-Hoseyn Nava'i (Tehran, 1349/1970), p. 187.

238. 'Attar, *Ilahi-nama*, p. 170.

239. Strauszens, *Sehr schwere*, p. 148; for these financial benefits see Jean Chardin, *Voyages*, ed. L. Langlès, 10 vols., (Paris 1811), vol. 6, pp. 17-18, 24-25.

240. Anonymous, *A Chronicle of the Carmelites in Persia and the Papal Mission of the Seventeenth and Eighteenth Centuries*, 2 vols. (London, 1939), vol. 1, p. 471; see also Engelbert Kaempfer, *Am Hofe des persischen Grosskönigs*, translated by Walther Hinz (Leipzig, 1940), p. 52, where he reports that Shah Soleyman, when he visited Jolfa, the Armenian suburb of Isfahan, also took

Day and night he was eager and without restraint in
eating and coition. At a test in one day and night he
ordered one hundred virgins to be taken into temporary
wedlock, in accordance with the *Shari'a* and with their
own and their father's consent. In twenty-four hours
as a result of a great aphrodisiac that Refuge of the
Nation and the Land deflowered all those lovely girls
and graceful and sugar-lipped sweethearts, and still like
an intoxicated bachelor was eager for more. Then, in
compliance with the law of the Prophet, he divorced and
sent them to their homes with legal marriage-portions
and with precious clothes and ornaments presented
by the Monarch of the World. As this story spread
throughout the land of Iran, whoever had a wife uniquely
beautiful would willingly and eagerly divorce and send
her to the royal court, which is renowned for justice,
out of expediency or in the hope of ample reward. The
Matchless Monarch of the World, in accordance with
religious rites, would marry and enjoy her, and then
he would similarly divorce and dismiss her. The lady,
being thus graced with royal favors, would return to her
husband with bounty and riches.[241]

Despite the financial and other rewards that such a relationship
with the royal court might bring the girl's relatives, not everybody was
happy with the manner in which this was brought about. For it seems
that this encroachment on his subjects' women had struck a negative
cord among part of the population, for Nader Shah, who himself took
whatever he wanted, took steps to announce that he would not behave
in such a manner.

Armenian girls that were to his liking. His grandfather, Shah Safi I, did the
same. Adam Olearius, *Vermehrte newe Beschreibung der moscowitischen und
persischen Reyse*, ed. D. Lohmeier (Schleswig, 1656 [Tübingen, 1971]), p. 664.

241. Mohammad Hashem (Rostam al-Hokama) Asaf, *Rostam al-Tavarikh* ed.
Mohammad Moshiri (Tehran, 1348/1969), pp. 81-83; the English translation is
by Javadi, *Satire*, pp. 208-09.

To ensure greater security of their property in their wives, the only one which Nadir seemed to have any regard to, on his coming to the crown he published an ordinance, which made it present death for any person whomsoever, who should attempt to corrupt another man's wife, or forcibly take a married woman from her husband; for which reason those who have beautiful daughters give them in marriage very young, that they may not be exposed to any violence. In the reign of Hussein, men of great distinction were wont to seize upon what woman they pleased, whether married or single.[242]

Nader Shah also imposed a demand for 50 girls on supporters of the rebel Mohammad Khan Baluch as a punishment for their participation in the 1734 uprising.[243] A similar demand was made by Karim Khan Zand during the early years of his reign, but he allegedly ceased such demands for fresh girls.[244]

BEDROOM DO'S AND DON'TS

Male superiority was a *sine qua non*, also in sexual matters.[245] Women were on the receiving end; they were dominated by their underlying position by the man, and this showed who was in charge. Because marriage gives the man the right to have sex with his wife, a woman can neither leave her husband's bed when she has been invited nor refuse to come; she even has to cut her prayers short when he wants

---

242. Jonas Hanway, *An Historical Account of the British Trade over the Caspian Sea* (London, 1753), vol. 1, p. 271.

243. Mohammad Kazem Mervi, *'Alamara-ye Naderi* 3 vols. ed. Mohammad Amin Riyahi (Tehran, 1369/1990), vol. 1, p. 350; M.R. Arunova and K. Z. Ashrafiyan, *Gosudarstvo Nadir-Shakha Afshara* (Moscow, 1958), p. 83.

244. John R. Perry, *Karim Khan Zand, A History of Iran, 1747-1779* (Chicago, 1979), p. 291.

245. Al-Ghazzali, *On Marriage*, p. 24 wrote "Men are set up over women (Q. 4:34). The men must always be dominant. The messenger said (pbuh) said: 'Wretched is (the man who is) the slave of his wife.'"

to sleep with her.[246] Furthermore, because a man has paid for his wife, (although payment of the *mahr* usually takes place on divorce), only he has the right to decide when and how he wants to have sex, which he also might want for medical reasons.[247] For only men are allowed to show sexual desire, also towards women with whom they are not married. If the latter happens the man will not be blamed, but the woman is, because she should not have found herself in a situation where another man could approach her. Moreover, there still is a strong belief that girls and women cannot say no to a man, if she happens to be alone with a man. The author of the *Qabus-nameh* wrote: "You must realize that a woman cannot steadfastly resist a man, however old or ugly he may be; so admit no male slave into the women's apartments, even though he is black, old and ugly."[248] The belief that women are unable to withstand a man's charms, because of her insatiable lust, was reinforced by the fact that, according to Imam Reza, women are 99 times lustier than men.[249] This belief was further enhanced by popular tales that confirmed and endorsed such attitudes. For example, in the popular tale of Hoseyn-e Kurd, the daughter of his captor, Sonbol,

---

246. Muslim, *Sahih*, 8, 3366-3368 (unless he cannot pay the dowry; see above); Avazeh, *Qanun-e Qovveh-ye Bah*, pp. 22; she also cannot go to sleep before her husband has had sex with her or has given her leave to do so. Ibid., pp. 21-22.

247. Avazeh, *Qanun-e Qovveh-ye Bah*, pp. 24-25 (e.g. in cases of high blood pressure, pains, weakness of the body, phleghm, etc.).

248. Kai Ka'us b. Iskandar, *Qabus Nama*, p. 118 (ch. XXVI); Vielle, "Iranian Women," p. 463. "The mark of a slave suited for employment in the women's apartments is that he should be dark-skinned and sour-visaged and have withered limbs, scanty hair, a shrill voice, little [slender] feet, thick lips, a flat nose, stubby fingers, a bowed figure and a thin neck." Kai Ka'us, *Qabus Nama*, p. 102. The same sentiments still prevailed in the seventeenth century. Eunuchs were often chosen for their ugliness so that women really had to be very desperate before they would overcome their disgust at their sight to desire them. But even this was not enough, for some of the eunuchs had not only their testicles removed, but also part of their penis. However, this was partly compensated by the attachment of a silver tube, which allowed them to urinate farther. Strauszens, *Sehr schwere*, pp. 154-55. Polak, "Die Prostitution," p. 563 reports that no Persian man will believe that his wife is innocent if she has been alone with another man without witnesses.

249. Avazeh, *Qanun-e Qovveh-ye Bah*, p. 42.

helps him escape because her father wants to kill him. Her motive was, as she told Hoseyn: "I will sacrifice myself for your handsome face and your shaved [and therefore appealing] penis."[250] This probably was as much male boasting as it was male uncertainty given their endless search for penis enhancement, about which later. Although allegedly much lustier than a man, a woman cannot show desire, even in marriage. She must follow and react to her husband's moves, which are aimed to reveal "the latent erotic powers of the woman. Only he arouses the desire of the woman and fulfills it. The woman before his intervention would not be able to desire; afterward she could not remain insensible without frustrating him in the result he expects from an act whose sole author he considers himself."[251]

But even if a man has been overcome by sexual desire he just cannot give in to his lust. For even when you are married, as a Moslem, you have to respect certain religious rules concerning if and when you may have sexual intercourse with your wife or slave girl. For example, it is unlawful to have intercourse with a woman during menstruation or who has a female complaint.[252] However, there are other constraints. Intercourse on the first night of the month, the last night of the month and the middle night of the month is considered to be an abomination by the jurists, because during those nights Satan is present during intercourse. Also, while having sex, one should neither face nor have one's back towards the *qiblah* or the prayer direction, while in general the place where the sexual act takes place should be care-

250. Rosemary Stanfield-Johnson, "Yuzbashi-ye Kurd and 'Abd al-Mu'min the Uzbek: A Tale of Revenge in the *Dastan* of Husayn-e Kurd," in Soussie Rastegar & Anna Vanzan eds. *Muraqqa'e Sharqi. Studies in Honor of Peter Chelkowski* (San Marino, 2007), p. 175. On the various reasons why bodily hair should be removed see Avazeh, *Qanun-e Qovveh-ye Bah*, pp. 80-81. Persians took hair removal seriously, for a man became very annoyed when he noticed that his wife had not shaved her pubic hair and said: "This is allright with me since I am your husband and intimate with you, but you should really be ashamed if a stranger finds you like this. Obeyd-e Zakani, *Ethics of The Aristrocrats*, p. 69.

251. Vielle, "Iranian Women," pp. 462-63. About the macho man see 'Obeyd-e Zakani, *Resaleh-ye Delgosha*, p. 245.

252. Julie Scott Meisami, *The Sea of Virtues (Bahr al-Fava'id) A Medieval Islamic Mirror for Princes* (Salt Lake City: Utah UP, 1991), p. 97.

fully chosen; e.g. not on the roof or under a fruit tree.[253] For a woman there is an additional impediment, for she cannot have intercourse with a male slave. Finally, incest is not allowed, which means that sexual relations with any of the so-called *maharem*, the close relatives, such as the father's wife, the wife's mother and the wife's sister and daughter, is forbidden.[254]

Once these impediments have been taken into account intercourse may begin. However, here the believer is counseled to behave properly, for sexual intercourse is after all sanctioned by religion and therefore, its spirit should guide one's behavior, including when having sex. The man is therefore given the very appropriate advice to "begin by pleasing her with talk, play, kisses, and embraces."[255] If this were not convincing enough the jurists have adduced a Tradition that makes these things even clearer and moreover have the additional weight of the Prophet's own words:

> The Prophet said, 'A man should not fall on his wife as on
> a mule; he must send a messenger before he lies with her.'
> They asked, 'O Prophet of God, what is this messenger?'
> He replied, 'A kiss.' Then when he wishes to begin he
> should say, '*In the name of God, Sublime and Mighty;*
> *God is Great, God is Great, God is Great.*' ... At the time
> of ejaculation he should think of this verse: 'Praise be
> to God; It is he who hath created man of water, and has
> made him to bear the double relation of consanguinity
> and affinity' (25:56), and then wait till the woman
> also ejaculates. For the Prophet said, 'Three things are
> weakness in a man: ... third, that he becomes busy with
> intercourse before kissing and embracing, and when his
> need is satisfied not wait until the woman's need is also
> satisfied.'"[256]

---

253. Meisami, *Sea*, pp. 163-64; Avazeh, *Qanun-e Qovveh-ye Bah*, pp. 27-30, 34-36; Khomeyni, *Tahrir*, p. 214..

254. Meisami, *Sea*, p. 226.

255. Meisami, *Sea*, pp.163-64; Avazeh, *Qanun-e Qovveh-ye Bah*, p. 30.

256. Meisami, *Sea*, pp.163-64; al-Ghazzali, *On Marriage*, p. 28. In another version the man should not behave like the birds, for sex should not be 'a

Such an advice would not be out of place in modern 'How to have good sex' manuals, although the approach is rather one-sided, i.e. only the male has the initiative. Although Imam 'Ali allegedly advised men to take heed and realize that women have sexual needs, having sex with one's wife, according to the prophet Mohammad, is like giving alms (*sadaqeh*), which puts it in a slightly different perspective.[257] Moslem authors certainly took their cue from this and other Traditions. The *Qabus-nameh* counsels:

> Do not have intercourse when you are drunk, for it may have detrimental effects. Moreover, it sets man apart from beast, when he selects both the time and proper season for intercourse, and is not ruled by passion. During the height of cold and warm season it was better not to have intercourse, in particular older men, on whom it could have a deleterious effect. Spring was the best season, when like the world, the body renews its vigor, "the blood in the veins increases together with the semen in the loins." Moreover, let your desires incline "During the winter towards women." But on this topic it is requisite that one's discourse should be brief, lest it engender appetite.[258]

Kay Ka'us b. Eskandar further advised his son:

> Once you have married a wife, being greatly in love with her, even though you may be infatuated with her, do not spend every night in her society. Let it be only from time to time, thus leading her to think that such

---

quickie', according to Imam 'Ali. Avazeh, *Qanun-e Qovveh-ye Bah*, pp. 39-41, which also provides more details on what constitutes good and desirable foreplay.

257. Avazeh, *Qanun-e Qovveh-ye Bah*, pp. 23, 39 ("Imam Sadeq said: The holy prophet asked a man: 'Did you fast this morning?' He said: 'No.' He then asked: 'Did you feed a poor person?' He said: 'No.' The holy prophet then said: 'Go back and have sex with your wife, which to her is like receiving alms.'").

258. Kai Ka'us b. Eskandar, *Qabus Nama*, ch. XV, pp. 77-78.

is the universal custom, so that if on occasion you have
reason for excusing yourself or wish to go on a journey,
your wife will be forbearing towards you. But if you
customarily visit her every night, she will acquire a
propensity for it and it will be difficult for her to exercise
forbearance.[259]

A late nineteenth century anonymous author in a booklet entitled
'The Education of Wives' (*Ta'dib al-Nesvan*) took a rather censorious
position towards women's behavior in marriage and he counseled his
readers that wives should prepare for bed, i.e. make toilet, wash up
and smell and look nice. "To my mind, a simple chemise of transparent stuff and a bright-coloured petticoat will advantageously replace
the day's apparel." In fact, the best way would be to dress the way the
man likes it. If the man wants his wife to come to him in a pleasant
manner, she should not discuss irksome matters of the day, but rather
make enticing remarks and above all do not wait for him to make the
first move. "Shamelessness is better in bed than prudery; therefore
do not imagine that your dignity will suffer if you surrender utterly
to love." Also, the author preferred no lamps, waiting maids and the
like in the bed room, while he opined that "the woman may undress
entirely at a certain moment." There should be, of course, no talking
about what happened in bed with the girl friends, which women often
did when going to the baths. He lectured his female readers as follows:
"Do not imitate the fashion of too many woman of our time, and
show all your friends the marks of kisses you have had on the neck or
breasts." Shocked, he further remarked that some women even went
further and wrote about it to their friends. Since the unknown author
considered sex very important he further opined:

Certain great ladies exact a multitude of preliminaries,
especially if their husband claims this favour in the day-
time. They have no idea of abandoning themselves except
in some place devoted to the purpose, and, once there,
they require the maid to come and spread the bed, to

---

259. Kai Ka'us b. Iskandar, *Qabus Nama*, p. 118, Ch. XXVI.

> bring in towels, and to shut all the doors before they will
> undress. After such long preparations the poor lover feels
> his flame die down and fall asleep, and even when the
> case is not as bad as this, there can be no great pleasure
> in love after such waiting. It is well then, I repeat, for
> the woman not to pay too much attention to those silly
> details. Let her rather be ever ready for her husband's
> amorous fantasy, and always have a yes for his advance,
> whether it be preceded by tender cajolery and exciting
> play or not.

In short, the author told his readers that the husband wants his wife to be uninhibited at these moments. In the morning, however, the wife should not tarry, but leave and wash up, clean her teeth and make her toiletry and make-up. Meanwhile, the husband's servants will take care of him. Only then present yourself again to him; sweet-smelling, good-looking and coquette. However, most women want to stay and smoke one water pipe after the other and then they expect to be showered with kisses and are astonished when that does not happen.[260]

Thus, women were not considered to have a sexual life of their own; they were just an object of sexual gratification for the man. The latter considered women like a farmer considers a piece of land, viz. a passive field to be used, ploughed and molded by him alone and of which only he had the right to try to get the most productivity (progeny, sexual gratification) by using his knowledge of the lay of the land.[261] If there were no children then it must be that the woman was infertile, not the man, unless he was impotent. If there were only children of the same sex, then it must be the woman's fault. Eslami-ye Nadushan in his childhood memoir 'Days' echoes this, for he writes:

---

260. Anonymous, "The Education of Wives" translated from the French by E. Powys Mathers, *Eastern Love* 3 vols. (London, New York, 1930), vol. 1, pp. 246, 248, 251, 253.

261. For the theme of comparing the beloved with a garden see Julie Meisami, "The Body as Garden; Nature and Sexuality in Persian Poetry," *Edebiyat* 6 (1995), pp. 245-74.

> Man/woman relations were either based on barter and settlement or on domination. There was no equality between the two sexes to generate love. Generally speaking, with the view a man held of a woman, he considered it below his dignity to feel himself obligated to satisfy her. In other words, he could not debase himself to the level of gratifying her. His fulfillment was bound with domination and possession, that is, taking by force and preponderance. This was called "enjoyment".[262]

This one-sidedness of the sexual act is also expressed in the terminology used (mostly Arabic terms in the texts) that tends to be derogatory and abusive in nature and most certainly does not convey the meaning of reciprocity, of a coming together of two equals trying to please both parties.[263] According to one Iranian female psychologist, writing in 2007, "In traditional Iranian society, the concept of sexual satisfaction for women is essentially without meaning. I have seen many such women who regard sexual intercourse as merely a means of satisfying the man, prolonging a shared married life and perhaps also guaranteeing continued financial support from their partner."[264] For women, of course, were/are not passive sexual partners, because they also know that they have to please their man. However, she is

---

262. Mohammad 'Ali Eslami-ye Nadushan, *Ruzha* (Tehran, 1363/1984), p. 272, quoted by Farzaneh Milani, *Veils and Words. The emerging voices of Iranian women writers* (Syracuse, 1992), p. 142. Women, of course, were not the passive sexual submissive non-person as seen by men; they had sexual feelings, which they often freely expressed in games and plays performed for and by women, see Safa-Isfahani, "Female-centered World Views," pp. 42-53 and Anthony Shay, "*Bazi-ha-ye Namayeshi*: Iranan Women's Theatrical Plays," *Dance Research Journal* 27/2/ (1995), pp. 16-24.

263. Javadi, *Satire*, pp. 198-99. A Persian verb *sopukhtan*, used in medieval times, meaning, among other things, 'to enter by force', also was used to denote 'to have sex.' 'Obeyd-e Zakani, *Resaleh-ye Delgosha*, p. 100. Even the rather neutral Persian term for having sex, *kardan*, expresses the one-sidesness of the sexual act, for it refers to the male role, i.e. doing, for the woman's part is but 'to give' (*dadan*). Milani, *Veils*, p. 142. The polished term for having sex, *nazdiki kardan*, is neutral on purpose and is one that may be used in polite society and text books.

264. [http://www.mianeh.net/en/articles/?aid=99].

not supposed to show her desire and does so only indirectly by pro-voking her husband's desire. Women apparently shared information to know what pleased men, for by binding her husband sexually she acquired marital security.[265] Nevertheless, it is also reported that many men were not sexually satisfied and they estimated that 30-40 percent of women were frigid. This male dissatisfaction with heterosexual rela-tions was/is expressed in "the lament of popular songs, the frequency of other forms of sexuality such as masturbation, homosexuality, and bestiality."[266]

Such conditions led to a situation where many women felt that marriage rather than a warm, safe nest was a cage, even if it was a gilded one. This sentiment was eloquently expressed by the poetess Forugh in her poem 'The Captive' (asir).[267]

> I am thinking that in a moment of neglect,
> From out this silent prison I will fly,
> Laugh in the face of the man who jails me,
> And then begin life over by your side.
>
> I am thinking this, and know that never
> Will I have the strength to leave from out this cage;
> Even if the man who jails should wish it,
> Breath for my flight no longer now remains.

---

265. Vielle, "Iranian Women," pp. 463, 468.

266. Vielle, "Iranian Women," p. 470. This may explain the satyrist's witty advice: "Do not waste your precious time on lawful but cold love-making." Obeyd-e Zakani, *Ethics of Aristocrats*, p. 77. This does not mean that there were not satisfied males or thought that they could be so, as evidenced by a popular Qajar streets song (Phillot, "Some Lullabies," p. 153):
"Now lip pressed lip and navel pressed against navel;
an aleph straightened up into qaf's round stable." Translation by Dick Davis.
For the metaphoric use of letters of the alphabet, in this case of the aleph and the qaf, see Paul Sprachman, *Language and Culture in Persian* (Costa Mesa, 2002), pp. 78-80.

267. Hasan Javadi and Susan Selleé, *Another Birth. Selected Poems of Forugh Farrokhzad* (Emeryville, CA, 1981), p. 9.

From the foregoing it is clear that male dominance in sexual matters did not necessarily result in sexual gratification for either husband or wife. It may be that the general phallic attitude is reinforced by the prevailing notion that, in the words of Rumi, "The creator is masculine and active in relation to creation, which is female and receptive." Love, therefore, has little to do "with mutual satisfaction and nuptial bliss." In the view of al-Ghazzali, one of the most influential Islamic thinkers, "the lover is an enemy and not a friend, and that the beloved, too, is not a friend." Therefore, both have two scripted roles to play, one who loves, the other who is beloved, but neither can or wants to assume the role of the other and reciprocate the feeling. [268]

Although sex was not performed in the nude, for usually both partners were/are still (partly) dressed, this is not due to passion which prevented the couple to divest themselves of their clothes. The most likely reason for clothed sex is religious in nature, for Imam Sadeq replied in the negative to the question whether a man could sleep with his wife naked. Moreover, one should not talk during sex as the child may be born mute.[269] The fact of clothed sex is evident from miniatures that depict couples in sexual embraces. This also holds for those miniatures that are explicitly pornographic in nature, i.e. those that show the genitals and the coitus. In these cases, both parties only have divested themselves of their bottom clothes, while the top ones are still worn. This practice of clothed sex also is borne out by sociological studies, which submit that "the lower classes do not undress to make love; the bodies remain covered; it is believed that nudity can bring on male impotence." In fact, foreplay, as strongly counseled by

---

268. On this issue in general see Michael Glünz, "The Sword, the Pen and the Phallus: Metaphors and the Metonymies of Male Power and Creativity in Medieval Persian Poetry," *Edebiyat* 6 (1995), pp. 232-33.

269. Avazeh, *Qanun-e Qovveh-ye Bah*, pp. 36-37, 39-41. Also the fact that Ayeshah reported that "I used to wash the traces of Janaba (semen) from the clothes of the Prophet and he used to go for prayers while traces of water were still on it (water spots were still visible)," indicates that sex was performed while clothed during the prophet's time. Bukhari, *Sahih*, 4.229-233. However, Khomeyni, *Towzih*, p. 511 (no. 2312) states that husband and wife can look at one another's body; Ibid, *Tahrir*, vol. 2, p. 217.

the prophet and some of the Imams, is usually absent and the same holds for making love. "There is no physical contact during the course of the sexual act other than that of the genital organs; other erogenous zones are not excited and used by sexuality. ... In addition, the caress is practically unknown; the sexual act begins with intromission and ends with ejaculation, so that man and woman are physically united only in coitus." The absence of sexual fore- and afterplay in rural areas is mainly due to "poverty, living arrangements, and the presence of family."[270] The usual living arrangement in rural areas until recent times was one room or tent that was shared by parents, their children and the farm animals.[271] In urban areas, where until recent times there was no separate bedroom either in most family homes, this situation may further have been enhanced by the fact that lower class married workers worked an average of eleven hours per day, and spent most of their spare time with other men, and thus could not spend much time in the company of their womenfolk.[272]

It is the man who not only decides when to have sex, but who also decides whether to practice birth control and by what method. However, coitus interruptus is only allowed with the wife's permission; such permission is not required when the woman is a slave girl.[273] Such rules offered food for satirists, such as the author of the *Latayef al-Tavayef.* He told the story of a man who had sex with his neighbor's slave girl and, as a result, she became pregnant. When the owner became aware of this he said to the neighbor: 'Oh enemy of God, you

---

270. Paul Vielle, "Iranian Women in Family Alliance and Sexual Politics," in Lois Beck and Nikki Keddie eds. *Women in the Muslim World* (Cambridge, 1978), p. 462. For a funny poem describing the frustration of a man with three wives, who wants to have sex with his wife, but cannot because his children seem never ever want to go to sleep read 'Ali Akbar Sabir, *HopHop-Nameh* translated into Persian by Ahmad Shafa'i (Baku, 1962), pp. 173-74 (*mard-e seh zan*).

271. Willem Floor, *Agriculture in Qajar Iran* (Washington DC, 2005), pp. 134-45.

272. Pakizegi, "Legal and Social Positions," p. 222.

273. Meisami, *Sea*, p. 164; Bukhari, *Sahih*, 62, 135-137; Muslim, *Sahih*, 8, 3371-3388. On birth control methods in medieval Middle Eastern society, see B.F. Musallam, *Sex and Society in Islam: Birth Control before the Nineteenth Century* (Cambridge, 1986); for the situation in the last 40 years see chapter five.

did this dirty deed; could not you at least have withdrawn so that the seed would not have entered the womb.' The fornicator replied: 'I learnt from the olama that withdrawing is 'not desirable' (*makruh*).' The owner then said: 'Did not you learn that fornication is forbidden (*haram*)!'[274]

Erotic Stimulants

As sexual performance was and is important and, in particular older, males worried and worry about their sex drive as well as erectile dysfunction, physicians and others came and come to the rescue.[275] For before there was Viagra, penis enlargement drugs and other similar enhancement remedies, physicians in Iran (and elsewhere) tried to meet market demand and developed medicines and methods to help sexually-challenged men.[276] Whether these remedies were really helpful has not been recorded, but despite the fact that this is unlikely, physicians and druggists continue to sell such products as they continue to make and sell love and fertility potions for women who want to ensure their husband's sustained affection. [277]

---

274. Ravandi, *Tarikh*, vol. 7, p. 410.

275. There is also a strong belief that being a good sexual performer makes one's wife more pliant and faithful to the husband. Male sexual performance can also be enhanced if he applies make-up such as through the use of henna, according to Imam Reza. Avazeh, *Qanun-e Qovveh-ye Bah*, pp. 62-64. The consumption of special food items also increases male sexual prowess. Ibid., pp. 66-73, 78-79.

276. For those interested in this aspect of sexual relations see, e.g., a twelfth century text by Habish b. Ebrahim b. Mohammad Teflisi, *Bayan al-Sana'at* ed. Iraj Afshar, *Iran Farhang Zamin*, pp. 279-458, chapter 20 (pp. 430-40). Herewith a sample, so that readers may get an idea of the kind of medicines and remedies offered ("If you take asafetida and cubebs in the mouth and you copulate and collect the saliva that it produces in the mouth and rub that on the penis and have sex it will give the woman pleasure. If you take honey with wild rue or ginger or pepper into the mouth and copulate and rub it on the penis it has the same effect," etc.).

277. The interest in and use of love potions was great and women were criticized for having recourse to them. Anonymous, "The Education of Women," p. 212. These love philters were sold in shops and in the streets by herbalists, including by peripatetic sellers. Phillot, "Some Street Cries," p. 285 (*Ay dava-yi*

Impotent men did not limit themselves to herbs and other medicines, but also had recourse to the products of the power of the pen.[278] One of the earliest examples of stimulating erotic literature, embellished with suggestive pictures, was that by the poet Azraqi, who allegedly wrote his *Alfiyeh Shalfiyeh*, a well-known erotic book of the time, to revitalize the sexual desires of his patron, the Seljuq prince Toghanshah Seljuq. The poet of food, Abu Eshaq (ca. 1400) described this in his 'Treasure of Appetite' (*Kanz al-Estiha*), and was inspired his example, when his sweetheart told him:

> I have no appetite whatever they give me as aliment
> I am afraid that this affliction will give me indigestion
> I told her this is just like the man who had become
>   impotent
> He went to a physician to tell him of his indisposition
>
> That physician to stimulate the sexual drive
> Wrote *Alfiyeh and Shalfiyeh* for that companion
> He made a few drawings of man and wife
> Made them copulate in many a position.
>
> The impotent man when seeing them got an erection
> Immediately he took a virgin girl to his bosom
> I now also will make for you [similar poetic]
>   alimentation
> So that once you have read it your appetite will
> blossom.[279]

The Kama Sutra-like *Alfiyeh shalfiyeh* also influenced illustrations of other poetic works where, in addition to non-erotic miniatures,

---

mihr u muhabbat, 'Oh medicine for love and affection.'); see also Willem Floor, *Public Health in Qajar Iran* (Washington DC, 2004), pp. 49-50.

278. On this subject and the various types of Persian love poetry see Djalal Khaleghi-Motlagh, "Erotic literature," *Encyclopaedia Iranica*.

279. Browne, *Literary History*, vol. 3. pp. 349-50; see also Ibid, vol. 2, p. 323.

sometimes quite explicit erotic ones were to be found. These kinds of paintings appealed to the baser nature of the art patrons and whetted their lust. The Dutch traveler de Bruijn observed as to the situation in the early 1700s: "Persons of condition there have also their books very well bound, and adorned with all sorts of figures, dressed in their manner, and also with representations of hunting-matches, companies, birds and beasts in miniature, and in charming colours. These books are also sometimes full of figures in immodest postures, which they are very fond of."[280] In addition to the home-drawn variety, Indian sexual paintings and drawings were also sold in the bazaar of Isfahan during the seventeenth century.[281]

Naser al-Din Shah (r. 1848-1896) had a spurious interest in lewd and titillating stories, for he asked Vali Khan, son of Sohrab Khan Gorji, who had spent his father's fortune on wine, youths, women, and songs, to write a so-called *Resaleh-ye Fojuriyeh* or a 'Treatise of Debauchery' in which he had to describe the escapades of the most famous male and female prostitutes of Tehran as well his sexual liaisons with 28 Qajar princesses. In this treatise he only introduced 65 public beardless youths (*amradan-e ma'ruf*) on whom he had spent and wasted all his wealth. The book was completed in 1872 and enjoyed a large readership, including that of the shah.[282] Around 1890, the shah asked Kamal al-Molk, the leading painter in Iran at the end of the nineteenth and the beginning of the twentieth century, to make paintings for him based on pornographic pictures that he gave to the painter. Kamal al-Molk, however, did not want to make such paint-

---

280. Cornelius Le Bruyn, *Travels into Moscovy, Persia and part of the East-Indies*, 2 vols. (London, 1737), vol. 1, p. 220. For a sample of these shocking pictures see Robert Surieu, *Sarve Naz, essai sur les représentation érotiques et l'amour dans l'Iran d'autrefois* (Geneva, 1976); S. C. Welch and Martin B. Dickinson, *The Houghton Shahnameh*, (Cambridge, 1981), vol. 1, p. 160 (a case of sodomy).

281. Olearius, *Vermehrte*, p. 518.

282. Mohammad Ebrahim Bastani Parizi, *Siyasat va Eqtesad-e 'Asr Safavi* (Tehran, 1348/1969), pp. 453-54. Mirza Mohammad Hasan Khan E'temad al-Saltaneh, *Ruznameh-ye Khaterat-e E'temad al-Saltaneh* Iraj Afshar ed. (Tehran, 1345/1966), pp. 577, 831.

ings and procrastinated and the shah did not press him further on the matter and there the matter rested.[283]

To stimulate the juices and senses further there was an abundance of erotic and pornographic material available. Erotic paintings were not only found to illustrate literary works of whatever nature, but also were applied to walls of homes and bathhouses. Amir Mas'ud (r. 1030-1040), the son of Mahmud of Ghazna had a palace built in Herat, which contained a relaxation room; this he had decorated from floor to ceiling with images of naked men and women depicted in scenes from the *Alfiyeh Shalfiyeh*.[284] In 1629, Herbert noted similar paintings in the house of Khvajah Nazar, the chief of the Armenians of Jolfa. "A Christian he professes himself, but (I must be bold to say) his house was furnished with such beastly pictures, such ugly postures as indeed are not fit to be remembered."[285] In a former palace of Karim Khan Zand in Shiraz, one of the rooms had "a great number of paintings of the ladies of that chieftain's time."[286] The paintings in the pleasure-house in *Haft Tan* garden in Shiraz were the ones that struck Europeans most. These included paintings from the Zand period about Sheikh Sa'nan, the classical tale of the old mystic who fell in love with a Christian girl.[287]

---

283. See Willem Floor, 'Art (*Naqqashi*) and Artists (*Naqqashan*) in Qajar Persia, *Muqarnas* 16 (1999), p. 138. In this article I also briefly discuss sensual and erotic art in the nineteenth century and provide a short biography of, among others, Kamal al-Molk.

284. Beyhaqi, *Tarikh*, p. 121f.

285. Thomas Herbert, *Travels in Persia, 1627-1629*, ed. W. Foster. (New York, 1929), p. 122.

286. Lieut. Col. Johnson, *A Journey from India to England through Persia, Georgia, Russia, Poland and Prussia in the Year 1817* (London: Longman, Hurst, Rees, Orme, and Brown, 1818), p. 61. Edward Scott Waring, *A Tour to Sheeraz* (London, 1807), p. 61 copied one of the ladies, viz. Shah Nowbat, the favorite mistress. See also Benjamin Burges Moore, *From Moscow to the Persian Gulf* (New York, 1915), pp. 383-84 for a description of the tile mosaics and some frescos, and p. 393 for a description three crumbling Zand frescos in the *Chehel Tan*. On frescos in general see Willem Floor, *Mural Paintings in Qajar Iran* (Costa Mesa, 2003).

287. William Hollingberry, *A Journal of Observations made during the British embassy to the court of Persia in the years 1799, 1800 and 1801* (Calcutta,

In the nineteenth century, according to Teule, the walls and ceilings of the homes of the rich were decorated with floral designs, birds or half-naked women.[288] The house of Amin al-Dowleh, one of the most important ministers of Fath 'Ali Shah, had "a room which, though small, was exceedingly pretty; … In one recess was the portrait of a beautiful Georgian girl; in another, of a handsome *b'iri'sh* or beardless boy."[289] In 1825, the *divan-khaneh* of the governor's palace in Tabriz was decorated with portraits of women striking voluptuous poses.[290] The Vali of Kurdestan had private room in his palace in Sennah. "Round it were pictures of women. One was said to be the portrait of a female slave, sent as a present to one of the Vali's ancestors by Shah Abbas the Great."[291] In 1812, Mirza Musa, the governor of Mazandaran had a room in his palace decorated with "several pictures of beautiful Georgian women, in various dresses, and of one effeminate boy."[292] The *talar* of the women's apartment of the house of the governor of Tabas, 'Emad al-Molk, was decorated with naked women. E'tesam al-Molk wrote that the governor spent much time on the construction of buildings and on embellishing them with paintings

1814 [Tehran: Imp. Org. f. Soc. Services, 1976]), pp. 34-35; James Morier, *A Journey through Persia, Armenia and Asia Minor in the Years 1808 and 1809* (London: Longman, Hurst, Rees, Orme, and Brown, 1812), p. 106; Lumsden, *A Journey from Meerut in India to London in the Years 1819 and 1820* (London, 1822), p. 97; Claude James Rich, *Narrative of a Journey to the Site of Babylon … with a Narrative of a Journey to Persepolis* (London: Duncan and Malcolm, 1839), pp. 227-228; R.B.M Binning, *A Journal of Two Years' Travel in Persia, Ceylon, etc.* 2 vols. (London: Wm. H. Allen & Co, 1857), vol. 1, pp. 229-230, 232; Lycklama, *Voyage*, vol. 2, pp. 510-511.

288. Jules Charles Teule, *Pensées et Notes Critiques extraites du journal de mes voyages dans l'empire du Sultan de Constantinople, dans les Provinces Russes, Géorgiennes et Tartars du Caucase et dans le royaume de Perse* (Paris: Arthus Bertrand, 1842), p. 321.

289. William Ouseley, *Travels in various countries of the East; more particularly Persia* 3 vols. (London, 1819), vol. 3, p. 124.

290. Charles Bélanger. *Voyage aux Indes-Orientales.* 2 vols. (Paris: Arthus Bertrand, 1838), vol. 2, pp. 294, 297.

291. Claudius James Rich, *Narrative of a Residence in Koordistan* 2 vols. (London, 1836), vol. 1, p. 218.

292. Ouseley, *Travels*, vol. 3, p. 156.

of bad taste, invariably of women engaged in dirty acts.[293] The building does not exist anymore, but according to a description from the
1960s, it contained wall paintings, which show a couple that embrace
each other, and hold a glass in one of their hands. In the background
there are two servants, one of whom is black. The other is similar, in
this case with three servants.[294] Private bathhouses sometimes were
decorated with erotic scenes, either with suggestive paintings and/or
with tiles, such as that of 'Emad al-Molk in Tabas. Its *talar* was covered with paintings. Each panel there was a group of naked women,
and their vaginas in particular were much in evidence.[295]

Lovely ladies appeared on all kinds of utensils such as the water
pipes. "Chillums (cups for the tobacco) being of enameled gold, with
portraits of fair Persian dames, &c."[296] But they were also found on
other items. "The graphic depictions on mirror boxes, pen-boxes and
above all on playing cards are such that they offend those with the
least strict morals. True, these depictions are much more common in
Persia than elsewhere in the world, and in their history and poetry
the search for the most sensual pleasures are to be met at almost every
line."[297]

Other female related themes, such as harem intrigues, also were
popular themes for artists. In 1817, Kotzebue "saw paintings repre-
senting something of that kind."[298] Worse, of course, in the mind of

---

293. E'tesam al-Molk, *Safarnameh-ye Mirza Khanlar Khan E'tesam al-Molk*. ed.
Manuchehr Mahmudi (Tehran, 1351/1972), pp. 248, 261 (here he mentioned
a large *talar* where each panel showed such scenes of lewd women. It is not
clear whether that is the same he mentioned earlier or that it concerned a
different building).

294. Iraj Afshar, "Bist Shahr va Hazar Farsang," in Iraj Afshar ed. *Savad va
Bayaz* 2 vols. (Tehran: Dehkhoda, 1349/1970), vol. 2, pp. 63-64.

295. E'tesam al-Molk, *Safarnameh* (Tehran, 1351/1972), p. 237.

296. Lumsden, *A Journey*, p. 101.

297. Allemagne, *Du Khorasan*, vol. 1, p. 191. On this theme in general see
Floor, "Artists (*Naqqash*) and Artistry (*Naqqashi*)," *Muqarnas*, p. 138.

298. Moritz von Kotzebue, *Narrative of a Journey into Persia in the suite of the
Imperial Russian Embassy in the year 1817* (Philadelphia: Carey & Sons, 1820),
p. 154.

the outwardly staid Victorians, was the kind of pictures that were for sale, for example, in the shops of Resht at the turn of the 20th century. These were "the vilest oleographs that the human mind can devise, only matched by the vileness of the frames." The hotel at Resht also boasted of "a couple of German oleographs, which set one's teeth on edge."[299] Brugsch observed as to the art sold in the bazaars of Iran, "Here one sees at one single shop in the bazaar the products of Persian [painting] art, and among these the vilest scenes, in front of which Persian women often stop, and to prove their participation by the pointing finger and the loud remarks."[300] All these stimulating media are banned under the Islamic Republic as they only will lead those, who watch erotic films and pictures or read erotic books, into temptation to commit sins.[301]

MARITAL BLISS

Although males and females were often married at a young age, and were sometimes part of a polygynous household, this did not mean that there was not appreciation and even love between husband and wife. Of course, just as in other culture areas it all depended on the character and circumstances of the persons concerned. Nezam al-Molk, the famous grand vizier of the Seljuq king Malek Shah, wrote: "In all the world I hold none dearer than this my wife; she is my mate and the mother of my children. My good is her good, and she more than all people desires my good." Nevertheless, such a man and other

---

299. E. Henry Landor, *Across Coveted Lands* 2 vols. (New York: Scribners, 1903), vol. 1, pp. 35-36, 41; see also Floor, "Art (*Naqqashi*) and Artists (*Naqqashan*)," p. 138. The pictures that hung in the shops were not all that vile, see, for example, a photograph of a bazaar shop that displays illustrations, Iraj Afshar, *Ganjineh-yi 'Aksha-yi Iran* (Tehran: Farhang-e Iran, 1371/1992), p. 279. For a picture of a Persian grocery store with a picture of an unveiled European woman showing bare shoulders, see J. Knanishu, *About Persia and its People* (Rock Island, Ill 1899), p. 153.

300. Heinrich Brugsch, *Die Reise der K.K. Gesandtschaft nach Persien 1861-1862*, 2 vols. (Berlin: J.C. Hinrichs, 1863), vol. 2, pp. 287-88.

301. Amini, *Entekhab*, p. 68.

men were strongly advised not to consult women in anything, not to do what they counseled and above all, never ever to allow them to assume power. This advice was underscored by examples of the experience of such luminaries as Adam (of Eve's fame), kings Key Kavus and Darius, and even the prophet Mohammad, who did the opposite of what his wife A'isha counseled him to do.[302] Likewise, Kai Ka'us counseled his son: If you marry a wife, my son, treat her with the utmost consideration. Even though material goods may be valuable to you, they are not more so than wife and children, to whom you should not begrudge them, at least if they are a good wife and obedient children.[303]

Despite the multitude of poems about love for girls, there also were authors who counseled men not to be ruled by love, because that would cause anguish, result in immature behavior, which would be indulged by youth, but not by a more mature man. Moreover, love was but passion and would not bring happiness. As the poet said:

Can passion's fire, my darling, comfort thee?
Who ever found relief in raging fire?[304]

Indeed, such advice is in harmony with the advice given by jurists, who, moreover, make it clear that it was the woman's main task to please her husband and not the other way round. "Know that the Prophet has said: 'God's pleasure rests upon the pleasure of the husband. When a woman dies whose husband is pleased with her, her lot is Paradise." To make sure that there is no misunderstanding, the jurists have spelled out the nine rights of the husband:

First: that (the wife) not leave the house except with his permission;
Second: that she not deny herself to her husband that time when she is clean;

302. Nizam al-Mulk, *Book*, ch. 42, pp. 185-92.
303. Kai Ka'us b. Iskandar, *Qabus Nama*, p. 117, Ch. XXVI.
304. Kai Ka'us b. Eskandar, *Qabus Nama*, ch. XIV.

Third:	that she not betray him (with respect to) his property;
Fourth:	that she pray for him;
Fifth:	that she not cause his distress;
Sixth:	that she help him as much as she can;
Seventh:	that she not boast to him of her own wealth;
Eighth:	that she not deny her wealth to him; and
Ninth:	that she cares for his relatives.[305]

From these rights of the husband it is clear that a wife has to devote her entire life to make her man happy. Some jurists even make it clearer where woman's place is. "For women were created from weakness and immodesty; the remedy for their weakness is silence, and the remedy for their immodesty is to make the house their prison."[306]

To keep the scales of marital justice in balance the jurists have detailed the eight rights of women, so that the men may know how to properly behave as well:

First:	that the husband fall not short in providing her expenses and support;
Second:	that he not beat or punish her except when she is disobedient;
Third:	that he not consort with her in that place which is repugnant;
Fourth:	that he not wrong her in the matter of her dower;
Fifth:	that he not prevent her from visiting her parents;

---

305. Meisami, *Sea*, p. 118.

306. Meisami, *Sea*, p.163. Also, "The Prophet said, 'Beware, honor your wives, for they are your prisoners.' Ibid., p. 118. According to al-Ghazzali, *On Marriage*, p. 21. The prophet Mohammad said: "Marriage is slavery; be careful about to whom you give your own child as a slave."

Sixth: that he instruct her in religion and customs of
              the law with respect to prayer, fasting, and
              the statutes concerning the menses;

Seventh: that he not be absent from his wife for more
              than four months; and

Eighth: that he not keep two wives in one house.[307]

Most of these rights speak for themselves. The 'repugnant place' in the third right concerns the practice of anal intercourse, which is an often practiced form of traditional birth control. This form of sexual congress may also have been preferred, because it was one that many men were used to when having sex with boys or other men. There is no agreement among jurists whether anal intercourse with one's wife is allowed or not, some allow it, others do not, as discussed above. The seventh right is an important one, because, implicitly, Islamic law acknowledges that not only men, but also women have sexual needs and therefore men were enjoined to have sex with their wife at least once every four months.[308] If a man has more than one wife he has to treat them equally and he cannot favor his young wife over his old wife, although he did, of course, in most cases. Therefore poets such as Nezami counseled:

> It suffices to have one wife
> A man who has many wives has none.

What these rights and duties tell us is that men are rational, capable, and, most importantly in charge. Women are fickle, emotional and lacking in self-control, and inferior; they need the firm guiding hand of a male, in this case the husband, to fulfil their role, i.e. to make the husband happy. In sexual matters that meant that she had

---

307. Meisami, *Sea*, p.119, 162-63; Khomeyni, *Towzih*, pp. 507-08 (nos. 2288-92).

308. Some men in the Bandar Lengeh area did not respect this Koranic injunction and practiced sexual abstinence for nine months per year, because of health reasons. Daneshvar, *Didaniha*, vol. 2, p. 11.

to be there for her husband. Because, in particular in sexual matters women needed to be controlled and her needs seen to, or else social chaos (*fitna*) might be the result. This control, of course, had to be provided by a male.[309] These are good intentions, if one-sided ones, because the wife has to make her life subservient in order to make that of her husband pleasant and without recrimination. As the chapter headings of the *Edification of Wives* (*Ta'dib al-Nesvan*), a treatise written in 1879, indicate, this means that a woman should:

(1) control her tongue; she should not be quarrelsome, rude, or scathing in her remarks;

(2) not grumble; complaints and whining only engender more of the same and therefore it is better to be gracious and gentle rather than bitter, for with nectar one attracts the bee;

(3) not sulk, for it is self-defeating and only hurts herself, while the husbands "have the right to peace within doors" so that they may forget the cares of the day;

(4) behave properly and with good manners in company;

(5) eat delicately and without making any noise;

(6) keep her body clean and be selective in the use of perfumes; and

(7) be dressed in clean and elegant clothes.[310]

It is interesting to note that these same sentiments are also offered in books by Ayatollah Amini, who, almost one hundred twenty years later, and more adroitly than the anonymous author of the *Edification*

309. Judith Tucker, *Gender and Islamic History* (Washington DC, 1993), pp. 3-13; Steven M. Oberhelman, "Hierarchies of Gender, ideology, and Power in Ancient and Medieval Greek and Arabic Dream Literature," in J.W. Wright Jr and Everett K. Rowson eds. *Homoeroticism in Classical Arabic Literature* (New York, 1997), p. 66. According to al-Ghazzali, *On Marriage*, p. 24, "Men are set up over women (Q. 4:34). The man must always be dominant. The messenger (pbuh) said: 'Wretched is (the man who is) the slave of his wife.'"

310. Anonymous, "The Education of Wives," vol. 1, pp., p. 242.

of Wives also counsels wives to respect their husband, have nice manners towards him, forgive husbands their errors, not to seek quarrels, to support their husband, be there for him not their mother, not to listen to gossip, when he is angry to be silent, to accept his rule; this is clear from his book on *The Rules of Marriage*.[311]

This salvo of behavioral guidelines for wives, which are completely based in and supported by the Traditions and therefore by religious teaching, demanded, of course, a female rebuttal, which, not long thereafter (in 1895) appeared as well, although it remained unpublished until 1992. Bibi Khanom Astarabadi argued in her riposte (*The Vices of Men*) that the author of the *Edification of Wives* only seeks to humiliate women and tries to cover all their good qualities with imaginary and false failings. Moreover, he considered all women slaves and servants and all men as kings and masters. Marriage for him only has a physical meaning and does not deal with love and life. Furthermore, men who have beautiful wives pay no attention to them and all the time are engaged in debauchery. Finally, Bibi Khanom argues that the anonymous author represents his own views and desires as those of all men, while this is not based in fact.[312]

These above mentioned formal rules certainly played, and still play, an important role as to how the relationship between men and women developed. But the formality of these rules only provides a framework and does not say anything about the actual content of the relationship. Despite the male-biased nature of these rules it did not prevent men and women feeling real mutual love. Examples of such instances are given, which, of necessity, always concern the upper classes, because until the end of the nineteenth century nobody wrote or cared about the majority of the population, the poor, where love also found and finds its way.

The father of the three Buyid brothers, Abu Shuja' had only one wife, whom he loved and when she died he publicly mourned her

---

311. Amini, *Ayin-e Hamsardari.*

312. Bibi Khanom, "Ma'ayeb al-Rejal."

death.[313] The Caliph al-Naser (r. 1180-1225) was totally and utterly besotted with love for Khalatiyeh, daughter of Arslan b. Soleyman. He pressed for her hand, but she was married and told him that she would only take him if her father accepted and made her husband divorce her. This finally happened and she married the caliph. However, the happiness did not last long, for she fell ill and died. Caliph al-Nasr was beyond grief, lamented her and then had her embalmed and he cried for a month, and it was only then that the courtiers were able to induce him to bury Khalatiyeh.[314] Qara Koz Begum, whom 'Omar Sheykh Mirza (d. 1495) married "was truly loved by him"[315] Soltan Ahmad Mirza (r. 1469–1494) adored Qataq Begum passionately, but she was utterly domineering. This unwomanly characteristic was made worse by the fact that she also drank wine. As a result, during her life-time Soltan Ahmad Mirza did not go to any of his other wives. Fortunately, he listened to his male relatives and put an end to this unnatural situation. "He had her killed and obtained release from disgrace."[316] Soltan Mahmud Mirza's (r. 1494–1495) chief wife was Khvanzadeh Begum. He loved her very much and grieved great when she died.[317]

There also were books that discussed what love meant and how to express it,[318] while poets and men of letters gave expression to their feelings on this subject. In the beginning of the twentieth century, for example, Mokhber al-Saltaneh wrote: "Love is a natural game, full of toil and little rest; it is also troublesome, mostly thoughtless give and take, and sometimes unbearable, if it veers to harmony it is bliss, if

313. Ibn al-Athir, *Kamil f'il-Tarikh* , vol. 8, p. 84 (ca. 900).

314. Hendushah b. Sanjar al-Sahebi al-Kirani, *Tajareb al-Salaf dar Tarikh* ed. 'Abbas Eqbal (Tehran, 1344/1965), p. 321.

315. Babur Padshah Ghazi, Zahiru'd-Din Muhammad. *Babur-Nama (Memoires of Babur)* translated into English by A.S. Beveridge 2 vols. in one (Delhi, 1989), 24.

316. Babur, *Babur-Nama*, p. 36.

317. Babur, *Babur-Nama*, p. 48.

318. Jamal al-Din Khalil Shirvani's *Nozhat al-Majales* ed. Mohammad Amin Riyahi (Tehran, 1366/1987) has several chapters with detailed advice what to say on what subject. See also Ravandi, *Tarikh*, vol. 7, pp. 350, 363.

the contrary is the case it is total lamentation."[319] But despite these considerations and soul searching some European observers held that "Love as a lofty moral sentiment as we understand it is unknown to the Persians. Love as sung by the poets of the golden age is a sensuous passion, and one not always inspired by women."[320] However, other European contemporaries, equally convinced, disagreed. "Notwithstanding the many peculiar laws and marriage customs of Persia, and contrary to what one might suppose, happy and permanent marriages are by no means uncommon; indeed, I am prepared to hazard the statement that there is but little more misery from this source there than in most Christian countries."[321]

ADULTERY

Although adultery is strongly forbidden by Islamic law it, of course, occurs. No quantitative data are available, but it would seem that men were the main culprits, as they had and still have more opportunity and possibilities than women. The very fact that male and female prostitution still thrives in Iran is proof of that. Also, men were the ones that were the least affected by the penalties of the law, because they were in charge of the women and society and thus, could turn its rules better to their advantage than women. Wives were not always stay-at-home persons, however. Muqaddasi has a negative opinion about women in Shiraz in the tenth century, while he opined about those of Herat" when the time comes that the heliotropes bloom, they come in heat like cats."[322] Men wanted to take advantage of such situations, such as a man who saw a beautiful woman, as told by the author of the *Latayef al-Tavayef*. He said to her: 'Hey lady, how about it, if the occa-

319. Mehdiqoli Hedayat Mokhber al-Saltaneh, *Khaterat va Khatarat* (Tehran, 1344/1865), p. 14.

320. Ponafidine, *Life*, pp. 319-20.

321. Benjamin, *Persia*, pp. 453-54.

322. Muqadassi, *Kitab ahsan*, pp. 427, 436.

sion arises, may I have a taste of you to see who is sweeter you or my wife.' She replied: 'Go and ask my husband who has tasted both!'[323]

More often, of course, adultery took place when the age difference between wife and husband was large, or when the husband was inattentive and abusive. The twelve century poetess Mahsati wrote:

> His wife with child, a judge began to wail and shout;
> From spite he wondered. 'What the hell is this about?
> I'm old and never does my peter raise its hoary head
> The whore's no Mary, so who made this baby sprout?'[324]

When a husband found out that his wife was pregnant and he believed it was not his, if he wanted to accuse his wife of infidelity, he had to make an oath of damnation (*li'an*) before an Islamic judge or qazi and either accuse her of infidelity or deny his fathering her child. The oath has to be repeated four times. If accepted by the religious authority, the spouses are irrevocably divorced or the child is declared illegitimate. To have been born out of wedlock (*haram-zadeh*), i.e. to an unmarried girl, divorcee, or widow was a terrible curse, although the jurists held and hold that such a child is not illegitimate.[325] However, popular belief and opinion did not agree with this. Usually, both mother and child were killed by one of the woman's male family members. Unmarried women who became pregnant therefore tried to get

---

323. Morteza Ravandi, *Tarikh-e Ejtema'i-ye Iran* 9 vols. (Tehran, 1368/1987), vol. 7, p. 410.

324. Paul Sprachman, *Suppressed Persian. An Anthology of Forbidden Literature* (Costa Mesa, 1995), p. 2. The reference to Mary is to the mother of the prophet Jesus, who, according to Moslems and Christians, allegedly had an immaculate conception, i.e. without intercourse with a man.

325. Polak, *Persien*, vol. 1, p. 217; Thot, "Das persische," p. 418. Under current Iranian law a child is illegitimate when it is the result of fornication. It is only illegitimate in the sense that it cannot inherit from its biological parents, although the other aspects of the relationship with its biological parents are not further defined in the Civil Code. To resolve this issue the Office Supreme Court in 1997 "declared that a child born outside wedlock will be considered the child of its biological parents (*farzand-e 'orf*) with the entire legal obligations that are attached to it, with the exception of inheritance," see Yassari, "Who is a child," p. 29.

their child aborted, in which midwives were very capable. Even in case of rape the child was killed by the family and in a reported case the mother was spared at the advice of a religious authority. However, she was expelled by her family and became mad. Even if bastard children were not murdered they were marked. For example, if a bastard would enter the holy shrine at Qom he would immediately get a nose bleed, because the holy person buried there, according to popular belief, cannot stand bastards.[326]

In case of adultery, the law required the death penalty in fact by stoning of the convicted adulteress. That this actually happened is clear from a story related by the poet 'Attar (ca.1142–ca.1220). He wrote that a chaste woman had been falsely accused by her brother-in-law of adultery, because she had not given in to his wicked demands, during the absence of her husband, and was then sentenced to be stoned by the qazi, after having heard the four lying male witnesses attesting that she had been guilty of adultery. "They took her into the open country on the high road and they cast stones upon her from all sides."[327]

The threat of the death penalty apparently had not much preventive impact on society, for apart from sexual drive, it was also difficult to find a couple in *flagrante delicto* witnessed by four male or eight female witnesses. As to marital fidelity, the satirical poet 'Obeyd-e Zakani (d. 1371) held opinion that:

> The Lady: She who has many lovers.
> The Housewife: She who has a few.
> The Virtuous: She who is content with one lover.
> The Real Lady: She who makes love gratis.

---

326. Polak, *Persien*, vol. 1 p. 217f; Serena, *Hommes*, p. 334; Bernard Kellermann, *Auf Persiens Karawanen Strassen* (Berlin, 1928), p. 51.

327. 'Attar, *Ilahi-nama*, p. 170. On the legal issues concerning adultery see al-Mawardi, *al-Ahkam al-Sultaniyya w'al-Wilayat al-Diniyya* translated into English by Wafaa H. Wahba as *The Ordinances of Government* (Reading, 2006), pp. 242-44. From his description it is clear that it is very difficult to prove adultery as the four male witnesses have to attest "that they witnessed the entry of the penis into the vagina as the kohl-stick enters the cosmetics jar."

The Charitable: A man who makes love to an old lady.

The Poor: She who is after strangers.

The Aphrodisiac: The leg of another's wife.[328]

Although 'Obeyd-e Zakani certainly exaggerated the situation, he assuredly would not have raised the issue if there had not been some smoke. 'Abbas Eqbal characterized the fourteenth century as one in which: "The mother of one of the kings was known for prostitution and promiscuity; the wife of another kills her husband in the most hideous way, since he had imprisoned her lover; another king blinds his father with his own hands and commits adultery with his mother; and a fourth monarch forces his enemies to divorce their wives so that he may woo them and write *ghazal*s of his love for them."[329]

In later centuries it is reported that adulterous relationships existed. For example, liaisons between Moslem widows and (probably married) Moslem men were reported in the sixteenth century. One case, involving the mother of Turanshah V, the king of Hormuz, and a son of Khvajeh Ebrahim, a high palace official, was the cause of a great public scandal in 1545.[330] In 1522, the ardor of Ra'is Shehab al-Din for the mother of Ra'is Shamsh led to the former's murder.[331] In these cases the women did not suffer, although there were designated locations to punish them for such a crime. In Shiraz, remiss loose women, who had been condemned to death were thrown into a deep well in the Qal'eh-ye Bandar. This place was already pointed out to Tavernier in the 1640s and still had this reputation at the end of the nineteenth century.[332]

---

328. 'Obeyd-e Zakani, *The Ethics*, p. 71.

329. 'Obeyd-e Zakani, *Kolliyat* ed. 'Abbas Eqbal (Tehran, 1353/1974), p. R.

330. D. João de Castro, *Obras Completas de D. João de Castro*, eds. Armando Cortesão e Luís de Albuquerque (Coimbra, Academia Internacional de Cultura Portuguesa, 1976), vol. 3-102, p. 103 (16/11/1545).

331. Gaspar Correia, *Lendas da India* ed. Rodrigo José de Lima Felner 4. vols. in 8 parts (Coimbra, 1860-66), II, pp. 701-02.

332. Forsat Hoseyni Shirazi, *Ketab-e Athar-e 'Ajam* (Bombay, 1314 AH/1896-97), pp. 416-17; Jean-Baptiste Tavernier, *Voyages en Perse et description de ce*

The reason that women sometimes sought love elsewhere was because their husbands were unable or unwilling to give it due to polygyny, homosexuality, or other inclinations that resulted in their neglect. They allegedly used procuresses and eunuchs to initiate liaisons,[333] and also purportedly took advantage of the greater freedom that going on a pilgrimage offered.[334] They also had non-penetrative sexual relations with their servants as related in the 'Vices of Men.' "A man had a slave and one day the master was going ahead of the slave to the roof. While they were going the slave 'fingered' the master and he turned back and said: 'you son of gun, why did you do that?' The slave was very afraid and wanted to give an excuse and said: 'Please forgive me, I made a mistake; I thought it was the mistress.'"[335]

Although one has to view with some skepticism claims by some European travelers that Persian women were not very chaste, except for tribal women; nevertheless, Polak, who eschews sensationalism, submits that adultery occurred frequently.[336] Adultery was a phenomenon that occurred in all classes of society. In the 1850s, Persians even went so far as to publicly claim that the queen-mother had been an adulteress, while similar aspersions were cast on the wives of the military and servant class.[337] But similar slander was banded about concerning women of the lower classes, who allegedly were not overly burdened

---

royaume (Paris, 1930), p. 305.

333. Polak, "Die Prostitition," p. 563 (they also signaled their interest in a liaison by holding a flower, an apple, an orange, the 'accidental' lifting of the face veil, etc.).

334. Brugsch, *Die Reise*, vol. 1, p. 30; Edward Stack, *Six Months in Persia* 2 vols. (New York, 1882), vol. 1, p. 293; Serena, *Hommes*, p. 62.

335. Javadi et al., *Do Ruyaru'i*, p. 199.

336. Binning, *Journal*, vol. 2, p. 407; Brugsch, *Reise*, vol. 1, p. 230; Ibid., *Im Lande der Sonne – Wanderungen in Persien* (Berlin, 1886), p. 240, 244; Dieulafoye, *Perse*, p. 261, 461; Wills, *In the Land*, p. 276; Polak, "Die Prostitition," p. 563.

337. J. A. de Gobineau, "Lettres Persanes," *Revue de la Littérature Comparée* (1952), p. 218; Wills, *In the Land*, pp. 202, 316; Mohammad Shafiʻ Qazvini, *Qanun-e Qazvini*. ed. Iraj Afshar (Tehran, 1370/1991), p. 122 (when the husbands frolicked with beardless youths their wives got their revenge [had sex] with the same youths).

by their own lewd behavior.[338] Likewise, aspersions were cast on the chastity of the mother of Mohammad 'Ali Shah (r. 1907-1910), who was referred to as *omm al-khaqan*, when his opponents referred to him as *pesar-e omm al-khaqan* or the 'son of the mother of the king.'[339]

It would seem that Qajar high-society was in a moral crisis in the early twentieth century, although it had started much earlier. Upper-class women, who had to share their husband with three other wedded wives and with any number of *sigheh*s, were very unsatisfied and therefore, sought sexual satisfaction outside the conjugal home.

> We can hardly wonder at the loose conduct of Persian women perpetually mortified by marital pederasty. During the unhappy campaign of 1856-7 in which, with the exception of a few brilliant skirmishes, we gained no glory, Sir James Outram and the Bombay army showing how badly they could work, there was a formal outburst of the Harems; and even women of princely birth could not be kept out of the officers' quarters.[340]

When in December 1894, Na'eb al-Saltaneh's mother had thrown a party, most upper-class women of the city turned up. The prince was there and walked around and feasted his eyes, but he never allowed his own wives to go there.[341] It would seem that this situation was aggravated during and after the reign of Mozaffar al-Din Shah, when even his own sisters had liaisons. Quite a few of the unsatisfied women of

---

338. X. Hommaire de Hell, *Voyage en Turquie et en Perse*. 2 vols. (Paris: P. Bertrand, 1856), vol. 2, p. 17; Binning, *Journal*, vol. 2, p. 401.

339. Ahmad Kasravi, *Tarikh-e Mashruteh-ye Iran* 3 vols. (Tehran, 1320/1941), vol. 2, pp. 84-85. An illegimate child was not named after his father, who formally was unknown, but after his mother. Whether there were grounds for this accusation or whether it was slander, which is more likely, is not known.

340. Richard Burton, "Terminal Essay" to his English translation of *The Arabian Nights* 10 vols. (London, 1885), [http://www.fordham.edu/halsall/pwh/burton-te.html].

341. Qahraman Mirza Salur 'Eyn al-Saltaneh, *Ruznameh-ye Khaterat-e 'Eyn al-Saltaneh* 9 vols. Iraj Afshar and Mas'ud Salur eds. (Tehran, 1374/1995), vol. 1, p. 667.

the upper-class had sexual relations with males of their own household staff or with other men. There was one woman who reportedly left her house in a droshke, the driver would take her to his house, have sex with her and then return her home.[342] Merritt Merritt-Hawkes also blames homosexuality as well as polygyny for Persian women's unsatisfactory sexual life, reason why some of them had lovers.[343] Dashti and Hejazi described the promiscuity of certain married women in Tehran's high society with deftness,[344] a development that had already started under the Qajars. Taj al-Saltaneh, sister of Mozaffar al-Din Shah gives some insight into these liaisons in which she and other similar dissatisfied women were engaged. Similarly, Merritt-Hawkes, who was a very good observer, noted the same phenomenon in the 1930s.[345]

Sometimes a man would not even bother to accuse his wife of adultery, even when he alleged that she had made off with his property with her much younger lover. This case shows that women indeed had liaisons and sometimes ran away with their lover. The man was a low government official and not a local and, therefore, pursuit of justice was more difficult. He did not even ask for justice against his wife, whom he had divorced, but for some financial support.[346] According to Bassett, referring to the situation in the 1880s, "If sodomy be a common vice of the men, adultery is said to be a special vice of the women, by which they retaliate."[347] The fact that women when going out of their home were incognito due to their all-concealing street clothes made this easier, because a man would not be able to recognize his own wife, while custom did not allow him to verify whether the

---

342. Hedayatollah Hakim-Olahi, *Ba man beh Shahr-e Now beya'id* 2 vols. (Tehran, 1326/1947), vol. 2, pp. 27-28, 32-33, 40.

343. Merritt-Hawkes, *Persia*, p. 288.

344. H. Kamshad, *Modern Persian Prose Literature* (Cambridge, 1966), pp. 72, 75-76.

345. Merritt-Hawkes, *Persia*, p. 286.

346. Irene Schneider, *The Petitioning System in Iran. State, Society and Power Relations in the Late 19th Century* (Wiesbaden, 2006), p. 195.

347. Bassett, *Persia*, p. 57; see also Qazvini, *Qanun*, p. 122.

chador hid his wife. Whether adultery was frequent or not, the penalty for it, stoning, was seldom applied in Qajar Iran. It was difficult to prove that it had occurred, while the authorities considered that pronouncing the divorce sufficed as punishment.[348] There were several places, nevertheless, in Iran that allegedly served as places of execution of adulterous women. Such places varied from a deep well near Shiraz where women were or had been thrown into or to a tower in Tabriz where they were thrown off.

With the establishment of a reforming regime in 1925 a number of laws were drawn up that aimed, among other things, to modernize the rules concerning sexual relations, including those dealing with adultery. Instead of the rules of Islamic law, the new Penal Code of 1925 laid down rules that, although pronouncing adultery a punishable act, no longer demanded the death penalty be applied. Article 212 specifically deals with adultery and punishes the convicted parties with 6 month to 3 years in prison, in the cases when:

(1) married woman has illicit sex with a man;

(2) married man has illicit sex with a woman;

(3) man has illicit sex with a married woman;

(4) married woman marries another man; and

(5) man marries a married woman.

The law considered the first three acts to be civil crimes, but the latter as felonies. In the former case punishment was determined based on charges made by concerned private citizens, while in the latter case the state itself determined the penalty.

In view of the rather relaxed position of the authorities vis a vis adultery, who considered it mostly a private family affair, it often happened that punishment was metered out by the family itself. Such family executions for adultery seem to have been common in southern

---

348. Bassett, *Persia*, p. 57; see also Binning, *Journal*, vol. 2, p. 405; Polak, "Die Prostitution," p. 563; Benjamin, *Persia*, p. 453.

Persia, according to Wills.[349] Often the family did without the legal process; just the suspicion of dishonorable behavior could result in a woman's death. Ponafidine, who was Russian consul in Mashhad and Tehran for many years, relates that in 1880 a villager of Zargandeh, the summer location of the Russian Legation, shot his sister on suspicion of improper conduct. Likewise in the village of Ne'matabad, used as summer quarters by Tehranis, a visiting Persian khan became acquainted with one of the village women. She secretly visited his house from time to time and one day when she left the house she was stabbed to death by a fellow villager, who was not even related to her. In the first case nothing was done, because, according to public opinion, the brother had done the right thing. In the second case the police *pro forma* arrested the man, who then 'escaped' and was allowed to go on with his life as if he had done nothing.[350] According to Mehrangiz Kar, in her home town of Ahvaz, during the 1930-1940s it was not uncommon to see in the morning a bloody head hanging from the door of a house in her neighborhood, although this account may be exaggerated. This head was from one of the womenfolk of the Arab tribesmen living in that neighborhood, one of whose male family members, because he suspected that the woman concerned had dishonored the family name, beheaded her and by hanging her head as a sign of justice done had regained honor.[351] Even in the 1970s, a husband who killed his wife, because she had a sexual relationship with another man was not prosecuted. In case of the killing of a daughter or sister, a man might at worst expect a few months of imprisonment.[352] In fact, the Penal Code (art. 179) of 1940 condoned

---

349. Wills, *In the Land*, pp. 96f., 276 (for the description of a case of poisoning by the mother and mother-in-law of the adulteress).

350. Ponafidine, *Life*, pp. 332; Papoli-Yazdi, *Khaterat*, pp. 138ff for a case that involved the continuous beating of the girl concerned by her brothers, although in the end all worked out well.

351. Mehrangiz Kar, "Rah va rasm-e shekastan-e sokutra beh man amukht," *Majalleh-ye Zanan* 29 [on line edition].

352. Pakizegi, "Legal and Social Position," p. 222. For a discussion of the phenomenon of honor and the act of deflowering see Nancy Lindisfarne, "Variant Masculinities, Variant Virginities: Rethinking 'Honour and Shame,' " in

such an act, "if the husband saw his wife with a strange man in a compromising position."[353]

However, killing an adulteress was not always believed to be necessary. Many women were simply divorced and almost invariably were forced into prostitution to ensure their and family members subsistence. Generally, there were no consequences for the adulterous man as adultery was considered to be the woman's fault.[354] Sometimes men were punished by a family member. A famous case is when Karim Khan Zand almost beat his nephew Taher Khan to death after his relationship with the wife of one of his courtiers had been discovered.[355] According to an unconfirmed report, statistics indicate that a fifth of all murders in Iran fall into the category of honor killings and other sexually-related murders.[356]

Nevertheless, the frequency of casual affairs (*sar o serr dashtan*) between men and women seems to be on the rise, although there are no hard quantative data to prove this. However, people have the impression that attitudes towards casual sex through affairs are becoming more acceptable to urbanized middle-class society. However, nowadays couples do not go out, because there is little scope for 'outings' due to the watchful eyes of the 'morality police' and thus they rather 'go inside', i.e. behind closed doors. There were and are also real love affairs, between partners who could not find the same within their own loveless marriage, such as the poetess Forugh Farrokhzad (1935-

---

Dislocating Masculinity: Comparative Ethnographies, eds. Andrea Cornwall and Nancy Lindisfarne (London, 1994), pp. 82-96.

353. Sedghi, *Women and Politics*, pp. 141-44, which also discusses honor killings in Iran in the 1970s.

354. Fischer, "Persian Women," p. 206; Vieille, "Iranian Women," p. 467; Erika Friedl, "Women in Contemporary Persian Folk Tales," in Lois Beck and Nikki Keddie eds. *Women in the Muslim World* (Cambridge, 1978), pp. 641, 645, 649.

355. Asaf, *Rostam al-Tavarikh*, pp. 216-19; Rezaqoli Khan Hedayat, *Tarikh-e Rowzat al-Safa-ye Naseri* 10 vols. (Tehran, 1339/1960), vol. 9, p. 126.

356. [http://www.mianeh.net/en/articles/?aid=99]. For the situation in the 1980s see Parvin Paidar, *Women and the Political process in Twentienth century in Iran* (Cambridge, 1995), pp. 353-54.

1967), who in her poem 'Sin' broke all conventions by announcing to the world that she reveled in her adultery and enjoyed it to the fullest extent. Rather than hiding the shame that, according to long established social mores, she had caused her family by her fornication, she announced that she had enough of this male domination of women, of this oppression of freely chosen love, and continued to live in sin with a man she had chosen and whom she choose not to marry. How more scandalous could a woman be?[357]

> I have sinned, a delectable sin
> In an embrace which was ardent, like fire
> I have sinned in the midst of arms
> Which were hot and vengeful, like iron
>
> I whispered the tale of love to his ear:
> I want you, O sweetheart of mine I want you,
> O life-giving bosom You, O mad love of mine

It was a sign of the times, of incipient modernization, that her behavior did not result in an honor killing or other repressive action. Other female poets also started to openly express their sexual feelings and the need for love in their works such as Tahereh Saffarzadeh (b. 1936) who wrote:

> Invite me to a sandwich of love
> Serve me in your hands
> Wrap my body
> In the warm paper
> Of your breath
> At the table of this cold winter night.[358]

However, with the establishment of the Islamic Republic of Iran such behavior and such expression of sexual feelings, whether by male or female poets, is no longer tolerated. The Pahlavi penal code was,

---

357. Javadi-Selleé, *Another Birth*, p. 11.
358. Milani, *Veils and Words*, p. 163.

of course, suspended and in 1995 a new one formulated and applied. The new penal code (Law of Retribution of *Qesas*) is but a codification of the rules of Islamic law and hence adultery is considered to be a heinous crime (articles 63-81). Punishment can only be pronounced if the perpetrators of the crime confess four times before the judge that they knowingly committed adultery, or where four male witnesses or three male and two female witnesses attest to having witnessed the crime. As commanded by Islamic law, adultery therefore is punishable either by execution, death by stoning or in a few cases by flogging. Execution is required in case of:

(1) fornication with a blood relative;

(2) fornication with one's mother-in-law;

(3) sex between a non-Moslem male with a Moslem female;

(4) rape (article 82).

Death by stoning has to be imposed in case of sex of an adult married male [female] with another woman [man], while having access to his wife [her husband] and being able to have sex with her [him] anytime he wants (art. 83). The same article further stipulates that stoning is not applied if either party does not have access to his/her spouse due to distance, imprisonment etc. It also states that if the adult married female has sex with a minor male, she will be punished by flogging. The punishment for adultery, in case articles 82 and 83 do not apply, is 100 strikes of the lash (art. 88). Should the adulterer repeat the crime after being punished four times, he or she will be executed. Execution will not be carried out as long as a female adulterer is pregnant or nursing a baby (art. 90). Articles 98 through 107 explain the provisions to carry out the punishment including who should cast the first stone. Article 103, for example, stipulates: the man should be buried in a pit up to his waist and the woman should be buried roughly to her chest. Should the person in the pit be able to escape, he or she will be brought back if the crime was confirmed by witnesses, but if (s)he was sentenced based on his or her own confession (s)he will not be brought back. The next article stipulates that the size of stones should not be so large that the person dies upon being hit by one or two of them, neither should they be so small that they cannot be called a stone (art. 104).[359]

It is not known how many persons have been executed by stoning in Iran. The practice, which formally was begun in 1985 (although with some early cases in 1979 and 1983) with the adoption of the new penal code, rose quickly from two cases in that year to as high as 43 in 1989. Thereafter, the number declined to ten in 1990 and in the following years they remained in the low single digits. In 1995 there was even a temporary halt to stoning, but thereafter, it was soon resumed, although the numbers remained low. In 2002, the judiciary again announced a moratorium on stoning, but the practice continued with cases varying between one and four per year. In 2007, as many as seven people were awaiting execution by stoning. Thus, over the last 22 years, up to 110 people have been executed by stoning, i.e. as far as Amnesty International has been able to determine.[360]

Divorce

Marriage, and thus the right to have lawful sexual relations, may be annulled for a variety of reasons (the theological schools, as usual do not agree on their number). These include infertility, insanity, emasculation, impotence, leprosy, and for the wife a blocked vagina. Either spouse, when becoming aware of the other's disability must act immediately, else they lose their right to annulment. Pre-existing disabilities are also cause for annulment. Marriage was and is the only lawful arrangement to provide sexual gratification, but its main objective was and is to multiply. As 'Attar wrote:

359. See for further discussion see Paidar, *Women and the Political Process*, pp. 349-51.

360. Amnesty International, *Country and International Reports*. For a detailed analysis of this aspect of punishment from a human rights point of view see Goudarz Eghtedari, *Islamic Republic of Iran and Execution for Adultery and Homosexuality*.
[http://www.eghtedari.com/vome/hr/DP_Paper.pdf%22%20/t%20%22_blank]

> The purpose of a wife is that a worthy son should be
> born,
> Because when a man has a peerless son there remains a
> good memory of him forever.[361]

These various reasons for annulment are not discussed, rather the focus is on divorce as the most important legal instrument to terminate a lawful sexual relationship.

The marriage contract (*'aqd*) expires with the death of one of the contracting parties, mutual consent, annulment (*faskh*) by either the husband or the wife and divorce (*talaq*). Today, only the man has the right to divorce his wife and that unilaterally and without cause; the wife cannot contest or refuse the divorce.[362] The theological schools, of course, disagree on the conditions that have to be satisfied, although they all agree that the husband has to speak a formula. The husband must employ words in the formula that denote divorce directly or indirectly, though the Shi'is hold that the word divorce itself must be employed. A man has to pronounce the formula three times, in case of the Shi'is in the presence of two witnesses, for the divorce to be irrevocable (*ba'in*). If he does it only once or twice then the divorce is revocable (*raj'i*). Irrevocable here means that a man may not remarry his wife unless she first marries another man, known as *mohallel*, who has to consummate the marriage.[363] If the latter thereafter irrevocably divorces the wife, only then she may remarry her first husband. In case of a revocable divorce, or rather separation, the husband may take his

---

361. 'Attar, *Ilahi-nama*, p. 58. See also Avazeh, *Qanun-e Qovveh-ye Bah*, p. 17.

362. For example, the prophet Mohammad "wanted to divorce Sawdah for she had become old. She said: 'O Prophet of God, I have given my turn [that you have to spend with me] to Ayishah. Do not divorce me so that I may remain among your wives until the Resurrection.' He did not divorce her, but spent two nights with Ayishah and one night with each of his other wives." Al-Ghazzali, *On Marriage*, p. 27.

363. For a description of such a case, involving the wife of a mullah, see Daneshvar, *Didaniha*, vol. 2, pp. 166-69. 'Obeyd-e Zakani, *Resaleh-ye Delgosha*, p. 244 called the irrevocable divorce the opening to freedom for the wife after much misery.

wife back and have sexual intercourse with her. Revocable means that the husband takes back his wife (even without her consent). She may not remarry during the obligatory three-months' waiting period. If he does not take her back he has to pronounce the divorce formula once or twice more to make the separation into an irrevocable divorce.

Today, wives still do not have the right to unilateral divorce. For "Divorce has been put in the hands of men, not women, because they are deficient in reason and lack judgment or foresight. They become angered quickly, and would give divorce at any moment, and the noble contract (of marriage) would become null."[364] They may, however, initiate legal proceedings to obtain dissolution, when the woman feels an aversion for her husband, but only with the consent of the husband. A wife may also initiate divorce proceedings when there is mutual aversion. In either case the woman has to pay an amount to the husband, which, in case of Shi'a Islam cannot be larger than the dowry. Thus, female-initiated divorce came at a high financial price as most men would only allow this if she relinquished her claim to part or all of her dowry.[365] Husbands were not always spiteful and greedy. One man who decided to divorce his wife paid her the dowry to which she was entitled, plus an additional 50 *tumans*.[366] As this type of divorce has the nature of a contract, there needs to be a formula spoken by the wife and the husband has to accept.

In case of divorce or death of a husband, the wife has to wait for a specific period before she can remarry and thus have sexual intercourse. In case of death, if she is not pregnant, she must wait four months and ten days. In case of divorce depending on the circumstances (e.g. if the wife is 9 years old; menopause had begun) the schools differ as to the length of the waiting period. Some schools say

---

364. Meisami, *Sea*, p. 226.

365. Hantzsche, "Haram," p. 431; Wills, *Persia*, p. 64; Ella Sykes, "A Talk About Persia and Its Women," *National Geographic Magazine* 21/10 (1910), p. 851. Non-payment of the dowry is considered to be one of the worst sins. Avazeh, *Qanun-e Qovveh-ye Bah*, p. 95.

366. 366. Reza'i and Azari, *Gozareshha*, p. 312 (consecutive numbering in both volumes).

that in the two cases mentioned there is no waiting period; others say that it is three months. However, the normal waiting period is also four months and ten days.

Not much information is available about the actual practice of divorce before the nineteenth century. In earlier periods, divorce, of course, occurred and followed the rules of Islamic law, but there is little information on the implementation details of divorce or how it was experienced. An interesting case is mentioned by Babur, the first Moghul emperor. He wrote that "shortly after the debacle of Tashkent in 1503, Ayishah Soltan Begum left me at her elder sister's instigation."[367] This relative freedom of women to enforce their divorce perhaps was due to the fact that these Timurid clans still retained their nomadic traditions, which differed from Islamic rules. This was also the case in remote rural areas where even as late as the 1940s traditional divorce rules applied that had nothing to do with Islamic law and, in fact, gave the wife the right to initiate a divorce.[368]

Among many groups divorce was rare or non-existent such as among villagers, tribes, the Ali Ilahi sect and non-Moslem minorities.[369] However, it was more prevalent in urban areas. Because most women were dependent for their livelihood on the good-will of their husband, their greatest fear was that he might divorce them. It is a theme that is not only repeated in books and articles by European observers, but also by Persian female authors, as soon as they started to write and publish. "The great trouble is the lack of confidence in mar-

367. Babur, *Babur-Nama*, p. 36.

368. Daneshvar, *Didaniha*, vol. 1, pp. 220-21; Barth, *Nomads of South Persia*, p. 32.

369. Malcolm, *History*, vol. 2, p. 610; MacBean-Ross, *Lady Doctor*, p. 67; Gobineau, *Trois ans*, vol. 2, p. 193 ; Loeb, *Outcaste*, pp. 117-20; Nancy Tapper, "The Women's Subsociety among the Shahsevan Nomads of Iran," in Lois Beck and Nikki Keddie eds. *Women in the Muslim World* (Cambridge, 1978), p. 378 ; Lois Beck, *Nomad. A Year in the Life of an Qashqa'i Tribesman in Iran* (Berkeley, 1991), pp. 379-80.

ried life; as it is a very rare thing to find a wife who can trust her husband not to divorce her, or not to add to his wives if he be able."[370]

From data from the nineteenth century it is clear that divorce was constrained by social and financial considerations, for it could mean loss in social standing as well as financial loss. Nevertheless, in some instances its frequency seems to have been relatively high, for according to an estimate by de Gobineau at the end of the 1850s, most women of 24 years of age had already been divorced once or more times.[371] It is difficult to believe that this observation was true for the whole of Iran as, for example, divorce in the rural areas was rare. It is therefore likely that this observation only concerned a particular class of people in Tehran about which de Gobineau may have had some detailed knowledge.

Although divorce is both socially and religiously disapproved it is the divine right of the husband (Koran 2:226-37). Thus, if the husband believed that a divorce might yield a net benefit for him he did not hesitate, nor did he, when he voluntarily or by order of the shah married a princess, for then he divorced all his other wives.[372]

> A wealthy nobleman, married to a young and beautiful lady of equal rank, the mother of both sons and daughters, and as reported, with a fair amount of wedded happiness, was dazzled by a proposed alliance with a princess of such rank as to brook no rival. The indispensable condition was a divorce and absolute separation from the wife he had. She knew nothing of her fate till one day, when visiting her brother's, word was brought to her that she need not return home. That night the wedding was celebrated with firing of cannon and great festivities, but the children were crying for their mother, and for her and them there was no redress.[373]

370. Van Sommer and Zwemer, *Our Moslem Sisters*, p. 229; Bibi Khanom, "Ma'ayeb al-Rejal," pp. 120, 181, 196.

371. Gobineau, *Trois ans*, vol. 2, p. 187.

372. Ponafidine, *Life*, p. 323.

373. Van Sommer and Zwemer, *Our Moslem Sisters*, p. 230. Because divorce

Divorce had social draw-backs for the wife, not the least of which was whether she might remarry someone else of the same social standing and wealth, because she was a "second-hand commodity."[374] This was not always the case and whether or not she remarried, the situation often resulted in dysfunctional families, in which children also suffered the consequences of the divorce. "Many of the divorced mothers remarry; other become beggars or maid-servants. As for the children, if the family be wealthy, they remain with the father; if poor, in case both parents find other partners, they are often cast adrift to fend for themselves."[375] For the payment of the dowry was not a real protection against divorce. In case of peasants it may be only five *qerans*, "enough to buy food for five days, and among the better off it is rarely more than a few hundred pounds [British], never enough to keep the woman for more than a few years." In that case the woman had no choice but to return to her family, for employment opportunities were almost non-existent. Also, her family, if it was poor, which was the case for 90 percent of them, was not happy to bear the burden of another dependent. As a consequence, "A considerable number of divorced woman go on the streets; hence a number of these 'public ladies' are socially different from those in Europe."[376]

---

gave rise to all kinds of disputes, in 1870, the governor of Gilan, Asaf al-Dowleh informed the two leading olama of the province that henceforth there should not be more than two divorce judges (*motalleq*) and four marrying ones (*'aqed*), who moreover should keep a marriage and divorce register. The same rule applied to Lahejan, Fumen and competent men from among the olama had to be appointed. In rural towns such as Masuleh, Tulem and Leshteh-Nesa competent jurists had to be placed there as well. Asaf al-Dowleh, *Asnad-e Mirza 'Abd al-Vahab Khan Asaf al-Dowleh* 3 vols. eds. 'Abdol-Hoseyn Nava'i and Nilufar Kasri (Tehran, 1377/1998), vol. 2, p. 45.

374. Julien de Rochechouart, *Souvenirs d'un Voyage en Perse* (Paris, 1867), p. 204; Benjamin, *Persia*, p. 450; Binning, *Journal*, vol. 2, p. 404; Wills, *Persia*, p. 64; Wishard, *Twenty Years*, p. 244; von Rosen, *Persian Pilgrimage*, pp. 100, 124; Sedghi, *Women and Politics*, p. 144.

375. Van Sommer and Zwemer, *Our Moslem Sisters*, pp. 230-31; see also Wishard, *Twenty Years*, p. 244.

376. Merritt-Hawkes, *Persia*, p. 281; see also chapter three.

As discussed above, adultery was not a cause for divorce, because, if convicted, the marriage was automatically annulled. Thus, if a husband failed to prove his claim that his wife had been an adulteress he had but little alternative than to divorce her. A man and his friend returned home to find his wife in *flagante delicto* with the friend's son. After some altercation the man divorced the wife, for he could not prove the adultery as he lacked the required four witnesses.[377] "If the man be plaintiff, and the cause, that she has 'played him false,' he then retains half her fortune. A certain number of oaths are required on the side of the husband, to establish her guilt; and an equal number on her part, in assertion of her innocence, are sufficient to free her from the punishment the law awards to adultery."[378]

Under the Pahlavis, changes were made that made divorce more difficult, a process that started in the 1930s with the gradual changes in the rules governing family, as discussed above. However, most of these changes left the unilateral right of the man to a divorce unchanged and thus, did not really provide much protection to wives. Also, payment of the dowry or *mahr* still was not made compulsory after the consummation of the marriage, as Islamic law requires. However, a woman could demand a divorce if she could show cause, such as her husband's impotence, non-support or desertion. It was only in 1967 under the Family Protection Law (*Qanun-e hemayat-e khanevadeh*) that this unilateral right of man was somewhat reduced, with a further slight adjustment in 1975.[379] The impact of the law

---

377. Reza'i and Zarai, *Gozareshha-ye Nazmiyeh*, p. 599 (for a case of adultery in the case of two Russians see Ibid., p. 611).

378. Robert Kerr Porter, *Travels in Georgia, Persia, Armenia, Ancient Babylonia* 2 vols. (London, 1821), vol. 1, p. 343.

379. The manner in which a woman's claim for divorce was handled could assume rather medieval overtones, because it was based on a method allegedly applied by Imam 'Ali and Imam Sadeq to establish whether a man's penis was long and strong enough to break the hymen. Avazeh, *Qanun-e Qovveh-ye Bah*, pp. 49-50. In 1947, Daneshvar, *Didaniha*, vol. 2, pp. 117-18 described a scene in Shiraz, where a naked man was swimming in a pool of water with his legs spread out so that his testicles could be seen, while a mullah and his wife were looking on. It appeared that the wife had asked for a divorce, because her husband had not slept with her for some time. She

was a reduction in the divorce rate. Whereas in the 1960s, the divorce rate in Iran (1.2 percent) had been much higher than in W. Europe (0.5- 0.8 percent), this changed significantly in 1970 when it stopped to 0.6 percent where it stayed until 1979.[380]

One of the reasons for the higher divorce rate was that women had not necessarily acquired many more rights, but it had become socially acceptable, in urban areas at least, that they stood up for themselves and made their views known, which often led to divorce. Simin Daneshvar (b. 1921), one of Iran's foremost female fiction writers of the twentieth century held the opinion that "heterosexual relationships are altogether sort of sick in Iran. They are patriarchical and androcentric. Most marriages in our country are unsuccessful. Two individuals with two different backgrounds, educations, and customs have to endure one another for a lifetime. Well, this very tolerance creates hatred."[381] That such feelings may result in divorce is clear. The anguish caused by marriage, as felt by many women, more particularly of one that remained loveless and where the wife does not have the right to divorce, is powerfully expressed by the poet Forugh Farrokhzad.

> With a smile
> The little girl asked:

---

had applied to a mullah to pronounce the divorce, who told the couple that to verify the truth of the wife's statement the man would have to swim in a pool of cold water. If his testicles would show up pendulous rather than normal then the wife was wrong and she would have to return to her husband's house, in the opposite case she would get her divorce. Given the fact that, according to Islamic law, one should not look at another person's private parts or nudity this scene was indeed shocking. It was similar to Mirza Saleh Shirazi's experience in England, where his stagecoach had an accident. He had fallen down and a female fellow-passenger stood above him. "English women wear nothing under their dresses, I looked up to see that she was wearing nothing at all from her knees to her waist; it was not a pretty sight!" Mirza Saleh Shirazi, *Majmu'eh-ye safarnamehha-ye Mirza Saleh Shirazi, ed. Gholam Hoseyn Mirza Saleh* (Tehran, 1364/1985), p. 350.

380. Akbar Aghajanian, "Some Notes on Divorce in Iran," *Journal of Marriage and the Family* 48/4 (10986), pp. 749-55; Woodsmall, *Moslem Women*, p. 126 ("divorce is quite a prevalent among the lower and middle classes in Iran" in the 1930s).

381. Milani, *Veils and Words*, p. 194.

'What is the secret of this wedding band
Circling me tightly on my hand?'

Years later, one night
A sad wife gazed at that golden band

And saw it its glowing design
Wasted days, wasted
In the hope of a husband's loving hands

Anguished, she cried
Out loud, and said;
'This luminous and glowing band
Is the band of tyranny and commands.'[382]

However, after the Islamic Revolution of 1979, this tolerant social climate was totally transformed to the opposite. Moreover, the new regime suspended the 1967 Family Protection Law and replaced it with a special civil court (*dadgah-e madani-ye khass*) that basically restored man's right to a unilateral right to divorce, in accordance with Islamic law. Nevertheless, the Islamic government was not unaware of the fact that men abused this right and therefore, in 1992 it amended the law to provide women with better protection against abuse. Among other things, the new regulations authorized the government to take away the right to unilateral divorce from a man in case of abuse of this right, or to make it conditional, while it also allowed wives to add conditions in the marriage contract that would give them greater freedom, such as the right to choose the place of residence, to study, to work, to travel abroad, etc. The court could verify whether these and other conditions had been properly respected and whether this constituted adequate grounds for the filing of a divorce by the wife. Also, no divorce could take effect, unless the man had obtained a court certificate and the couple had submitted to an arbitrage process, which had resulted in non-reconciliation. The arbiters also verified whether the man had

382. Milani, *Veils and Words*, p. 194.

respected all other legal requirements (such as payment of the dower) and only then the man was allowed to register the divorce.[383]

Although these changes do not significantly reduce a man's right to divorce his wife, it nevertheless opens the door to better protection of wives. However, it would seem that women are not demanding that divorce be made easier for them. In a sample of educated women in Tehran, only 24 percent agreed that this should be the case, thus indicating that divorce is still seen as socially undesirable.[384] This is indicated by the fact that although men can get a divorce easily, the average divorce rate in Iran is still rather low (10%) compared with Western countries (50%). This low figure is mainly due to the fact that divorce is still rare among villagers and tribal people. For in urban areas the rate is much higher and, moreover, is rising. In fact, according to one recent report the divorce rate in Iran is even as high as 25 percent.[385]

DISCUSSION

It is striking that whether in Zoroastrian or Islamic Iran women had no real persona, but through their male guardian (father, brother, uncle, husband, son). She was either a daughter, sister, niece, wife or a mother, but not herself. Her standing in society was determined by who her guardian was. In short, her persona is a derivative of that of her male guardian, it is only through him that she emerges from obscurity. "The relationship between father and daughter is based on essentially the same principles as that between husband and wife. The father cares for his daughter, protects her, and marries her off; the

---

383. For more details on divorce arrangements in Iran see, e.g., Ziba Mir-Hosseini, *Marriage on trial: Islamic family law in Iran and Morocco* (London, 2000), and her excellent documentary *Divorce Iran Style*.

384. M. Hojat, R. Shapurian, H. Nayerahmadi, M. Farzaneh, D. Foroughi, M. Parsi, and M. Azizi, "Premarital Sexual, Child Rearing, and Family Attitudes of Iranian Men and Women in the United States and Iran." *The Journal of Psychology* 133 (1999), pp.19–31.

385. Nassehi-Behnam, "Change and the Iranian Family," p. 560; Aghajanian, "Some Notes," p. 751; Amini, *Ayin-e Hamsardari* (section *Talaq*).

daughter in turn is obedient and industrious and keep's her father's honor intact."[386] Consequently, for an Iranian man there was and even now there is no free access to women and vice-versa, and hence pre-marital sex was rare, although this is changing. A man only can get access to a woman through her 'guardians', and then only as a groom, for a girl or a woman otherwise is out-of-bounds. As such he has to submit to the dictates of the girl's father, uncle, or brother as well as the demands by his own family. In short, a man's choice is subject to the "hierarchies of alliances of families and groups of the locality."[387] It is implied in all this that it is unthinkable, and from an Islamic point of view unlawful, that a girl decides to establish her own access to a man, for this upsets the hierarchy of power relations and casts a smear on the honor of her family. This is to some extent possible for divorcees and widows, who, unlike women in Zoroastrian Iran, for-mally did not need the permission of a guardian to remarry. In reality, of course, women heeded their family's wishes in this matter, most of the time.

Marriage therefore was and is a family decision and hence the preference for consanguineous marriage. Apart from religious param-eters (contract, equality, degree or consanguinity) parents also applied socio-economic criteria (virginity, age, family, wealth, beauty, etc.) in selecting a spouse for their child. Because of the high value set on virginity - even a rumor could endanger a girl's reputation - girls were carefully watched and kept secluded and were married off as soon as possible. This explains the young age at which girls in the past married, although in the last two decades the age of marriage for both boys and girls has risen dramatically, due to the modernization of Iranian soci-ety. One of the reasons of marriage at a later age is the high dowry that has to be paid, although the dowry is never paid when the marriage is concluded, for men marry their wives on credit, as they only have to pay when they divorce their wife. This development of late marriage has created a problem for both pubescent boys and girls, for they have

---

386. Friedl, "Women in Contemporary Persian Folktales," p. 646.

387. Vielle, "Iranian Women," pp. 467-68.

no lawful outlet for their sexual feelings, which engenders frustration and results in premarital sex as well as prostitution.

While polygyny was and is allowed and practiced in reality, it was and is only less than one per cent. of men who had/have more than one wife simultaneously. In discussion of these male rights the consequences for women, in particular their sexual needs, are never addressed. However, monogamous marriage was and is the rule.

Although women have to submit to man's guiding hand (he is the superior being after all), they have to make him happy (even is he is a jerk) and to support him rather than make life difficult for him, men in return have to take good care of their wife. Such an ideal situation does not exist, of course, and, like in marriages all over the world there are ups and downs between husbands and wives in Iran. These situations sometimes led to adultery and divorce, and the latter increasingly so at present. Divorce is an exclusive and unilateral right of the husband and dreaded by wives as this means loss of financial security, separation from her children and difficulty to find a new husband. Since the legal, religious and societal rules favor the husband over the wife, even when he does not live up to his obligations, modernizing women have tried to improve women's lot since the end of the nineteenth century, a process that is still ongoing.

CHAPTER TWO

TEMPORARY MARRIAGE: A FORMAL AFFAIR

TEMPORARY MARRIAGE
A FORMAL AFFAIR

Narrated 'Abdullah:

We used to participate in the holy battles led by Allah's Apostle and we had nothing (no wives) with us. So we said, "Shall we get ourselves castrated?" He forbade us that and then allowed us to marry women with a temporary contract and recited to us [Koran 5.87]:
—'O you who believe! Make not unlawful the good things which Allah has made lawful for you, but commit no transgression.[1]

In this chapter temporary marriage as practiced in Iran is discussed. Although temporary marriage existed in Imperial Iran, it is not discussed here, because (a) very little is known about its actual practice, and (b) this variant of Zoroastrian marriage is discussed in chapter one and (c) it had a different purpose than its Islamic counterpart. Therefore, in what follows, the religious justification for this exclusive Shi'ite form of concubinage *casu quo* legalized prostitution is discussed. Furthermore, the various forms of temporary marriage and the parties involved are analyzed, while societal appreciation as well as the fact that Christians also practiced this typical Shi'ite custom are discussed. Finally, attention is drawn to the fact that temporary

---

1. Bukhari, *Sahih*, 62.13. See also Koran 4.24.

marriage is touted by the Islamic Republic of Iran as a desirable and sensible institution that, moreover, may prevent prostitution.

ISLAMIC IRAN

WHAT IS TEMPORARY MARRIAGE?

With the advent of Islam after the conquest of the Sasanian Empire by the Arabs, besides covenanted marriage (*'aqdi*; see chapter one), the notion of a simultaneous contracted or temporary marriage (*mut'ah*) became an additional part of a Moslem male's menu that allowed him to satisfy his sexual appetite. In Sasanian times the possibility of a temporary marriage had existed, but that was a marriage of the covenanted type and its main purpose was not sexual gratification. The purchase or the acquisition by other means of slave girls for sexual purposes remained lawful. This custom existed under the Sasanians and thus, remained an additional option for sexual gratification. The owner had absolute authority over his property. He could use her for any purpose, including sex, which, in addition to menial work, was the usual reason for buying a slave girl. A man could buy any number of slave girls and he could have sexual intercourse with all of them.[2]

For the slave girl in question, to be elevated to share the master's bed was not something to look down at. On the contrary it usually meant that she received much better treatment and clothes, and, in particular if she bore her master children, she received living quarters separate from the other slaves. In fact, her treatment would improve even further as her allowance would be increased and she would have her own servants, just like the master's other wives.[3] However, unless her master freed her, she remained a slave even if she had given birth to a son. When her master died and he had not freed her, then, for Sunnis, she would be freed automatically, and for the Shi'is, if she had a living

---

2. For Koranic verses allowing the sexual use of slave girls see 6/3; 23/6; 33/50; and 73/30.

3. Jean Chardin, *Voyages*, ed. L. Langlès, 10 vols. (Paris 1811), vol. 2, pp. 223-24.

child, her freedom would be bought by deducting her value from her child's inheritance right.[4]

In accordance with Sura 4.24: *And those of whom ye seek content (by marrying them), give unto them their portions as a duty. And there is no sin for you in what ye do by mutual agreement after the duty (hath been done)*, Shi'ite religious law allows that a man can avail himself of any number of legal concubines, by entering into a temporary marriage with an unmarried woman, either a Moslem or those of the Book. In books on jurisprudence the terms *mut'a, al-nikah al-munqati'* (term-limited marriage), and *al-nikah al-muwaqqat* (temporary marriage) are all employed, while in some works the term *musta'jara*, or rented woman is used, because a man rents a woman's body for the purpose of sexual pleasure. The basis for the validity of this type of union is the contract (*sigheh*; literally, 'form' [of the contract]), the two parties who accept (*ijab*; *qabul*), the precise time period (*ajal*) and the definite measurable recompense (*mahr*; *ajr*).[5]

As to the formula or *sigheh*, the jurists have argued that the same ones that are used for covenanted marriage should be spoken out loud, although there has been much difference of opinion about the substance of the formula, including whether it should be spoken in the imperfect or perfect tense. In general, the marriage formula is simple: "The woman says, 'I [name] will pleasure thee, for the amount of [money] and for such and such period,' and the man says, "I accept.'"[6] After this, the contract is concluded and has validity and can be enforced. Given the importance of the formula or *sigheh* over time the term also

---

4. R. Brunschvig, "'Abd," *Encyclopedia of Islam*2.

5. The description of the legal characteristics and requirements of temporary (*mut'ah*) marriage is based on Sachiko Murata, *Temporary Marriage in Islamic Law* (MA thesis Tehran University 1974)—for the electronic version of this study see [http://www.al-islam.org/al-serat/muta/], Shahla Haeri, *Law of Desire. Temporary Marriage in Shi'i Iran* (Syracuse, 1989); Khomeyni, *Tahrir*, pp. 258-89; Ibid., *Towzih*, pp. 499, 508-10; W. Heffening, "Mut'a," *Encyclopedia of Islam²*; and Avazeh, *Qanun-e Qovveh-ye Bah*, pp. 101-34. See also I. K. A. Howard, "Mut'a marriage reconsidered in the context of the formal procedures for Islamic marriage," *Journal of Semitic Studies* 20/1 (1975), pp. 82-92.

6. See Bricteux, *Au Pays*, p. 228 for the formulas used in 1905.

denoted the subject of the contract, i.e. the woman. Divorced and widowed women do not need a guardian (*vali*) to obtain permission. In case of a virgin, the olama are divided, although all seem to agree a guardian is preferred. The contract may be verbal or written, in any language (as long as both partners understand and agree to the terms of the contract), no witnesses are needed, nor is registration, although the latter two items became necessary in the Pahlavi period with changing requirements over time.

A Moslem man can only conclude a temporary marriage with a free Moslem woman or a Christian, Jewish or Zoroastrian woman, but not with idolater women, those who are enemies of the prophet's family or with relatives with whom marriage is not permitted. But if a man happened to marry an idolater woman anyway there is a way out without having to break the contract. "In case a man has been deceived and has married a woman belonging to none of these religions, he must be careful that during that time of their union she does not drink wine, and does not eat any of the elements considered unclean." These forbidden unclean articles of diet include "pork, hare, crustaceans, and so on."[7] In the nineteenth century, it appears that temporary marriage of Moslem men with Christian, Jewish and/or Zoroastrian women seldom occurred.[8] This type of marriage must have been higher in previous centuries when these minority groups were much larger; one way of reducing their number was to take their daughters, often by force, as a temporary wife.

In the contract, the time period needs to be made explicit (e.g. one hour); a *sigheh-ye 'omri* or lifetime contract, for example, is illegal, as many a misled woman has found out to her loss, as it is not time-specific. The explicit purpose of this contract is to have sexual relations during an agreed fixed period (*ajal*), ranging from a fraction of one day up to 99 years, in exchange for a specified and unambiguous form of

---

7. Benjamin, *Persia*, p. 453; Eustace de Lorey & Douglas Sladen, *Queer Things About Persia* (Philadelphia-London: J.B. Lippincot Co, 1907), 130; Ibid. *The Moon of the Fourteenth Night: Being the Private Life of an Unmarried Diplomat in Persia during the Revolution* (London: Hurst & Blacket, 1910), p. 74.

8. Häntzsche, "Haram," p. 432.

payment (*ajr*), i.e. such that it can be weighed or measured, although that does not have to be actually done.[9] Failure to specify the amount of payment renders the contract invalid. After having concluded the contract the woman receives the entire payment, whether her husband has intercourse with her or not. Her duty is to make herself available for sex, whenever called upon, his duty is to pay. The situation has been likened to that of renting a house; whether you use the house or not you have to pay the rent. Contrariwise, the temporary wife does not have the right to sex with her husband.

Given that the objective of the contract is sexual gratification, not the production of progeny, the burden of preventing pregnancy is solely that of the woman. Also, for that reason she cannot use a condom to prevent being infected by venereal disease, unless with the man's permission. Children born to the woman belong to the man, even if he practiced coitus interruptus. Because there is a legal contract, eventual progeny (but not the *sigheh*) have equal inheritance rights with the progeny from the man's covenanted marriage[s]. However, if the man denies paternity, the law supports him based on his simple say-so; no oath of damnation (*li'an*) is required as in the case of covenanted marriage but maybe today, the option of DNA testing may change that.[10]

Because the contract stipulates a time period for the temporary marriage this marriage cannot be dissolved through divorce.[11] However, this is semantics, because a man has the right to end the contract at any time, "subject to his ability to pay the price."[12] This price to be paid, i.e., the agreed upon sum, varied with the length of the unexpired time of the contract. "Should the man, who alone can dissolve this union, decide to break with the woman before the expiration of half the term

---

9. Benjamin, *Persia*, p. 453; Henri-Réné d'Allemagne, *Du Khorasan au Pays de Bakhtyaris*, 4 vols. (Paris, 1911), vol. 1, p. 213.

10. Haeri, *Law*, pp. 33-48; Murata, *Temporary Marriage*, chapter two. See also James Basset, *Persia, the Land of the Imams* (New York: Charles Scribner's Sons, 1886), p. 288; Dieulafoy, *La Perse*, p. 200 for remarks by contemporary observers.

11. D'Allemagne, *Du Khorasan*, vol. 1, p. 214.

12. A.C. Forbes-Leith, *Checkmate and Fighting* (London, 1927), p. 180.

agreed upon, then he is obliged to pay the Sigha half the amount specified in the dowry; if this period is exceeded when they part, he must
pay the amount in full."[13] Moreover, the price is further influenced by
the nature of the execution of the contract; he has to pay only half of
the agreed amount if the marriage has not been consummated, but the
full amount is due if consummation has taken place.[14] If the man does
not consummate the marriage, but keeps the *sigheh* for the entire length
of the contract full payment is due, just like when you rent a house, but
do not occupied it.

The woman, however, does not have the right to end the contract ahead of time. If the *sigheh* leaves her husband before the end
of the contracted period, she not only forfeits all right to payment,
but, moreover, the man is owed compensation. "Frequently the poor
women are obliged to do this owing to the cruel treatment of the husbands, who take this means of avoiding payment."[15]

Temporary marriage automatically ends with the expiration of the
contract or with the death of either partner. There is no divorce ceremony; the sexual partners just part ways. Even if the length of the contract was only for one hour, the woman is required to abstain from sex
during a waiting period. There was much discussion and disagreement
among the *olama*, whether the waiting period should be the usual one
of four months and ten days, as in the case of covenanted marriage, or
three months (two months and five days for a slave), which time was
considered sufficient to determine whether she were pregnant. However, normally the waiting period consists of two menstrual periods,
provided she menstruates. If she does not, then the waiting period is

---

13. Lorey and Sladen, *Queer*, p. 129; Ibid, *Moon*, p. 74; 'Eyn al-Saltaneh, *Ruznameh*, vol. 2, p. 1452; Forbes-Leith, *Checkmate*, p. 180; Khomeyni, *Towzih*, p. 510 (no. 2307) states that irrespective of the remaining time, if the husband has slept with his wife he has to pay the full contractual amount; if he has not slept with her then only half that amount is due.

14. E'temad al-Saltaneh, *Ruznameh*, p. 277 (although there had been no consummation of the temporary marriage, he paid in full).

15. Ponafidine, *Life*, p. 322; Van Sommer and Zwemer, *Our Moslem Sisters*, p. 235.

45 days. In actual practice, it would appear that the waiting period was much lower, of the order of 25 days to one month before she could re-marry. When the woman remarries the same man, she has no waiting period. However, those women who were just legal prostitutes could ill afford to wait for long; after all they were hiring out their bodies not because they liked it, but because they needed the money. As a result, ways around this obstacle were found with the help of the mullahs, who also had a financial interest in the women's annual earnings.

> But many of these women may be said to follow the profession of Sigha, with the connivance, for a pecuniary consideration, of the officiating mullas, and since this period is prejudicial to their sinful traffic, the Mullas have discovered a way of evading the law. When the stipulated term of the union has expired, the woman manages to persuade the man to renew for a very short period. This second marriage is, of course, legal without any time of probation, the contracting parties being the same, whilst, on the other hand, since it is purely nominal, there is nothing to prevent the Sigha from entering, at its expiration, into a fresh arrangement with another man at once, or so soon as she can find one.[16]

Other travelers reported the same dilemma. Dieulafoy tells that the mulla encouraged the *sighehs* to remarry as soon as possible and also brought them new husbands, for a pious donation. "They do not ask much: 'earn a pittance, but marry often,' is their motto."[17]

The full array of Islamic rules governing temporary marriage did not exist during the early decades of Islamic rule, for they, like all oth-er legal rules, needed to be developed, a process that took place during the first 200 years after the prophet Mohammad's death. Therefore,

---

16. Lorey & Sladen, *Moon*, p. 75 (It is not entirely clear to me what the legal basis for this ploy is). According to Imam Reza, the waiting period should be 45 days. Avazeh, *Qanun-e Qovveh-ye Bah*, p. 121; Khomeyni, *Towzih*, p. 527 (no. 2390).

17. Dieulafoy, *Perse*, p. 200; d'Allemagne, *Du Khorasan*, vol. 1, p. 214.

it is likely that the rules that initially applied where those that reflected pre-Islamic practices, about which little information is available. However, from these practices and the Traditions it is clear that a woman had to be asked and accept to have sexual intercourse with the man; she then asked for a stipulated payment (a cloak; a handful of flour or dates).[18]

As is often the case, the Traditions are contradictory as to the lawfulness of temporary marriage. They report that the prophet Mohammad allowed his men to use temporary marriage to find sexual relief, "when it is very badly needed and women are scarce."[19] However, other Traditions state that the prophet later forbade temporary marriage, which must have been the reason that during the reign of the Caliph 'Omar (r. 634-644) a conflict arose about the legality of the practice.[20]

> Jabir b. 'Abdullah reported: We contracted temporary
> marriage giving a handful of tales or flour as a dower
> during the lifetime of Allah's Messenger (may peace be
> upon him) and during the time of Abu Bakr, until 'Umar
> forbade it in the case of 'Amr b. Huraith.[21]

The second Caliph 'Omar explicitly banned temporary marriage and denied that the relevant verse (4:24), on which Shi'ites based this practice, was actually part of the Koran, a position that later was adopted by all Sunnis.[22] Nevertheless, Sunnis initially allowed such temporary unions and it was only during the second century AH/eight

---

18. For a discussion of the available data, see Heffening, "Mut'a."

19. Bukhari, *Sahih*, 62-13, 50, 51; Muslim, *Sahih*, 8.3243-3248; Heffening, "Mut'a."

20. Bukhari, *Sahih*, 62-52; Muslim, *Sahih*, 8.3251-3267.

21. Muslim, *Sahih*, 8. 3249.

22. Muslim, *Sahih*, 8, 3249-3250; Heffening, "Mut'a." All the Companions accepted the ban, including the prophet's nephew 'Ali, although the Shi'ites claim that he did so out of *taqiyeh*, i.e. to hide his true feelings. Murata, *Temporary Marriage*, chapter two; Werner Ende, "Ehe auf Zeit (*mut'ah*) in der innerislamischen Diskussion der gegenwart," *Die Welt des Islams* 20 (1980), pp. 1-43.

century CE that most Sunni scholars declared this type of union unlawful. Others, however, such as al-Shafi'i, still allowed it, provided
there was the unuttered intention to marry for a stipulated period,
and that this was not written down in the marriage contract. Nevertheless, Sunnis in general did and do not practice temporary marriage,
although there were exceptions and actual Sunni practice to have lawful sexual relationships outside covenanted marriage often differs little
from Shi'ite temporary marriage.[23]

Temporary marriage was quickly adopted in Iran as a legal way to
have more wives, because this option was in harmony with the country's pre-Islamic customs, which, moreover, had a kind of Sasanian
counterpart. Some European observers even argued that it may have
been a time-honored Persian institution.[24] However, they made this
error because of copies of the *Shahnameh*, which had been rendered
religiously correct by later copyists. When Tahmineh and the epic
hero Rostam just spend the night together (at Tahmineh's behest, resulting in the birth of their son Sohrab), later manuscripts have them
first go though a hastily arranged marriage ceremony, something that
is absent from the older manuscripts.

SAFAVID–AFSHARID–ZAND PERIOD (1501–1794)

There is very little information available about the practice and prevalence of temporary marriage until the nineteenth century. This is

23. Heffening, "Mut'ah"; Murata, *Temporary Marriage*, chapter 4. On the
practice in the Sunni Middle East of the so-called *misyar*, or traveler's marriage,
see Aluma Dankowitz, "Pleasure Marriages in Sunni and Shi'ite Islam" (MEMRI,
Inquiry and Analysis Series - No. 291 (August 31, 2006). [http://memri.org/
bin/articles.cgi?Page=archives&Area=ia&ID=IA29106].
For the practice of so-called *'orfi* marriages in Egypt, which are perceived as
a cover for pre-marital sex, see Hoda Rashad, Magued Osman, and Farzaneh
Roudi-Fahimi, *Marriage in the Arab World* (Washington, DC: Population
Reference Bureau, 2005). On the legitimacy of temporary marriage among
Chinese Sunnis, see Linda Benson, "Islamic Marriage and Divorce in Xinjiang:
The Case of Kashgar and Khotan," *Association for the Advancement of Central
Asian Research* 5/2 (Fall 1992), pp. 5–8.

24. Lorey and Sladen, *Queer*, p. 129.

understandable, because until about 1600, Iran was a majority Sunni country and Sunnis condemn the practice of temporary marriage, which therefore, occurred infrequently. There were only a few pockets of Shi'as in Iran until 1501, when Shi'ism was declared to be the country's official religion by the first king and founder of the Safavid dynasty. However, it took another 100 years or so, before Shi'ism became the majority religion, but large parts of Iran, notably in the areas adjacent to the borders still remained mostly Sunni, although over time Shi'ism made inroads there. Therefore, little evidence has been unearthed concerning the occurrence of temporary marriage in contemporary Persian histories, except for one case. In 1607, Shah 'Abbas I (r. 1587-1629) concluded a temporary marriage with the daughter of Sorkhay Shamkhal.[25] A few European travelers mention the existence of temporary marriage during the seventeenth century, but most of them provided little detail.[26]

The Italian traveler Pietro Della Valle, who gathered information in Shiraz in 1620, qualified temporary marriage as one in which the man had the usufruct right of the contracted woman, for a limited period, while the children born of the union were legitimate. He saw it as a kind of trial marriage, which he believed might actually be transformed into a covenanted marriage. He understood that it was most common for women who had already been married to enter into such union. Girls from good families would never consent to such unions, however, unless it was with a man from a family more prominent than hers. Della Valle was further told that temporary marriage was in fact the most common form of marriage in that city and there was even a joke among the Shirazis about two women friends meeting each other and the other pitying the other that she

---

25. Molla Jalal al-Din Monajjem, *Ruznameh-ye 'Abbasi ya Ruznameh-ye Molla Jalal*, ed. Seyfollah Vahidniya (Tehran, 1366/1967), p. 324 ('*aqd-e monqate*').

26. L. Leupe ed., "Beschrijvinge van de coninclijcke stadt Spahan," in Ibid., "Stukken over den handel van Perzi' en de Golf van Bengalen, 1634," *Kronijk van het Historisch Genootschap gevestigd te Utrecht* X (1854), p. 204 mentions that Persians may marry women for a fixed period after which they can abandon them as they like.

was still living with the same husband after two months.[27] Given the fact that marriage was a family affair, it is unlikely that the prevalence of temporary marriage was higher than covenanted marriage, and perhaps the joke about the quick turn-round time of husbands was an indication about the high frequency of divorce, which seems unlikely. Thus, it may be an indication of the short-lived nature of these temporary unions, which is more in harmony with reality, as is clear from what follows.

Gemelli-Careri is another Italian author who took the trouble to learn more about temporary marriage during his stay in Iran in 1694. He reported that Persian men may take as many concubines as they want, whom they select from among prostitutes. Slave-girls also could become concubines. From the fact that Gemelli-Careri further noted that this relationship was for a definite period only and based on a contract before a judge, indicates that he described the custom of temporary marriage. He further noted that these women were referred to as "motha" (*mut'ah*). The fact that children born from this union had inheritance rights also makes this clear.[28] To express their love for their concubine, some Persian men went so far as to mark their forearms with a hot branding-iron, "perhaps to express that this torture was nothing compared with the torment that they felt in their heart [for her]." Gemelli-Careri related that one Persian gentleman showed him many of these amorous marks on his arms that he had made on account of a concubine, which had resulted in a constant dispute with his wife.[29]

---

27. Della Valle, *Voyages*, vol. 3, pp. 568-69. The same story is parrotted by Bembo, *The Travels*, p. 353.

28. Giovanni Francesco Gemelli Careri, *Giro del Mundo* 6 vols. (Naples, 1699), vol. 2, pp. 181-82; Tavernier, *Voyages*, p. 287 (only mentions "amoutha, i.e., the leased wives," of whom Persians could take as many as they wanted).

29. Gemelli, *Giro*, vol. 2, p. 182. Chardin mentions the same custom (see below), but in this case it was in connection to beautiful prostitutes. It is likely that Gemelli-Careri also meant prostitutes rather than concubines, for he is not quite certain about the status of the *sighehs*, who, he writes, were recruited from among prostitutes.

According to Chardin, who was in Iran during the 1660-1670s, the Moslem clergy, as well as men of the highest standing, were among those who availed themselves of the opportunity to partake of the forbidden fruits offered by the banquet made available by the courtesans and their lower class sisters: like the lay Moslems they also visited the fleshpots with great frequency. At night veiled courtesans could be seen, accompanied by their servants, or alone, visiting the mosques and seminaries (*madrasehs*) and staying overnight in the small rooms that housed the priests and seminary students (*tollab*).[30] These must have been *sighehs* or temporary wives, for elsewhere Chardin writes that the Moslem religion does not consider fornication to be a sin, which is erroneous and this was due to the fact that he saw no difference between prostitutes and *sighehs*. In fact, he later confirms that fornication and prostitution are forbidden by Islamic law.[31] Chardin was astonished that Persians actually believed that they 'married' a prostitute, which, as he described, they called "*sike koudim* [sic; *sigheh kardam*], which means word by word: I make the contract of pleasure, i.e., I am married." He called this type of union a lease contract, and the women involved were called "moutaa, which means concubine, and also domestic." In Isfahan, the contract price for a young and beautiful girl was 450 *livres* per year, excluding the obligation of providing her with clothing, food and shelter. Such unions were concluded per contract before a judge, and were renewed if the parties agreed. Otherwise all the rules of Islamic law as well as the contractual obligations, as descibed above, were respected.[32]

---

30. Chardin, *Voyages*, vol. 2, p. 222.

31. Chardin, *Voyages*, vol. 7, pp. 413-14. Elsewhere Chardin writes that the olama considered prostitution to be a sin and contrary to religious precepts. Chardin, *Voyages*, vol. 2, pp. 221-22.

32. Chardin, *Voyages*, vol. 2, pp. 223-27. It is interesting that Chardin mentions that *mut'ah* also means domestic help, which is not the case. However, it indicates, as in later centuries, that the *sigheh* usually worked in the man's home as a domestic. This is partly because the husband had the temporary wife serve as the servant of his covenanted wife or wives, which made the temporary wife more acceptable to them.

Du Mans observed that in Safavid Iran, prostitution was considered less shameful and dishonorable than in contemporary Europe. This has to do with the fact that he, like Chardin, also considered temporary marriage as not being different from prostitution.[33] The picture commissioned by Kaempfer, depicting a mullah with a prostitute, is probably based on the same misunderstanding. The woman in the picture most likely is a *sigheh*, rather than a prostitute as noted by the accompanying text. The picture shows an almost domestic scene, where the two parties are in fact quite comfortable with one another, probably waiting for a customer to contract a temporary marriage with the woman.

Figure 2.1 Mullah and *Sigheh*, from the *Kaempfer Album*, 1684–85

Little information is available about the situation in the eighteenth century. Hanway, who was in Iran in the 1740s, reports that temporary

33. Francis Richard, ed., *Raphael du Mans, missionnaire en Perse au XVIIè s.* 2 vols. (Paris, 1995), vol. 2, pp. 372-73.

marriage still existed and he briefly describes the main characteristics (contract with a time period, payment, and waiting period at the end of the contract). He adds, however, a piece of information that seems to be at odds with the Islamic rules governing this type of union, although it may represent actual social custom. Hanway wrote that "If she is pregnant, the man is obliged to support her for a year; and if the child is a male, it is his; if a female, hers."[34] Gmelin, who traveled in Northern Iran between 1770 and 1774, reported that Moslem men could "hire unmarried women, as many as their purse allows. Therefore, rich people believe that when they keep a large number, it is meritorious in the eyes of God, because they maintain that so doing enables them to render service to the human race, because otherwise these women would remain useless members of society." Gmelin did not consider these hired or contracted women as being married, for he further submitted that "Unmarried women are also let go without any divorce ceremony. He rents them either for a fixed or indeterminate period; one often for years, the other only for months or weeks."[35]

Qajar Period (1794-1925)

The information on temporary marriage is relatively copious for the nineteenth century and European travelers were struck by its almost universal presence. Unfortunately, there are no reliable statistics about the number of women who made a living as a *sigheh*. Referring to the situation around 1920, Forbes-Leith reported that "Many hundreds of women in every city and town in the country, making a living by becoming temporary wives of travelers or casual visitors."[36] In 1922, according to a census carried by the Municipality of Tehran, there were 430 *sigheh*s in Tehran, or only 1% of the number of covenanted wives,

---

34. Jonas Hanway, *An Historical Account of the British Trade over the Caspian Sea* (London, 1753), vol. 1, p. 266. According to Imam Sadeq, the child born from a temporary marriage belongs to the mother. Avazeh, *Qanun-e Qovveh-ye Bah*, p. 120.

35. Samuel Gottlieb Gmelin, *Travels through Northern Persia 1770-1774*, translated and annotated by Willem Floor (Washington DC, 2007), p. 94.

36. Forbes-Leith, *Checkmate*, p. 181; see also Basset, *Persia*, p. 288.

which seems to underestimate the number of such temporary unions.[37] As far as is known, no further quantified data are available.

Although still mostly impressionistic, data about who was working as a *sigheh* are more numerous. According to these data, *sigheh*s were mostly women of the lower class and all the available evidence, both Persian and foreign, agree on this point. "It is the women of the lower class, called *Sighehs*, or more exactly *Mouti*, who devote themselves to it. Their patrons are travelers, or those who fear the monotony of a prolonged union, or simply those whose wives are ill, and also those betrothed to girls not yet of an marriageable age, who have several years to wait before they can marry."[38]

Not every woman wanted to enter into a temporary marriage and that included prostitutes, who often were the recruiting grounds for this kind of union. A friendly prostitute (*zan-e ma'rufeh*) in Isfahan refused to become Yaghma'i's *sigheh*, because she did not want to be locked up in the house, but to be free to go where she wanted and told him that in this way he could focus on his work rather than thinking about where she would be all day.[39] But not every *sigheh* was from the lower class. "As the law forbids divorce to those who marry temporarily, it happens sometimes that women of a better social position have recourse to this marriage in order to ensure the permanence of their union."[40] A variant thereof involuntarily happened to one of the wives of Naser al-Din Shah. When he wanted to marry another wife,

37. Ja'far Shahri, *Tarikh-e ejtema'i –Tehran dar qarn-e sizdahom,* 6 vols. (Tehran, 1368/1989), vol. 1, p. 63.

38. Lorey and Sladen, *Queer*, p. 130. "It is mostly practiced by the poor who do not see anything reprehensible in this type of union." Henri Moser, *A Travers l'Asie Centrale* (Paris, 1885), pp. 389, 401; "usually only those in the lower classes, or in dependent circumstances, form such connexions. Justin Perkins, *A Residence of Eight Years in Persia* (Andover, 1843), p. 294. John Malcolm, *A History of Persia* 2 vols. (London, 1820), vol. 2, p. 591; Sheil, *Glimpses*, p. 143.

39. Esma'il Honar Yaghma'i, *Jandaq va Qumis dar avakher-e dowreh-ye Qajar,* ed. by 'Abdol-Karim Hekmat Yaghma'i (Tehran, 1363/1984), pp. 50-51.

40. Lorey and Sladen, *Queer*, pp. 131, 75; d'Allemagne, *Du Khorasan*, vol. 1, p. 214; Sheil, *Glimpses*, p. 143; Benjamin, *Persia*, p. 452; Wills, *In the Land*, p. 326; Curzon, *Persia*, vol. 1, p. 165, note 1.

already having four, he divorced one and made her a *sigheh*, to be able to marry the new wife.[41]

Although, according to Shi'ite law, no formal contract is required between the two contracting parties, written contracts usually seem to have been the norm. According to Southgate, an American missionary, "A regular contract is made, and the conditions and duration of the connection specified. Many of the inferior sort of Mollahs gain, in good part, their livelihood by negotiating these contracts."[42] These mullahs, both as procurer of the women and the notary of the contract, based their claim for a fee partly on the fact that they drew up the contract. Some important men made sure that the legal niceties were indeed respected, although others seem to have flaunted them. For example, 'Abdol-Hoseyn Farmanfarma wrote to a friend asking him to be his agent (*vakil*) for his temporary marriage.[43] When the contract had been established, the woman's agent asked the man's agent: 'Do you accept the conditions that have been agreed upon?' When he confirmed this, the seals of the mullah and the two agents were put on the contract, which was given to the woman and the marriage then might be consummated.[44] Varjavand has reproduced the text of such a *sigheh*-contract, which, as expected, is in complete agreement with the legal requirements.[45]

41. E'temad al-Saltaneh, *Ruznameh*, p. 601. Another *sigheh* of Naser al-Din Shah became one of the most influential women at court. Ibid, p. 126. In fact, Naser al-Din Shah had many *sighehs* concurrently in his harem. Ibid., pp. 244, 261, 490, 513, 696, 903.

42. Horatio Southgate, *A Tour Through Armenia and Mesopotamia*, 2 vols. (New York: D. Appleton & Co, 1840), vol. 2, p. 38; Van Sommer and Zwemer, *Our Moslem Sisters*, p. 234; Häntzsche, "Haram," pp. 431-32.

43. 'Abdol-Hoseyn Mirza Farmanfarma, *Siyaq-e ma'ishat dar 'ahd-e Qajar – Hokmrani va Molkdari* eds. Mansureh Ettehadiyeh and Sirus Sa'dvandiyan 2 vols. (Tehran, 1362/1983), vol. 1, p. 64.

44. D'Allemagne, *Du Khorasan*, vol. 1, p. 214.

45. Varjavand, *Sima*, vol. 2, pp. 927-28.

He is the Author between the hearts

In the name of God the compassionate and the merciful

Praised be to God who exalts marriage and enjoyment and forbids adultery

May God's blessings be on Mohammad and his family.

The performer of the solemnities of the temporary marriage (motamatte') is His Honor Mr. 'Azizollah Beyg, son of the late Qorban 'Ali Amiri Rudbari.

The provider of pleasure (motamatta') is the pure-like Ahaneh Khanom, daughter of Kheyr al-Zovvar Karbala'i 'Abbas, villager.

The rent is an amount of five Mozaffar al-Din dinars.

Witnessed by the Slave of Reason, Mohammad, son of the late Mullah Mohammad 'Ali Amiri

The date: 23 (twenty-three) Dhu'l-Qa'deh Tushqan'il in the year 1321 [10 February 1904]

In the margin on top of the document:

In the name of God, may the contract come to pass and witnessed by the least

[seal = Mohammad]

Figure 2.2 *Sigheh* contract

To have a written contract was important, given the woman's financial interest, because sometimes a client wanted to renege on the terms of the oral contract. In 1908, the governor of Astarabad, Amir Mokarram, wanted a woman and thus, his barber brought him secretly at night the miller's daughter, who had been promised a cash payment and the purchase of a house. Moreover, after one night they would marry in the morning and she would get 50 *tumans*. In the morning the governor gave the girl ten *tumans* and sent her home without having married her or fulfilled the other promises made. The parents then complained and were given another 10 *tumans* and that concluded this business.[46] In another case, a woman in Tehran agreed to become a man's *sigheh* and went with him to his house. However, there it became clear that he wanted her to be a prostitute and he brought a client to have sex with her. This led to a loud altercation, so that the neighbors called the police, which put an end to the man's lying scheme.[47] Payment was usually less rewarding than the above examples may seem to suggest. In Resht, the *sighehs* had to pay half of what they earned to the mullah who arranged for the 'husband,' if the marriage lasted less than one day or part thereof. What they earned was little in such cases, only half a *qeran*.[48]

There were many reasons why men acquired a *sigheh*. What all of them had in common, and the only thing that really mattered to them, was that they wanted to have sex, but with a lawful sexual partner. In particular, men wanted uncomplicated sex. According to the author of the Education of Wives (*Ta'dib al-Nesvan*), men did not like it when their wives told them: "Leave me in peace! Am I a sighah to amuse you when you are wearied and cannot sleep?"[49] No, they wanted female attention whenever, wherever and however, with no why, discussion, buts or ifs. According to the same author:

46. Hoseyn Qoli Maqsudlu Vakil al-Dowleh, *Mokhabarat-e Astarabad* eds. Iraj Afshar and Mohammad Rasul Daryagasht 2 vols. (Tehran, 1363/1984), vol. 1, p. 87. To give an idea of the purchasing power of this payment, one needs to know that one *tuman* is equal 10 *qeran*s. Prices for *gerdeh* rice, the staple food of the people of Astarabad, was 75 *qeran*s for 132 kg (20 Astarabad *man*) in 1909, or 0.56 *qeran*/kg. H.L. Rabino, "Trade of the Persian Caspian Provinces (Consular District of Resht and Astarabad) March 1909-March 1910", *Diplomatic and Consular Reports* no. 4828 (London, 1912), pp. 12-13.

47. Reza'i and Azari, *Gozareshha-ye Nazmiyeh*, vol. 1, p. 380 (16/03/1887).

48. Häntzsche, "Haram," p.432; see also Vambery, *Meine Wanderungen*, p. 71.

49. Anonymous, "The Education of Wives," p. 249. For the Persian text see Hasan Javadi, Manzheh Mar'ashi and Simin Shakarlu eds. *Ruyaru'i-ye zan va mard dar 'asr-e Qajar. Du resaleh. Ta'dib al-Nesvan va Ma'ayeb al-Rejal* (Bethesda, 1371/1992).

Men prefer the most ordinary sighah to such great ladies,
as being more simple and not playing the empress. The
sighah is ever content to yield to an amorous fantasy,
even in a corridor or other less comfortable place; to say
jestingly: 'It seems to me, dearest, that the place might
have been better chosen,' is enough for her. This is why
Hajji Jahandar Mirza called the sighah Madam Ever-
ready. [50]

In short, the exclusive purpose of temporary marriage is sex. It
could be for one hour, if somebody did not want to visit a prostitute,
it could be for a longer period, if the union served, for example, the
purpose to get sexual gratification while awaiting marriage, or even
longer, up to 99 years, if the man wanted to have the immediate option of uncomplicated sex, rather than having to pay attention to the
wishes of his covenanted wife. Therefore, "As soon as a youth arrives
at the age of maturity, and if his parents are affluent or he himself is
a wage earner, he takes a segar [sic; *sigheh*] wife."[51] Some men like
prince Rokn al-Dowleh could not live without a woman and thus, for
example, when he was staying in the Jahannama garden outside Shiraz
without his wives, they brought him a *sigheh*.[52] Naser al-Din Shah
when he was traveling in Europe had left his wives behind in Iran,
but he was accompanied by a Circassian slave girl. She was dressed as
a Persian boy. "When I saw her she was in a room with the two eunuchs." His entourage was not so fortunate and therefore, on arrival
in London the first thing they asked their British counterparts "where
they could go and amuse themselves in the evening? They had, it ap-

---

50. Anonymous, "The Education of Wives," vol. 1, p. 249.

51. Forbes-Leith, *Checkmate*, p. 180; Van Sommer and Zwemer, *Our Moslem
Sisters*, p. 236 (usually the mother selected the servant girl). According to
Gobineau, *Trois Ans*, vol. 2, p. 187 wealthy parents usually gave a son a
temporary wife at age seven or eight. She was to be his wife when he reached
puberty, and, because he could end her contract any time, this 'wife' had an
incentive to make herself liked by her 'husband.'

52. Hoseyn Qoli Khan Nezam al-Saltaneh Mafi, *Khaterat* [...] 2 vols. Ma'sumeh
Nezam-Mafi, Mansureh Ettehadiyeh, Sirus Sa'dvandiyan and Hamid Ram-
pisheh eds (Tehran, 1361/1982), vol. 1, p. 160.

peared, had a very lively time in St. Petersburg and were anxious to know whether the girls were likely to be as free and easy as those they had met there, also, were there dancing places open all night?"[53] Apart from affordability, not every man took a *sigheh*, of course. Of one man it was said that he was not a womanizer (*khanom-baz*), because he only had had one or two *sigheh*s at times.[54]

For wealthy men it was very easy to get a *sigheh*, if they chose them from lower class families.[55] There usually were attractive daughters and nieces to be found in the families of their servants, or there were young girls already working in the household, who probably had been hired with that purpose in mind.[56] Na'eb al-Saltaneh, the governor of Tehran, went each year to the same rural district to pick a few new *sigheh*s, to replace the ones he had, which gave 'Eyn al-Saltaneh the idea that he might do the same.[57] Sometimes, the wealthy man did not have to make any effort at all, for people came to offer their daughters, like the middle-class father, who was trying to get his daughter accepted as *sigheh* for a prince.[58] Peasants did the same when important men passed through their village.[59]

For the less wealthy there often were special streets where *sigheh*s lived, in particular in cities that were centers of pilgrimage, such as Mashhad and Qom, and in all major towns, and in particular those

---

53. Neville, *Unconventional Memories*, pp. 207, 205. The Circassian was a slave girl, not a temporary wife.

54. Yaghma'i, *Jandaq* 97.

55. If they did not, it could result in problems. E'tesam al-Molk, *Safarnameh*, p. 292.

56. E'temad al-Saltaneh, *Ruznameh*, p. 1017 (a prince married as *sigheh* the daughter of the uncle of one of his servants); 'Eyn al-Saltaneh, *Ruznameh*, vol. 1, p. 830 (19-year old girl working in the household), see also p. 628; Häntzsche, "Haram," p. 432.

57. 'Eyn al-Saltaneh, *Ruznameh*, vol. 1, p. 830.

58. 'Eyn al-Saltaneh, *Ruznameh*, vol. 2, p. 1052; Van Sommer and Zwemer, *Our Moslem Sisters*, p. 234.

59. Dieulafoy, *Perse*, p. 200.

that were stops on important commercial routes.[60] In Miyaneh, an important stop on the well traveled route between Tehran and Tabriz, women from all over Iran came to offer their services to travelers.[61] In Rasht and Qom, the *sighehs* lived in a special street, just like prostitutes in other cities. The women lived in simple reed huts. A mullah was seated in front of the huts and conducted the prospective husband into the hut to present him with his future wife. He then went quickly with the couple through the reading of the contractual formula and pocketed his share of the sum agreed upon. He then left the hut and sat down again, waiting for other clients.[62] The houses in which the *sighehs* lived were run by so-called *khanoms*, "whose business it is to receive *Sighas* desirous of marriage."[63] One of them, an old crone, recommended a client, de Lorey's Arab servant named Mansur, an Abyssinian woman, whose alluring qualities she described.

> Mansur enquired if the 'lady' were young.
> 'Young!' was the reply. 'By your death, if I told you she were born yesterday, you would not believe me. But I can assure you that our Padishah has not many younger in the royal anderun! I take for witness Her Highness, Fatima the Pure, sister of Imam Reza, that I speak but the truth when I say that she is like the rose in the paradise of sweets, a sugar-eating parrot!'
>
> 'I suppose she is white then?'
>
> 'White is perhaps an exaggeration, although she is known as Nur Jehan, the Light of the World,' answered the matchmaker. 'She is not black, but the warmth of the sun, as you know, is felt considerably in Abyssinia-my lord is somewhat brown of colour himself-we will put it that she is the same.' And to counteract whatever evil

60. Curzon, *Persia*, vol. 1, p. 165; Polak, *Persien*, vol. 1, p. 208; Ibid, "Die Prostitution," p. 563.
61. Arminius Vambery, *Meine Wanderungen und Erlebnisse in Persien* (Pesth, 1867), p. 71.
62. Häntzsche, "Haram," p. 432; Brugsch, *Im Lande*, p. 300.
63. Lorey and Sladen, *Moon*, p. 70.

impression this admission might have produced, she added hastily, with an eye to the weak spot of an Arab's fancy, 'She is as fat as a sheep's tail!'

Mansur gathered that the woman in question was a lady of colour; he had no objection to that, his first wife having been the same, and, indeed, the coloured women are much better housekeepers than their white sisters, and more docile and reliable, more devoted and affectionate. And, in short, so satisfactory did it all seem that the matter might have been ordered beforehand by Destiny."

These *khanom*s competed with mullahs who provided similar services, because *sigheh*s were found in large numbers at caravan stations and they were one of the main sources of income for the low-level clergy that concluded these marriages, as mentioned above.[64] In Mashhad with its tens of thousands of pilgrims every year,

A flourishing business is carried on by mullahs, who have a large number of women living in their houses ready to be married. The mullah on finding a candidate for his protégé's hand gets paid for the marriage contract as well as for her board while she lived in his house. At the end of the term, and having received from her husband the promised sum, the woman returns to the house of her spiritual benefactor and impatiently awaits the expiration of four months that must pass before a new contract can be concluded. This term is, however, not always as strictly observed as it should be. The Shariat permits a woman marrying only three times, but the obliging mullahs are always ready to overlook such a small matter.[65]

---

64. Moser, *A Travers*, pp. 389, 401; Bricteux, *Au Pays*, pp. 228-39; Southgate, *Narrative*, vol. 2, p. 38.

65. Ponafidine, *Life*, pp. 322-23; see also Perkins, *A Residence*, p. 295 ("the Moollahs—the priesthood—are themselves the licensers and managers of the public brothels, and regard them as an important source of income").

Indeed, through technicalities, mullahs aided and abetted their stable of *sigheh*s to reduce the legal waiting period between husbands and make money. It was because of this and other reasons, of course, that the populace made little distinction between a *sigheh* and a prostitute.[66] In fact, Häntzsche, who lived and practiced as a physician in Iran for many years, and knew the difference between contemporary marriage and prostitution, nevertheless opined that the difference between the two was sometimes blurred, such as in the Sunni town of Kermanshah, where the mullahs acted as intermediary between prostitutes and clients.[67]

Lonely husbands posted far away from their family also felt the need for sexual comfort and acted upon those feelings. Indeed, friends sent a Tehrani girl to a man who was temporarily in the city as a *sigheh* to console and divert him.[68] Mohsen Sadr relates how, when he was alone in Hamadan in 1903, he concluded a temporary marriage with a girl whom he loved very much. Suddenly, after one and a half year his covenanted wife arrived with his family and he did not want to keep his second, be it temporary, marriage a secret any longer for his family, which he had done thus far. He believed that having the *sigheh* to stay in his house with her mother as servants to his covenanted wife would not be objectionable to the latter and he therefore tried to explain the situation to his wife, who told him 'either divorce me or send her home.' With pain in his heart he did the latter, although he loved his temporary wife very much.[69] Ehtesham al-Saltaneh had a similar dilemma, because when his wife left for Tehran, he took not one, but two *sigheh*s. But, for family reasons, he gave them up with regret when he also left Khamseh.[70] Some women forestalled their husband's need for sexual gratification when they were away. For ex-

66. Hantzsche, "Haram," p. 432; George Nathaniel Curzon, *Persia and the Persian Question* 2 vols. (London, 1892), vol. 1, p. 165, note 1.
67. Häntzsche, "Haram," pp. 431-32.
68. Yaghma'i, *Jandaq*, p. 93.
69. Mohsen Sadr, *Khaterat-e Sadr al-Ashraf* (Tehran, 1364/1985), p. 162.
70. Ehtesham al-Saltaneh, *Khaterat-e Ehtesham al-Saltaneh* (Tehran, 1366/1987), pp. 153-54.

ample, some wives of those who went on pilgrimage, a journey that would last several months, and who could afford it, provided their husband with one or more girls as concubines to stand in for them during their absence.[71] Religious students also kept *sigheh*s, invariably women above the child-bearing age, because they had to spend many years studying and could not afford "to interrupt their studies and bring up their children on air."[72]

The anguish was more often felt by the women, who usually were also in love with their 'husband', in particular when their union was not that merely of a sex worker, who had been contracted through a madam or mullah. In the latter case, "The woman often passes from one husband to another in the course of a few months."[73] However, there were also cases where the temporary marriage lasted for a number of years and the wife loved her husband. In Latgah (Hamadan province), for example, the Sardar had a *sigheh*, with whom he had three children and the oldest boy was his heir. However, when the Sardar married the daughter of an important national politician he got rid of his *sigheh* wife, paid her and kept the children, even going so far as to forbid her even to see them.[74] Na'eb al-Saltaneh for financial reasons all of a sudden threw out 12 *sigheh*s and thus totally disconsolate he had to find his pleasure with fewer women.[75]

It would be wrong to think that temporary marriage was a bad deal for the woman in all cases. It all depended on the circumstances. Of course, the majority of those that basically were sex-workers were in the worst position. Their situation, apart from the legal aspect, was not much better than that of a prostitute. But some of those who were able to contract a marriage with a rich man often found that they had made a good deal. About one such rich man Merritt-Hawkes wrote,

---

71. Van Sommer and Zwemer, *Our Moslem Sisters*, p. 239.

72. Von Rosen, *Persian Pilgrimage*, pp. 134-35.

73. Bassett, *Land*, p. 288 (a *sigheh* often moved from one man to the other, and not always as *sigheh*, but as a mistress); Yaghma'i, *Jandaq*, pp. 50-51.

74. Forbes-Leith, *Checkmate*, p. 182.

75. 'Eyn al-Saltaneh, *Ruznameh*, vol. 1, p. 971.

that he was "an old and moral Moslem who had a household of one hundred and twenty-two persons. He has never let down any of his *sighehs* and is, quite rightly, proud of himself.[76] Mostowfi relates the case of his nanny, Naneh Mensa, one of whose granddaughters was very beautiful. At one time she was accepted as a concubine of an important man. Later she returned to her mother's house with a substantial dowry. This led to a better marriage for her to someone of her own age and status.[77] Von Rosen likewise reported that she was told that when these girls returned to their village, "they are invariably much sought after wives, partly because it is thought that they have learnt nice manners and partly because they bring money with them."[78] This is what parents hoped for, but it was not what happened in most cases. According to Doctor Wishard, who knew, because he treated many of them in his hospital, *sighehs*:

> Are easily cast off, and the result is that many hardships
> are thus inflicted. Sometimes they are able to find
> employment in large households as maids, or, as they are
> called in Persia, bodjees. Not infrequently they are taken
> as plural wives of some other man, in order to get their
> services as maids for the more favoured ones. Often, after
> years of struggle, sickness overtakes them and they are
> cast out by some wicked master into the street. ... These
> poor women may often be seen sitting by the roadside
> with no place to go, every door, seemingly, closed against
> them.[79]

Social status in Iran was and is based on factors such as socioeconomic standing, reputation, kinship affiliation, occupation and

---

76. Merritt-Hawkes, *Persia*, pp. 285-86.

77. Mostowfi, *Sharh-e zendegani*, vol. 1, p. 157. An Armenian woman who had been married by her father, (who had lost his capital due to the Russian revolution), to a high-placed Moslem for five years, had given birth to two boys during that time. After that period her husband had remarried her. Janet Miller, *Camel-Bells of Baghdad* (Boston-New York, 1934), p. 141.

78. Von Rosen, *Persian Pilgrimage*, p. 134.

79. Wishard, *Twenty Years*, pp. 211-12.

level of education. Family status was of overriding importance. Interconnection among families was carefully planned from birth and parallel or cross-cousin marriages were preferred and therefore quite common. Therefore, a marriage with a socially inferior woman, or in other words a temporary marriage, was not an event a man or his family wanted to advertise. According to Merritt-Hawkes, "Usually the *sighehs* are women of a lower class, and, amongst the women, of another tribe."[80] Some *sigheh* wives, however, were able to occupy a role of some influence in elite society, for as long as they were able to keep male attention and admiration. For example, Rhubaba, a *sigheh*, played a courtesan role in Tabriz society and was the confidante of the revolutionaries, and in 1909 she was "the most important personage in Tabriz at the present moment, Sattar Khan and the Russian Consul-General included."[81]

However, these were the exception to the rule. For despite the legality of temporary marriage and its religious approved nature, *sigheh* wives, in general, were neither accepted by society as equal to covenanted (*'aqdi*) wives nor had their children, in practice, automatically the same rights as children from a covenanted marriage, be they monogamous or polygamous. A telling case is that of Mas'ud Mirza, Zell al-Soltan, the eldest son of Naser al-Din Shah, who was excluded from the succession (*vilayat-'ahd*), because his mother was a *sigheh*. Therefore, a younger brother, son of an *'aqdi* mother, was selected as crown prince.[82] In some elite families one finds both an *'aqdi* (therefore also called *asli*) and a *sigheh* branch, originating in the nature of the marriage of their ancestress. What is interesting is that this fact is still known and socially significant today, more than 100 years after the fact! Although, the children have legally the same rights, despite the nature of their mother's marriage, children of a *sigheh* often found it difficult to obtain their rightful share of their father's inheritance,

80. Merritt-Hawkes, *Persia*, p. 285.

81. Lionel James, *Side-Tracks & Bridle-Paths* (Edinburgh-London, 1909), pp. 33-36.

82. Polak, *Persien*, vol. 1, p. 230.

according to Polak.[83] However, de Lorey reported that "the children are generally acknowledged by the father, who provides for their maintenance until they can support themselves," which is confirmed by other contemporary travelers.[84] Nevertheless, it might give rise to problems when a child went to find his father, and the more so in case of an inheritance. For there were swindlers who tried to get part of an inheritance, while it also happened in legitimate cases that the other children might not want to share with somebody of unknown and uncertain provenance.[85] Probably, these kinds of problems mainly arose in case of children born to travelers, who had a sexual relationship with the mother for a limited period only. The situation was, of course, different when both partners had been 'married' for a number of years and co-habited in the same village or town, where the children were part of the father's household.

The children of the *sigheh* marriages were often referred to by the members of the *asli* family as *pesar-e* (or *dokhtar-e*) *kolfat*, or the maid's son or daughter, indicating the difference in social status and background as well as the fact that *sigheh*s often doubled as maids. One cannot say that marrying a *sigheh*, or being one, implied social stigma. However, a *sigheh* often found herself an outsider in the family into which she had married. In short, there was little pride in this family connection. Kazemi relates an event of his youth, when during a family festive gathering his uncle's 'wife' sat apart and did not participate in the merriment. He then found out that she secretly was his uncle's *sigheh* (*dar khafa sigheh-ye u*).[86] It is therefore, not surprising that late nineteenth and early twentieth century social reformers

---

83. Polak, *Persien*, vol. 1, p. 208; see also Forbes-Leith, *Checkmate*, pp. 181, 185.

84. Lorey and Sladen, *Queer*, p. 131; d'Allemagne, *Du Khorasan*, vol. 1, p. 214.

85. Moser, *A Travers*, pp. 389, 401; Hugo Grothe, *Wanderungen in Persien* (Berlin, 1910), pp. 154-55.

86. Mortaza Shafaq Kazemi, *Ruzegar va Andisheh* 3 vols. (Tehran, 1350/1971), vol. 1, p. 56. See also Ehtesham al-Saltaneh, *Khaterat*, pp. 153-54; Merritt-Hawkes, *Persia*, p. 285 ("there is a strong sentiment against this form of marriage."); Van Sommer and Zwemer, *Our Moslem Sisters*, p. 235.

wanted to abolish the institution. Mirza Aqa Khan Kermani argued that temporary marriage was a barbaric hold-over from pre-Islamic Arabia, when that part of the world was still immersed in the Age of Ignorance (*jaheliyat*).[87]

TEMPORARY MARRIAGE AND CHRISTIANS AND JEWS (1520S-1900)

Temporary marriage not only occurred among Shi'ites in Qajar Iran, but also among Christians and Jews. Among the latter, however, it was "not as common [as] with Mohammedans."[88] In particular, expatriate Europeans availed themselves of this opportunity to have sexual relations without legal covenanted marriage. The first time that this is reported was in the sixteenth century, in the kingdom of Hormuz, where concubinage of Portuguese men and Moslem women was a widely accepted practice.[89] It was not acceptable to João III, however, who, in vain, tried to do something about it, in particular about the adultery committed by Portuguese men as well as about the illegitimate children born from these adulterous unions.[90]

It also occurred during the seventeenth century, when there was an influx of mostly unmarried European males, albeit in limited numbers, who often remained there for many years. Because they could not have sexual relations with Moslem women, some of those living in Isfahan married Armenian ones. It is reported that these marriages were concluded according to the Armenian or Nestorian rite, but in the light of the information about this in later periods, these marriages indeed may have also been temporary rather covenanted marriages.[91]

---

87. Camron Michael Amin, *The Making of the Modern Iranian Woman* (Gainsville, Fl., 2002), p. 29.

88. Bassett, *Eastern Mission*, p. 67.

89. Joseph Wicki ed., *Documenta Indica* 16 vols. (Rome, 1948-84), vol. 1, pp. 606-06, 612, 620, 657; vol. 2, pp. 250, 333-34.

90. António da Silva Rego ed., *Documentação para a história das missões do padroado português do Oriente* 12 vols. (Lisbon, 1947-58), vol. 3, pp. 19-23.

91. Léon Mirot, "Le Séjour du Père Bernard de Sainte-Thérèse en Perse (1640-

Dutchmen, who were all employees of the Dutch East Indies Company (VOC), had to ask the Company for permission to marry and they hardly ever did, because the Company did not like their male employees to be married and usually refused permission. Moreover, if and when it was found out that they had married without permission they were shipped out, leaving the women behind.[92] Rodolphe Stadler, a Swiss watch-maker (d. 1638), had a Nestorian woman in his house, probably as a concubine, because her sister was also living with him and they had servants, thus suggesting that they had a household together.[93]

The practice also existed in the nineteenth century, be it only between European men and non-Moslem women.

> Concubinage may be practiced in other countries, by such
> as are cast out of the pale of all decent society, without
> implicating the moral healthiness of public sentiment. But
> here it exists under circumstances, which plainly show the
> mass of the Armenian community to be infected with its
> corrupting influence. Public opinion does not frown upon
> it. Parents even sell their daughters into concubinage;
> and not only, we are assured, are these victims of lust
> admitted to the communion and the other privileges
> of the church as good Christians, but their priests have
> to be found to share in the gain. This sad state of moral

1642)," *Études Carmélitaines. Mystiques et Missionnaires* 18 (1933), p. 227, n.1, reports that Dutch, English and French men with the use of money corrupted Catholic [Armenian or Arab] girls. "The parents of these girls are so poor that they even sell them in the hope to gain" from such unions. But when a Protestant Dutchman wanted to marry a Catholic Arab girl Père Bernard de Sainte-Thérèse forbade the marriage for "reasons that concerned the glory of God." Ibid., p. 228.

92. H. Dunlop, *Bronnen tot de geschiedenis der Oostindische Compagnie in Perzië* (The Hague, 1930), p. 425, 568 (after his death, Visnich's concubine married an Italian); A. Hotz ed., *Journaal der reis van den gezant der O.I Compagie Joan Cuneaus naar Perzi' in 1651-1652* (Amsterdam. 1908), pp. 310-11; Chardin, *Voyages*, vol. 2, pp. 219-20 noted that in the 1660-1670s, Shi'ite religious dignitaries would refuse to conclude a temporary marriage between two consenting Christians, because their religion forbade polygyny.

93. Tavernier, *Voyages*, pp. 173-74.

does not exist among the Armenians of Tebriz alone. In Erzroom, Erivan, and Nakjchevan, Armenian parents have been known to sell their daughters, for the same criminal purpose, for a limited time.[94]

Southgate confirmed that the practice of temporary marriage was "practised to a very considerable extent by the foreigners in the country, the females, in this case, being generally, if not always Armenians."[95]

[They sell them] to the embraces of any man who will pay the price. With this view, they watch the arrival of every European; and having made the necessary enquiries respecting the length of his purse, and probable sojourn in the country, few days elapse before his private ear is sought by succession of mothers, soliciting his approbation of one of their daughters. Should he be inclined to comply with the too common fashion in the East, and select a girl, the bargain is made by her parents. They first demand the price of her pretended services to them; then settle what her protector is to allow her for clothing, &c.; while she lives with him; and what sum he is to leave with her, when he quits the country, to purchase her a respectable husband amongst her own people, should she be inclined to take one.[96]

Bélanger and other contemporary authors make similar observations as to the willingness of Armenian priests to conclude *sigheh* marriages; the parents selling their daughters as of 13 years of age. He implies that these were sold to Russians and Englishmen living in Iran, who did not bother about the children born from these unions.[97]

---

94. E. Smith & H.G.O. Dwight, *Researches of the Rev. E. Smith. & Rev. Dwight, H. G. O in Armenia* 2 vols. (Boston, 1833), vol. 2, pp. 153-54.

95. Southgate, *A Tour*, vol. 2, p. 38.

96. Porter, *Travels*, vol. 1, p. 425.

97. Bélanger, *Voyage*, vol. 2, p. 207; see also Porter, *Travels*, vol. 1, pp. 425-26 (Jolfa); Henry A. Stern, A. *Dawnings in the East; with biblical, historical, and statistical notices of persons and places visited during a mission to the Jews*

This was the major difference with the Islamic form of concubinage where the children were not illegitimate and the fathers usually acknowledged their fatherhood. Edward Burgess, for example, wrote his parents to inform them that his brother Charles, who had left him in the lurch in Tabriz, also had left "an illegitimate family in Persia, this consisted of the mother and two children." Edward Burgess therefore had assumed responsibility for his brother's family and supported them for many years and saw to it that his niece made a good and a happy marriage to a Roman Catholic Persian.[98] Edward Burgess was not the only European who acted honorably and responsibly, other Europeans also concluded a proper covenanted marriage with Christian girls.[99]

Porter was very much upset about these temporary arrangements, "not only breaking the ordinances of their [Christian] faith, but adding to that offence a breach of the law of nature, by deserting the offspring of their temporary engagements."[100] But his moral outrage did not stop many a European man, who could afford to, from indulging himself in such dalliances. Although he described the situation in Jolfa, the largest concentration of Europeans in Iran in the 1830s probably was in Tabriz, where Greek and Russian merchants, Russian diplomats and a few British or other European males constituted the European community.

> Some of these Greek [merchants at Tabriz] were married
> men, but had left their wives behind in Constantinople.
> Most of the members of the Russian embassy had also
> come here as bachelors. In both cases, the new comers

---

in Persia, Coordistan, and Mesopotamia (London, 1854), pp. 191-93; James Edward Alexander, Travels from India to England (London, 1827 [New Delhi, 2000]), p. 98. ("[Armenian] mothers not unfrequently sell their daughters."); Hommaire de Hell, Voyage, vol. 2, p. 17.

98. Benjamin Schwartz ed., Letters from Persia. Written by Charles and Edward Burgess 1828-1855 (New York, 1942), pp. 109-110.

99. See, for example, father and son John and William Cormick, who both married Armenian women. Denis Wright, The English Amongst the Persians (London, 2001), p. 124.

100. Porter, Travels, vol. 1, p. 427.

had followed a long established practice of Europeans in Persia, and contracted temporary marriages with Nestorian women. ... Its members have not the least scruple, on religious, national, or ethical grounds, to give their daughters in marriage to Europeans, for a limited period (be it six years or six months,) and for a stipulated sum. The affair is generally arranged in the most regular and formal manner, always in the presence of the parents and the nearest relation of the girl, and often under the sanction of a Nestorian priest, acting, perhaps, as notary. In fact, there is a complete competition for the preference of every newly arrived European, who is supposed to be about to take up his residence for some time in the country. The wealthiest strangers have the best selection. As soon as they have agreed about the duration, and the terms of these matromonie alla carta, the bride is brought to her husband with due ceremony, by her relations. It is usual for the family of the lady to take up their residence in the house of the temporary lord, who must naturally maintain them all. This arrangement is often expressly stated in the marriage settlement. Not only all the Greek merchants, but most of the members of the Russian General Consulate, were married in this manner, and the practice is so usual and long established, that public morality is not at all shocked at it. The persons concerned ask each other, without the least embarrassment, how their wives and children are. Each of these gentlemen had set apart a portion of his house for the women, and called it the harem. The ladies retained the mode of life, and costume of native females, covered their faces when strangers appeared, kept away from table when guests were invited, filled up their leisure hours like Turkish women, with devotion to the toilette, and visiting baths, and when they went abroad, appeared like the other women, in long envelopes, extending from head to foot.

It cannot be disputed that these females are faithful and affectionate to their children, but being totally deficient in cultivation and refinement, notwithstanding their beauty, they cannot compensate for the life of intelligent female society in Europe. It was evident, from the regrets expressed by the gentlemen, for the tender reminiscences in the West, that these Perso-Frankish weddings did not satisfy the affections and the imagination. Young M. Mavrocordato longed for Parisian grisettes, M. Osserof, for the refined females of the Petersburgh salons. The physical beauty of these Nestorian women, which is quite undeniable, was lost sight of, in comparison with the delicacy and spiritual refinement of the cultivated class of European women.

So soon as the interval, specified in the contract, has elapsed, another agreement is made, unless the gentleman is tired of his partner, when he forms a new one. The deserted lady is sure of a settlement at home, because she brings a good sum with her, whereas most Nestorians have to pay dearly in purchasing a wife. The children of these short-lived marriages, almost invariably follow their mothers, and I was told that the Nestorian females love them almost more than those born in subsequent alliances. The step-fathers are, also, said to treat them very kindly. Nor is it less remarkable, that the European fathers are said to feel no scruple in abandoning their offspring, without taking a farther thought about their destiny. A long residence in the East appears to blunt the sense of duty, honour and affection, even in the most upright characters.[101]

Although married to Europeans, the Persian women behaved in the same manner as they would have if their 'husbands' had been Armenian or Assyrian, i.e. they were neither seen nor heard. Wagner relates that when he was going with a group of Europeans for an outing in the village of Liwan, "M. Osserow, and the gentlemen of his suite, had arrived before us. ... The party had brought their Nestorian women with them, these ladies occupying each a small tent beside

101. M. Wagner, *Travels in Persia, Georgia, and Koordistan*. 3 vols. (London, 1856 [Westmead, 1971]), vol.3, pp. 112-15. Porter, *Travels*, vol. 1, p. 427 was much more pessimistic about the future of these children.

that of their lords. Nor did the fair inmates venture to unveil the chars of their countenances, notwithstanding the solitude of the place."[102]

Not every European wanted to follow the route of temporary marriage to find sexual gratification. M. Richard, who had come to Iran 1848, to teach French at the *Dar al-Fonun* choose a more direct way. Rather than a temporary marriage he bought a Kurdish slave girl and dressed her in male clothes.[103] He told everybody that the 'boy' was his servant, but at night, unbeknown to the world, she was his body servant. When his relationship was divulged by one of his servants, he claimed that she was the wife of that servant, but he later admitted his 'involvement.' Moreover, when she was found to be pregnant, Richard fled to Shah 'Abdol-'Azim to seek sanctuary. He then had himself circumcised as proof that he was a Moslem and declared that the young woman was his wife.[104] The French ambassador in Tehran may have learnt from this experience that had befallen his compatriot, for he, in 1877 only had a mistress, a Christian woman named Zartar, who lived in a garden where he had rented a bungalow.[105]

Sometimes the initiative to suggest a temporary marriage to a European was taken by Iranians. In December 1908, when Arnold

---

102. Wagner, *Travels*, vol. 3, p. 186.

103. This was unusual, because usually "the Kurds sell their daughters, but to serve as domestics." Bassett, *In the land*, p. 287; see also *Ponafidine*, Life, p. 320.

104. For a detailed account of this case see Adrienne Doris Heytier ed. *Les dépêches diplomatiques du comte de Gobineau en Perse* (Geneva, Paris, 1959), pp. 83-87, 93; Momtahen al-Dowleh, *Khaterat-e Momtahen al-Dowleh* ed. Hoseynqoli Khan-Shaqaqi (Tehran, 1353/1974), p. 45, note. Wills, *In the land*, pp. 36-37, further relates that when he met Richard in his old age, that he still was a satyr (i.e., a man with uncontrollable sexual desires). He changed women, of whom he had two, every year in the spring, to which end he went each year to Hamadan to find two new ones. This suggests that these women were *sigheh*s. Richard thus heeded the famous Persian poem that states: 'Oh master, every spring get a new wife/ That old calendar needs a new life.' According to Polak, "Die Prostitution", p. 564, a number of Europeans were entrapped by prostitutes and forced to convert to Islam to escape the death penalty. However, he is the only one who reports this.

105. Momtahen al-Dowleh, *Khaterat*, p. 245. For the yearnings of another French diplomat for 'love' and presumably sex, see Lorey & Sladen, *Moon*.

Wilson was staying in Dezful a young Iranian chief of his acquaintance lamented Wilson's bachelor existence, "and urged me, in presence of his henchmen, to take a temporary mate to relieve the intolerable tedium of long winter evenings. I could not, of course, take a wife about with me, but *sub pro tem.* He would find the right girl, and place a nice little house in a garden at my disposal."[106] When Wilson was robbed by Chigini Lurs in June 1911, its chief first wanted to hold him to ransom. "I must stay some days with him—a week a month—he would give me fine shooting and a *sigha,* temporary wife, with eyes like a gazelle, breasts like the udders of a yearling ewe."[107]

Pahlavi Period (1925–1979)

Under Reza Shah the institution of temporary marriage was socially frowned upon. When asked about it, upper-class women blushed and men might even deny its very existence. Therefore, the feminist monthly *'Alam-e Nesvan* (The World of Women) predicted that the new Marriage Act of 1931, which had continued to permit temporary marriage, nevertheless would result in the disappearance of temporary marriage, because (a) men had to publicly register their name, and (b) there was a growing stigma among the upper- and middle-class concerning temporary marriage. The journal claimed that there was already a drop in such unions of 10 percent in the first year after the publication of the new Marriage Act.[108] One year later, Merritt-Hawkes noticed two phenomena, viz. (1) that the number of temporary marriages was going down, and (2) that at least among the upper class temporary wives were replaced by mistresses. This seems to bear out the trend that Khal'atbari, the author of the article in *'Alam-e Nesvan,* foresaw, or, which is more likely, because she spoke to persons who thought like him. As to the middlemen Merritt-Hawkes observed:

---

106. Arnold Wilson, *South West Persia. A Political Officer's Diary 1907-1914* (London, 1941), p. 73.

107. Wilson, *South West Persia,* p. 166

108. *'Alam-e Nesvan* 12/3 (May 1932), 97-103; Woodsmall, *Moslem Women,* p. 120.

"Formerly the *sigheh*-marriage was lucrative for the mullahs, for they knew all the available girls and took fees for the introduction as well as for the marriage ceremony,"[109] implying that demand had gone down. The *sigheh* women themselves also had less demand for their business, in particular from their most lucrative clients, rich men.

> Mistresses are now replacing sighehs; they have the disadvantage that they cannot be taken into the man's house, cannot be treated merely as possessions, demand more consideration and are therefore more expensive, but, on the other hand, the man is not responsible for their children. The Moslem wife accepts the European mistress quite calmly, as the husband will probably soon tire of her and is unlikely to marry her, but she dreads the Moslem mistress, who may easily become the next wife.[110]

As a consequence, it would appear that both the clerical middlemen and the women, who facilitated this sexual service on demand, suffered financially. In modern economic terms, they had lost market share. While there are no quantified data, this possible downward trend was not counter-balanced by a new trend of *sigheh*s that came into being, viz. European women. Merritt-Hawkes observed that "A Moslem cannot, at present, contract a permanent marriage with a non-Moslem woman, so he marries a European for the longest possible *sigheh*-marriage, ninety-nine years."[111] There also were European men who concluded temporary marriages with local women, but given the small number of such marriages, its frequency must have been limited.[112]

Under Mohammad Reza Pahlavi temporary marriage was discouraged and was something that was mainly associated with sites

---

109. Merritt-Hawkes, *Persia*, p. 285.

110. Merritt-Hawkes, *Persia*, p. 285.

111. Merritt-Hawkes, *Persia*, p. 285.

112. Arnold T. Wilson, *Southwest-Persia. Letters and Diary of a Young Political Officer 1907-1914* (Oxford, 1941), p. 11.

of pilgrimage (Mashhad, Qom, Karbala). Some young men from wealthy families contracted temporary wives to avoid military service. Information on *sigheh*s was obtained either from a certain type of mullahs or from friends and colleagues in a manner similar to that of obtaining the address of prostitutes, who still constituted the recruiting grounds for *sigheh*s.[113] Socially it was something that men did not want to become known and was frowned upon. In a number of literary works devoted to the subject, temporary marriage was depicted as a wretched business for the *sigheh* (see, for example, the works of Moshfeq-e Kazemi; Sadeq Chubak, Jamalzadeh, Golestan, and Al-e Ahmad), while Ebrahim Golestan in his short story "Esmat's Journey" describes how a vulnerable young woman on a pilgrimage to a holy shrine was taken advantage of by a sayyed and induced to become a member of his stable of women, whom he offered as temporary wives to pilgrims.[114] Just prior to the Islamic Revolution the government tried to make temporary marriage even more restrictive. On January 3, 1976 the Ministry of Justice sent a circular to all notaries public instructing them to refuse registry of a *sigheh*-marriage, if the man concerned could not prove that at the time of the temporary marriage he was not already married.[115] Of course, many temporary marriages were not registered (with all possible legal problems as to the rights of eventual children) and thus evaded official scrutiny.

Shahla Haeri has shown that so far the characterization of the institution of *mut'ah* has been male-oriented resulting in the picture of a *sigheh* solely as that of a votary of pleasure. Haeri's research has shown that, because women like sex as much as men and therefore have the same sexual needs, an indeterminate number of unmarried women seek temporary marriage as a means to obtain sexual satisfaction. It

---

113. Ellen Rydelius, *Pilgrim i Persien* (Stockholm, 1941), pp. 111, 120; Woodsmall, *Moslem Women*, pp. 119-20.

114. Ebrahim Golestan, "Esmat's Journey," translated from Persian by Carter Bryant in Heshmat Moayyad ed. *Stories from Iran: An anthology of Persian short fiction from 1921–1991* (Washington DC: Mage, 2002), pp. 131-35.

115. Echo of Iran, *Iran Almanac 1976*, p. 351.

may be that this form of temporary marriage rather than prostitution is also that which Buckingham referred to when he wrote:

> Shut out from that open intercourse with men, which the females of Europe enjoy, and denied the benefit of education, the only pleasures they know are those of the passions, a love of novelty in suitors for their favours, and a fondness for finery in dress. As, however, they seldom entertain any decided preference for particular individuals, and would find it generally difficult to indulge their choice, all affairs of this nature are conducted by inferior agents, and money is the only standard by which the claims of the solicitors are measured. When the sum is once fixed, the rest is easily accomplished; and whole nights are passed by supposed faithful wives in the arms of others, without their being missed by their husbands since it is not the fashion of the country for married people to share constantly the same bed. Three thousand piastres, or about one hundred and fifty pounds sterling, were currently named as the price of the daughter of the Dufterdar Effendi, one of the Secretaries of State.[116]

Ponafadine and Bricteux mention another variant of this kind of temporary marriage that was initiated by older women (*ya'eseh* or in menopause) rather than by men, the purpose of which was sexual gratification. It is the single instance where women were allowed to take the initiative to get access to men for their sexual gratification. It is also quite clear that this option concerned a small group of women only and then only older women, who could act without a guardian, who had no real covenanted marriage prospects anymore and who had money.

> A contract between a bachelor and women who are deprived of the hope of becoming mothers, *'yaesé—* hopeless. In this case the religious ceremony performed

---

116. Buckingham, *Travels*, vol. 1, pp. 84-85.

by a mullah is unnecessary. A certain formula is simple
repeated by both, naming the sum decided by mutual
consent and the duration of the term of marriage-from
hours or days, to months-upon which they have agreed.
At the end of the term, the couple separate and the
'yaesé' [sic; ya'eseh] is again free to marry in the same
way. Such partnerships are looked upon in being quite
honourable.[117]

Although female sexuality has, of course, been the subject of
scholarly studies, its existence nevertheless is usually ignored in studies
outside the realm of psychology, let alone the published information
available to the general public. Even in so-called women's magazines
this dimension of a woman's life is usually left unspoken. An exception was a translated article that appeared in *Khvandaniha* in 1947
that pointed out, among many other things, and probably shocking
only some of its readers, that women after menopause still have a
sexual appetite.[118] However, the laws and social custom governing
contacts between men and women are still male-centered and entirely
ignore female needs.

Apart from the explicit sexual objective of a *sigheh* marriage other
uses of the institution of temporary marriage existed in Iran, viz., there
is the option of a non-sexual relationship with a woman. This type of
union is known as *sigheh-ye mahramiyat*, which arrangement is used to
make somebody who is normally not among the *maharem*, i.e. those
who can see a woman without a veil, one of the *maharem*. This procedure is used when maids are working in a house where there are non-

---

117. Ponafidine, *Life*, p. 324 (the religious ceremony mentioned in the quote
is not a requirement, as discussed in the beginning of this chapter); see also
Bricteux, *Au Pays*, p. 229. This class of women often 'married' seminary
students. Von Rosen, *Persian Pilgrimage*, pp. 134-35. See also Khomeyni,
Towzih, p. 514 (no. 2333), who states that you should not accept it for the
purpose of marriage, when a woman says that she is *ya'eseh*, but only when
she says that she has no husband.

118. Anonymous, "Zanhara beshanasid," *Khvandaniha* 8/55 (1326/1947),
pp. 18-20.

related males, or, when a frequent male visitor (e.g. a religious elegist or *rowzeh-khvan*) is allowed to see the womenfolk, whom he entertains and/or instructs. This is done to make life easier for everybody, because normally all the women would be without a veil indoors. A man whose wife went on pilgrimage and neither he nor a male relative could accompany her, would divorce his wife. She would become the *sigheh* of what seems to have been a professional *mohallel* or middleman, who would accompany the woman on her pilgrimage. On her return the middleman would divorce her and her ex-husband would marry her again.[119] Or when a woman had to go on a journey with her daughter and no male relative could accompany them. In that case, an unrelated man, probably also a professional, might be employed for the duration of the journey to accompany the women and to that end he contracted a temporary marriage with the daughter, whose mother then became his 'mother-in-law.' A surviving contract detailing such a case bears this out, "complete with names, dates, length of the marriage term, amount of the *mahr*, and on the back the date of termination with the testimony of the husband that the woman was still *ghayr madkhula* (literally 'not penetrated')."[120] These types of arrangements were still regarded as 'risky' by some male members of the family, for sometimes these men abused their status to take advantage of young beautiful girls to whom they now had unhindered and even preferential access. In 1947, there was such a case where the man, a *rowzeh-khvan* or religious elegist, who had thus been included among the 'relatives' took advantage of this situation and of the nine-year old daughter.[121]

More common were the arrangements made to allow women to work in an environment where they would come in regular and daily

119. Anonymous, "Die moderne Perserin," *Das Ausland* 1880, p. 848 [847-49]; Gobineau, *Trois ans*, vol. 2, p. 187; Dr. Saad, La frontiere turco-persane et les pelerins de Kerbela," *Journal asiatique* V (1885), p. 544.

120. Michael M.J. Fischer and Mehdi Abedi, *Debating Muslims. Cultural Dialogues in Postmodernity and Tradition* (Madison, 1990), p. 276.

121. Anonymous, "Sar-anjam-e shigheh-ye mahramiyat," *Khvandaniha* 8/62 (1326/1947), p. 13.

contact with one or more non-related men. Wilson, e.g., reports that "In the rice fields of Mezanderan a man engages as concubines for the season as many women as are required to harvest his crops, abandons them during winter; and the next year contracts with the same or different ones, as the case may be."[122] It is not clear whether these *sigheh*s also were required to have a sexual relationship with their 'husband.' It is unlikely, but not impossible, given the existence of a similar kind of situation in urban areas. Mahdavi in his biography relates that when he came to Tehran as a bachelor and wanted to hire a maid to clean his house he was referred by friends to an 'employment agency' in South Tehran. When he arrived at the 'agency' he was asked to wait for the 'Madam' in a room, where a number of women were sitting, arranged according to age, who were eying him. When Madam finally arrived and he asked for a maid, she told Mahdavi: "to-day it is not the day for maids, to-day is the day for *sigheh*s. If you take a *sigheh* she will be a maid as well." Because Mahdavi was opposed to the institution of temporary marriage he left the 'agency' and did not avail himself of this two-for-the-price-of-one offer.[123] The latter case resembles prostitution, for which temporary marriage is often mistaken.

ISLAMIC REPUBLIC OF IRAN (1979–TO DATE)

With the establishment of the IRI, the new religious leadership tried to improve the social status of temporary marriage, but without much success. Its positive aspects were stressed (divine roots; moral and public health benefits; and at the time of war, social responsibility), in

---

122. S.G. Wilson, *Persian Life and Customs* (New York, 1895), p. 263; see also Lorey and Sladen, *Queer*, p. 132; Ibid., *Moon*, p. 76; d'Allemagne, *Du Khorasan*, vol. 1, p. 214. Haeri also mentions this example, which seem to run counter to her argument that "a temporary's social and legal responsibilities toward her temporary husband are less restrictive than are those of a [permanent] wife." Haeri, *Law*, pp. 59, 88-89.

123. Mo'ezz al-Din Mahdavi, *Dastanha'i az panjah sal* (Tehran, 1348/1969), p. 199. Another case is that of maids who accept to become *sigheh*s, often of a non-sexual nature, and were abandoned by their employer-'husband' when they became too old for work. The time frame of their contract is not known. Wishard, *Twenty Years*, p. 210.

particular during the 1980s with the growing number of war widows due to the high number of men killed. It was and is touted as being the Islamic morally superior answer to satisfy sexual needs in a socially responsible and healthy manner. Men were incited to marry war widows, and war widows were told to marry soldiers, either as legal or temporary wives. Another argument used is that for those who cannot afford covenanted marriage, temporary marriage is the perfect and affordable solution to find sexual relief and avoid committing fornication. Although, the awareness of the institute of temporary marriage was certainly raised, this did not mean that societal reluctance to embrace it as a God-given solution for the relations between the sexes was overcome.[124] Although Iranians still have not embraced the idea in large numbers it would seem that the Iranian government has more success across its borders where in Iraq and Afghanistan the practice seems to attract more interest.[125]

In 2007, temporary marriage was once again launched as solution to some of Iran's societal problems, i.e. the trend towards later marriage, due to the high cost of establishing a family, thus depriving young people of sexual gratification or driving them to fornication. In June of that year, Mostafa Pur-Mohammadi, the minister of the interior, argued that temporary marriage should be promoted to give younger people easier access to lawful sex.[126] It is fairly certain that temporary marriage will continue to play a role in Iran, although

124. Haeri, *Law*, pp. 7-8. This book discusses the situation and different forms of temporary marriage in the Islamic Republic of Iran in detail. Amini, *Entekhab*, pp. 52-55. According to a report in the Village Voice of 28 March 2001, "Children born of temporary marriages face difficulties in getting the identification papers needed for school and work. Without these papers, they are shut off from family inheritance and from government assistance normally available to poor or orphaned kids." [http://www.uri.edu/artsci/wms/hughes/prostitution_holy_men]. If this report is true the described activity clearly is in contradiction of the law.

125. US To-day 5/4/2005 'Pleasure marriages' gain popularity in Iraq again, while they are being introduced into Afghanistan by returning refugees, see: [http://www.bbc.co.uk/persian/iran/story/2006/04/060424_mj-afghan-short-marriage.shtml]

126. Robert Tait in Tehran (Monday, June 4, 2007) [http://www.guardian.co.uk]

maybe not in the manner that the government has advocated. For, contrary to what the government seems to believes, not having a husband is not what drives women to prostitution. This is one of the topics that is addressed in the next chapter.

DISCUSSION

Although much more sociological research will have to be done to adduce additional data about the *modus operandi* and above all the socio-economic origin and status as well as the quantitative aspect of temporary wives, I believe, that the above mentioned facts indicate that these were mainly, if not exclusively, women from the lower classes, forced by economic necessity, to hire out their bodies in a legal way to make a living for themselves and their family. In these cases the borderline between legal *mutʿah* and illegal prostitution is, as Malcolm puts it, "simply a legal quibble."[127] This was also the point of view of the villagers of Davarabad (Khorasan) in the 1950s. Although they made a difference between a *sigheh* and a prostitute, this distinction was a legal rather than a moral one. To them, both kinds of women sold their sexual favors to make a living, and, if they had been good women they would have been *ʿaqdi* wives, they argued. "Thus they are considered 'not bad—but not really good.'" For the same reason those men in the village and adjacent ones who had a *sigheh* did not advertise the fact, but kept it quiet, also not to upset their *ʿaqdi* wife.[128]

Thus, in practice, the legal sheen has not prevented the vast majority of Iranians from considering temporary marriage as a legalized form of prostitution. This view is based on (a) the manner in which *sigheh*s operate, (b) the purpose of the union (sexual gratification), (c) the social standing of *sigheh*s, as well as (d) the fact that religious groups in Iran other than Shiʿites practiced temporary marriage.

---

127. Napier Malcolm, *Five Years in a Persian Town* (London: John Murray, 1905), p. 177; Bassett, *Eastern Mission*, p. 66 ("It is legalized prostitution sanctified by a brief religious rite").

128. Alberts, *Social Structure*, vol. 2, p. 671; see also Borhanian, *Die Gemeinde Hamidieh*, p. 133.

Europeans invariably acted morally superior towards Persians as to the position of women and all other matters, but that was undeserved. Although the Persians wanted to modernize and adopt more ideas and institutions of the European way of life and thinking, they were also aware that European criticism of temporary marriage was somewhat hypocritical and self-serving. Merritt-Hawkes reported the following interesting anecdote about these sentiments. "When a Western newspaper has a big headline, 'Persians purchase wives', Persians reply quite justifiably, 'What about people in glass-houses throwing stones? Don't heiresses ever sell themselves to young lords? We are at least honest about our extra women and you are not. Who is the hypocrite and who's the villain in the play?'[129]

It is not known how many temporary wives were or are purely sex workers, i.e. legalized prostitutes, which question brings out the next point. Did temporary marriage lead to prostitution, or was it an institution that reduced its prevalence? This question is not without merit, since the Shi'ite clergy argues that the institution of temporary marriage is precisely to prevent prostitution.[130]

> The legitimization of temporary marriage in Islam is
> done with the aim of allowing within the sacred law
> possibilities that minimize the evils resulting from
> the passions of men, which if not channeled lawfully
> manifest themselves in much more dangerous ways
> outside the structure of religious law.[131]

---

129. Merritt-Hawkes, *Persia*, p. 285. Wilson also held a more nuanced opinion about temporary marriage: "This Persian system of allowing men to marry, temporarily, a woman who may later be divorced sounds immoral but, human nature being what it is, it is a compromise between the impracticable ideal of celibacy and the undesirable practice of promiscuity." Wilson, *South West Persia*, p. 290

130. Lorey and Sladen, *Queer*, p. 129; Ibid., *Moon*, p. 72; d'Allemagne, *Du Khorasan*, vol. 1, p. 212; Woodsmall, *Moslem Women*, p. 121.

131. 'Allamah Sayyid Muhammad Husayn Tabataba'i, *Shi'ite Islam*, translated by Seyyed Hossein Nasr (Albany, 1975), p. 229; Avazeh, *Qanun-e Qovveh-ye Bah*, pp. 107, 109-110.

It is therefore no surprise to learn that currently members of the government of Iran consider mounting a program aimed at transforming prostitutes into *sigheh*s so as to eradicate the existence of what is considered to be immoral behavior.

Southgate, an American Presbyterian missionary in Iran, also believed that it prevented prostitution. He stated that temporary marriage is "a custom which prevents, in some measure, the great prevalence of a more public and common vice." In actual practice, however, we find no evidence for such a belief, and observe that prostitution was common throughout Iranian history.[132] According to Forbes-Leith, who had lived for many years in Iran and had taken a careful look at the institution, "Such a custom as the segar [sic; *sigheh*] marriage is naturally open to a great deal of abuse, and inasmuch as the public prostitution of women is a sin according to Mohammedan scriptures, 'segarism' is nothing more or less than a form of this vice."[133] According to Woodsmall, 75 percent of the *sigheh*s became prostitutes, a circumstance which, given the manner in which this institution was and is operated, is not surprising, even if this figure is not entirely correct.[134] Like Woodsmall, Merritt-Hawkes and others also noted that "The *sigheh*s are the recruiting ground of the prostitutes."[135] She reported on a young *sigheh* woman about to give birth who was nearing the end of her contract. "With luck she might find another husband, and, without luck-there is only one industry for women in Persia."[136] In the 1890s, an Isfahani *luti*, Rahim Khan, told the court that would sentence him to death, that making girls into *sigheh*s led to

---

132. Southgate, *Narrative*, vol. 2, p. 38. The fact that Imam Reza held that a Moslem should not marry a prostitute, temporary or otherwise has nothing to do with that, because Imam Sadeq was all in favor of it. Avazeh, *Qanun-e Qovveh-ye Bah*, pp. 122-23.

133. Forbes-Leith, *Checkmate*, p. 181.

134. Woodsmall, *Moslem women*, p. 119.

135. Merritt-Hawkes, *Persia*, p. 285; Rydelius, *Pilgrim*, p. 111; Häntzsche, "Haram," p. 432.

136. Merritt-Hawkes, *Persia*, p. 56.

prostitution.[137] It was especially against this form of temporary marriage that the nineteenth century reformer Hajj Sayyah fulminated,
accusing the mullahs, who made a living out of the misery of destitute
women, of immoral behavior.[138] Indeed, when we consider the *sigheh*
who operates as a sex worker then, apart from her legal status, she
does not do anything different from what a prostitute does and did.[139]
However, this begs the question whether it was not having a husband,
or having the wrong one, that drives women to prostitution or is it
something else? That is one of the questions that is addressed in the
next chapter.

---

137. Yaghma'i, *Jandaq*, p. 55.

138. Hajj Sayyah, *Khaterat-e Hajj Sayyah ya Dowreh-ye Khowf va Vahshat*
ed. Hamid Sayyah (Tehran, 1347/1968), p. 164-65. Haeri, *Law*, pp. 88f,
105ff. argues that for many different reasons women may take the initiative
themselves to become a *sigheh*. That may be true, but they seem to be the
exception to the rule, and they are outpaced by the ambivalence, if not negative
notions, that people generally feel towards this institution.

139. Since temporary wives need to make money it is alleged that the
significant rise in abortions in Iran is partly due to the fact that men do not
want children from these unions [http://www.uri.edu/artsci/wms/hughes/
prostitution_holy_men].

CHAPTER THREE

PROSTITUTION: AN EXTRA-MARITAL AFFAIR

PROSTITUTION
AN EXTRA-MARITAL AFFAIR

This chapter discusses the prevalence of female prostitution, its causes, its workers and their *modus operandi*, as well as societal response in both trying to ban and regulate it.

IMPERIAL IRAN

Achaemenid–Parthian–Sasanian Period (559 bce–651 ce)

Prostitution is usually described as providing sexual intercourse in exchange for payment. If this sexual intercourse is between a woman and only one (married) man over an extended period, who, moreover, is her main economic support, then such a woman is usually described as a mistress. This definition clearly displays a male-centered bias, because a critical reader might ask, but what about women, did they not have the need for an extra-marital affair? Of course they did and do, but female prostitution was there to serve male clients. Those women who felt the need to get extra-marital sexual satisfaction had recourse to males (hired or not) and the available information is discussed in chapter one in the section of 'adultery' and 'pre-marital sex.' Married women were engaged in prostitution as well, as discussed in this chapter, and thus also had extra-marital affairs, sort of. There were, however, no brothels that served the sexual needs of women, according to available information.

In adjacent Babylonia and Sumeria, which were part of the Iranian Achaemenid Empire, something known as a holy marriage (*hieros gamos*) existed where each year every woman had to go to the shrine of Militta (Anahita) to have sex with a foreigner, as a sign of hospitality, for a symbolic price.[1] There is no evidence that the same practice existed in Iran proper, despite the fact that the Anahita cult also thrived there. In fact, there is hardly any information available about the prevalence of prostitution under the Achaemenids, Parthians and Sasanids, although it existed.

In the Avesta, the sacred texts of Zoroastrianism, mention is made of a demon referred to as the *jahi*, i.e., the person who does not chant the Gathas, and who is the antagonist to the Zoroastrian religion. The same demon stood as a model for the notion of corruption and immorality. *Jahi* or *jahika* (the second is derogative) is generally rendered into English as 'whore.' But its meaning varies per its context and, therefore, it may refer to a barren and post-menopause woman, as well as one engaged in prostitution and witchcraft.[2] Not only having intercourse with a woman other than one's legal wife, but also even marrying a non-Zoroastrian was and is considered to be prostitution, although some contest this particular exegesis of Vendidad 18.62.

Despite the religious condemnation of the practice, prostitution existed under the Achaemenids. This included the so-called *hetaira*s, who, just like in Greece, entertained all-male banquets with their song, dance, music and conversation, during the Achaemenid period.

---

1. Herodotus, *Histories*, I.199. For a discussion of the institute of the divine prostitute in antiquity see E.M. Yamauchi, "Cultic Prostitution: A Case Study in Cultural Diffusion," in H.A. Hoffner ed. *Orient and Occident* (Kevelaer, 1973), pp. 213-22.

2. Yashts 3.9,12,16; 8.59; Vendidad 18.62; 21.1, 17 for *jahi*, and Yasna 9.32; Yasht 14.51; 17.54, 57.58; Vendidad 18.54; 13.44,48 for *jahika*. For the Yashts and Yasna see James Darmesteter and L.H. Mills in Max Müller ed. *Sacred Books of the East* (New York, 1898), vols. 23 and 31. For the electronic version of the Vendidad see [http://www.avesta.org/vendidad/vd_tc.htm].

These courtesans probably had been bought in the slave markets and were then sent to 'finishing schools' to be trained in the arts of make-up, singing and dancing. These *hetairas* would use their position to capture the heart of a wealthy man so as to move up to the ranks of the concubines, if not that of a wedded wife. The beautiful Aspasia was such a *heatera* who seduced Cyrus the younger (d. 401 BCE). Other girls, who did not make the cut so to speak, probably were put to use in other services, amongst which was prostitution.[3] It was not only slavery that led to prostitution, but also poverty. This was the case, for example, in Babylonia, which was part of the Persian Empire.

> In every village once a year all the girls of marriageable age used to be collected in one place, while the men stood round them in a circle; an auctioneer then called each one in turn to stand up and offered her for sale. ... Marriage was the object of the transaction. The rich men who wanted wives bid against each other for the prettiest girls, while the humbler folk, who had no use for good looks in a wife, were actually paid to take the ugly ones, for when the auctioneer had got through all the pretty girls he would call upon the plainest, or even perhaps a crippled one, to stand up, and then ask who was willing to take the least money to marry her-and she was knocked down to whoever accepted the smallest sum. The money came from the sale of the beauties, who in this way provided to the ugly and misshapen sisters. ... This admirable practice has now fallen into disuse and they have of late years hit upon other scheme, namely the prostitution of all girls of the lower classes to provide some relief from the poverty which followed upon the conquest with its attendant hardship and general ruin.[4]

It may be assumed that the prevalance of prostitution during Parthian times was not dissimilar to that of the preceding period. After all, the Roman-Parthian wars, as well as other military conflicts and

3. Briant, *From Cyrus*, pp. 278-79.
4. Herodotus, *Histories*, I. 196-197.

rebellions, resulted in an enormous number of slaves. The capture of Ctesiphon, for example, was particularly devastating. Septimius Severus gave his soldiers the liberty to plunder the city. According to Cassius Dio, as many as 100,000 women and children were sold into slavery.[5] Clearly these slaves ended up in the Roman Empire, but "the Persians under Chosroes thrice invaded the rest of the Roman territory and razed the cities to the ground. Of the men and women they captured in the cities that they stormed and in the various country districts, some they butchered, others they carried away with them, leaving the land completely uninhabited wherever they happened to swoop."[6] These captives did not end up in Rome, but in Parthia, where slaves were used for all kinds of services. One of the services for females was to become a dancing or music-playing girl for which there was a great demand. Parthian banqueting was always accompanied by music, and the party was ended by dancing, which they loved very much. Although Ammianus Marcellinus, writing in the late fourth century CE, does not mention prostitution, he implies it, when he wrote:

> Most Persians are inordinately addicted to the pleasures
> of sex, and find even a large number of concubines hardly
> enough to satisfy them; they do not practise pederasty.
> A man has many or few wives according to his means,
> and his affections, being divided between a number of
> objects, is lukewarm.[7]

His statement, of course, only applies to the elite, because most men could not afford to have many concubines or wives, and monogamy, given the male-female ratio in the population, must also have been the norm. Whether most Persians had an extra-ordinary sexual appetite is difficult to establish as Marcellinus linked this statement

5. Cassius Dio Cocceianus, *Roman History*, Books 75, 76, 79.

6. Procopius *The Secret Histories*, translated by G.A. Williamson, (Harmondsworth, Penguin, 1981), 18.20-35. See also Ibid. 3.15-31.

7. Ammianus Marcellinus 23.6, translated by J. Rolfe as Ammianus Marcellinus, *History* (Cambridge MA, Harvard University Press, 1963).

to the number of concubines, which may or may not have been employed solely for household activities, for example.

The prevalence of prostitution in Sasanian Iran is also implied by the fact that in the Pahlavi language there was a name for such a woman—*rospig* (prostitute).[8]

ISLAMIC PERIOD

> Narrated by Abu Mas'ud:
>
> *The Prophet prohibited taking the price of a dog, the earnings of a soothsayer and the money earned by prostitution.*[9]

Prostitution, like dogs and soothsayers, continued to be part of life in Iran after the imposition of Islam as the official religion, despite the fact that both social custom and religious precepts saw to it that there were few unmarried men and women, as discussed in chapter one. Adultery existed, which was corroborated by the fact that Islamic law required such incontrovertible proof that it was almost impossible to prove. Young unmarried men engaged in fornication, despite the option of temporary marriage. Prostitutes were known by a variety of names such as *jendeh, fahesheh, qahbeh,* and *ruspigar,* while during the early decades of the twentieth century they were called *zan-e ma'rufeh* (public woman) and later were also referred to as *zan-e valgerd* (street walker).

CALIPHATE UNTIL THE MONGOL PERIOD (653–1258)

'Attar in his *Ilahi-nameh* mentions that there were prostitutes in Mecca and sums up their qualities and depravities as follows:

---

8. Grenet, *La geste*, pp. 70-71.

9. Bukhari, *Sahih*, 63-258.

> There was a prostitute in Mecca whose entire stock in
> trade was vice and depravity. Whenever someone had a
> mind to debauchery that woman would offer herself as
> his partner. She had a melodious voice, was graceful in
> her movements and pleasant of speech; and there was
> never a moment when she was not singing.[10]

From this and the subsequent description, it is clear that singing-girls and prostitutes were basically considered to be one and the same persons. The reference to the prostitute may have been a literary prop to help 'Attar make his point, when eulogizing the prophet Mohammad, who led this poor woman onto the right path, but the fact is that fornication existed in Mecca during Mohammad's lifetime. Not only do the Traditions mention that the prophet banned the practice, but, for example, it is mentioned that Someyya, the grandmother of 'Abbad b. Ziyad, the governor of Seystan in 673, had been a prostitute in Mecca.[11] Also, there were female musicians and singers in Mecca, who performed erotic songs accompanied by lascivious movements, whose experiences allegedly gave rise to the anti-musical sentiment expressed in the Traditions (*hadith*), such as that music leads to debauchery (*al-ghana raqiqah al-zana*).[12] No wonder that in the so-called 'Aqaba agreement of 621, the prophet Mohammad's adherents undertook, amongst other things, to refrain from fornication and lewd behavior.[13]

The wars of conquests, the revolts that followed later, as well as religious uprisings and other events that led to military intervention, resulted in a growing number of slaves. In all of these cases many of

---

10. 'Attar, *Ilahi-nama*, pp. 19-20.

11. Abu'l-'Abbas Ahmad b. Abi Ya'qub al-Ya'qubi, *Kitab al- Buldan* ed. M.J. de Goeje (Leiden, 1892), p. 298, translated by Gaston Wiet as *Les Pays* (Cairo, 1937), p. 119. Anonymous, *Tarikh-e Seystan* ed. Malek al-Sho'ara Bahar (Tehran, 1314/1935), p. 69.

12. P.H. Lammens, *La cité arabe de Taif à la vieille de l'hegiré* (Beyrouth, 1922), p. 268; see also Ibid., *Le Mecque a la vieille de l'hegire* (Beyrouth, 1924), p. 275.

13. Frants Buhl, *Das Leben Muhammads* (Heidelberg, 1961), p. 186.

the men were usually killed, while their wives and children were taken captive and sold at auction.[14] Eventually, some of these women and children were employed in brothels. In 912, a pious Moslem traveler to China described that country's organized system of prostitution and taxation thereof and exclaims that fortunately "God has purified us of such seductions."[15] However, the Persians were very familiar with the nature of this seduction as the *Hudud al-'Alam* (982) refers to the existence of brothels (*rusipi-khaneh*) in India: the fact that they had a word for it implies that they had experience with it.[16] Moreover, the pious Moslem traveler was mistaken, because half a century later the Shi'ite Buyid ruler, 'Azud al-Dowleh (d. 982), established an official brothel (*dar al-qebah*) in Baghdad to (a) improve his revenues and (b) protect his subjects against the unruly passions of his soldiers, who had neither wife nor page with them. He also imposed taxes on prostitutes and dancers and farmed out its collection.[17] 'Azud al-Dowleh allegedly forced the Abbasid princess Jamilah to serve as a prostitute there when she refused to marry him. However, rather than give in to his advances she drowned herself in the Tigris.[18] Elsewhere within the Moslem Empire, similar establishments existed such as in Shush, where the brothels were situated next to the mosque, as well as in Fars, where they were all taxed.[19] The Fatimids, who, like the Buyids, were Shi'ites, followed suit in Egypt and established brothels that

---

14. Nizam al-Mulk, *The Book*, pp. 239-42; Narshakhi, *The History*, pp. 37-38, 49.

15. Mez, *Die Renaissance*, p. 341.

16. Minorsky, *Hudud*, p. 88. A ninth-century Zoroastrian text mentions that a prostitute (*zan-i rospig*) was excluded from *sturih* marriage (see chapter one) and thus the institution was well known in Iran. Gignoux, *Le Livre d'Arda Viraz*, pp. 89 (para 81.3); [http://www.cais-soas.com/CAIS/Law/family_law.htm].

17. Mohammad b. Ahmad al-Biruni, *India*, translated into English by Edward C. Sachau (London, 1888), vol. 2, p. 157; al-Muqadassi, *Kitab ahsan*, p. 44.

18. Mez, *Renaissance*, p. 341.

19. Biruni, *India*, vol. 2, p. 157; Muqadassi, *Kitab ahsan*, pp. 407, 441; Schwarz, *Iran im Mittelalter*, vol. 2, p. 46.

were taxed.[20] The brothels were easily recognizable, because the clients hung their sandals on their doors.[21]

Probably it was during that time, if not earlier, that the *mohtaseb*, whose task it was to supervise standards in the market place, in particular with respect to weights and measures, was made responsible for the regulation of public morals and decorum in the cities. Henceforth, it was the *mohtaseb* who had to ensure that action would be taken against all activities that were contrary to Islamic law, in particular drinking, gambling and prostitution. From the mid-eighteenth century or thereabouts, this task passed from the *mohtaseb* to the *darugheh*, the police chief.[22]

Of course, these 'immoral' activities gave rise to opposition from religious people, who presumably did not frequent such places. In Baghdad, for example, fanatic Hanbalis attacked the houses of the elite, where they beat up the female singers, destroyed their instruments and bashed the wine jars. They banned men going about in streets accompanied by women and boys.[23]

As in pre-Islamic times, covenanted wives were not part of the social scene and the height of a social *faux pas* was to ask the host to call his wedded wife to come and eat with them.[24] Those women who attended otherwise all-male meetings were courtesans, who by their beauty, wit, musical and other qualities were more than welcome at these gatherings. Most of them were slaves, although some were freeborn, but were attracted by the high pay that these women could command. A famous lute player asked two dinars during the day and

---

20. Mez, *Renaissance*, p. 342.

21. Heribert Busse, *Chalif und Grosskönig. Die Buyiden im Iraq (945-1055)* (Beirut, 1969), p. 267, n. 2.

22. For information of this official see Willem Floor, "The office of muhtasib in Iran," *Iranian Studies*, vol. 18 (1985), pp. 53-74.

23. Ibn al-Athir, *Kamil*, vol. 8, p. 230; on this issue see al-Mawardi, *al-Ahkam al-Sultaniyya w'al-Wilayat al-Diniyya* translated into English by Wafaa H. Wahba as *The Ordinances of Government* (Reading, 2006), pp. 270-71.

24. Mez, *Renaissance*, p. 342.

one dinar during the night.[25] The fact that singing girls and musicians were very much sought after by Buyid rulers and officials explains these high fees.[26] This reality may explain a poem by Shahid Balkhi (d. 936 CE), one of the earliest known poets writing in Persian, who, in one poem has a prostitute say:

> If you, Sir, neither have high position nor big business
> Take a sickle and go cut fodder.[27]

Indeed, from this poem it is clear that this class of women was not cheap and you need not inquire after her services, if you did not have the wherewithal in which case you were a hayseed and had better stick to farming. Another of his poems also emphasizes the danger of having your heart ensnared by such women.

> An impure, unclean and Ahriman-like woman
> take heed before you visit this leman,
> for she will inflame you.[28]

The fact that these women were also attractively, if not seductively, dressed, while their use of male gonad-enhancing odors applied to their person added to their allure, immediately put them in a class apart. For the prophet had said: "Any woman who puts perfume and musk upon herself and passes among men so that they will smell her is a fornicator, and every eye that looks on her is a fornicator."[29] This danger was well understood by Abu Hanifah, the great jurist and founder of one of the main Islamic schools of thought (*madhhab*)

---

25. Mez, *Renaissance*, p. 342.

26. J. Christoph Bürgel, *Die Hofkorrespondenz der Adud ad-Daulas* (Wiesbaden, 1965), pp. 10, 19, 46, 77, 103.

27. Gilbert Lazard, *Les premiers poètes persanes* (Paris, 1964), p. 65.

28. Lazard, *Les premiers*, p. 69; see also Ibid., pp. 71-72 for poems by another early Persian poet, Faravali, on the same subject.

29. Meisami, *Sea*, p. 207.

named after him, for he considered "singing and music unlawful, for women listen, disobey their husbands, and temptation arises."[30]

People, of course, did not pay heed to such wisdom and there was a growing trend of loose morals in the Abbasid state that found its expression in the increasing use of coarse and very explicit sexual language in written communications.[31] Allegedly in 933, to stop the rising tide of immoral behavior, the caliph al-Qahir banned the drinking of wine and singing and ordered people to sell their singing slave girls. Prices for the latter dropped precipitously thereafter and the caliph, through intermediaries, bought them for a song, because he loved female singers.[32] Others were more forthright in their condemnation, such as the author of the *Bahr al-Fava'ed*, a twelve-century text of the 'Mirror for Princes' genre, who quoted a Tradition (*hadith*) stating that among the 15 things that were absolutely unlawful were "the hire of female mourners, singers," and likewise "the playing the the drum, harp, or lute.[33] Such condemnation was superfluous because debauchery prevailed. In the royal palaces and houses of the Ghaznavid elite, and in particular in their pleasure houses, where they threw parties, if not had orgies, there were wall paintings showing pornographic pictures. Indeed, Kai Ka'us b. Eskandar, mentions that his father, the Ziyarid king of part of Gilan, had intercourse with Khayzuran, the famous woman lute player, thus underscoring the wisdom of the admonitions not to hire female singers and musicians, which in vain were trumpeted by religious leaders.[34]

The inmates of brothels were mostly those women who had been captured during war or pacification expeditions. They were bought by slave traders (*nakhkhas*), who sold many of them to brothel owners, while there were also slave traders who started their own brothels. Of the latter kind was Ibn Ramin, who was a slave trader in Kufah.

---

30. Meisami, *Sea*, p. 188.

31. Mez, *Die Renaissance*, pp. 334-45.

32. Ibn al-Athir, *Kamil f'il-Tarikh*, vol. 8, p. 204.

33. Meisami, *Sea*, pp. 138-39.

34. Kai Ka'us b. Iskandar, *Qabus Nama*, p. 233, ch. xlii.

He established a tavern with singing girls, who were accomplished in poetry and other arts. His establishment was frequented by many of the leading intellectuals of his time, such as Ibn Moqaffa', and Ibn Ramin made much money.[35] The slave traders not only prostituted their slaves, but also sold any children born to them. However, these pimps did not want their slave-girls to become pregnant as that would mean a loss of income and hence the women were forced to use contraceptives. The jurists, therefore, explicitly condemned the use of such measures (for the purpose of) the prostitution of slaves.[36]

It was not that people were unaware that the jurists, who had developed the body of Islamic law, had condemned prostitution, because it entailed sexual relations outside of marriage. This constituted fornication and adultery and hence a prohibited (*haram*) practice, but men (and some women who chose prostitution as an occupation because they liked it) could not help themselves; human nature was and is stronger than religious tenets. The same religious condemnation held for the service providers (even those who are forced into prostitution), for not only the direct partners involved in the act of fornication were guilty of a crime, but so was the pimp, madam, or owner of the woman, who received the money that she earned through prostitution.[37]

Not only Moslems were liable to punishment, but so were *dhimmi*s, i.e., the adherents of the other monotheistic religions (Christianity, Judaism, and Zoroastrianism), who, in theory, were protected in the exercise of their faith. However, they would lose this protection, if they engaged, *inter alia*, in fornication.[38]

But the flesh is weak and therefore Kai Ka'us b. Eskandar, ever the very practical man of the world, advised his son that: "If you

35. Ravandi, *Tarikh*, vol. 7, p. 473 quoting Ahmad Amin, *Partow-e Islam*, vol. 2, p. 140.

36. Meisami, *Sea*, p. 139 (*qofl bar del va shekam zadan va nakhkhasi-ye gholam va kanizak*)

37. Meisami, *Sea*, p. 138 ("the price of a prostitute is absolutely unlawful"), 139; Bukhari, *Sahih*, 63.258-260.

38. Meisami, *Sea*, p. 128.

commit a forbidden act, let it be with a beautiful partner, so that even though you may be convicted of sin in the next world, you will at any rate not be branded as a fool in this."[39] Fortunately, as decreed in the Koran (24:13), to prove fornication requires the testimony of four male witnesses. As discussed in chapter one, the proof of adultery was very difficult to obtain and in actual practice was hardly ever realized. But, if you were caught, the best way to avoid punishment for fornication was to repent of this criminal act, as this was and is acceptable to the jurists.[40]

For those willing to 'sin' there was plenty of opportunity, for under the Seljuqs, the local governors had established brothels and taverns (*kharabat va khomr-khanha*), where the entire range of lewd and lascivious deeds were performed and enjoyed. Sometimes they even had more than one brothel (*qavvad-khaneh*) in the same town.[41] Other terms used to denote a brothel include youth hostel (*'azab-khaneh*) and hidden house (*khaneh-ye nehani*). The girls in those houses were managed by a woman, who was referred to as the madam, procuress or *lanban*.[42] The pimp, *qaltaban* or *qartaban*, was the madam's opposite, although this term often referred to one who pimped his own wife.

> You won't make money unless you've a penchant for
>   vileness
> The ignorant becomes a beggar because of his baseness
> Vileness and the world are both bad and linked
> The one is a harlot, the other is a pimp[43]

Poets such as Mas'ud Sa'd Salman and Suzani Samarqandi wrote about prostitutes and their environment as part of the social fabric

---

39. Kai Ka'us b. Iskandar, *Qabus Nama*, p. 62, ch. xii.

40. Meisami, *Sea*, p. 184.

41. Mohammad b. 'Ali Ravandi, *Rahat al-Sodur fi Ayat al-Surur* ed. Mojtaba Minovi (London, 1921), p. 30.

42. *Farhang-e Dehkhoda*, q.v. Lanban.

43. Ravandi, *Tarikh*, vol. 7, pp. 485. The poem is by the poet Sana'i.

of society of the eleventh and the twelfth century and confirmed the licentious was a way of life prevailing at that time. Sa'di (1194-1292) in one of his verses in the *Golestan* says:

> Rulers say that four persons fear four other persons
> The criminal fears the king; the thief the watchman
> The fornicator the informer; the harlot the *mohtaseb*.

For it was the inspector of public moral or *mohtaseb*'s task to see to it that prostitution did not occur. However, the reality was that the *mohtaseb* allowed them to remain in business who paid him. In those days, such an official prostitute was known as *zan-e dasturi* or 'a woman with a license'.

> By nature, a woman is respectable and more
> If she is neither then she's a whore.[44]

MONGOL–ILKHANID–TIMURID–TURKMAN PERIOD (1258–1500)

In the period following the Mongol conquest down to the rise of the Safavids, prostitution remained a fact of life. The harsh economic reality, due to the murder of millions of people by the Mongols and thus the destruction of the economic base of the conquered areas, in particular of Iran, combined with the vast number of slaves and the demands that the Mongols made of these slaves, meant that prostitution was one way to gain a honest living. Even after the conquest, the Mongols came down hard on any rebellion or just disobedience of a town or tribe, in which case the men were either killed and their womanfolk were raped, or of the remaining some were enslaved and the rest killed.[45] In one peculiar case, a tribe that had disobeyed orders

---

44. Ravandi, *Tarikh*, vol. 7, pp. 482-83. The poem is by the poet Owhadi.

45. 'Ata Malik Juvaini, *The History of the World Conquerer* translated by John Andrew Boyle 2 vols. (Manchester, 1958), vol. 1, pp. 161-62, 107, 127 ("their small children, the children of the nobles and their womenfolk were reduced to slavery."); vol. 2, pp. 385-86; Rashid al-Din, *Jame' al-Tavarikh* 2 vols ed. Bahman Karimi (Tehran, 1362/1983), vol. 2, p. 973.

had all its girls over seven gathered; the daughters of emirs were raped in public. Of the rest,

> such as were worthy thereof were dispatched to the
> [imperial] harem, while some were given to the keepers
> of cheetahs and others to the various attendents at the
> court, and others again were sent to the brothels and the
> hostels of the envoys to wait upon travelers. As for those
> that still remained it was decreed that all present, whether
> Mongols or Moslems, might carry them off.[46]

This was a standard operating procedure for the Mongols; in case of conquest the choiciest girls went to the ruler, part of which he distributed among his courtiers, then another part went to brothels, and then the army camp got the rest to be divided among them.[47] Slavery was a thriving business that brought much profit to important courtiers as well as merchants. In many towns there were slave markets.[48] The availability of so many girls was too much for some rulers such as Soltan Mohammad, who forgot the state affairs for he was too busy "pulling down the garments of his wives," and spent too much time with his singing-girls such that his vizier considered himself a pimp (*qavvad*) instead of attending to the business of governance (*qovvad*).[49]

Ghazan Khan (r. 1295-1304), the first Mongol ruler of Iran who turned Moslem, banned the presence of prostitutes near mosques, monasteries, and madrasehs and made an effort to reduce the prevalence of fornication by banning the establishment of new brothels. One of the rules that he imposed was that if a slave girl refused to serve in a brothel she could not be sold to it. Those already serving

46. Juvaini, *History*, vol. 1, p. 235.

47. Juvaini, *History*, vol. 1, p. 235; vol. 2, p. 468; Mohammad b. Khavandshah Mir Khvand, *Tarikh-e Rowzat al-Safa* 10 vols. (Tehran, 1339/1960), vol. 4, p. 166 (*ta khedmat vared va sader konand*).

48. Rashid al-Din, *Jame' al-Tavarikh*, vol. 2, p. 1113; Ibid., *Geschichte Ghazan-Khan's*, p. 364.

49. Juvaini, *History*, vol. 2, pp. 379-80.

there and wishing to abandon that life would be bought from their master by the government and taken away from there. To prevent cheating a pricelist was established based on their condition, beauty, and the like.[50] Ghazan Khan apparently wanted to implement the Koranic injunction (24/33):

> But force not your maids to prostitution when they desire chastity, in order that ye may make a gain in the goods of this life. But if anyone compels them, yet, after such compulsion, is Allah, Oft-Forgiving, Most Merciful (to them).

It was a good idea that did not work, of course. Ghazan Khan was not the only one who realized at that time that the women working in brothels were not there because they liked it, but because they had no choice. As quoted above, the poets Sa'di and Baha' al-Din Valad lamented their lot. Baha' al-Din Valad, who, being a Sufi, wanted of course to give his words an existential if not spiritual bent, wrote: "A whore had gone among drunkards as a companion and wept ... It is sad that the happiness of this woman, who has one *man* (about 2.9 kg) of cotton, and sits in the corner with the spindle and in peace desires the tools of other women."[51]

Because Ghazan Khan's ban remained ineffective it had to be revived again by his nephew Soltan Abu Sa'id (r. 1316-1335). One of the alleged positive aspects of the latter's rule was that he apparently had made all his lands free from the sin of brothels (*kharabat*) and taverns (*mastabah*). This in spite of the fact that every day the state had collected a few *tuman*s from the Soltan Suq in Baghdad, the Timancheh in Tabriz, the Long Street in Soltaniyeh, the brothels

---

50. Rashid al-Din, *Jame' al-Tavarikh*, vol. 2, pp. 1113; Ibid., *Geschichte Ghazan-Khan's*, p. 364. He did not ban all brothels because since ancient times these had shown to have some societal benefits.

51. Ravandi, *Tarikh*, p. 481.

(*beyt al-lotf*) of Shiraz, the Bayan Street in Kerman and the brothels in Khvarezm.[52]

However, this ban was mostly wishful thinking as had been the earlier ones, although the Mozaffarids of Shiraz made a short-lived successful effort to put an end to brothels and taverns. Hafez characterized that period as follows:

> I am a drinker of wine, a *rend* and lover of beauties,
> Who is not like me in this city? Show me one.

In the time of Hafez (ca. 1325-1389), Shiraz had many brothels, with both male and female sexworkers; the latter were known as *zan-e dasturi*.[53] These brothels became an object of political discourse and action, when Mobarez al-Din Mohammad, the fundamentalist Mozaffarid opponent of the governor Sheikh Abu Eshaq, who was accused of being a corruptor (*mofsed*) of the people, took the city in November 1352. Mobarez al-Din Mohammad immediately after the conquest of Shiraz took drastic action. Not only did he bring justice to all Moslems, honored the olama and embellished religious buildings, but he also destroyed all brothels (*kharabat*) and wine-houses (*mey-kadeh*s) in the city. Shah Shoja' called his father Mobarez al-Din jokingly the inspector of public morality (*mohtaseb*) and he made reference to the situation and the sobriquet in an appropriate poem.[54]

> Closed are now the taverns throughout the land
> Zither and harp and tambourine are banned
> Banned is wine worship to the libertine
> Only the *mohtaseb* is drunk, though not with wine.[55]

---

52. Samarqandi, *Matla'-ye Sa'deyn*, vol. 1, p. 148.

53. 'Abdol-Hoseyn Zarrinkub, *Az Kucheh-ye Rendan* (Tehran, 1364/1985), p. 85; Ravandi, *Tarikh*, vol. 7, p. 481.

54. Ebn Zarkub, *Shiraznameh* ed. I. Va'ez Javadi (Tehran, 1350/1971), p.122; Mahmud Kotbi, *Tarikh-e Al-e Mozaffar* ed. 'Abdol-Hoseyn Nava'i (Tehran, 1364/1985), pp. 64-65. Later the drinking began again. Ibid,. pp. 111, 113, 132; Samarqandi, *Matla'-ye Sa'deyn*, vol. 1, pp. 293-94.

55. E. G. Browne, *A Literary History of Persia* 4 vols. (Cambridge, 1963), vol. 3, p. 164.

Around the same time, Shams al-Din ʿAli (r. 1347-1353), the ruler of the Shiʿite Sarbadar state in Western Khorasan banned bhang, drinking and prostitution, and to show how serious he was he had 500 prostitutes buried alive. It is not clear how effective this ban was as he fell from power due to its very strict enforcement.[56] Elsewhere in Iran during the subsequent Ilkhanid period prostitution continued to thrive as indicated by the fact that the revenues from the bordellos were considerable, both for the owners of these houses as well as the governors in whose areas they were established. Many of the women serving in them were bought at the slave markts in the urban bazaars.[57] Brothels were so prevalent such that to attract customers prostitutes would spread out into the streets and even would accost passers-by. Around 1360, the olama of Ardabil asked the ruler in a letter to intervene and prevent these women from bothering people in public. In reply the ruler issued the following order:

> The emirs, governors, sayyeds, *qazis*, *motasarrefan*,
> *bitekchiyan* of Ardabil are informed that at this time a
> number of sheikhs, pious men, and literati have come
> here and after having paid their obligatory respects and
> well-wishing they submitted that in the past it was not
> customary that prostitutes (*favahesh*) and evil-doers
> (*monkerat*) were sitting in the streets so that respectable
> people during their walks did not see them. [Now] there
> is a group of people who make their slave-prostitutes sit
> in the streets contrary to custom and the eyes of pious,
> devout and God-fearing men fall upon these impious
> and unlawful persons, which is not in accordance with
> Islamic law.

56. J.M. Smith Jr., *The History of the Sardibar Dynasty, 1336-1381 A.D. and Its Sources* (The Hague/Paris, 1970), p. 133; Ilya Pavlovich Petrushevsky, *Keshavarzi va monasebat-e ʿarzi dar Iran-e ʿahd-e Moghul* 2 vols. translated by K. Keshavarz (Tehran, 1355/1976), pp. 877-80.

57. Rashid al-Din, *Jameʿ al-Tavarikh*, vol. 2, p. 1113; Ibid., *Geschichte Ghazan-Khan's*, p. 364.

The order further noted that there were those who drank wine and became drunk and then bothered respectable people in the ba-zaars. As it would be in accordance with the precepts of Islam and no great loss to the royal treasury, the ruler commanded the *motasarrefan* and *betikchiyan* that, as of the 59th Khani year,[58] the collection of taxes from prostitutes and of the alcohol tax (*tamgha-ye sharab*), which rep-resented an amount of 10,000 dinars annually, had been abolished. If after that date, prostitutes would be seen in the streets, or somebody would be making and selling wine, or would be asking for prostitutes he would be seriously punished and called a sinner and his property would be confiscated.[59]

Immoral activities not only occurred in Ardabil, but also in the neighborhood of the tomb of Sheykh Salah al-Din Musa where peo-ple were selling wine and offered prostitutes in the streets. The pious and faithful who came to pray at the tomb had to see all this, which darkened the purity of their experience. The Soltan therefore ordered the governors and *motasarrefan* to force the sellers of wine and the pimps of prostitutes (*favahesh*) and whores (*qehab*) out of the town and have them take up residence at a certain location, so that those who wanted to have intercourse with these people could go there and the pious and devotees would not bothered by them in their coming and going.[60]

Pious petitioners had drawn the ruler's attention to the fact that prostitutes were driven to their unlawful and illicit activities by pov-erty. The Soltan therefore issued an edict stating that governors and

---

58. The Khani era, established by Ghazan Khan, started with 1 Rajab 701/2 March 1301.

59. Mohammad b. Hendushah Nakhjevani, *Dastur al-katib fi ta'yin al-maratib* 2 vols. in 3 A. A. Ali-zadeh ed. (Moscow, 1964), vol. 2, pp. 289-91.

60. Nakhjevani, *Dastur*, vol. 2, pp. 291-92. There was already a "bad house (*khaneh-ye bad*), i.e. a brothel (*beyt al-favahesh*)" in the days of Sheikh Safi al-Din Ardabili (1252-1334), the founder of the Safavid order, who apparently was not upset about this as it has not been reported that he took action against it. After his death both the brothels and wine taverns continued to operate in Ardabil. Ebn Bazzaz Ardabili, *Safvat al-Safa* ed. Gholam Reza Tabataba'i-Majd (Tabriz, 1373/1994), pp. 807, 1055.

qazis had to examine the situation of these women and if they were Moslems they had to take steps to put a stop to their illicit activities, give them a husband, and if some of them needed to be settled in a place (presumably a place to live) then funds could be drawn from the treasury (*mal-e divan*), which the *motasarrefan* had to execute.[61] Indeed, this was a good idea, but like the earlier plan decreed by Ghazan Khan, nothing came of it as shown by reality on the ground. As so often, rulers and other politicians confuse intent with execution, and therefore, they usually forget to implement programs aimed at helping poor people, because that costs money.

Another problem that contributed to prostitution was the sending of emissaries or *ilchiyan* and their often numerous accompanying suite, who had to be housed, fed and taken care of by the people among whom they stayed or in the hostels for envoys (*ilchi-khanehha*) that dotted the major routes. The services offered to them also included the use of their women as is clear from a story related by a man in the ruler's *divan*.

> I am an old man and I have a young wife. My sons are
> travelling. All of them have left young wives behind
> in my house; I also have daughters. Then emissaries
> (*ilchi*s) came to my house; they were nice and handsome
> young men; they are in my house for a long time and
> saw all these women, who I and my children, who were
> travelling, were not able to satisfy. Because we are with
> these emissaries all in one house I cannot watch them day
> and night and most people are in the same situation. As
> I see it, within a few years in this town you will not find
> one child that is not a bastard, and all of them will be the
> sons of Turks or mongrels.[62]

Under Timur the situation did not change that much. Due to the many conquests he made, his army took captive women to be

---

61. Nakhjevani, *Dastur*, vol. 2, pp. 292-93.

62. Rashid al-Din, *Jame' al-Tavarikh*, vol. 2, p. 1110; Ibid., *Geschichte Ghazan-Khan's*, pp. 358-59.

the sex object of the soldiers.[63] He and his successors also enslaved families of those that he punished and conquered.[64] Timur and his successors, like the Mongols before them, also, in particular, targeted the women of his conquered foes. Timur made the wives and concubines of the captured Ebn Othman the cupbearers at a drinking party for his conquered foe.[65] Timur also made use of "witty singers, aged procuresses and crafty old women, as spies.[66] He furthermore had his palaces embellished with paintings of "his public feasts and the goblets of wine and cup-bearers and the zither-players of his mirth and his love-meetings and the concubines of his majesty and the royal wives."[67] His grandson Shahrokh even went so far as to abase Shadi Molk, the beloved of Soltan Khalil his rival for the throne, whom he prostituted to her own guards.[68]

Under the Timurids, prostitution prevailed as well, while troops after having taken a city, such as Maragheh in 1407, would commit untoward acts with women and children.[69] There was much debauchery and carousing going on, where wine flowed freely and the presence of cup bearers and female dancers/singers/musicians provided a

---

63. Ahmad ibn Arabshah, *Tamerlane or Timur. The Great Amir* translated by J.C. Sanders (London, 1936), pp. 53, 67, 69, 157, 192. For the sale of prisoners at Baghdad, when there were so many that the slave brokers gave "the same price for an 80-year old as for an 8-year old boy," see Samarqandi, *Matla'-ye Sa'deyn*, vol. 1, p. 882.

64. Arabshah, *Tamerlane*, pp. 231, 269. Sometimes, these prisoners were treated in the most degrading manner as happened to the children of the Tabrizis in 1386, who had been made prisoner by a Timurid army, so that even Samarqandi was shocked, when he noted that "it is indescribable and unfit to be written and told." It must have been really revolting as he had no problem describing with some glee the murder of 100,000 Hindu prisoners by Timur. Samarqandi, *Matla'-ye Sa'deyn*, vol. 1, p. 585.

65. Arabshah, *Tamerlane*, p. 188.

66. Arabshah, *Tamerlane*, p. 300. The same was done under the Ghaznavids, see C. E. Bosworth, *The Ghaznavids, Their Empire in Afghanistan and Eastern Iran, 994-1040* (Edinburgh, 1963), p. 96.

67. Arabshah, *Tamerlane*, p. 310.

68. Arabshah, *Tamerlane*, p. 290. Soltan Khalil (r. 1405-1409) was another grandson of Timur.

69. Samarqandi, *Matla'-ye Sa'deyn*, vol. 2, p. 83.

stimulant of another kind. One of Abu Sa'id Mirza's courtiers, Ahmad Hajji Beyg, described one aspect of this life style as follows:

> I'm drunk, *mohtaseb*. Punish me on a day that you find
> me sober.[70]

Under Olugh Beyg (r. 1411-1449) there were singing women who sat among the men who attended the opening of a new bath-house and were singing, which shocked respectable people, who asked that he take action against this immediately.[71]

Although little is known about prostitution during this period, some courtesans became very rich. One of them had good contacts with her colleagues who visited the homes of the notables and gran-dees. Apart from providing their services they also observed the inte-rior arrangements in the homes. This woman collected all that infor-mation from her colleagues and then when invited to a patron's home would astonish him by her ability to tell exactly how the interior of his house looked like, although she had never been there. In this man-ner she was given much money by her admirers and during a ten-year period she amassed much wealth, more than anyone else in Khorasan. Perhaps it was for this reason, and not because she was a courtesan, that Sheybani Khan, the Uzbeg leader, had her killed when he took Qa'en.[72]

Prostitution continued to be taxed under the Timurids and their successors. An inscription in Shiraz dated around 1450 mentions sev-eral taxes that were levied in that city, which included taxes on broth-els, wine-shops, opium dens and gambling houses.[73] Likewise under Uzun Hasan (r. 1467-1478), the Aq-Qoyunlu ruler of Western Iran, there was religious pressure to ban brothels and other dens of iniquity,

70. Babur, *Babur-Nama*, p. 38. The *mohtaseb* is the officer in charge of public morals in a city.

71. Ghiyath al-Din Khvandamir, *Tarikh-e Habib al-Siyar* 4 vols. ed. Mohammad Dabir-Siyaqi (Tehran, 1362/1983), vol. 4, p. 35.

72. Zeyn al-Din Mahmud Vasefi, *Badaye' al-Vaqaye'*, 2 vols. ed. Aleksandar Baldruf (Tehran, 1350/1971), vol. 2, p. 396.

73. John Limbert, *Shiraz in the Age of Hafez* (Seattle, 2004), p. 72.

(that paid taxes), to which he positively reacted. The edict that he issued, dated 1470-71, was chiseled in stone and erected at mosques, such as at the Friday Mosque of Yazd.[74] It is doubtful that this ban was ever implemented, because Uzun Hasan had good relations with prostitutes and he needed their tax money; moreover, he died shortly thereafter. At other times, such as in 1447, he had a better use for prostitutes. In that year, a battle had taken place between Uzun Hasan Aq-Qoyunlu and the troops of Jahanshah Qara-Qoyunlu, which the latter lost. The men of Diyarbekr, who were part of Jahanshah's army, had lost their turbans in battle and these were picked up by the men of Uzun Hasan. Then they gave these to the prostitutes, who put these turbans on their head to mock the vanquished.[75] From the fact that drinking and untoward sexual activities took place at Soltan Ya'qub's court (r. 1478-90), it is highly unlikely that the ban was still in effect.[76]

SAFAVID PERIOD (1501-1736)

WHO WERE THE PROSTITUTES?

According to Olearius, the prevalence of prostitution was due to the Persians' nature. "In lustfullness and lack of chastity the Persians are second to no other nation, for aside from taking many wives they are much given to whoring."[77] In short, the Persians could not help themselves. However, this statement only concerns the demand side, for 'the Persians' refers to males. What about the females? Du Mans ascribes the prevalence of prostitution to the high divorce rate; men forced their wives to ask for a divorce so that they do not have to

74. Modarresi Tabataba'i, *Farmanha-ye Torkmanan-e Qara-Qoyunlu va Aq-Qoyunlu* (Qom, 1352/1973), p. 76; V. Minorsky, "The Aq-Qoyunlu and Land Reforms," *Bulletin of the School of Oriental and African Studies* 17/3 (1955), p. 450.

75. Rumlu, *Ahsan al-Tavarikh*, p. 277. For a similar use of prostitutes by Shah 'Abbas I see below.

76. Sam Mirza, *Tadhkereh-ye Tohfat-e Sami* ed. Rokn al-Din Homayunfarrokh (Tehran, n.d.), p. 176 (see also chapter four).

77. Olearius, *Vermehrte*, p. 592.

pay the dowry. This left such women with no source of income and obliged them to sell their bodies in the official brothels, where the youth of Isfahan lost their innocence.[78] Chardin confirms the reason for women asking for a divorce, although he estimates that the divorce rate was not that high, in fact divorce was rather uncommon.[79] Indeed, it would seem that Du Mans is right, irrespective of whether he is right concerning the level of the divorce rate which may only refer to the situation in Isfahan, for it was either economic necessity or forced labor that drove women to sell their bodies to lustful males. For most of the women working as prostitutes did so because they had no choice, not because they liked it. If they were not destitute divorcees, they were slaves, whose masters had turned many of them into sex workers. The frequent Safavid campaigns in the Caucasus resulted in the enslavement of many Caucasian women (Georgian, Armenian, Circassian), who in particular were sought after for this profession, which they also seemed to have dominated.[80] The Portuguese friar Dos Anjos reports the purchase of Armenian women, captured during 'Abbas I's campaign in Armenia in 1604, to be put to work in brothels. Although 'Abbas I intervened so that these particular Armenian girls were not sold to the brothels, this must have been an exception.[81] Shah Safi I was wont to transfer womenfolk of some of the groups that he conquered to the brothels.[82] That prostitutes mostly were slaves may also be deduced from an observation made by Fryer, viz., "if a Curtezan conceive, and it proves a Girl, she

78. Richard, *Raphael du Mans*, vol. 2, pp. 371-75.

79. Chardin, *Voyages*, vol. 2, p. 241.

80. de Silva y Figueroa, *Comentarios*, vol. 2, p. 233, 235; Arak 'el of Tabriz, *The History of Vardapet Arak'el of Tabriz* 2 vols. translated into English by George A. Bournoutian (Costa Mesa, 2005), vol. 1, pp. 27, 40, 52, 56, 58, 64, 78, 220; Abu'l-Qasem Hoseyn b. Mohammad Raghib Esfahani, *Navader - Mohazarat al-Odaba va Mohavarat al-Sho'ara va'l-Bolagha*; translated into Persian by Mohammad Saleh b. Mohammad Baqer Qazvini edited by Ahmad Mojahed (Tehran, 1372/1993), p. 58 wrote that "Islam was Arab, but now it is non-Arab (*'ajam*) due to the influx of Georgians and Turks."

81. Roberto Gulbenkian, *L'ambassade en Perse de Luis Pereira de Lacerda* (Lisbon, 1972), pp. 100-01; Chardin, *Voyages*, vol. 7, p. 414.

82. Olearius, *Vermehrte*, p. 661.

is registered by her Mothers Profession."[83] This conclusion is further borne out by the fact that these children could not inherit from their biological fathers. If the woman had been a freewoman her children automatically would also have been free and could not be assigned to what is an unlawful occupation. However, if the woman was a slave then legally all her children belong to her owner and she had to earn her living. Women were also led astray by procuresses. According to a story told by Ragheb Esfahani, in old age, a prostitute repented of her way of life and then started to sell female accoutrements. In this way she gained access to people's homes and she "corrupted most of the daughters and women of Moslems."[84]

In which Towns Did Prostitutes Work?

Despite the ban of 1471, European travelers are unanimous in their observations that prostitution was very widespread in Safavid Iran in the first decade of the sixteenth century, which implies that the ban was not really effective. Don Juan, a Shi'ite Moslem who had converted to Catholicism when he went to Spain in 1602, takes exception, for he writes that

> In Persia, unlike other countries among the Mahomedan
> nations, there is never seen any great number of public
> women. The gypsies, or Egyptians, however, who live in
> the provinces of the frontier that neighbors Persia, enter
> our country in bands and troops and they bring in their
> families with them; and among them these their women
> make a livelihood by prostitution. ... I myself at one
> time took occasion to enquire of the Egyptian folk who
> inhabit the country where these public women come
> from, and they told me that no man there would marry

---

83. John Fryer, *A New Account of East India and Persia Being Nine Years' Travels, 1672-1681*, 3 vols. (London, 1909-15), vol. 3, p. 130.

84. Raghib Esfahani, *Navader*, p. 326. Della Valle, *Voyages*, vol. 3, p. 105, also mentions that Persian men did not want influential courtesans such as Dallaleh Chizi to visit their womenfolk at home, because "they were not so certain about their wives's chastity. "

a girl unless she would promise and undertake to feed and clothe her future husband with gains made in this abominable commerce.[85]

Don Juan clearly still had stong and positive feelings for his homeland, but he was in total denial of the reality of prostitution in Iran. He is correct that the *kowlis* or gypsies indeed were present in Iran and Chardin, for example, estimated that in Isfahan there were about one thousand men and women. They went about in rags and lived in a state of squalor, sloth and sexual promiscuity and the term *kowli*, Chardin maintains, therefore was synonymous with a despicable, incestuous person.[86] However, as in later centuries, the gypsies were not the problem, for they were only a very small group that stood out because of their peculiar bohemian habits. Moreover, they also operated in the rural areas providing many services to all and sundry, who were willing to pay for them.

The bulk of the prostitute population was not supplied by gypsies, but by the urban population or rural immigrants, in both cases slaves and free women. It was a phenomenon that from the very beginning of the Safavid state's establishment, prostitution continued to exist and thrive. Indeed it would appear that prostitution occurred everywhere in Safavid Iran and throughout the entire reign of the Safavid dynasty, despite the occasional bans. An anonymous Venetian traveling in Iran in 1514 states that after the conquest of Tabriz, Shah Esma'il I had 200 to 300 harlots killed.[87] However, many others stayed in business, for the same merchants writes: "Also the harlots, who frequent the public places, are bound to pay, according to their beauty, as the prettier they are the more they have to pay ... All the money they collect

---

85. Don Juan of Persia, *A Shi'ah Catholic* translated into English by Guy Le Strange (New York-London, 1926), p. 57.

86. Chardin, *Voyages*, vol. 7, pp. 478-80.

87. Josef Barbaro et al., *Travels to Tana and Persia by Josef Barbaro and Ambrogio Contarini* 2 vols. translated into English by Lord Stanley (London, 1873), vol. 2, pp. 52, 191.

is for the private advantage of the revenue-farmers."[88] Whatever moral compunction Shah Esma'il I may have had against prostitution, it certainly did not prevent him from farming out the revenues of the brothels, keeping dancing girls as well as working his wicked will on the most beautiful youths of Tabriz.[89] Again, there were many prostitutes in Herat, the old Timurid capital. The Uzbeks in 1532, when laying siege to the town, allowed the people to depart, but not before they were relieved of their valuables. Qomi writes that he abhorred the fact that the Uzbegs used prostitutes (*fahesheh*) to check respectable women to look for jewellery and other costly items, even going so far as searching their underwear.[90]

Fr. du Iarric wrote that the Hormuzians were a voluptuous people, who liked music and dressed pompously. Both men and women used much make-up,[91] jewelry and trinkets. The use of perfumes was widespread among the city's population. Sellers of aromatic liquids and perfumes were found in the streets and bazaars as well as perfume shops, while the rich were trailed by a small slave who carried a perfume bottle.[92] Voluptuous they were indeed, for morals were tolerant.

---

88. Barbaro, *Travels*, vol. 2, p. 172.

89. Barbaro, *Travels*, vol. 2, pp. 202, 207.

90. Qomi, *Kholasat*, vol. 1, pp. 220, 177.

91. P. Pierre du Iarric Tolosain, *L'histoire des choses plus memorables advenues tant ez Indes Orientales, qu'autres pais de la descouverte des Portugais* 2 vols. (Bovrdeavs, 1610-14), p. 363; Damião de Góis, *Crónica de felicissimo rei D. Manuel.* 4 vols. (Coimbre, 1949-55), II/32, p. 108; António Tenreiro, *Itinerários da India a Portugal por terra.* António Baião ed. (Coimbra, 1923), p. 5. On what constituted make-up at that time see Fatema Soudavar-Farmanfarmaian, "Haft Qalam Arayish: Cosmetics in the Iranian World," *Iranian Studies* 33/3-4 (2000), pp. 285-326.

92. N. Orta de Rebelo, *Un voyageur portugais en Perse au début du XVII siècle* ed. J. Verissimo Serrão (Lisbon, 1972), p. 96; Duarte Barbosa, *The Book of Duarte Barbosa* translated by M. Longworth Dames, 2 vols. (London, 1918-21), vol. 1, pp. 91, 96; Correia, *Lendas da India*, vol. I, p. 185; Tomé Pires, *The Suma Oriental of Tomé Pires, an account of the East, from the Red Sea to Japan, written in Malacca and India in 1511-1515* translated and edited by Armando Cortesão 2 vols. (London, 1944), vol. 1, p. 23 (this was also common in Persia). For a contemporary picture see P. Schurhammer, *Gesammelte Studien* II, Orientalia (Rome, 1963), p. 115.

Prostitution, both male and female, thrived in Hormuz, which was only to be expected in a cosmopolitan sea port. A Jesuit wrote that to pay five *deniers* for a virgin was considered to be expensive.[93] When the commercial function of Hormuz passed to Bandar 'Abbas after 1622, officially licensed brothels were to be fond everywhere in that port as well.[94] Lockyer wrote that the *kutval* or police chief, "makes a profitable farm of whores."[95]

In Qandahar, in 1622, von Poser observed the presence of brazen and lewd prostitutes.[96] According to the Dutch ambassador Jan Smidt, writing in 1629, "Common women here [in Shiraz] have a great deal of freedom and are much inclined to unchaste behavior."[97] To some extent, it would seem that this held for Zoroastrian girls as it is told that a learned man in Yazd had relations with Zoroastrians girls, whom he led astray. The relationship with Zoroastrian girls probably was brought about by the fact that Moslems in Yazd, in need wine, had to go to the quarter of the Zoroastrians, who were the only one in the city allowed to make wine. And, as it has been seen on other occasions and times, and as the jurists have pointed out, wine drinking and untoward behavior go together.[98] If there is still somebody who doubts whether there were prosititutes in Safavid Iran, they have not read Olearius, who, reporting in 1637, wrote that all towns of Iran

---

93. Wicki, *Documenta Indica*, vol. 4, p. 202 (He also wrote that men were avidly sought after by these women).

94. Herbert, *Travels*, p. 47.

95. Charles Lockyer, *An Account of British Trade in India* (London, 1711), p. 239.

96. von Poser, *Als Schlesischer Adliger*, p. 46 (Qandahar was still in Moghul hands at the time of his visit, for it was only a few months later that Shah 'Abbas I would conquer the city. However, it is unlikely that this aspect of the city would have changed, given that the shah and his troops were welcomed into the city by the prostitutes orchestrated by the shah himself).

97. Dunlop, *Bronnen*, p. 736.

98. Mohammad Mofid Mostowfi-ye Bafqi, *Jame'-ye Mofidi*. 3 vols. ed. Iraj Afshar (Tehran 1340/1961), vol. 2, pp. 344-45; Mir Mohammad Sa'id Moshiri Bardsiri. *Tadhkereh-ye Safavi*, ed. Ebrahim Bastani Parizi (Tehran, 1369/1990), p. 448. Those who bought wine in that quarter, when returning, hid the jar[s] under their cloak.

had brothels, which were protected by the authorities (with the exception of Ardabil, where 'Abbas I had recently banned them).[99]

The largest concentration of prostitution in Iran at that time was
in the capital city of Isfahan. According to an anonymous Dutch
author, writing in the 1630s, there were more than 12,000 public
women in Isfahan, who had to pay monthly a considerable sum, pro
rato their beauty and how often their services were asked for.[100] The
same figure is later mentioned by Chardin, but he also mentions that
this number does not include those who provided more private and
expensive services, a group that he estimated at some 1,500 persons.[101]
At another instance, Chardin writes that there were 14,000 prostitutes in Isfahan in 1666, who were registered in a special office, which
is the figure that is also given by Du Mans. However, Chardin adds
that he was told that there were probably as many prostitutes in Isfahan, who were not registered. This happened with the connivance of
the relevant authorities who lined their own pockets with the pay-off
that these women gave them, which was higher than the official fee.[102]
This then explains the much higher number given by Fryer, according to whom the number of prostitutes in Isfahan was 30,000, which
otherwise seems a little on the high side compared to other data.[103]
Given the fact that Isfahan was the largest city of Safavid Iran, with
possibly 500,000 inhabitants, it is not surprising that it had the largest
number of prostitutes. This is reflected in the revenues they yielded,
for Isfahan accounted for two-fifth's of the total of the taxes of trades
of ill-repute.[104]

99. Olearius, *Vermehrte*, p. 592.

100. L. Leupe ed., "Beschrijvinge," p. 205.

101. Chardin, *Voyages*, vol. 7, p. 417; vol. 5, p. 371.

102. Chardin, *Voyages*, vol. 2, pp. 211-16; vol. 5, p. 371; Richard, *Raphael du Mans*, vol. 2, pp. 373-74; Bembo, *The Travels*, p. 353 (12,000 who pay taxes plus "as large a number of unofficial courtesans who pay no tax.").

103. Fryer, *A New Account*, vol. 3, p. 129.

104. Chardin, *Voyages*, vol. 2, p. 211. On the population of Isfahan see Willem Floor, *The Economy of Safavid Persia* (Wiesbaden, 2000), p. 3.

Prostitution was not limited to large urban areas, but even occured in large villages and caravanserais. The role of the *kowli*s, mentioned above, should not be forgotten in this connection, since they were a nomadic group that moved from village to village. In 1685, Kaempfer mentions that in Sabeshah, south of Jahrom, a prostitute plied her trade in a caravanserai.[105] Likewise, the manager of the caravanserai of the village of Myrgascun, which was half a *farsakh* from Persepolis, was an old ugly prostitute, who offered her services to the passing travelers.[106] The small town of Jahrom had a miserable bazaar, and a large caravanserai Shah Hoseyn, in which the prostitutes seemed to be in charge.[107] Finally, not only married women joined their husbands when the army marched, for non-married ones also followed the army to offer their services to soldiers and other males.[108]

THE WAGES OF SIN

Prices varied; Fryer claims that there were "costly whores in this city who will demand an hundred thomands for one nights dalliance, and besides, expect a treat of half the price."[109] According to Chardin, courtesans were often referred to by their price, for example, the 'two-*tuman*' or the 'five-*tuman*' girl.[110] He further mentions the famous case of a house known as the 'twelve-*tuman* house', in remembrance of the courtisan who had lived there and whose artistic name was 'twelve-*tuman*', because that was the price she charged for the first visit to her house, which was luxuriously laid out and decorated and

105. Karl Meier-Lemgo ed., *Die Reisetagebücher Engelbert Kaempfers* (Wiesbaden, 1968), p. 114.

106. Meier-Lemgo, *Reisetagebücher*, p. 96.

107. VOC 1157, f. 359-85, "Dagh Register gehouden bij den oppercoopman Leonard Winninx 'tsindert den 6 Julij anno 1645 dat uijt Gamron naer Spahan vertreckt, tot den 24e November, daeraen volgende, als wanneer in gemelte Gamron wederom gearriveert is.", entry on July 18 (Sjaron; sic, = Jahrom).

108. De Silva y Figueroa, *Comentarios*, vol. 2, pp. 335, 345; della Valle, *Voyages*, vol. 2, pp. 127, 348, 617; Olearius, *Vermehrte*, p. 592.

109. Fryer, *A New Account*, vol. 3, p. 130.

110. Chardin, *Voyages*, vol. 2, p. 211.

painted in azure and gold colors.[111] Chardin reports that indeed, the dancing courtesans in Isfahan sometimes asked 15 to 20 *pistoles*, or 3 to 4 *tuman*s, although elsewhere he writes that they charged 10 *pistoles*, or 2 *tuman*s, but never less than one *tuman*.[112] Thevenot reports that a courtesan had danced so well that 'Abbas II, who was drunk, gave her a caravanserai in recompense for her services, which building yielded considerable revenues in rents. The next day the grand vizier counseled the shah to cancel the gift and instead give her 100 *tuman*s. She at first insisted upon her right to the gift, but finally gave in when told that otherwise she would get nothing.[113]

These prices were, of course, exorbitant as salaries were not that high. From the data it is clear that these rates only applied to high class prostitutes or courtesans. The average salary of a Qezelbash officer was just 6 *tuman*s per year[114] and thus, only the highest officials of state could have afforded their services, which means that the number of these high-cost courtesans must have been limited. Chardin relates an interesting story that highlights this:

> A governor of a district in Gilan was totally enamored of a dancing girl, whom he had seen dancing, that, in accordance with custom, he sent her the next day [a present, consisting of] two horses and five *écus* [or one-third of a *tuman*] and asked her to come to his house. For him this was a considerable sum, but the girl replied that she would only come to his house if he paid 30 *écus*. He then sent 10, 15 and 30 *écus*, but she refused to come. Finally, totally frustrated he sent her 10 *pistoles*, telling his friends he would teach her a lesson. The girl finally came and the governor asked if she had received the money. 'Yes,' she said. 'I have

---

111. Chardin, *Voyages*, vol. 7, pp. 410-11.

112. Chardin, *Voyages*, vol. 5, p. 371; vol. 2, pp. 211-12; vol. 9, p. 211.

113. Monsieur de Thevenot, *The Travels of [...] into the Levant into three parts* (London, 1686 [Westmead, 1971]), part. 2, p. 100.

114. For the wages of the military class see Willem Floor, *Safavid Government Institutions* (Costa Mesa, 2001), pp. 154-55, 175, 187; for wages of the lower classes see Ibid., *Economy*, pp. 6-7.

given it to my servants, because I do not sell myself that cheaply.' I have only come out of consideration for you. The governor nevertheless wanted that she dance and sing for his friends; he kept her till mid-night without giving her food or drinks. He then took her to a room where he and his friends had their way with her, one after the other until the morning. In the morning she thought that she would finally be allowed to depart, but the governor gathered all his staff in a room, from the steward to the groom, brought the girl and said to her: 'My beauty, I am only a minor governor, who cannot afford to pay 10 *pistoles* for one night; my people are part of the expense, but therefore they also will have to be part of the pleasure.' They kept her the entire following day and night. She made a lot of noise about this treatment, and it looked as if the governor would be in trouble. Because he saw that the tide was against him, he told the affair the king, in a burlesque manner, who took care of the matter with a second payment of 10 *pistoles* that he had to give, because he had kept the courtesan two in stead of one night.[115]

Some officials indeed spent much of their time drinking and frolicking with prostitutes such as Khvajeh Mohammad Saleh Betekchi Astarabadi, who was a rich man.[116] In fact, men made entire fools of themselves over this or the other beautiful woman and many a nobleman ruined himself because of this. Don Juan related that

> A Persian youth who wishes to pose as a faithful lover ... must painfully burn himself in various parts of his person with a slow match made of linen stuff, that in effect acts like the caustic which, with us in Spain, the surgeons apply for opening issues such as may be needful in the

---

115. Chardin, *Voyages*, vol. 2, pp. 214-15.

116. Qazi Ahmad ibn Sharaf al-Din al-Hoseyn al-Hoseyni al-Qomi, *Kholasat al-Tavarikh*, 2 vols., ed. Ehsan Eshraqi. (Tehran, 1363/1984), vol. 1, p. 283. For another example, in this case the vizier of Yazd, see Bardsiri, *Tadhkereh*, p. 448.

legs and arms. Then the lover displays himself in the sight
of the lady, he being a very Lazarus for the number of
his sores: whereupon she will send him cloths, napkins
and bandages of silk or holland, with which to bind his
wounds, and these he wears until they are cured. Later, he
can show most signs of these cauteries is [sic; to] the one
most beloved of the fair dames, and he most promptly
will come to matrimony.[117]

Some 70 years later, Chardin knew men of probity and good sense
who had totally lost their head over such women. They gave as their
excuse that they were bewitched and believed that if they really wanted to break off the relationship that they could. These slaves of love,
as they were known, could be recognized by the burns on their body,
in particular on their arms. They made these burns with a red hot iron
and pressed so hard that it gave a burn the size of a piece of 30 *sols* (ca.
2 cm). They did this when they were totally impassioned to show their
mistress that the fire of their love rendered them insensitive to fire.
The more burns a man had the more passionate he was. There were
men who made them over their entire body, in particular at the level
of the kidneys.[118] Gemelli-Careri some twenty years later observed
the same custom, but in his case the amorous object were *sigheh*s or
temporary wives (see chapter two).[119]

---

117. Don Juan of Persia, *A Shi'ah Catholic 1560-1604* translated by G. Le
Strange (New York-London, 1926), pp. 54-55. These damsels were not, of
course, women with whom these young men contracted a covenanted marriage,
but at best a temporary marriage, if they bothered at all with such formalities.

118. Chardin, *Voyages*, vol. 2, pp. 212-13; likewise della Valle, *Voyages*, vol. 2,
p. 334 and Bembo, *The Travels*, p. 301. Even princes applied these love burns,
such as in the case of 'Omar Sheikh Mirza, Babur's father, of whom his son said
that "he bore many a lover's mark." Babur, *Babur-nama*, p. 16.

119. Gemelli, *Giro*, vol. 2, p. 182. For pictures showing this kind of scarification
as well as the implements to make such burns (pl. 16 ; left hand) see Anthony
Welch, "Worldly and Otherwordly Love in Safavi Painting," in Robert Hillenbrand
ed. *Persian Painting From the Mongols to the Qajars* (London, 2000), plates
16-18. It is doubtful whether the origin of this type of scarification was religious
in nature as suggested by Welch as tattooing for non-religious purposes was
widely practiced in Iran, see Willem Floor, "Tattooing" *Encyclopedia Iranica*.

There were several other ways to shows one's passion. In Hamadan, in the same year of 1608, a prostitute repented her ways and became the wife of 'Abdali, a herbalist. The woman's lovers were so upset that in one night they cut all the trees in 'Abdali's garden, and did in one night the work requiring 50 people and two weeks! Later they broke into 'Abdali's shop and broke all his jars and shelves and mixed all his herbs and liquids. Then during another night they dug up his father's corpse from the cemetery and burnt it in the square of Hamadan. Because 'Abdali and his wife were both good-looking and sweet-voiced they made a song about it, which attracted the royal court's attention and the shah bade them to come to Isfahan, recompensed them and punished the perpetrators of these evil deeds.[120] Passions could indeed run high when several suitors loved the same woman. In this case, in 1676, Kohneh-Qadam was the woman, the enamored man was Mansur Beyg, the vizier of Yazd, who was always deeply immersed in wine and prostitutes, and the rival was his own brother Rafi'a. The latter took the lady to a friend's house opposite the mosque to spend the evening and Mansur Beyg learning of this, instructed his men to lie in wait and when Kohneh-Qadam would leave the house to grab her and immediately take her to him.[121] A similar case was that of the courtier Nasr 'Ali Beyg who had so much fallen in love with one of the Shah Soleyman's most favorite dancing girls that he had been able to entice her to stay at his house for eight days rather than perform at the royal palace. When the shah asked her why she had not shown up, she replied that she had been indisposed. The shah said that she looked quite healthy to him, which was due to wine that she had drunk, she told him. The shah then asked where had she drunk the wine? She then caved in and told the shah that she had been with his courtier. The shah became furious that Nasr 'Ali Beyg had had the nerve to enjoy himself with his dancing girl and then decided that, in return, he would have his fun with the wives of the courtier. He immediately ordered his men to seize Nasr 'Ali Beyg's wives, concubines and slave girls and take them to one of the city's brothels. His wives and

120. Monajjem, *Ruznameh*, p. 345.
121. Bardsiri, *Tadhkereh*, pp. 448-51.

slave girls were immediately put backwards on donkeys, unveiled and bared-headed, and taken to the brothel. Because the shah had arisen early the next morning people interceded with him, arguing that the wives and slave girls were innocent, so beautiful and accomplished. These arguments made the shah change his mind who then decided to add them all to his own harem.[122]

It was not everybody who could afford to loose his head, the majority of the clients were interested in a quick visit. This meant that the majority of prostitutes neither charged nor received such high rates, otherwise their fiscal revenues would also have been much larger. The common run-of-the mill prostitute, who served everybody, worked in a brothel, from home or plied her wares in the streets for a modest payment. Whatever the price level, it is clear from the large numbers of sex workers that there was a great demand for their services and that they did not lack for clients.[123]

WAS THERE A RED LIGHT DISTRICT?

Yes, indeed. While women walked the streets and did anything in between to attract customers, in Isfahan there was a red light district. According to Gemelli-Careri, you had "the quarter of the Cacpe [sic; *qahbeh*] or prostitutes, who are known in Isfahan as Bazarnouche and who pay taxes to the shah."[124] Chardin provides more information; he relates that the *Madraseh-ye Safaviyeh* was situated at the entrance of the red light district of Isfahan. The district itself consisted of three streets and seven large caravanserais, which were known as the caravanserais "of the uncovered or unveiled ones, because that is the Persian name for prostitutes." Respectable people neither wanted to live there, because of its reputation, nor to pass through it, because they

122. Chardin, *Voyages*, vol. 9, pp. 210-13; on pp. 111-12 the same story with a different ending.

123. Strauszen, *Sehr Schwere*, p. 172 and Mohammad Taher Vahid Qazvini, *Tarikh-e Jahanara-ye 'Abbasi* ed. Sayyed Sa'id Mir Mohammad Sadeq (Tehran, 1383/2004), p. 415 state that the price was small.

124. Gemelli, *Giro*, vol. 2, pp. 181-82.

did not like to hear the cat-calls that the prostitutes made at those who refused to come into their dens.[125] Some of the houses where high-class prostitutes lived and worked were quite beautiful, according to Chardin. This is clear from his description of some of these houses where, in each one, some six Georgian slave girls were kept, who were prostituted by their Madam.[126] Those prostitutes not working in the red light district rented rooms, in such places as in the Meydan-e Bozorg, where its upper galleries were rented to travelers and other foreigners.[127] Unregistered prostitutes worked from home.[128]

In Ardabil, prostitutes were active in a caravanserai in the Ur-sumi Mahalleh. The women, according to Struys, some were quite accomplished in reciting poetry, odes to Imam 'Ali and the Shah, while others would dance naked before the governor of the city. "They are utterly shameless and they allow [men] to kiss their breasts and what I cannot say, fondle and caress them, even in the public streets. Young men do not consider this work of Venus bad or dishonorable, and they are not even punished."[129]

Less fortunate females had to make do with more modest surroundings. In 1656, the quarter of the prostitutes in Bandar 'Abbas, its red light district, was very simple. They all lived in "huts made of thatch of date tree branches with square openings in the 'walls' to get some wind into the hut."[130]

125. Chardin, *Voyages*, vol. 7, pp. 416-17; vol. 2, p. 215.

126. Chardin, *Voyages*, vol. 7, pp. 413-14.

127. Kaempfer, *Am Hofe*, pp. 95, 156; Tavernier, *Voyages*, p. 37; see also Mohammad Taher Vahid Qazvini, *Tarikh-e Jahanara-ye 'Abbasi* ed. Sayyed Sa'id Mir Mohammad Sadeq (Tehran, 1383/2004), p. 415 (text royal order of Shah 'Abbas II).

128. Chardin, *Voyages*, vol. 2, p. 215.

129. Strauszens, *Sehr schwere*, p. 164.

130. VOC 1224, f. 403.

Streetwalkers and Others

Nevertheless, women in Isfahan and elsewhere walked the streets, because, in 1607, Diego di Santa Anna reported that prostitutes were seen everywhere in the streets and shops plying their wares.[131] Chardin writes that in the past, before the 1645 ban (see below) prostitutes went out into the streets like a swarm of crows in the evening, and from there they spread over the entire city and the caravanserais.[132] However, that was marketing, because the business deal was concluded in nearby dwellings. Olearius reported that in Qazvin at sunset merchants appeared at the east side of the square displaying their goods as well as prostitutes who lined up in a row with their faces covered.[133] Struys in 1671, described this location in Qazvin as a major concentration of prostitutes, where during the day jewels and other costly goods were sold. After sunset, for a small payment, an old woman or go-between (*dallaleh*) acted as an intermediary for the prostitutes who were lined up in rows. The *dallaleh* stood behind the women with their tools of trade, to wit: a pillow, a blanket of cotton or down, holding a lantern in her hand. When a customer arrived she would shine the light on the prostitute who would uncover her face, so that the man could inspect her. If he liked what he saw and agreed on the price she would follow him, presumably either to his home or some rendez-vous nearby. This happened in almost total quiet, so that one might think that the commerce concerned one of the most honorable trades, Struys remarked.[134]

Gypsy women found their clientele in a different manner, usually as a result of their dance performances, as well as being in or near caravanserais, when one or more of the spectators or travelers expressed the wish to sleep with a specific woman.

---

131. Carlos Alonso, "Due lettere riguardanti i primi tempi delle missioni agostiniane in Persia," *Analecta Augustiniana* 24 (1961), p. 160.

132. Chardin, *Voyages*, vol. 2, p. 216.

133. Olearius, *Vermehrte*, pp. 482-83.

134. Strauszens, *Sehr Schwere*, p. 172. He may have copied this from Olearius, *Vermehrte*, p. 483.

It is the custom on these occasions for their husbands
to take them to the house of any Persian with whom
the woman has engaged to pass the night; and on the
morrow the husband will duly appear to carry away his
wife, with her looking-glass and paints and headgear
and pins and belts, and he then receives the price
stipulated for.[135]

What about Non-Moslem Males?

Many prostitutes were Christians, who were forced by their Moslem
slave masters or mistresses, as the case may be, to work as whores.
Their work has been discussed already and therefore, there is need to
take a look at non-Moslem male clientele, as there was a considerable number of foreign, non-Moslem males in Safavid Iran, mainly
concentrated in the capital and some ports, who also sought an outlet
for their sexual desires. In particular, this held for sailors in Hormuz
and later in Bandar 'Abbas, who were on shore-leave, and, married or
single, they had been without women for a long time. In Hormuz,
during the period of the Portuguese protectorate, there were brothels
on the island. There were many Moslem women who, after the Portuguese takeover, had asked to be baptized, so that they also could ply
their trade to a Catholic clientele.[136] In Bandar 'Abbas, with the large
number of Dutch, English, and other European as well as numerous
Asian sailors there was a strong demand for women. Hence, there
were many prostitutes, mostly from India, during the trading season.
Mostly, for not only Indian women, but also Moslem women worked
there as prostitutes, which the castellan (*kotval*) allowed, because they
paid him.[137] In Bandar-e Kong, in 1674, Portuguese officers took the
Venetian traveler Bembo to parties "with women, to whom they are
much inclined, even though there is not one there who is worth it.

135. Don Juan, *A Shi'ah*, p. 57.

136. Afonso de Albuquerque, *Cartas de Afonso de Albuquerque, seguidas de
documentos que as elucidam* 7 vols. eds. Raimundo António de Bulhão Pato
and Henrique Lopes de Mendoça (Lisbon, 1884-1935), vol. 6, p. 287.

137. Herbert, *Travels*, p. 47; Lockyer, *Account*, p. 239.

Some soldiers sell their clothes and all they have in order to satisfy themselves."[138]

The sailors in Bandar 'Abbas hired ponies or *yabu*s when they came ashore, which walked them straight to the whorehouse "as if they know that the sailors have to be there."[139] But non-Moslem males didn't find solace only in port cities. In Tabriz, under Shah Esma'il I, non-Moslems could frequent the brothels, because "no difference is made between Christians and Musulmans in going to the prostitutes."[140] An unnamed Portuguese friar, "who was lodged in Sir Anthony's house found the means to have a Persian courtesan to lie with him, and had night by night during his continuance there…"[141] It was apparently quite normal to arrange for women to visit one's home. De Bruijn wrote that despite "the care they take to hide themselves from the eyes of men," Armenian women were not as chaste as you would think. "For there are a number of them who prostitute themselves for money, and who, disguising themselves as men, go on horseback with their mothers to *Ispahan*, where they drive on a little trade, while the poor husband thinks them proof against all temptation, because they never unveil themselves."[142] Chardin remarked that nobody took offense at this nor when these same women visited foreign merchants in the caravanserais.[143] Foreigners also visited the brothels and nobody raised

---

138. Bembo, *The Travels*, p. 288. He does not relate where these women were from (locals, or more likely from Sind).

139. François Valentyn, *Oud en Nieuw Oost-Indien* 5 vols. (Dordrecht, 1726), vol. 5, p. 250.

140. Barbaro, *Travels*, vol. 2, p. 171.

141. Anthony Sherley, *Anthony Sherley and His Persian Adventure*, ed. Sir E. Denison Ross (London 1933), p. 126 [in Isfahan].

142. Le Brun, *Travels*, vol. 1, p. 230 [234]. If these Armenian women were really married, as Le Brun implies when referring to their husbands, this quote should be part of chapter three. However, I think that this was his assumption rather than a fact, for temporary marriage liaisons with Europeans better fits with the reality both for the seventeenth as well as the nineteenth century and is in harmony with the existing patterns.

143. Chardin, *Voyages*, vol. 2, pp. 222-23.

objections.[144] However, these women must have been non-Moslems, because della Valle reports a case of a Venetian merchant in 1620 who had been badly treated by the governor of Isfahan, because he had spent time in the company of a Moslem woman.[145]

Some foreigners were more fortunate than others, because it was not unusual for the shah to give a girl to a foreign visitor, either because he believed that a man should not be without a woman, and/or, because he wanted to have the foreigner sire a child. In 1515, this fate befell the first Portuguese ambassador.

> The King desired Miguel Ferreira to sleep with [a]
> woman so that he would leave [a] son or daughter
> behind. He dispatched a white and very beautiful woman
> of his house, with rich jewels and cloths, and two female
> servants with her; and he declared it appeared to him
> to be a bad thing for a man not to have a woman; for
> this reason he dispatched that woman, who was [a]
> woman of his house, and she would serve him in all
> matters to his will. Miguel Ferreira returned great thanks
> and courtesies, asking him very circumspectly not to
> send her to him, because he was married in Portugal,
> and when he had departed, he had made an oath and
> had promised never to touch another woman until he
> returned, asking many pardons for not doing what His
> Highness had commanded. The King considered his
> virtue commendable.[146]

This royal gesture is reminiscent of a similar gesture made by Genghis Khan, who gave a woman to Pahlavan Fila, "to beget children between" them.[147] Other foreigners were likewise honored. 'Abbas I

---

144. Tavernier, *Voyages*, p. 252.

145. Della Valle, *Voyages*, vol. 3, p. 142.

146. Ronald Bishop Smith, *The First Age. Of the Portuguese Embassies, Navigations and Peregrinations in Persia (1507-1524)* (Bethesda, 1970), p. 26 quoting Correa, *Lendas*, II, ch. 48.

147. Juvaini, *History*, vol. 1, p. 228.

gave Robert Sherley "out of his seraglio, in marriage, a *Cirassian* [sic; Circassian] lady of great esteem and regard. But that he should have a child in *Persia* and that the king should be the Godfather."[148] While he was staying in Shiraz, the governor offered the Spanish ambassador Don Garcia da Silva y Figueroa a few women, while Shah 'Abbas I did the same in Isfahan, which offer the ambassador declined saying that he was too old for such company.[149] Huybert Visnich, the first director of the Dutch East Indies Company in Iran, reported how in 1625 in Shiraz he and his staff were fêted by Emamqoli Khan with music and dance; the governor later that night sent the same women to Visnich's room for more "singing and enjoyment."[150] In 1664, 'Abbas II offered Tavernier a woman after a banquet with much carousing.[151] An interesting case is reported in the VOC documents. Mattheus van Leijpsigh, the VOC (Dutch East India Company) chief in Isfahan, had died in 1739. During the Afghan occupation in the 1720s he had bought what he believed was a Georgian Christian woman. After the defeat of the Afghans in December 1729 the woman declared herself to be a Moslem. Although she had a child fathered by him, van Leijpsigh put her out of his house to avoid being accused of having had relations with a Moslem woman. To prevent legal claims on van Leijpsigh's estate, the VOC asked the Sheikh al-Eslam of Isfahan in 1739 for a verdict whether van Leipsigh's natural child had a claim on her father's goods. The legal decision stated that a child of a prostitute could not inherit from her biological father, according to Islamic law.[152] The Polish ambassador Bogdan, when he was in Shamakhi in 1671, waiting for a reply from Shah Soleyman, bought two Georgian girls for a total of 100 *Reichsthaler*, whom he used for sexual intercourse and to liven

---

148. Cartwright, *The Preacher's Travels*, p. 738. This was Teresa, a Circassian lady. For details see Bernadette Andrea, "Lady Sherley: The First Persian in England?" *The Muslim World* 95/2 (2005), 279–295.

149. De Silva y Figuroa, *Comentarios*, vol. 2, pp. 47-48, 388.

150. Dunlop, *Bronnen*, pp. 271-72.

151. Tavernier, *Voyages*, p. 131.

152. VOC 2511, f. 1929-31; see also Olearius, *Vermehrte*, p. 609.

up the company when he had guests with their dancing.[153] Persian ambassadors abroad likewise saw nothing untoward in solliciting the attention and the accosting of unmarried women much to the horror of Dutch (in the case of Musa Beyg) and English authorities (in the case of Naqdi Beyg).[154]

DID PROSTITUTES WEAR SPECIAL DRESS?

Courtesans not only dressed differently and daringly than other women, but also they behaved as such. High class courtesans were a group apart and they went about with their face unveiled, riding on horseback and accompanied by servants.[155] During the month of mourning (*Moharram*) everybody dressed in black, except for the courtesans, according to da Silva y Figueroa. In fact, they even went about unveiled on the high day of the mourning ceremonies (*'Ashura*), dressed in yellow or tan clothes embellished with silk and gold thread.[156] Many of them became wealthy, were dressed in gold cloth and the like and were embellished with gold and pearls; those who could afford it were frequently seen riding horses in town. The horses were decked out with silver and golden tack and other golden attachments, while the courtesans were accompanied by three to four servants on foot.[157] Herbert described the clothes of courtesans as follows: "their habit ... is loose and gaudy, reaching to their mid-leg; under which they wear drawers of cloth of gold, satin, and tissued stuffs, or costly embroidery."[158] He described the prostitutes of Bandar 'Abbas, who in his words, "infested" that town, as follows:

---

153. Strauszens, *Sehr Schwere*, p. 137.

154. Dunlop, *Bronnen*, p. 207; Denis Wright, *The Persians Amongst the English* (London, 1985), p. 7.

155. Della Valle, *Voyage*, vol. 3, p. 22.

156. De Silva y Figueroa, *Comentarios*, vol. 2, pp. 345-46.

157. Leupe ", Beschrijvinge," p. 205.

158. Herbert, *Travels*, p. 237; see also Olearius, *Vermehrte*, p. 480.

> For albeit their hair be neatly plaited and perfumed,
> and about their cheeks are hung ropes of oriental pearl,
> about their necks carcanets of stones, in their ears many
> rings (some of which are headed with ragged pearl) one
> by another, in their noses a brooch or piece of gold three
> inches or more in length and half-an-inch in breadth
> embellished with turquoises, rubies, spinels [gemstones],
> sapphires, and like stones of value... their arms and legs
> are chained with manillos [bracelet; Port. manilho] and
> armlets of silver, brass, ivory and the like ...[159]

Common prostitutes did not go out unveiled, and to the unwary eye they could not be distinguished from other women that went outside. However, they wore veils that were shorter, thinner and less tight, while, and this really set them apart, they would open them to attract customers.[160] Under the veil prostitutes allegedly wore clothes that set them apart, such as dresses with a large seam, whereas "honest women have no borders to their sheets."[161]

PROSTITUTION: A TAXING AFFAIR

Lasciviousness and fornication are the result of strong human needs and despite religious and secular royal prohibition to be engaged in such things, illicit and unlawful activities thrived. Government therefore, had to keep an eye on such activities to ensure that they either were suppressed, or, what usually happened, kept under some measure of control. To that end, subsequent governments appointed an official to look after public morals, who, until the end of the sixteenth century, was the *mohtaseb*.[162] For reasons unknown the function of the *mohtaseb* became subservient to that of the *darugheh* (city governor; chief of police). In this task, the *darugheh* was supported by

---

159. Herbert, *Travels*, p. 47.

160. Chardin, *Voyages*, vol. 2, p. 211; Herbert, *Travels*, p. 47.

161. Fryer, *A New Account*, vol. 3, p. 128.

162. On this official see Floor, "The office of muhtasib in Iran," pp. 53-74.

a number of officials, amongst which the head of the royal lighting department (*mash'aldar-bashi*). The latter supervised all houses of ill-repute, coffee-houses and all "dishonourable professions" (musicians, artists, etc.), while he was the beneficiary of the taxes to which these professions were subjected. He was also the recipient of such fines as those levied on musicians playing in the streets, while he also kept the register of all prostitutes.[163]

Exercising control over unlawful activities costs money, and therefore, the government charged a fee to those engaged in such activities. Della Valle mentions that "Aga Haggi", Shah 'Abbas I's chamberlain (*mehtar*) and his 'secretary for royal entertainment', was the superintendent of the courtesans in Isfahan, to whom they paid a tribute.[164] In the 1630s, the Dutch reported that "it is said that in this city [Isfahan] there are 12,000 loose women over and above the married ones, who must appear before the *darugheh* each month and who have to pay a great tribute according to their beauty and the extent to which they are in demand."[165] Like other travelers, Fryer states that: "They give him [the Shah] so much for their License when they first set up, and annually as long as they practice."[166] It is unlikely that all 14,000 prostitutes presented themselves monthly at the *darugheh's* office. It is more likely, as there was some kind of trade organization, that the managers of the prostitutes, the pimps, madams, brothel keepers and the like did so, which kept the numbers visiting the office every month manageable.

163. Willem Floor and Mohammad Faghfoory, *Dastur al-Moluk, a Safavid State Manual* (Costa Mesa, 2007), pp. 300-06; Vladimir Minorsky, *The Tadhkirat al-Muluk, A Manual of Safavid Administration*. (Cambridge, 1980), p. 82; Chardin, *Voyages*, vol. 5, p. 371; Floor, *Safavid Government*, pp. 115-22.

164. Della Valle, *Voyages*, vol. 3, p. 178. It is possible that the *darugheh* managed the collection of the tribute on behalf of this and subsequent court officials, who held a similar supervisory position over the courtesans.

165. Leupe, "Beschrijvinge," p. 205.

166. Fryer, *A New Account*, vol. 3, pp. 129-30, 395; Vahid Qazvini, *Tarikh*, p. 415.

The revenues from these unlawful activities and dens of iniquity were considerable. In 1532, or thereabouts, the total national revenue collected from brothels, gambling and opium dens, taverns, etc. was an estimated 12,000 *tumans*.[167] In the early part of the seventeenth century, the national revenue collected from brothels only was estimated at 3,000 *tumans* or 25 percent of all illicit activities.[168] Olearius reports that levies on bathhouses and prostitutes yielded more than one ton of gold per year.[169] Chardin estimated the total revenue at 200,000 *écus* or 13,000 *tumans* per year.[170] According to Kaempfer, the tax on prostitutes yielded an annual income of about 10,000 *tumans* of which 6,000 came from Isfahan alone. Chardin estimated the total payment in Isfahan at 8,000 *tumans* per year.[171] In 1694, the treasury officials estimated that a ban would constitute a loss of 10 *mann-e shah* or 59 kg in gold per day (valued at US\$ 53,000 per day or US\$ 19 million/year!), which seems to be much too high. The shah, however, allegedly angrily dismissed these arguments, saying that ill-gotten gains could never be used for pious ends.[172] A decade or so later, Nasiri mentions a much lower and more realistic amount, viz. 3,000 to 4,000 *tumans* per year.[173]

Assuming that the revenue from the dishonorable professions amounted to 12,000 *tumans* per year in ready cash, then these revenues represented 1.7 percent of the total annual revenue of the Safavid state, which, according to some estimates amounted to 700,000

167. Qomi, *Kholasat*, vol. 1, p. 225; Qazi Ahmad Qazvini Ghaffari, *Tarikh-e Jahanara* (Tehran 1343/1964), p. 287.

168. Ebrahim Dehgan ed., *Tarikh-e Safaviyan. Kholasat al-Tavarikh- Tarikh-e Molla Kamal* (Arak, 1334/1955), p. 102.

169. Olearius, *Vermehrte*, p. 669.

170. Chardin, *Voyages*, vol. 2, p. 212.

171. Kaempfer, *Am Hofe*, p. 94; Chardin, *Voyages*, vol. 7, p. 417.

172. Ehsan Eshraqi, "Shah Soltan Hoseyn dar Tohfat al-'Alam," *Tarikh* 1/1 (2335/1976), pp. 90-91

173. Mohammad Ebrahim b. Zeyn al-'Abedin Nasiri, *Dastur-e Shahriyan*. ed. Mohammad Nader Nasiri Moqaddam (Tehran, 1373/1995), p. 40.

*tuman*s, which were mostly in kind.[174] This is a considerable share of the state's finances and thus, it is understandable why subsequent governments were loath to forego these finances. Moreover, this income was in ready cash, which was always in very short supply, and was promptly paid every month. This is one of the reasons why the bans never lasted very long.

These same figures tell us something indirectly about the level of the price that prostitutes demanded for their services. Assuming a monthly payment of 40 per cent (Isfahan represents that share in total revenues of illicit trades) of 4,000 *tuman*s by 12,000 prostitutes, this means an average monthly payment of 0.22 *tuman* or 220 dinars per Isfahani prostitute. However, this is an average, for some sex workers paid more and others paid less, because the license fee was pro rated according to their beauty and market position. This figure makes it very unlikely, as argued above, that two or more *tuman*s per night was asked. This may have been the case for some high-class performers, but the bulk of the working girls made much less and it may be concluded that they paid someting in the order of 50 to 100 dinars per month in tax, reflecting their relatively low prices, which must have been a minimum of 20 dinars per visit.

Because this money was unclean from a religious point of view, it was allegedly not always received by the royal treasury. Sanson states that Shah 'Abbas I felt that, although he did not ban prostitution and other illicit activities, he could not, in good faith, accept their ill-gotten gains. 'Abbas I making a virtue out of necessity, therefore, circumvented this moral dilemma by purifying the tainted money. To that end he allegedly gave orders that these monies had to be collected by the chief of the royal lighting department (*mash'aldar-bashi*), who spent these funds on the lighting of the royal palaces and on fireworks for various festivities.[175] However, this money purification scheme

174. Willem Floor, *A Fiscal History of Iran in the Safavid and Qajar Periods 1500-1925* (New York, 1999), pp. 67-68.

175. M. Sanson, *The present state of Persia* (London, 1695), p. 100; TM, p. 139; a fee called *zar-e mash'aldar-bashi* is mentioned. Masih Dhahibi and Manuchehr Setudeh, *Az Astara ta Astarabad* 10 vols. (Tehran, 1366/1987), vol.

that the Safavid state sorely needed seems to be a fabrication, because the *mash'aldar-bashi* was already in charge of these disreputable trades, including their revenues, in Timurid times.[176] Moreover, according to Olearius, 'Abbas I

> had made it a rule that he preferred to give no other
> money more to the poor than the revenues that he
> received from the brothels. Because he had said: 'That
> which one gives to the poor should not have been
> extorted from others and not have been received
> reluctantly. The subjects do not give their taxes
> voluntarily, but there is no one more willing [to give]
> than those who frequent the brothels.'[177]

Both are excellent and inspiring stories and it was good public relations, something the sinning shah did not eschew at all. They are similar to the stories told that some shahs allegedly refused to accept the argument that they could not afford the financial loss that they would incur, if brothels and taverns would be banned (see below). Also, Shi'ite divines were less picky, because during the panegyrics and elegies declaimed and spoken during the month of mourning, it is customary to give money, fabrics or other valuables at the mosque. Women in particular made such contributions and the ones that gave most were the courtesans.[178]

WERE PROSTITUTES PROTECTED?

Because most prostitutes were registered and paid their monthly fee, they could count on some measure of protection. In 1637, when one of the Holstein soldiers did not pay his fee, the prostitute who was bilked lodged a complaint. The governor insisted that the soldier pay,

---

6, doc. 20.

176. Hans Robert Roemer, *Staatsschreiben der Timuridenzeit* (Wiesbaden, 1952), p. 174.

177. Olearius, *Vermehrte*, p. 648.

178. De Silva y Figueroa, *Comentarios*, vol. 2, p. 347.

stating that since the kachbae (*qahbeh*) had to pay taxes, it was only reasonable that she also should receive her fee.[179] This protection was even given by the shah. When one of the shah's soldiers was disporting himself with a courtesan in a garden at Kashan she was displeased with his behavior, and "cried out so loudly that the King heard, forthwith had her brought before him and asked why she called so lustily, to which she replied that he was using force." The soldier was brought before the king who butchered him with his own hands.[180]

Although considered a profession of bad repute, some prostitutes overcame this social handicap. Della Valle relates the story of an old unattractive courtesan called Felfel (Pepper) who commanded much respect as she had been one of Shah Abbas I's favorite performers.[181] But she was, of course, an exception to the general rule. Therefore, to become more socially acceptable, these women engaged in pious acts. De Silva y Figueroa reported that the courtesans:

> Went about town, alone or only accompanied by a single servant, well dressed, without mantle and face uncovered except for a gauze veil of gold and transparent silk, which covers their head, face and bosom but through which it is easy to discern all their beauty. In their hands they carry wooden or gilded box, and they approach men and halt before them without saying a word, with much modesty, with lowered eyes, until they give them alms, which they subsequently distribute among the poorest and the neediest they know.[182]

One of these Madams, after having earned a considerable sum, had found religion; she repented her way of life, did penitence, made the pilgrimage to Mecca and became respectable. In this case it did not help her much. Because she was still a beautiful woman, although

---

179. Olearius, *Vermehrte*, p. 592.

180. Sherley, *Anthony Sherley*, pp. 160, 213-14.

181. Della Valle, *Voyages*, vol. 2, p. 50.

182. De Silva Figueroa, *Comentarios*, vol. 2, p. 350.

not young anymore, the young debauches of Isfahan on one occasion tried to force entry into her house to get to know her intimately, so that she had to defend herself with a dagger.[183]

Their accepted role in high society was confirmed by the fact that the balcony of the gallery of the great mosque of Isfahan was reserved for the courteans and leading public women, whom "one honors and esteems here more than other women because the king gives them great privileges and considerable exemptions, both because of the profit they yield for him and because there are those who follow the army, which would not be able to operate without them"[184] Courtesans accompanied Shah 'Abbas I wherever he went, whether on social visits or to war. Usually, they were led by one of the older women, who had influence with the shah such as Dallaleh Chizi, and who 'managed' the other younger ones.[185] The shah and his courtiers indeed were lavish in their appreciation, which allowed these women to live luxuriously.[186]

WERE DANCING AND SINGING GIRLS PROSTITUTES?

Although dancers, singers and female musicians are often mentioned as a separate group, in their behavior, comportment, clothing, and services rendered, they differed little if at all from prostitutes and the difference, therefore, can only be ascribed in the eye of the beholder, who recorded his impressions. According to Chardin, only prostitutes and public women danced, and therefore, dancing was even more dishonorable and contrary to religious precept than singing and making music.[187] Nevertheless, dancers were part of court life from the very beginning of Safavid rule. It is stated that for Shah Esma'il I, "The King ordered beautiful female musicians to sing and dance inside the

---

183. Chardin, *Voyages*, vol. 7, pp. 413-14.

184. De Silva y Figueroa, *Comentarios*, vol. 2, p. 345.

185. Della Valle, *Voyages*, vol. 3, pp. 22-23, 104-05, 567.

186. De Silva y Figueroa, *Comentarios*, vol. 2, pp. 210-11.

187. Chardin, *Voyages*, vol. 4, p. 309; Tavernier, *Voyages*, pp. 264-65; della Valle, *Voyages*, vol. 3, p. 23.

house, and they spoke and jested with Miguel Ferreira [the Portuguese ambassador] freely; but he dispatched them with gifts and courteous words, without ever to understand with them."[188] Tahmasp I also employed them and so did 'Abbas I. When he received the deposed Uzbeg ruler Vali Mohammad Khan "rose colored beauties", melodious singers and dancers entertained the guests.[189] In Kashan the shah gave a party in 1016/1607 where dancing women performed.[190]

In fact, dancers were so much part of public and political life that "There are no banquets in Persia without music and courtesans."[191] The leading men of the state, from the shah down to the grandees and lesser officials always had some dancing girls, who danced, made music and sang for them and their friends and guests-even foreign guests, including non-Moslem Europeans. Most of these women were of Caucasian origin.[192]

The group of dancing girls at the royal court numbered twenty-four and they were the most famous courtesans of the country. They were placed under one of the old female members of the royal band, but usually, they did not live together as a troupe, but lived in different parts of Isfahan. It was the task of the old woman to assemble them, arrange for performances, settle disputes, punish them if need be, protect them if they were insulted, and keep an eye on the finances of the troupe. Punishment was given with a whip, and in the case

---

188. Smith, *The First Age*, p. 24.

189. Eskander Beyg Monshi, *Tarikh-e 'Alamara-ye 'Abbasi*. Iraj Afshar ed. 2 vols. (Tehran 1350/1971), pp. 837-38; Anonymous, *'Alamara-ye Shah Tahmasp*, ed. Iraj Afshar (Tehran, 1370/1991), pp. 136-37.

190. Molla Jalal, *Ruznameh*, p. 330.

191. Sherley, *Anthony Sherley*, p. 156.

192. Chardin, *Voyages*, vol. 2, pp. 205, 211 (a dancing group in the provinces usually had not more than 7 to 8 girls); Hotz, *Reis*, p. 87 ('Abbas II); António de Gouvea, *Jornada do Arcebispo de Goa Dom Frey Aleixo de Meneses Primaz da India Oriental* (Coimbra, 1606), 145b (performance by Circassian female dancers); Silva y Figueroa, *Comentarios*, vol. 1, pp. 343, 359, 361, 366, vol. 2, pp. 366, 381; Herbert, *Travels*, pp. 47, 129, 236-37 ('Abbas I); Barbaro, *Travels*, vol. 2, p. 202 (Esma'il I); Leupe, "Beschrijvinge," p. 205; Olearius, *Vermehrte*, pp. 510, 516-17, 532; Dunlop, *Bronnen*, p. 272 (Safi I).

of a second offense the girl concerned was expelled from the group. The old woman also took care of their wages; she saw to it that they had costly clothes, had appropriate furniture, in short that they were properly equipped for the tasks they had to perform. Each girl had a support staff of two maids, a valet, a cook, a groom with three horses, and if they traveled with the court they had four additional horses for their luggage. They received payment of 1,800 francs per year, with a certain quantity of fabrics for their dresses, and a food allowance for themselves and their staff. Some of them made as much as 900 *écus*; but the level of their salary depended on the shah's appreciation of their art. This was not their only source of income, for some nights they might be paid as much as 50 *pistoles*. As a result, they were very finely dressed. In 1665, Chardin saw two dancing girls in dresses studded with precious stones, whose value he estimated at 10,000 *écus*. These court dancers were well paid for their services. According to Kaempfer, the standard price amounted to two to three *tuman*s per night; hence they were also referred to by the amount of money they demanded for each performance (the two *tuman* or ten *tuman* girl). None asked less than one *tuman*, and when they could not command that much, they were let go and another took her place. However, despite the riches that they received, many spent the money as fast as they acquired it and, often, they ended up being poor and destitute.[193]

One of their major functions was to welcome the shah, a governor, foreign visitors and a victorious army, whether in the national capital or in provincial capitals. In 1651, during the official entry of Joan Cuneaus, the Dutch ambassador to Shiraz, some eight dancing girls were performing on a gallery built over a gate through which the cavalcade passed.[194] In Qazvin, the Sherleys rode out of the city,

---

193. Chardin, *Voyages*, vol. 2, pp. 205-11; Olearius, *Vermehrte*, pp. 531-32; Kaempfer, *Am Hofe*, p. 193. Tavernier, *Voyages*, p. 134 relates how one dancing girl slapped another one at court; Shah 'Abbas II heard it. After having asked who had done so, he dismissed her on the spot and sent her to the *darugheh* with instructions to replace her with another, to give her 100 *tuman*s and to marry her to somebody.

194. Hotz, *Reis*, p. 87. Likewise was the Holstein embassy welcomed by 15 dancers at Qazvin. Olearius, *Vermehrte*, pp. 480-81.

"Where in a while after, we might see a great troop of courtesans of the city come riding richly appareled to salute the King and to welcome him from his wars, their apparel little differing in fashion from the men's, but only in their head attire and upper coats. They wear breeches and ride astride as men do, and came with such a cry as the wild Irish make. The multitude of people was so great (consisting of actors and spectators) that we had much ado."[195] At a triumphal entry of troops with the heads of the vanquished, there was also a large group of courtesans "riding astride in disorder, and shouting and crying in every direction as if they had lost their senses, and frequently they embraced the King."[196] Occassionally, entertainers in general, and female dancers in particular, were used to mock vanquished enemies. When 'Abbas I took Qandahar in 1622, he first had a group of courtesans led by Dallaleh Chizi enter the fort to make it appear that the Moghul had been defeated by a group of soft women.[197] It was usual to decorate the bazaar to mock a conquered foe while the storytellers (*qavvalan*), dancers (*mokhannathan*), buffoons (*mozahhekan*) and jesters (*maskharahha*) welcomed him with their derisory mockeries such as in 943/1536-37.[198] This implies that he had a group of such female dancers with him, just like his grandson Safi I did, as did his successor, whenever they left on campaign.[199]

After the triumphal entry, usually a banquet was organized later at the bazaar with "all kinds of music, singing and with boys and courtesans dancing strange kinds of jigs and lavoltas [an old Italian dance popular in England]: without which courtesans no banquet, be it never so costly, hath any relish with them. Howbeit, no man's wife comes thereat."[200] Prostitutes were also present at other public

195. Sherley, *Anthony Sherley*, pp. 117-18.

196. Sherley, *Anthony Sherley*, pp. 154-55.

197. Della Valle, *Voyage*, vol. 3, p. 567

198. Rumlu, *Ahsan*, p. 356.

199. Olearius, *Vermehrte*, p. 592; Tavernier, *Voyages*, p. 275.

200. Sherley, *Anthony Sherley*, p. 119. Although of bad repute when there was a party in the streets "the children dance with the courtesans." Sherley, *Anthony Sherley*, p. 156.

festivals, including Christian ones. Struys noted that on the occasion of the Baptism of the Cross, an Armenian festival, there were at the site where the festivities took place, a group of prostitutes who, by performing seductive dances, were able to draw clients.[201] "There was also at that feast [in Qazvin] ten women very gallantly appareled, and very beautiful, who did dance according to their country manner, and sing all the time we were feasting."[202]

According to Du Mans these dance troupes performed at weddings and other parties where these "qahbehs [harlots] for rent" would engage in all kinds of dances, their faces unveiled, before the men. This was an expensive service, however.[203] Dancing was also done by Georgian boys, who engaged in prostitution as well (see chapter four). Indeed, the dancing, singing and drinking often led to other things. These women amused the company by displaying their beauty and wealth. Moreover, "they are very sweet voiced and witty so that men are seduced by this and the married ones fail [in their obligation]."[204] For female as well as male dancers not only danced but also were available for sexual intercourse. In particular, those dancers employed at court performed both functions. At these banquets side rooms were available where guests and dancers could seek privacy and be engaged in sexual congress. Afterwards, both returned to the banquet; the man to his seat, the woman to resume dancing.[205] Dancers, therefore, were also referred by less neutral terms such as *luli, luri* and *lavand,* which all three connote people who sing and beg in the streets, are shameless, impudent, as well as conveying the notion of nice, delicate, and pretty, but to make sure that these albeit alluring aspects were but signals for entrapment of the unwary; the terms also meant gypsy, prostitute, and loose woman.[206]

---

201. Strauszens, *Sehr Schwere*, p. 141.

202. Sherley, *Anthony Sherley*, p. 203.

203. Richard, *Raphael du Mans*, vol. 2, p. 90; Tavernier, *Voyages*, p. 262.

204. Leupe, "Beschrijvinge," p. 205.

205. Olearius, *Vermehrte*, p. 532.

206. *Borhan-e Qate'*, vol. 3, p. 1916.

With the changing religious climate under Shah Soleyman, when less doctrinarian, Sufi-tolerant Islam was on the wane, slowly being ousted by orthodox Imami Shi'a Islam, tolerance for frivolous activities such as dancing and singing was considered not to be permissible, if not plain unlawful, and thus it disappeared from the public, but not the private, life of the court.[207] In 1704, de Bruyn wrote that dancing by public women was something of the past. "Nor do they any longer allow dancing women and courtezans, who formerly abounded on all sides."[208] John Bell and Ketelaar confirmed this in 1717 and noted that there were no dancers during the official audience.[209]

However, female dancers still continued to perform at private parties as well as on occasion of some special public events. In 1674, Carré attended a party thrown by the governor of Bandar 'Abbas. There was a banquet; toasts were given, followed by conversation, after which the dinner ended. Then musicians appeared with dancing girls; this lasted for two hours during which time the governor conversed with the Frenchmen.[210] According to Lockyer, in the country houses at 'Essin at seven miles from Bandar 'Abbas they had musicians, dancing girls from Madras and elsewhere in India as well as jugglers, but these were not up to Indian standards.[211] In Bandar-e Kong people also knew how to have fun. In 1694, Gemelli-Careri saw a Moorish show with female dancers.[212] The Banyans celebrated their annual Devali festival, which was enlivened with a *nautch* of Sindi female dancers, which pleased Gemelli-Careri so much that "he wanted to see them again and

207. For an analysis of the discussion among the olama concerning the propriety of singing, see Rasul Ja'fariyan, "Tarikh-e mas'aleh-ye ghana dar dowreh-ye Safaviyeh," in Ibid, *Safaviyeh dar 'arseh-ye din, farhang va siyasat* 3 vols. (Qom, 1379/2000), vol. 2, pp. 697-722, also Raghib Esfahani, *Navader*, p. 174.

208. Le Bruyn, *Travels*, vol. 1, p. 196.

209. John Bell, *Travels from St. Petersburgh in Russia* etc. 2 vols. (Edinburgh, 1788), vol. 1, pp. 118ff.

210. Carré, *Travels*, vol. 3, pp. 804-05; for a description of the French at the governor's dinner see Ibid., vol. 3, pp. 816-18.

211. Lockyer, *Account of Trade*, pp. 134-35.

212. Gemelli-Careri, *Giro*, vol. 2, pp. 307, 311 (female dancers' clothing).

again."[213] In 1717, Bell was entertained at the home of one of the court officials with music, dancing boys, and puppet players. No wine was served "as it was not then used at court."[214] In urban areas it appeared that men did not dance, although it occurred in rural areas. In 1684 Kaempfer describes public dancing in southern Iran in which both men and women participated.[215]

BANS ON PROSTITUTION

The shahs would regularly submit to religious pressure and ban brothels, taverns and other dens of iniquity or when they themselves repented their own lewd activities they invariably performed. Such was not the case with Shah Esma'il I when he, on assuming power in Tabriz, had a number of harlots executed, but he allowed many others to live and continue their trade, which prospered thereafter. He also continued to be engaged in all kinds of unlawful activities (sodomy, adultery, imbibing wine, eating pork), thus failing to set a good example.[216] However, Shah Tahmasp I, who, at 20 years of age (in 1532) on finding religion, banned brothels and abolished all taxes on public houses, gambling dens and brothels and struck them from the financial registers.[217] Uncharacteristically, there was even some follow-up activity, because the *sadr*, the head of the religious establishment, was active in destroying various dens in iniquity.[218] As was customary the text of the royal edict was erected on the wall of the Friday mosque or

---

213. Gemelli-Careri, *Giro*, vol. 2, pp. 296-302, 305.

214. Bell, *Travels*, pp.132-33.

215. Detlef Haberland, *Von Lemgo nach Japan. Das ungewöhnliche Leben des Engelbert Kaempfer 1651 bis 1716* (Bielefeld, 1990), p. 168.

216. Jean Aubin, "L'Avènement des Safavides reconsiderée" (Etudes Safavides III), *Moyen-Orient et Océan Indien*, 5 (1988), pp. 41-54.

217. Qomi, *Kholasat*, vol. 1, pp. 226, 233; 'Abdi Beyg Shirazi. *Takmeleh al-Akhbar*, ed. 'Abdol-Hoseyn Nava'i (Tehran, 1369/1990), p. 167. See also Rasul Ja'fariyan, "Amr beh ma'ruf va nahi az monkar dar dowreh-ye Safaviyeh" in Ibid., *Maqalat-e Tarikhi* 5 vols. (Qom, 1378/1999), vol. 5, pp. 19-26.

218. Qomi, *Kholasat*, vol. 1, p. 314; Monshi, *Tarikh*, vol. 1, p. 201.

another important one in the major cities.[219] Shah Tahmasp I was very proud of his edict, because he wrote Soltan Soleyman about it, implying that the leader of the Sunni world had so far failed to take similar steps.[220] Initially, Shah Tahmasp I verified the application of the edict and when it came to his notice that the governor of Mashhad had failed to do so he was dismissed in 1555. Ebrahim Mirza, the shah's nephew and his successor was explicitly instructed to see to it that the regulations of Islamic law be adhered to.[221] In 1569-70, Shah Tahmasp I sent a similarly worded order to another governor.[222] After this event there is no further mention of this ban and it does not seem as if prostitution had disappeared.[223] According to two seventeenth century Armenian sources, the ban had a positive impact, for the authors lists as one of the late Shah Tahmasp I's accomplishments the fact that he had banned prostitution and that orders had been given to kill anyone who nevertheless performed as such. However, the Armenian authors did not state that prostitution had been eradicated.[224]

Even Shah 'Abbas I felt obliged to to make a token gesture towards the religious establishment, when in 1620 wine drinking was banned; albeit temporarily. In 1608 prostitutes were given the choice to repent or leave Isfahan within three days. If they repented, loans that had been given to them were cancelled, and therefore they all re-

---

219. Surviving texts are to be found in Kashan, Isfahan and Ardabil, see 'Abdol-Hoseyn Nava'i ed. *Asnad va Makateb-e Tarikhi-ye Iran az Timur ta Shah Esma'il* (Tehran, 1341/1962), pp. 513-14; Lotfollah Honarfar, *Ganjineh-ye Athar-e Tarikhi-ye Esfahan* (Esfahan, 1350), p. 82; Sayyed Jamal Torabi Tabataba'i ed., *Athar-e Bastani-ye Adharbayjan* 2 vols (Tehran, 1355), vol. 1, pp. 134-35; Ja'fariyan, "Amr beh ma'ruf," pp. 22-25.

220. 'Abdol-Hoseyn Nava'i, *Asnad va Makateb-e Tarikhi-ye Iran az sal-e 1038 ta 1105* (Tehran, 1360), p. 225.

221. Qomi, *Kholasat*, vol. 1, p. 380; see also Rumlu, *Ahsan*, pp. 508-09; Qazvini, *Tarikh-e Jahanara*, p. 302; Monshi, *Tarikh*, vol. 1, p. 201.

222. Klaus-Michael Röhrborn, *Provinzen und Zentralgewalt Persiens im 16. und 17. Jahrhundert* (Berlin 1966), p. 71.

223. It was referred to again in 1564, see Qomi, *Kholasat*, vol. 1, 450.

224. M. F. Brosset, *Collection d'Historiens Armeniens* 2 vols. (St. Petersburg, 1874-76), vol. 1, p. 554; vol. 2, p. 8.

pented.[225] It was a good show, of course, as is clear from the prevalance
of prostitution and wine dinking under 'Abbas I as well as his warm
relations with them. Under his immediate successors, prostitutes were
to be found in taverns and in the streets, as discused above.

When Khalifeh Soltan became grand vizier in October 1645, he
was offered a gift in the form of the national revenues of the brothels
(*beyt al-lotf*). Khalifeh Soltan asked 'Abbas II instead to be allowed
to ban prostitution and brothels. Orders were sent to the outlying
districts to ban alcohol and wineshops. This was part of a general
purification campaign including the banning of alcohol, the closing
of all taverns and the ban on Armenians to be any longer engaged in
the making of fur cloaks, which they sold to Moslems. The shah supported the ban despite the fact that he was offered much money by
the owners of the taverns to stay in business.[226] To celebrate this event
poets wrote laudatory pieces praising the shah for this important step
to protect religion.[227] In the beginning there was severe suppression of
all prostitutes and taverns. They only could go to clients if they had
been asked to their houses. To set an example, Khalifeh Soltan had a
woman, who had prostituted her daughters, thrown to man-eating
dogs.[228] Unfortunately, it was in vain, as fornication, betting, wine
drinking and other untoward activities continued even by the shah
himself, by Khalifeh Soltan and the populace at large.[229]

---

225. Molla Jalal, *Ruznameh*, p. 356.

226. Dehgan, *Tarikh-e Safaviyan*, p. 102; Vahid Qazvini, *Tarikh*, p. 415; Chardin, *Voyages*, vol. 2, p. 216; Keyvani 129; Rasul Ja'fariyan ed., *Mirath-e Eslami-ye Iran* 10 vols. (Qom, 1373/1994), vol. 6, pp. 236-37; Ja'fariyan, "Amr beh ma'ruf," pp. 28-29.

227. Ja'fariyan, "Amr beh ma'ruf," pp. 29-32. The *Saqi-nameh* was addressed to 'Evaz Beyg, which leads me to believe that the poem was written not in 1653, as submitted, but rather in 1663 when he was Lord High Justice (*divan-beygi*) of Iran.

228. Chardin, *Voyages*, vol. 2, p. 216; Tavernier, *Voyages*, p. 253.

229. Khalifeh Soltan sometimes drank so much alcohol that he had to be held on his horse by two servants, who kept him in his saddle. Willem Floor, "A Note on the Grand Vizierate in Seventeenth Century Persia," *ZDMG* 155 (2005), p. 463.

In 1685, after a failed effort to give up wine in 1668, Shah Soleyman banned wine at his court for medical reasons, while dancing girls and musicians were no longer present when foreign ambassadors were received in audience in that year.[230] In 1694, when Shah Soltan Hoseyn acceded to the throne, shortly thereafter he banned the sale of intoxicating liquor and of that most deleterious drug, *bhang*, which is made from hemp seed. Houses of ill-repute were to be closed, and pigeon racing, cock-fights, ram-fights, and bull-fights were to cease; the edict further admonished women to behave modestly, not to mingle with non-related men and not to appear in public. The royal edict was chiseled in stone and erected at the entrance of mosques.[231] To give more weight to the execution of the edict, Shah Soltan Hoseyn had a written agreement (*vathiqeh-nameh*) drawn up, in which the olama undertook to see to its execution and to which a number of the highest-ranking olama put their seal plus a short statement of intent.[232] There is, of course, also the inspiring story that government officials tried to convince the shah not to issue the edict, because of the large financial loss involved, a loss that the state's finances could ill afford and that were needed for the defense of the realm. It is doubtful whether this really happened (for one thing, the amount mentioned is not credible) and it is more likely that it was a deliberate embellishment of the religious epiphany that the shah experienced to make him even look better than he already was. Whatever the truth, this moment of religious fervor did not last long, as government officials knew, of course, given the need for money, wine and

---

230. Kaempfer, *Am Hofe*, pp, 281-82. For the text of the edict see Ja'fariyan, "Amr beh ma'ruf," pp. 37-38.

231. Nasiri, *Dastur*, pp. 50-51; H. L. Rabino, *Mazandaran and Astarabad* (London, 1928), p. 37 (Amol); Sayyed Jamal Torabi-Tabataba'i, *Athar-e Bastani-ye Adherbaijan* (Tehran, 2535/1976), vol. 1, p. 276-82; Hajj Hoseyn Nakhjavani, "Masjed-e jame'-ye Tabriz va sharh-e katibehha-ye an," *Nashriyeh-ye Daneshkadeh-ye Adabiyat-e Tabriz* 6/1 (1333/1964), pp. 36-38; Hamid Izedpenah, *Athar-e Bastani va Tarikhi-ye Lorestan* 2 vols. (Tehran, 1363), vol. 1, pp. 137-42 (Khorramabad); Ja'fariyan, "Amr beh ma'ruf," pp. 39-43.

232. Nasiri, *Dastur*, pp. 43-44; Ja'fariyan, "Amr beh ma'ruf," pp. 43-50.

women.[233] Therefore, wine continued to be produced, exported and drunk, while prostitution as well as a large variety of other untoward activities remained a fact of life. In 1721, almost at the end of Shah Soltan Hoseyn's reign, a two-month long appearance of a red sun was interpreted by the olama as a bad omen. They asked people to repent and used this as an argument to convince and induce the shah to expel the prostitutes from Isfahan.[234]

Whereas the previous bans were aimed at bringing about an environment that was more in line with religious precepts, in October 1726, a Safavid pretender in the Bandar 'Abbas area believed that the removal of prostitutes and other evil-doers might bring an end to the Afghan occupation. Therefore, he gave orders to his deputy-governor of that port, Mohammad Zal Beyg, to kill dancing girls, male dancers, gamblers, drunkards, etc. "so that God's punishment would not weigh heavier over this country."[235] The order was not executed.

Afsharid–Zand Period (1736–1794)

Under Tahmasp II (r. 1723–1732) and Nader Shah (r. 1736-1747), the situation concerning prostitution remained unchanged. Tahmasp II set an excellent example, because he devoted all his time in adoration of Bacchus and Venus, and thus caroused constantly. Things were not better under his usurping successor. One might say that Iran during Nader Shah's reign was one big brothel, where wine flowed freely. In Shiraz in 1734, "a town abounding with exquisite wine and although it was the time of Ramazan, i.e. of their fasting, he [Nader] gave permission to his entire army to drink it and, as they numbered 90,000 men, they emptied the wine-houses in a few days"[236] No boy

233. Eshraqi, "Shah Soltan Hoseyn," pp. 90-91.

234. Hajj Mirza Hasan Hoseyni Fasa' i, *Farsnameh-ye Naseri*. 2 vols. ed. Mansur Rastgar Fasa'i (Tehran, 1378/1999), vol. 1, p. 497.

235. Willem Floor, *The Afghan Occupation of Safavid Persia 1721-1729* (Paris, 1998), p. 303.

236. Anonymous, *A Chronicle of the Carmelites in Persia and the Papal Mission of the Seventeenth and Eighteenth Centuries*, 2 vols. (London, 1939), vol. 1, p. 601.

or girl was safe from the lustful hands of his soldiers, while in case of rebellion, the women and boys of the rebels were enslaved. Additional sources of women, girls and boys were those sold by their family to pay taxes.

In 1730, while operating in Khorasan, Nader's troops raped many women and girls in Mashhad, against which no measures were taken.[237] In April 1732, fights had broken out between the population of Qazvin and Nader's troops because they had raped some Qazvini women. Each side lost about 75 dead and the Qazvinis said that they would not suffer the presence of Nader's troops anymore.[238] Mohammad 'Ali Khan, who had arrived with Wakhtang Mirza in January 1733 in Bandar 'Abbas on inspection was accompanied by a rough and undisciplined lot, who committed all kinds of untoward activities such as the rape of women and girls, the stealing of cattle and extortion of food.[239] On the 25 January 1733, it was reported that the Persians had abandoned their plan to attack Basra and were enslaving many women and children in Hoveyzeh, who were sold for 15-20 *mahmudi*s per person.[240] On the 26 November 1733, the *sardar* Tahmaspqoli Beyg Jalayer forbade married women to be outside their homes, because he probably knew what was coming. On the 23 December 1733, he decamped and his soldiers took women away and stole all they could when going into the houses. The same happened when marauding tribesmen made their regular incursions into parts of Iran, such as Baluch and Afghans in the south and Lezgis in the North: one of their objectives was to capture women, girls and young boys, who were sold as slaves. Also, when an occupying force had to

---

237. VOC 2255 (28/01/1731), f. 2280-82.

238. VOC 2322 (26/07/1732), f. 283vs, 288.

239. VOC 2269, Gamronsch Dagregister (04/01/1733 and 10/011733) f. 6604 vs; .VOC 2232, de Cleen to Batavia (30/09/1733), f. 36vs-38r.

240. VOC 2269, Extract Daghregister Bassoura, f. 6612-12 vs; VOC 2322, Basra to Gamron (05/08/1733), f. 425; On July 12, 1733 tax collectors arrived in Isfahan to demand 24,000 *tumans*, and even government officials were given the bastinado to get money, for the city and villages were almost empty of people (many of whom had fled). VOC 2584, Beschrijvinge, f. 2007-08.

abandon a town, they would grab anything of value that they could and in particular, they targeted girls and boys.[241]

After the war with Turkey in 1730, Nader moved to Khorasan where he defeated the rebellious Turkomans. He then dealt with the Abdali Afghans who had made common cause with Hoseyn Khan Ghalzai. They had massacred some 12,000 men, women and children (even cutting open the bellies of pregnant women), enslaved many people and left with a large booty.[242] In case of rebellions, the rebels were heavily punished and their wives and children sold to the brothels and/or given to the conqueror's soldiers or staff.[243]

In October 1741, Emamverdi Khan, the admiral of the Persian fleet, sent the Arab mutineers a peace proposal. If they did not accept it, he threatened to kill them all and enslave all their women and children and destroy their islands.[244] After Mohammad Taqi Khan Shirazi's failed revolt in 1744, Nader Shah gave his wives and children to his soldiers.[245] On many occasions when he had conquered a foe, Nader Shah would sell the female prisoners at public auctions.[246] No wonder that when the Dutch estimated the size of his army marching to Qandahar in 1736 at 200,000 men, in addition, they found there were 20,000 women.[247]

---

241. VOC 2323, Extract van 'tSpahans Dagregister (Summary of the Isfahan Diary), f. 908-11, 930-34; Floor, *Afghan Occupation*, pp. 50, 68.

242. VOC 2255 (28/01/1731), f.2280-82.

243. Anonymous, *Hadith-e Nader Shahi*; ed. Reza Sha'bani (Tehran, 2536/1977), p. 28; Hanway, *An historical account*, vol. 1, p. 296.

244. VOC 2584, Ibrahim Sahid (Congo) to Koenad (Gamron) (18/11/1741), f. 2229-34; VOC 2584, Zion and Deeldekaas to Koenad (11/11/1741), f. 2692-96; VOC 2584, Mohammad Taqi *darya-beygi* to Koenad (11/11/1741 received), f. 2134-35.

245. Mohammad Kazem Mervi, *'Alamara-ye Naderi* 3 vols. Mohammad Amin Riyahi ed. (Tehran, 1364/1985), vol. 3, p. 946.

246. 'Abdol-Razzaq Maftuni Donboli, *Tajrabat al-Ahrar va Tasliyeh al-Abrar* 2 vols. Hasan Qazi Tabataba'i ed. (Tehran, 1349/1970), vol. 1, p. 467.

247. VOC 2416, Isfahan to Gamron (26/12/1736), f. 3942-51.

In April 1734, the Dutch reported that Nader Shah had become an alcoholic and allowed his army to drink wine. He gave full reign to prostitution and recommended it as a good thing for his soldiers. This may explain the rumor, that somebody in Isfahan was said to have farmed out the bordellos and wine-houses for 5,000 *tuman*s per year.[248] To show how immoral he had become, the Dutch reported him having said: "Who is God; I have declared all women to be common property." Also by force, he had Armenian girls taken from Jolfa to enjoy his carnal lust.[249] Beyram 'Ali Khan, a well-known courageous man was strangled by Nader, because, during a wine-drinking get-together (*majles*), he asked that unfortunate man what kind of children would be born to women who had had sex with 10 soldiers. He then had answered: "One just like you, a Nader dourou [sic; *nader-e du-ru* or a rare two-faced (child), i.e. a bastard]. This Nero did not tolerate that."[250]

However, the same freedom to use women was not accorded to foreigners. On the 1 January 1734, the governor of Isfahan told the Banyans that henceforth they were forbidden to drink wine or brandy and that they were not allowed to bring women into the caravanserais for pleasure.[251] These women undoubtedly were non-Moslems, otherwise that would have resulted in all kinds of trouble for them, as the Dutch found out in August 1730, when they were accused of sometimes talking to Moslem women and sometimes keeping them in their houses as if they were their wives.[252] Fortunately, for them they were able to show that the accusation was a frivolous one, having been made to spite them.

---

248. VOC 2323, f. 988 (30/03/1734).

249. VOC 2323, f. 998-90; VOC 2584, Beschrijvinge, f. 2016; VOC 2323, f. 990. On April 8, 1734 Nader behaved most improperly with prostitutes and young male dancers.

250. VOC 2416, Isfahan to Gamron (26/10/1736), f. 2534-64; VOC 2584, Beschrijvinge, f. 2022-23.

251. VOC 2323, f. 936-41.

252. VOC 2253, f. 551-59.

It was not only war that supplied the slave markets with boys and girls. The tax burden was so heavy under Nader Shah that urban and rural tax payers were beaten with sticks and chains to force them to pay. When this did not help, the tax collectors forced them to sell their wife and/or children. In 1747 the price of a girl was 15 rubles or 22.5 *tumans* and one woman 10 rubles or 15 *tumans*; these were then taken to serve the soldiers.[253] Otter reports a case of a man in Kurdestan who faced the dilemma either to find money to pay the tax collectors or to sell his own daughter to raise that money.[254] Astarabadi relates that, on his way to Iraq, Nader killed so many people as punishment for perceived misbehavior that the price of a 14-year old boy and an 11-year old girl went down to 1,500 dinars in 1746.[255] But the slavers did not take anyone, for there seems to have been a surfeit on the market. If the slave buyers did not like what they saw, even when the girls were virgins, they refused to buy them and the tax payer had to find money elsewhere.[256]

Apart from war, rebellion, lack of money, and slavery, another source of women was that of donations. In the aftermath of the Safavid dynasty's fall, there was a large number of Safavid pretenders who claimed to be heir to the throne. Their rural adherents to get a whiff of presumed royalty, offered their daughters to these pretenders in the hope, of his success, to better their life. As all these pretenders failed, their harems were up for grabs, thus adding to the slave population.

This same situation continued under the Zands, but to a lesser extent.[257] Karim Khan was well aware that he had to provide his soldiers

253. Arunova and Ashrafiyan, *Gosudarst'vo*, p. 102.

254. Jean Otter, *Voyage en Turquie et en Perse* (Paris, 1748) translated into Persian by 'Ali Eqbali as *Safarnameh-ye Zhan Uter* (Tehran, 1363/1984), p. 181.

255. Mohammad Kazem, *'Alamara*, vol. 3, p. 180.

256. Mohammad Ebrahim Bastani-Parizi, *Khatun-e haft qal'eh: majma'-ye maqalat-e tarikhi* (Tehran, 1344/1965), p. 395.

257. For a case of the kidnapping of women by the Turkmen see Abu'l-Hasan Ghaffari Kashani, *Golshan-e Morad* ed. by Gholamreza Tabataba'i-Majd (Tehran, 1369/1990), p. 314.

with the means to find sexual gratification. When he went on a multi-annual campaign to Azerbayjan, he, therefore, provided his men with the needed votaries of pleasure. One option was to keep a tribe of gypsies (*foyuj*) always with his army, because he knew "that mankind is captured in the hand of lust." He also knew that in case of need, people made use of animals, but he wanted to give his troops something better. He therefore, decided to keep not only gypsies attached to his army, but also prostitutes, accompanied by female dancers and musicians.[258]

Like any other general, Karim Khan Zand realized the importance of having female camp followers to keep the army happy, but during periods of peace that same army had no other outlet for its energy and he thus wanted to provide a channeled outlet for it. Also, it would prevent rape and other untoward activities aimed at the urban population. Karim Khan Zand, therefore, assigned a special quarter of Shiraz for prostitutes so that the general population and in particular, the virtuous, the pious and God-fearing would be not be led into tempation and the evil of the depraved and the corrupt. In this district with its brothels and winehouses, soldiers, courtiers, townspeople and guests of the court found solace and amusement. Here a wide arrangement of women were found, numbering in the thousands, from the simple whore to the cultured courtesan, to serve his army and hangers on as well as civilian clients. Karim Khan, himself a sensual man who liked women, allegedly was said to have commented that "a town without its brothels (*kharabat*) was like a town without a lavatory or a garbage dump."[259]

Donboli scathingly commented: he thus made the Abode of Discourse (*Dar al-'Elm*) into an Abode of Intercourse (*Dar al-'Eysh*) and the Residential House (*Dar al-Maqameh*) into a Public House (*Dar al-Qamameh*).[260] In fact, it was said that Karim Khan had arranged

---

258. Asaf, *Rostam al-Tavarikh*, pp. 329-31.

259. 'Abdol-Razzaq Maftuni Donboli, *Tajrabat al-Ahrar va Tasliyeh al-Abrar* 2 vols. Hasan Qazi Tabataba'i ed. (Tehran, 1349/1970), vol. 2, p. 43.

260. Donboli, *Tajrabat*, vol. 2, pp. 42-44.

for the establishment of the red light district in Shiraz to provide all kinds of amusement to the many hostages that were kept in Shiraz to prevent them conspiring against him.[261] In the red light district of Shiraz, which was known as *Kheyl,* lived some 6,000 sex workers as well as female acrobats, dancers and musicians and all of them had names of which the Rostam of *Rostam al Tavarikh* lists about seventy.[262] Mullah Fatima, of whom he gives a detailed idealized description, knew 20,000 verses by heart of both old and new poets, which she recited accompanied by music. She said about herself and her colleagues:

> I and girls like me are always infertile. We apply a medicine so that we do not become pregnant. For someone who is infertile there is no waiting period [of two months]. One thousand men can sleep with an infertile one. Apart from that we satisfy all Moslem precepts. We are caring, industrious, earnest, keen and zealous, and concerning good welfare institutions, we give alms and spend them for the greater glory of God and we never fail to support good works.[263]

Karim Khan himself availed himself of the services offered in the taverns by inviting women to perform at his court. One of them, Shah-Nabat, a witty courtesan, who also was a poetess, became his mistress in his later years. When she fell ill, he had her bed surrounded by other women hoping that by prayers her malady might be transferred to one of them. When she died, he had her portrait painted and an epitath composed by Mirza Sadeq Nami.[264] Karim Khan was

---

261. Asaf, *Rostam al-Tavarikh*, p. 339. Female dancers performed at festivals such as Nowruz and marriages, while rich men had groups of Georgian boys for singing and music making. Hardford Jones-Brydges ed., *The Dynasty of the Kajars* (London, 1833), p. cxlix; Edward Scott Waring, *A Tour to Sheeraz* (London, 1807), p. 53.

262. Asaf, *Rostam al-Tavarikh*, pp. 340-41. A well-known prostitute aka *Chakmeh-ye zard* or yellow boots. Ibid., 322.

263. Asaf, *Rostam al-Tavarikh*, pp. 342, 348.

264. Asaf, *Rostam al-Tavarikh*, p. 341; Donboli, *Tajrabat*, vol. 2, pp. 49, 56-58; Waring, *Tour*, p. 61. For the prayer rite to transfer illness from a sick person to

not alone in this, for all governors had many woman attached to their court. For example, in 1770, Hedayat Khan of Rasht kept "a very large number of hired strumpets and women in his harem."[265]

QAJAR PERIOD (1794–1925)

Mainly due to lack of alternative remunerative employment opportunities, many women, girls and boys had to earn money for their family by providing their personal sexual services to those who stood in need of them. Given the extent of poverty in urban areas, prostitution was rampant. Although data are dispersed, there is convincing evidence that prostitution remained a structural part of social and economic life in urban Iran. In Tehran there was a special city quarter for prostitutes during Fath Ali Shah's reign (1797-1834),[266] and likewise in Shiraz, a holdover of Karim Khan Zand's reign.

> The people who pay the heaviest tax to the government, are the female dancer, and the votaries of pleasure. They exercise their professions under the immediate patronage of the governor; their names, ages, &c. are carefully registered, and if one should die or marry, another instantly supplies her place. They are divided into classes, agreeably to their merits, and the estimation they are held in; each class inhabit separate streets, so that you may descend from the *doo Toomunees* to the Polli Seeahs, without the chance of making mistakes.[267]

Some 30 years later the situation had not changed that much in Shiraz, for "Wine is often drunk in private parties: and public women are in greater numbers here than even at Ispahan."[268]

---

somebody else see Willem Floor, *Public Health in Qajar Iran* (Washington D.C., 2005), pp. 98-99 as well as chapter five.

265. Gmelin, *Travels*, p. 100.

266. Polak, "Die Prostitution," p. 517.

267. Waring, *Tour*, p. 80.

268. Buckingham, *Travels*, vol. 2, p. 312.

Prostitution was thus a widespread custom that was practiced in all towns and major caravan halting stations.²⁶⁹ Nevertheless, Porter maintains that "The existence of such infamous places [brothels], is now hardly known in the country."²⁷⁰ However, other travelers saw it differently. At the caravanserai at Baba Hajji, Dupré met a prostitute, face uncovered, who had been expelled from Shiraz.²⁷¹ At the caravanserai of Bajgah (near Shiraz), Morier saw "seated among the rubbish three women, a man and two greyhounds. The women had their faces uncovered, and soon informed us, (though they bore a most haggish appearance,) that they were *kowlies*, or courtesans by professions. They seemed to form one community with the rahdars [road-guards]."²⁷² Important men, as in previous centuries, also made use of the services of high-class and expensive courtesans, who, *inter alia*, enlivened parties with their beauty and wit, and even Naser al-Din Shah was said to have had a few at his beck and call. Consequently, their pay was quite high and they received, for example, expensive shawls in payment for their participation in debaucheries.²⁷³

These *kowlis* were elsewhere called "Suzemaneeah, or courtezans."²⁷⁴ There were in fact two groups; one, which was that of the gypsies, who were referred to by a large variety of names, and the other the Suzmanis, a group of Kurdish origin. Both were nomadic, performed music and dance, while the women were willing and available for lusty males. Because of this, both groups had a bad reputation. Of the gypsies it was said that "the women living entirely by thieving

269. Moser, *A Travers*, p. 389. According to Hommaire de Hell, *Voyage*, vol. 2, p. 17, about half of the women in the streets had loose morals, due to their husbands' interest in youths, who, moreover, did not mind their wives' behavior. Persian men, according to Gobineau, *Trois Ans*, vol. 2, p. 185, opined that apart from their own womenfolk all other women were of doubtful chastity and they said so in the most outrageous terms.

270. Porter, *Travels*, vol. 1, p. 349.

271. A. Dupré, *Voyage en Perse fait dans les années 1807, 1808, 1809*, 2 vols. (Paris, 1819), vol. 1, pp. 463, 466.

272. Morier, *A Second Journey*, p. 90.

273. Polak, "Die Prostitution", p. 517.

274. Buckingham, *Travels*, vol. 2, p. 149.

and prostitution."[275] These groups were not the only ones, because the Khitur tribe around Qahnu, north of Minab, also had the reputation to prostitute their women, including the married ones.[276]

Before the Qajars, dancing girls were always part of the group of people that welcomed a grandee when he arrived at a city, "but this is strictly forbidden nowadays," according to Goldsmid.[277] Clearly, the ban on this type of frivolity imposed by Shah Soleyman in 1685 had survived the regime changes and the passage of time. However, in some outlying districts of Iran local officials apparently were not aware of such a ban. For example, around 1820, consul Rich was in Kurdestan and he "was at the exhibition in the meidan yesterday at noon. Principally, it consisted of a dance, performed by all the most disreputable town's women, who were drunk. The Shahzadeh, who was looking at them, was drunk also, as were two or three favourites who were standing around him."[278] Baluchi women danced for the governor, gladdened by the distribution of money.[279]

There continued to be groups of female dancers and singer/musicians in addition to the more numerous male ones. They performed in the harems of the wealthy as well as for private male parties. About 1840, Layard attended a private party given in the harem of the governor of Isfahan. He observed that "many of these girls were strikingly handsome-some were celebrated for their beauty. Their costume consisted of loose silk jackets of some gay colour, entirely open in the front so as to show the naked figure up to the waist. Their movements

---

275. Harry de Windt, *A Ride to India across Persia and Baluchistan* (London, 1891), p. 107; Brugsch, *Im Lande der Sonne*, p. 169; Lycklama à Nijeholt, *Voyage*, vol. 4, pp. 52-54; Polak, *Persien*, vol. 1, p. 293; Ibid., "Die Prostitution", p. 564; Hommaire de Hell, *Voyage*, vol. 2, p. 17.

276. K. E. Abbott, "Geographical Notes taken during a Journey in Persia in 1849 and 1850" *JRGS* 25 (1855), p. 51.

277. Sir Frederic J. Goldsmid, Eastern *Persia, An Account of the Journeys of the Persian Boundary Commission 1870-71-72*, 2 vols. (London, 1876), p. 108.

278. Rich, *Narrative of a Residence*, vol. 1, p. 231 (on the occasion of a marriage of a prince).

279. Percy M. Sykes, *Ten Thousand Miles in Persia or Eight Years in Iran* (New York, 1902), p. 141.

were accompanied by female musicians."[280] In the 1850-60s, the Susmanis still provided dancing, singing and music and led a dissolute life, such as the practice of prostitution "with the utmost repugnant audacity."[281] Some 20 years later, Binder reported that the Susmani girls danced lasciviously with a transparent mousseline shirt that did not cover much of the breasts, for the shoulders and breasts were almost bare; they were followed by male dancers dressed in female dress.[282] Around 1880, C. J. Wills and some other Europeans had been invited to a dinner party in Shiraz, where pretty Susmani girls performed. After dinner, the Persians began to drink heavily; "in fact, their frequent acceptance of cupfuls of raw spirits from the hands of the dancers had made them see things generally in a rosy light. They wept when we left!"[283] By the end of the nineteenth century, Persian hosts in Tehran did not invite Europeans for such frolicking anymore, for female dancers only danced in the harems, "but this was all strictly private and not accessible to European visitors."[284] However, for those who were interested in this kind of alluring spectacle there was, "In a low quarter, just outside Tehran, a number of Kurdish girls belonging to a tribe which had a peculiar morality (or rather immorality) of its own, squatted, unveiled, in tawdry finery designed to attract the passer-by."[285] By 1907, there were some 40 female troupes with more than 400 dancers and singers, who, like their male colleagues, paid

---

280. A. H. Layard, *Early Adventures in Persia, Susiana, and Babylonia* (London, 1894 [Westmead: Gregg Int., 1971), p. 125

281. Lycklama, *Voyage*, vol. 4, pp. 52-54; Polak, *Persien*, vol. 1, p. 293; Ibid, "Die Prostitution," p. 564; Brugsch, *Die Reise*, vol. 2, p. 304; Häntzsche, "Haram," p. 431. According to Polak, "Die Prostitution", p. 564, the cost of hiring the dancing girls was high. Usually a shawl was given with a value between 16 to 40 ducats.

282. Henry Binder, *Au Kurdistan* (Paris, 1887), pp. 389-90.

283. Wills, *In the land*, p. 115. He also reported them en route between Kangavar and Kermanshah, where under a roadside grove, "the woman, gaily dressed, with her face painted and without any veil, her hair in long tails, strung with coins, importunately solicited us. The man remained under the umbrella, and took no notice. They were 'Susmanis,' or gypsies." Ibid., p. 108.

284. Neville, *Unconventional*, p. 147.

285. Neville, *Unconventional*, p. 147.

taxes to Ehtesham al-Khalvat, a court official.[286] Naser al-Din Shah had his own female musicians and singers for entertainment in his women's quarters.[287]

In Tafreejan, outside Hamadan, many courtesans "had fixed their abodes there."[288] In Yazd in 1879, with an estimated population of 40,000, reportedly there were 500 prostitutes registered in the government's fiscal records, or 1.2 percent of the population.[289] According to Najm al-Molk, at that time there were 40 prostitutes in Dezful, which also had a population of 40,000.[290] In Rasht they were to be found as well,[291] and even in a small town such as Senneh (Kurdestan).[292] In Kermanshah, the prostitutes lived in the house of the public executioner. "The monopoly of whom [i.e. the prostitutes] was the largest source of this man's revenue."[293] A similar situation existed in Shiraz in the 1880s, where prostitutes, "are, as a rule, tolerated. They are under the absolute jurisdiction either of the daroga or the public executioner."[294] Hajj Sayyah, a nineteenth century reformer and world traveler, described the fate of poor women in the Kerman area towards the end of the 19th century as follows. The men, driven by poverty,

> Lease their wives and daughters, or even sell them, as
> *sigheh*. This activity is carried on in the madrasehs by the

---

286. J.C. Häntzsche, "Spezialstatistik von Persien," *Zeitschrift der Gesellschaft für Erdkunde* 1869, p. 440; Brugsch, *Reise*, vol. 1, p. 187; Eugene Aubin, *La Perse d'aujourd'hui* (Paris, 1907), p. 230.

287. Momtahen al Dowleh, *Khaterat [...]* ed. Hoseyn Qoli Khan Shaqaqi (Tehran, 1353/1974), p. 106.

288. Buckingham, *Travels*, vol. 1, p. 169.

289. A. H. Schindler, "Reisen in südlichen Persien 1879," *Zeitschrift der Gesellschaft für Erdkunde zu Berlin* 16 (1881), pp. 320-321.

290. 'Abdol-Ghaffar Najm ol-Molk, *Safarnameh-ye Khuzestan*. ed. Mohammad Dabir-Siyaqi (Tehran, 1342/1963), pp. 21, 93 (just across the Shatt al-Arab was Basra with its Red Light district aka Kataneh).

291. Asaf al-Dowleh, *Asnad*, vol. 3, p. 233.

292. Mirza Mohammad 'Ali Khan Farid al-Molk, *Khaterat-e Farid* ed. Mas'ud Farid Qaragozlu (Tehran, 1353/1975), p. 257.

293. Wills, *In the Land*, p. 110.

294. C.J. Wills, *Persia as it is* (London 1886), p. 40.

seminary students *(tollab)*. The type of woman (young or old), the price and terms were concluded, and she was fetched or came to one's house. The women dallied with the seminary students in their rooms *(hojreh)* in the evenings. The earnings were taxed by the government as well as a fee *(khedmateneh)* taken by government officials. This custom is not limited to Kerman but practiced all over Iran in all cities by the young (25-40 year old) seminary students. However, what is peculiar to Kerman is that the women are given to others and hired out. The gunners who have money run gambling dens [in the city] where peasants come to bet to get money to pay their taxes. They bring their wives and daughters with them who serve as security for the loan they get.[295]

There was a simple reason for the continued existence of prostitution. First, there was a strong market demand due to the high number of unmarried men, and of married, but unaccompanied, travelers and transients in the cities and towns. Second, for desperate poor people, prostitution was sometimes the only opportunity to earn some money in the urban areas. Third, prostitution provided an important source for income to the authorities.

As in former times, the financial interest of the local authorities in the prevalence of untoward behavior remained high. In the beginning of the nineteenth century, Waring wrote that prostitutes were among the highest taxed professions in the country. This did not change throughout the century, for Polak in the 1850s and Hajj Sayyah in the 1880s, reported that prostitutes were allowed to be in business in exchange for a monthly fee.[296] De Monteforte,[297] the chief

---

295. Hajj Sayyah, *Khaterat*, pp. 164-65.

296. Polak, "Die Prostitution", p. 564 (in Tabriz, Qazvin, Hamadan, Isfahan, Qom and Shiraz); Hajj Sayyah, *Khaterat*, p. 482; Wills, *Persia*, p. 40; 'Ali Akbar Sa'idi Sirjani, *Vaqaye'-ye Ettefaqiyeh* (Tehran, 1361/1982), p. 609.

297. Antonio Conte di Monteforte came to Iran in 1879 as part of an Austrian military mission that had been requested by Naser al-Din Shah in 1878. Because he had worked in public security of Vienna he was tasked by the shah to establish a new police force in Tehran. See Helmut Slaby, *Bindenschild und*

of police of Tehran received an annual payment of 14,000 *tumans* from the prostitutes.[298] In Senneh (Kurdestan) in the 1880s the revenues from the brothels (*fahesheh-khaneh*) amounted to 100 *tumans* or 10% of total cash revenues.[299] It also happened, of course, that clients who visited prostitutes were 'arrested' by the police and then released after payment of a hefty fine.[300] The authorities also used prostitutes for political ends. Because the women had access to the private quarters of their male clients, they reported on what they learnt about the house as well as took compromising documents. The police also used prostitutes to steal other wanted items as well as send them into homes of Europeans or other persons, who then were heavily fined by the police.[301] In 1907, Sa'd al-Dowleh, one of the supporters of Mohammad 'Ali Shah, organized a protest by a group of unveiled prostitutes, who chanted the slogan: "The constitution has given us freedom to abandon our religious duties and live as we like." This was an attack on the reformists who, *inter alia*, advocated women's emancipation, or, according to the conservatives, immorality and prostitution.[302]

The connection between the urban authorities and prostitutes was not limited to a purely financial or political one. E'temad al-Saltaneh recorded in his diary that Hajji Mullah 'Ali demanded the dismissal of some government officials in Tehran, because they kept prostitutes in their office (it is possible that this was a politically motivated accusation because some religious leaders considered any woman outside the home to be wanton). Naser al-Din Shah remarked that if he would throw the prostitutes out of the city gates they would be allowed back through another gate.[303] In 1906, the house of the *Emam-e Jom'eh* of

Sonnenlöwe (Graz, 1982), pp. 162-68, 181-87.

298. E'temad al-Saltaneh, *Ruznameh*, pp. 159, 236, 997 (between 1882 and 1893).

299. Farid al-Molk, *Khaterat-e Farid*, p. 257.

300. Wills, *Persia*, p. 40; Polak, "Die Prostitution," p. 564.

301. Polak, "Die Prostitution", p. 564.

302. Mehdi Malekzadeh, *Tarikh-e Enqelab-e mashrutiyat-e Iran* 7 vols. (Tehran, 1328/1949), vol. 3, p. 62.

303. E'temad al-Saltaneh, *Ruznameh*, pp. 159, 236, 997.

Rasht was said to be a brothel and a tavern, while other government authorities were accused of doing or causing evil things.[304] In Astarabad in July 1921, the governor was accused of keeping prostitutes in the Government House.[305] This also happened in Isfahan, where the house of clients, who had visited a prostitute, had been robbed. The clients accused the woman Sanam aka Khar-kesh, who was one of the official prostitutes in Isfahan, of having organized the robbery. The deputy governor then imprisoned her for 24 hours, but that night he slept with her and made her his official paramour. Therefore, he did not want to keep her at Government House, but sent her home and visited her house in secret. But his enemies found out and exposed him.[306] As in previous centuries pimps were referred to as *qavvadi* and *ja-kesh*; they usually had a 'stable' of boys and girls for their clients' entertainment.[307]

Formally, the Qajar government followed religious law for the punishment of prostitution and the imposition of the death penalty was theoretically on the books.[308] However, matters hardly ever reached such a stage. It would seem that in Urmiyeh around 1880, the local authorities took the ban on prostitution seriously. The normal punishment was that prostitutes were put in a bag and then were given the bastinado. Thereafter, their head was shaved, their face blackened with soot, and then they were taken around the streets seated on a donkey.[309] Sometimes, they were buried alive. This is what happened

---

304. Nazem al-Eslam Kermani, *Tarikh-e Bidari-ye Iraniyan* 5 vols. in 2 parts Sa'id Sirjani ed. (Tehran, 1362/1982), part 1, pp. 610-11.

305. Vakil al-Dowleh, *Mokhabarat-e Astarabad*, vol. 2, p. 768.

306. Yaghma'i, *Jandaq*, p. 26.

307. E'temad al-Saltaneh, *Ruznameh*, p. 947. When a notorious 17-year old dancing girl, who was employed at the royal palace, and had a reputation of being a loose woman and having contacts with European men, was executed at the Queen-Mother's orders, this was not because of her loose morals, but due to her sharp tongue and a "tu coque" attitude towards her royal employer, whom she had called a "fellow-sinner". Wills, *Persia*, p. 40; Ibid., *In the land*, p. 202.

308. Häntzsche, "Haram," p. 378.

309. Polak, "Die Prostitution", p. 564; Sirjani, *Vaqaye'*, p. 73. At times the

in 1881, when seven prostitutes were arrested, because they were running after the soldiers. Two of them were strangled in the sewer of the bath-house, five others were buried alive.[310] However, the normal situation was that, as in previous centuries, the authorities once in a while would show their concern for public morality and religion by suppressing prostitution and ancillary activities such as wine drinking. In 1809, the young governor of Shiraz, Hoseyn 'Ali Mirza, was induced by his mother and a local sheikh to expel all prostitutes and close down all taverns. His order was executed rather brutally. The ill-treated prostitutes moved to the villages around Shiraz, while the taverns were closed and their wine jars broken. The sheikh then left Shiraz, quite pleased with himself, but he was showered with the curses of the merchants, whose business was hurt, and of the wise, who did not consider it prudent to expel the prostitutes, fearing that this would create greater immoral problems. Shortly thereafter, the *darugheh* or police chief of Shiraz asked the prince to allow the prostitutes to return and the taverns to be re-opened. He allegedly received four to five *tuman*s from each prostitute and ten *tuman*s from each tavern, while he had to pay the prince-governor 2,000 *tuman*s per year for his function. The *darugheh* pointed out that he would be unable to pay that amount and supported his request with a sum of money, both these compelling arguments had the desired effect, viz. that the prostitutes returned to Shiraz and the taverns were opened again.[311] Polak reports that Mohammad Shah (r. 1834-1848) had ordered the closure of the prostitutes' quarter in Tehran. However, it is doubtful whether this had the desired result. Although, during his son's reign (Naser al-Din Shah, r. 1848-1896), "prostitution was strongly banned, but despite or better because of this ban, it was able to maintain itself in even greater size." Nevertheless, if a scandal or some other political event occurred, this required that they were temporarily expelled from

---

authorities also took action against pimps. Ibid., p. 134.

310. Rubens Duval, *Les dialects néo-araméens de Salmas* (Paris, 1883), pp. 36-37.

311. Dupré, *Voyage*, vol. 1, pp. 464-66.

the city.[312] In 1897, Hajji Sayyed Kamal, a religious dignitary, made much trouble for the authorities and after his arrival in Qazvin, 10-20 houses were destroyed that were suspected as brothels.[313] In 1900, the governor of Shiraz, at the instigation of his wife (to thwart her brother who had a prostitute dance in their mother's clothes), had all prostitutes in town arrested, which yielded him the pretty sum of some 400 *tumans*.[314] In May 1911, the local *anjoman* at Astarabad banned the sale of alcohol by Armenians and the deputy governor also expelled two prostitutes from the city at his orders.[315]

Neighbors alerted the police in case they believed that women of loose morals were working in their street or if one had taken up residence with a man, thus committing fornication. In some cases, the police came to arrest the man and the woman, whom neighbors had reported were living together. It then appeared that the woman was the man's *sigheh*.[316] However, the situation was different when men had brought one or more prostitutes into their home, caravanserai or to an abandoned building to have sex (*'eysh va nush*). When neighbors were aware of such happenings they would warn the police, who usually arrested the woman, when she exited the house, and less often the man. The woman invariably was expelled from the city, while the man was also punished, but usually no details are given. Sometimes it could be imprisonment for two weeks. Another case concerned a pimp, who promised not to engage in pimping anymore.[317] The same action was

---

312. Polak, «Die Prostitution», pp. 517, 564. He also reports that some women prostituted themselves to Europeans to earn money to enable them to go on pilgrimage to Karbala. These same women therefore faithfully respected all other Moslem purity and other religious requirements.

313. 'Eyn al-Saltaneh, *Ruznameh*, vol. 2, p. 1240.

314. Sirjani, *Vaqaye'*, p. 609.

315. Vakil al-Dowleh, *Mokhabarat-e Astarabad*, vol. 1, p. 265.

316. Reza'i and Azari, *Gozareshha-ye Nazimiyeh*, vol. 2, pp. 656, 682-83. In another case a young man had made a prostitute his *sigheh*. Ibid, vol. 1, p. 114; Ibid., p. 83 (the woman had been divorced and the 'client' had paid for the cost of the waiting period or *'eddeh*).

317. Reza'i and Azari, *Gozareshha-ye Nazimiyeh*, vol. 1, pp. 42, 50, 65, 137, 186, 248, 315, 355, 360 (a Christian merchant was the client), 370, 372,

taken when neighbors had the idea that loose women (*zanha-ye bad-kareh*) had invited men into their home to have sex (*shani'eh*) or when a man tried to rape a neighbor's wife, or when a man prostituted his wife and daughter and brought clients home.[318] Police intervention depended, of course, on the rank of the person who received women.[319] It sometimes also happened that a wife caused such a row when she took her husband to task after she found out that he had been with a prostitute that the police had to intervene.[320]

But all these measures only had a temporary impact, because they did not address the main underlying cause, poverty, which gave the poor no other choice but to sell themselves. Moreover, as a result of the growing influx of rural migrants after 1870, in particular in Tehran, "Loose women are to be found everywhere in each quarter in Tehran or other cities. The *kadkhodas* and *babas* [chiefs] of the city quarters know this and receive money from them."[321] According to Neville, although a few Armenian women were believed to be "of dubious morality, there was no regular demi-monde in Teheran."[322] Some of these women gained great popularity, such as Moti Jan, an Indian courtesan, whose departure to Shiraz was bemoaned in a song composed by of one her admirers.[323]

394, 407, 411, 416, 419, 421; vol. 2, pp. 430, 461, 475 (*jakeshi*),481, 511, 540 (client was a drunken sayyed), 568, 583 (pimp), 598, 602, 631 (Christian clients), 632, 650, 653, 673 (female pimp), 676 (female pimp), 694 (female pimp), 681, 691, 706, 709.

318. Reza'i and Azari, *Gozareshha-ye Nazimiyeh*, vol. 1, pp. 26, 50, 73, 371 (rape attempt); vol. 2, 518, 600 (a divorcee and her daughter invited men into their home), 646 (also Jewish clients).

319. See for an interesting case 'Raportha," *Yaghma*, Ordidbehesht (1339/1960), p. 96.

320. Reza'i and Azari, *Gozarehsha-e Nazmiyeh*, vol. 1, p. 4.

321. Qazvini, *Qanun*, pp. 121-22.

322. Neville, *Unconventional*, p. 146. Bricteux, *Au Pays*, p. 286 suggests that, due to the fact that many Armenian men in Jolfa were working abroad, there were many lonely Armenian women, which resulted in licentiousness.

323. Phillot, "Some Lullabies," pp. 52-52; Polak, "Die Prostitution", p. 563.

Also, the court itself set a very bad example, due to the licentious life at court and among the nobility with their liaisons and love affairs.[324] Taj al-Saltaneh provides several instances of the moral laxity at court. Shortly after Naser al-Din Shah's death, when his relatives were still in mourning, her brother, Mozaffar al-Din Shah was found throwing a party. "Around this king were scattered two or three groups of female minstrels, while women of ill repute sat on the fringes of the rug. In the middle, a number of heavy, unshapely women were dancing and making vile gestures or lewd comments. Awful screams of laughter and inane, ludicrous shouts could be heard on all sides."[325] This was not an exception, but this type of behavior became normal at Mozaffar al-Din's court. His sister Taj al-Saltaneh wrote that: "Among the many immoral things that stirred murmurings and caused wonder was the constant coming and going of female musicians and prostitutes who disguised themselves as musicians. For a time my brother's [Mozaffar al-Din Shah] attention was drawn to a paltry, ugly girl from the troupe of Haj Qadam-Shad."[326] As a result of these nocturnal debauches Mozaffar al-Din Shah was derisively called 'sister Mozaffar' (*baji Mozaffar*) by the man-in-the-street.[327] It was, therefore, no surprise that in 1909, a visitor from Khoy, who was of a puritan and conservative bend of mind, considered Tehran to be a den of iniquity with its freedom of drinking alcohol and that like London and Paris it had become an *azad-khaneh* or a Libertine's House, where loose women were seated with their clients in a droshke or horse carriage and circulated through the streets of Tehran."[328] According to

---

324. See for a description of some evenings of pleasure-making and drinking with women, see E'temad al-Saltaneh, *Ruznameh*, pp. 125-26, 342-43, 947.

325. Taj al-Saltaneh, *Crowning Anguish: memoirs of a Qajar princess from the harem to modernity 1884-1914*, translated into English by Anna Vanzan and Amin Neshati (Washington DC, 1993), p. 230.

326. Taj al-Saltaneh, *Crowning*, p. 234.

327. Gu'el Kuhan, *Tarikh-e sansur dar matbu'at-e Iran* 2 vols. (Tehran, 1362/1983), vol. p. 245; Ebrahim Teymur, *Qarardad-e 1890 rezhi-ye tahrim-e tanbaku* (Tehran, 1328/1949), p. 153.

328. Amin al-Shar' Khu'i, "Safarnameh-ye 'Atabat," ed. 'Ali Sadra'i Khu'i in Rasul Ja'fariyan ed. *Mirath-e Eslam dar Iran* 10 vols. (Qom, 1373-78/1994-99), vol. 7,

the poet 'Aref Qazvini, when Aqa Bala Khan Sardar was chief of police of Tehran he forced many girls to become prostitutes. When he saw a nice girl he instructed a procuress to harass the woman and besmirch her reputation. At a certain moment she would be arrested by the police and taken to the Sardar's house and kept there and then released. The husband would not believe his wife's story of her arrest, because he thought she had committed adultery and, therefore, did not want her anymore in his house. As a result, the poor woman, in more than one sense, had no choice but to give in to the Sardar's wishes and joined the army of prostitutes. 'Aref Qazvini further writes that he knew of at least 100 of such cases where women had been forced into prostitution.[329]

Normally, these women and/or boys walked (*valgerd*) the streets and alleys, in particular in some designated city quarters. In Tehran, at the end of the Qajar period, usually they were to be found in the dwellings made in the city moat. For boys, the pick-up place was at the beginning of the Qazvin road in the newly established *Shahr-e Now* quarter.[330] There were other places, such as the garden surrounding the Imamzadeh-ye Da'ud. It was not only a magnet for pious people, but for people who wanted to make an outing, because there was merry making by acrobats and the like as well as coffee-houses offering all kinds of services. It attracted lovers of all kinds, such as catamites, pimps, whoremongers, and prostitutes, due to its many quiet and private spots.[331]

---

p. 519. The order by he governor of Tehran given in 1903 that droshkes should henceforth not any longer transport women wearing the *neqab* (face cover) and prostitutes clearly had become a dead letter. Sepehr, *Vaqaye'*, vol. 2, p. 222.

329. Abu'l-Qasem 'Aref Qazvini, *Kolliyat-e Divan* (Tehran, 1337/1958), pp. 123ff.

330. Ja'far Shahri, *Tarikh-e ejtema'i -Tehran dar qarn-e sizdahom*, 6 vols. (Tehran, 1368/1989) vol. 1, pp. 468-9; Ibid, *Tehran-e Qadim*, vol. 1, p. 28, vol. 3, pp. 394-96. Earlier, *Shahr-e Now* had been known as Mahalleh-ye Qajariyeh, because most of the Madams of the prostitutes were Qajar women who lived in that area. Hakim-Olahi, *Ba man*, vol. 2, p. 40.

331. Shahri, *Tehran-e qadim*, vol. 3, p. 429.

In addition, there were, of course, brothels (*'azab-khaneh*), which provided services on a varying price scale. The latter were among the cleanest and the nicest places in Tehran, according to Shahri.[332] However, unlike the preceding periods, under Mozaffar al-Din Shah, the authorities did not oppose the establishment of several brothels inside the city of Tehran. Despite complaints and protests from people living in the concerned streets, nothing happened. The police officer (*na'eb*) of the affected city quarter told the protesters: "Come and fix a price of your homes and I'll buy them," implying that he wanted to use and turn them into additional brothels. As a result these people did not dare to say anything anymore.[333] Brothels were found elsewhere in Iran. According to Rice, "There are many houses of ill-fame in the cities, and such can often be recognized by the sight of an unveiled woman peeping out of the door."[334] Outside of the Shah 'Abdol-'Azim gate, Nan-e Khanom, who was described as a bad woman of course, had a house, where men could find all kinds of women for hire, not unlike, and may be the same as the women who kept a house with temporary wives or *sigheh*s (see chapter two). Everybody knew about this place and the poor, as a last resort, often would bring their daughters to work there and in order to support their family.[335]

There is very little information available on the pimps and procuresses, who supplied women and provided protection to the brothels as well as their inmates. There was close cooperation as is clear from the case of Rahim Khan, the rowdy (*luti*) who was accused of having killed a mullah in Isfahan, while drunk. He was condemned to death, but his friends, amongst whom were the prostitutes of Isfahan, raised

---

332. Shahri, *Tarikh*, vol. 1, p. 470; vol. 3, p. 400.

333. "Raportha," *Yaghma* Farvardin (1341/1962), p. 48. It also was reported that two Englishmen were seen in a house with Persian women, which is contrary to Islamic law. Mehdi Qoli Hedayat Mokhber al-Saltaneh, *Khaterat va Khatarat* (Tehran, 1344/1965), p. 350.

334. Clara Rice, *Persian Women and Their Ways* (London, 1923), p. 92.

335. Momtahen al-Dowleh, *Khaterat*, p. 245.

sufficient money to change (at least temporarily) Zell al-Soltan's decision to execute him.[336]

In the brothels, which in the early 1920s, if not earlier, were already
concentrated in *Shahr-e Now*; the prostitutes were 'managed' by a so-
called *na'eb-khanom* or *khanom aqa*, meaning the Madam. The entire
red light district was under a *kadkhoda* or chief to whom one could
address complaints in case of mistreatment. The red light district consisted of houses with six to seven rooms, while there were eateries and
shops for the visitors and inhabitants. At night only the eateries provided lighting for the visitors. The sex workers, some of who were very
young, performed dances, accompanied by music. They were forced
by circumstances to work there, and in many cases had been sold by
their parents or husbands to the Madam. "Whenever a new guest
came in, the hostess [Madam] called a girl and commanded her to
show herself to the man, fetch a mattress and a coverlet from a room
which stood empty, and then they would go off to whichever room
the guest preferred."[337] According to the Swedish general Westdahl,
who was in charge of the police of Tehran, the taxes on prostitution
were his department's most important source of income. Their fiscal
rates were scheduled in accordance with their attractiveness, ranging
from 50 øre to 20 crowns per month.[338] In addition to these working
boys and girls, there were also high-class call girls, whose market often
included more than one city. They were well-known among the elite,
who made use of their service. Some of them also performed at parties accompanied by musicians.[339] These independent courtesans were

---

336. Yaghma'i, *Jandaq*, 54.

337. Von Rosen, *Persian Pilgrimage*, p. 106.

338. P. Nystrom, *Fem år I Persien som gendarmofficer* (Stockholm, 1925),
p. 34; Anonymous, "Raportha," *Yaghma*, Ordibehesht (1339/1960), p. 96.
Nevertheless, Westdahl sometimes also punished prostitutes. In one case,
who later became a famous music playing courtesan, Shams al-Zehi, was given
some lashes in front of the police office in the Meydan-e Tupkhaneh. 'Abdol-
Hoseyn Mas'ud Ansari, *Zendegani-ye Man* 4 vols. (Tehran, 1352/1973), vol. 1,
p. 52.

339. E'temad al-Saltaneh, *Ruznameh*, pp. 465, 1056. Von Rosen, *Persian
Pilgrimage*, p. 104 visited a house of a *demi-mondaine* in Tehran, called Shirin,

referred to as *khatun* and one of them was even able to conclude a marriage with one of her clients.[340] A census carried out in Tehran in 1301/1922, indicates the following.[341]

Women who sold themselves (*zan-e khod-forush*)	1.5%
Girls (*dokhtar-e khod-forush*)	1.0%
Zan-e takparan (occasional prostitute)	2.0%
Known boy prostitutes (*pesar-e khod-forush*)	1.5%
Unknown	1.0%
Pa-andaz-e zan (go-between or *dallal*)	305
Pa-andaz-e mard (go-between for men)	60

This meant that, given a population of some 240,000 people, about five per cent of the population of Tehran had to earn their living through prostitution. This number excludes the number of *sigheh*s, who legally were not prostitutes, but provided the same sexual services. In 1922, there were 430 *sigheh*s in Tehran, according to the census, or only one per cent of the number of covenanted wives, a number, as noted in chapter two, that seems somewhat on the low side.[342]

Modern Persian literature depicted Tehran, the epitome of urban life, as being rife with disease, prostitution and immorality and thus an obstacle for progress and emancipation. Moshfeq Kazemi's 'Horrible Tehran' (*Tehran-e Makhfuf*) is a good example of this new trend, but,

---

in 1934. "As far as I could see, the house had two rooms and both served as bedrooms. The first room we entered was empty, very dimly lighted and unfurnished except for a big bed. In the next room there seemed to be a gay party going on. Three girls, who all spoke French, came forward and welcomed us."

340. Momtahen al-Dowleh, *Khaterat*, p. 242.

341. Shahri, *Tehran-e Qadim*, vol. 1, p. 87.

342. Shahri, *Tarikh*, vol. 1, p. 63. According to Nystrom, *Fem År I Persien*, p. 34, there were 20,000 prostitutes in Tehran, which had a population of 300,000 or almost 7% of the population.

although he is good at describing the problems, he is not good at analyzing them. "His analysis of prostitution and other social problems shows little understanding of basic economic and social factors; his approach is descriptive rather than deductive. There is a constant appeal to the emotion with plenty of platitudinous moralizing."[343] A contemporary of Kazemi, 'Abbas Khalili likewise writes much about "women's rights, compulsory marriages, prostitution, and moral lapses of youth." Rabi' Ansari takes the subject matter a little farther in his 'Human Traffickers of the Twentieth Century' (*Adam-forushan-e qarn-e bistom*) and describes the fate of two girls kidnapped by a gang of white-slavers, their mistreatment and tragic death.[344] Most social reformers, moreover, considered prostitution as a threat to marriage, because of the possibility of the contraction of venereal diseases and their transfer to a future or actual wife. Both phenomena were seen being on the rise, in particular among the upper class.[345] An exception was Mirza Aqa Khan, who, although he otherwise favored emancipation of women, argued that prostitution offered men the option of "friendship and companionship," which they apparently could not possibly develop with their wives.[346]

The almost universal presence of prostitution occasionally gave rise to protests, which usually were due to political rivalry rather than to moral outrage. In March 1906 (Moharram 1324), Tehran was in uproar; one of the reasons was that the son of Qa'em-maqam had killed a sayyed in a brothel, of which both were clients.[347] Political rather than moral outrage also turned up the heat when a non-Moslem was known to have received a visit from a Moslem woman, which, of course, was highly immoral. In 1914, in Mashhad a Russian merchant allegedly had taken a woman into his house; this enraged the people

343. H. Kamshad, *Modern Persian Prose Literature* (Cambridge, 1966), p. 60.

344. Kamshad, *Modern Persian*, p. 61.

345. '*Alam-e Nesvan* 3/1 (Sept 1922), pp. 29-34. For a discussion in detail see chapter five.

346. Amin, *The Making*, p. 28.

347. Yusof Moghith al-Saltaneh, *Namehha-ye Yusof Moghith al-Saltaneh* ed. by Ma'sumeh Mafi (Tehran, 1362/1983), p. 201.

تبریز مجهدینك آغا زادەلرىنك مكەدن قایدەندە تعلیمدكى عادتلری

Figure 3.1: Hajjis returning from Mecca

who 'spontaneously' attacked the house, plundering and destroying it.[348] However, if true, it is rather likely that this was not the first time that such a woman had visited the Russian merchant and that the outrage was more aimed at Russian political and military interference in Khorasan than against a Russian's moral turpitude. Different in approach and objective was the line taken by the women's journal *'Alam-e Nesvan*, which took the position that prostitution was a social evil that needed to be eradicated.[349]

Although people frequented prostitutes, they usually did not want their friends to know about it. Yaghma'i tells the story of his friends, with whom he was sleeping on the roof of their house. When they thought he was asleep they left, one of them putting on Yaghma'i's clothes so as to appear, if he was seen, that Yaghma'i, not he, was going out for some womanizing (*khanom-bazi*).[350]

PAHLAVI PERIOD (1925–1979)

Under the Pahlavi regime prostitution was exclusively found in urban areas. In 1934, according to Merritt-Hawkes, "Every town has prostitutes, although there are none in the villages. In Shiraz, Ispahan and Tehran their great number even shocks the knowing student just back from Paris."[351] Prostitution was indeed rampant in the urban areas. Services offered were not only for men, but also for women.[352] As in previous times, prostitutes worked in brothels, from hotels, or had their own house. In Tehran, the brothels continued to be concentrated in a suburb called *Shahr-e Now*. In the early 1930s an attempt was "made to keep a register of the women. It is said that in October 1933 a law was passed, but not signed by the Shah, making it illegal to keep a brothel and that by the end of December all would be closed. A

---

348. Moghith al-Saltaneh, *Namehha*, p. 86.
349. *'Alam-e Nesvan* 3/2 (Nov 1922), pp. 1-3.
350. Yaghma'i, *Jandaq*, 24.
351. Merritt-Hawkes, *Persia*, p. 289.
352. Merritt-Hawkes, *Persia*, p. 289.

further clause ordered the arrest of any officer found with a prostitute, but it is open to doubt that this order was obeyed."[353] This implies that apparently the ancient system of licensing and taxing prostitutes, a system that had existed at least since 950, had been abandoned. It probably had been replaced by a system of regular pay-offs to the police.

In Shiraz, Merritt-Hawkes, found two women in black *chadors* standing in the grounds of her hotel warming themselves at a charcoal brazier. One lived in the hotel, the other only stood at the gate trying to attract clients. "When they had done well they had breakfast together on the verandah, and they always shared the food with the two maids."[354] She further noted that in the same street where she stayed in Tehran a public lady received guests and had parties during the night enlivened by music.[355] Such a use of the house could be a problem for the next person who rented it as Kellerman found out, when he had rented a house in Isfahan. He was then regularly woken up at night when clients knocked on his door. They were unaware that the previous female occupants of the house had moved away.[356] Merritt-Hawkes further noted that "A considerable number of divorced women go on the streets."[357] The street-walkers, of course, had to attract attention. "Prostitutes also wear the *chadar*, which, in suitable places, they pull aside to show their faces and gay bespangled dresses."[358]

European men visited the brothels, where, according to Merritt-Hawkes, they might be exposed to anti-European feelings, by the unbalanced behavior of the hashish smoking women. Scrupulous observant Moslem women refused to have intercourse with uncircumcised men, while others would demand a double fee "that she might give

353. Merritt-Hawkes, *Persia*, p. 289.
354. Merritt-Hawkes, *Persia*, pp. 51-52.
355. Merritt-Hawkes, *Persia*, p. 120.
356. Kellermann, *Auf Persiens Karawanstrassen*, p. 65.
357. Merritt-Hawkes, *Persia*, p. 281.
358. Merritt-Hawkes, *Persia*, p. 289. One prostitute in Isfahan drew attention by singing loudly and exposing her dress to advertise her wares. Ibid., p. 107.

half to the mullah to expiate her sin. But an Italian courtesan always turned her statue of the Virgin with its face to the wall when she received a client. Are the West and the East really so far apart?"[359] Some European men in the oil fields seem to have come to an arrangement with local women for spending the night together.[360]

The new generation of writers that wrote in the 1920s wanted Iran to change and modernize and one of the many social ills that they treated in their writings was that of prostitution. The next generation of writers of the 1930s continues with the same themes as their predecessors, be it in a more talented and crafted manner. Jahangir Jalili describes the story of a 'fallen' girl from the educated middle class. Mohammad Mas'ud also deals with prostitution in his 'Night Diversions' (*Tafrihat-e Shab*) all within the context of a rudderless youth, who had neither hope, ambition nor moral scruples and in the evenings flitted from bar to bar looking for women, to end up in brothels.[361]

The main reason for a woman to start working as a prostitute was that she had no choice. The newspaper *Mard-e Emruz* published a number of articles in 1945, arguing that because men were unable or unwilling to provide for their families, women were forced to be engaged in prostitution to make ends meet.[362] About 80 percent of the brothels in North Tehran had been closed in 1947, but each night the police arrested some 300 prostitutes, who were lining up at building sites along the Karaj River, showing the desperate need among poor women to make money.[363] Poor women in urban areas did not have

---

359. Merritt-Hawkes *Persia*, p. 290.

360. Daneshvar, *Didaniha*, vol. 1, p. 82. As had Indian surveyors before them, who all had taken temporary wives. Wilson, *South West Persia*, p. 98. Wilson further reports that when serving on the Boundary Commission in Azerbaijan in 1914, "Our Indian [Moslem] officers and some sergeants have each acquired a *sigha* who unobtrusively accompanies the baggage like a *vivandière* and is referred to politely as a 'cook'." Ibid. *South West Persia*, p. 290.

361. Kamshad, *Modern Persian*, pp. 64-67

362. Amin, *The Making*, p. 222.

363. Anonymous, "Etella'at-e geranbaha-ye ejtema'i darbareh-ye Iran," *Khvandaniha* 8/33 (1326/1947), p. 15.

many employment opportunities. Mainly they worked as seamstresses, spinners, darners, sewers, knitters, weavers, maids, midwives, healers, preachers, matchmakers, oil-makers, attendants in public baths and mortuaries, beggars, singers, dancers, and musicians.[364] The last three occupations were difficult to distinguish from prostitution with which they overlapped. However, according to Merritt-Hawkes and others, "The prostitutes are not at present as low a type as in Europe, and, because they are free to see the world and talk to many people, some men find them more satisfactory than their wives."[365] When they became older and unattractive these women had to find employment elsewhere, if they did not want to be reduced to begging. "There were two women servants in the hotel who did some of the work that the men didn't. The employment of women is difficult, as no decent woman can be a hotel maid, so these two were worn-out prostitutes, and when they were worn-out maids, they would then be qualified to be midwives. That is one way of keeping down the population."[366]

Usually prostitutes were divorcees, abandoned women, and those from unstable family backgrounds. It even happened that their husband took them to *Shahr-e Now* to make money.[367] One village girl became pregnant, was abandoned and was picked up by a friendly woman, who helped her cope with the pregnancy and the birth of her daughter and then told her she had to start working. She did not really care for the girl, for she was a Madam (*ra'iseh*) of a brothel who had been scouting for new girls.[368] In 1947 it was estimated that there were about 12,400 prostitutes in Iran excluding those in Tehran.

---

364. Ernst Höltzer, *Persien vor 113 Jahren* (Tehran, 2535/1977), p. 22.

365. Merritt-Hawkes, *Persia*, p. 290; Hakim-Olahi, *Ba man*, vol. 2, pp. 427ff., also indicates that many prostitutes were divorcées from middle- and even high-class backgrounds; see also Anonymous, "Arzu-ye yek dokhtar-e Shahr-e Now," *Khvandaniha* 8/50 (1326/1947), pp. 19-20.

366. Merritt-Hawkes *Persia*, p. 50.

367. Anonymous, "Du dokhtar-e Shahr-e Now," *Khvandaniha* 8/34 (1326/1947), pp. 21-23; Anonymous, "Avval daf'eh shoharam Amir Khan mara beh Shahr-e Now bord," *Khvandaniha* 8/40 (1326/1947), pp. 21-23.

368. Anonymous, "Arzu-ye yek dokhtar-e Shahr-e Now," *Khvandaniha* 8/50 (1326/1947), pp. 19-20.

These were mostly managed by 1,250 madams or so-called *sarkardeh* or *ra'iseh* and 100 pimps (*koskesh*) who were the bosses. The number of convictions for brothel keepers is shown in Table 3.1.

Table 3.1: Number of women by age, marital status, literacy and employment that have been convicted of operating a brothel

Age group	Number of women	In percentage
20-30 years	50	30
31-40	100	60
41-50	17	10
Total	167	100
Literate	15	9
Illiterate	152	91
Total	167	100
Married	25	15
Unmarried	142	85
Total	167	100
Free occupation [shoghl-e azad]	55	33
Unemployed	112	67
Total	167	100

Source: Hejazi, *Barrasi*, pp. 148-49.

The ages of the prostitutes varied between 12 and 25 years, and most likely higher. Some 90 percent were villagers and 10 percent had come from urban areas. The former had been forced to prostitution, because they suffered from bad treatment by their husbands; most (9%) of the city girls gave the same reason, while one percent were in this business because they liked having sex.[369] In 1949, it was

369. Anonymous, "Chand amar-e tazeh va jaleb-e tavajjoh az zanan-e Iran," *Khvandaniha* 8/37 (1326/1947), pp. 14-15; Anonymous, "Chera zanamra talaq dadam," *Khvandaniha* 8/56 (1326/1947), p.17. Brothels also were

estimated that there were 4,000 prostitutes in *Shahr-e Now* plus an
unknown number in the rest of Tehran.[370] These did not include small
children. In 1946, little girls of 6-8 years were bought from their parents for 30 *tumans* by the Madam (*khanom-aqa*) or the female brothel
keeper in *Shahr-e Now* indicating that there was a market for such
little girls.[371] According to Hejazi, during the 1950s, prostitution represented about 25 percent of the crimes committed by women in Tehran.[372] At the time of Hejazi's study it was estimated that there were
about 3,000 licensed prostitutes in the walled district of *Shahr-e Now*
in South Tehran.[373]

Not only did Tehran have a red light district, but so did Bandar
'Abbas and many other towns. The district was situated at two *farsakh* from Bandar 'Abbas, where it was cooler. Most of the leaders
and wealthy men of Bandar 'Abbas, therefore, had a 'girl friend' there,
as did many truck drivers, because the district was situated on the
road to Kerman. In the afternoon many cars from the town could be

---

reported to operate in Ahvaz and Abadan. Daneshvar, *Didaniha*, vol. 1, pp. 40,
98, while there was one prostitute in Shushtar. Ibid., vol. 1, p. 44.

370. Overseas Consultants, *Report on seven year development plan for the
Plan Organization of the Imperial Government of Iran* 5 vols. (New York, 1949),
vol. 2, p. 42.

371. Hakim-Olahi, *Ba man*, vol. 2, pp. 47ff. (with pictures). For one case of a six-
year old that had already been infected with VD see Anonymous, "Fahesheh-ye
Shesh-saleh," *Khvandaniha* 7/96 (12 Mordad 1327/1948), p. 16.

372. Qodsiyeh Hejazi, *Barrasi-ye jara'em-e zan dar Iran* (Tehran, 1357/1978),
pp. 148-49. For a discussion see Khosrow Khosrovi, "Tahqiqi dar bareh-ye
jorm-e zanan dar Tehran," *Masa'el-e Iran* 1/9 (1342/1963), pp. 343-47;
see also Shahpur Rasokh, "Sokhani-ye chand dar bareh-ye hara'em-e zan,"
Masa'el-e Iran 3/4-5 (1344/1965), pp. 103-08.

373. Echo of Iran, *Iran Almanac 1965* (Tehran, 1966), p. 494; Ibid., *Iran
Almanac 1964*, p. 374. For a discussion of living conditions and other
problems of prostitutes in *Shahr-e Now* see Hakim-Olahi, *Ba man*. There were
prostitutes in small towns such as Malayer in 1965 (21,000 people), where
several brothels were found in a poor neighborhood in the south of the town.
Badri Zahereddini, *Medizinische Topographie der iranischen Stadt Malayer*
(Erlangen, 1966), p. 31. For a description of some aspects of the operation of a
neighborhood brothel and how it was well-embedded into the social fabric, see
Gholam-Hossein Sa'edi, *Dandil. Stories from Iranian Life* (New York, 1981),
pp. 1-28.

seen, with men dallying with their girls. The entire district consisted of houses made of reeds, which were called *saqu* by which name the district also was known. These women all seem to have been married, but their husbands did not seem to mind their money-earning activity, for it allowed them to loll about all day and devote their time to sleeping and eating. The women with 'boy-friends' wore a face-mask (*borqeh*) when they went outside, so that, as they said, unrelated men would not see them.[374]

A very detailed survey-based sociological study of 1548 prostitutes in Tehran in 1969 showed that they operated in five kinds of milieus: (1) in *Shahr-e Now*; (2) as street walkers; (3) in assignation houses; (4) in night clubs and bars; and (5) in the Holes (*gowd-neshinha*). These five milieus were as follows:

(1). *Shahr-e Now* was a quarter in the south of Tehran near the Farabi Hospital with a surface area of 135,000 m2. Because now it does not exist, having been leveled in 1979, a description of it follows. It was founded in 1881 and from its very beginning became the red light district and amusement center of Tehran. The quarter was situated next to the old Qazvin city gate, which was a busy assembly point for travelers and rural migrants as well as a transport center. In 1953 the quarter was walled and the municipality forced all streetwalkers to take up abode there, but after the wall was completed it prevented

---

374. Daneshvar, *Didaniha*, vol. 1, pp. 176-205. The entire atmosphere in Bandar 'Abbas was rather relaxed as both men and women went about half naked, because of the heat. Ibid., pp. 166, 170. In Shiraz, Moslem prostitutes, serving only Moslems, had settled in the Jewish quarter despite opposition from the Jewish population. The Moslem men, who stood in line waiting their turn to be served sometimes harassed neighbors or were a nuisance at the nearby synagogues. There also seem to have been some Jewish prostitutes, although that may have been gossip. Loeb, *Outcaste*, p. 72. In Tabriz, the red light district was known as *Dash Maghazaler* and was situated in the Armenian quarter. In Enzeli, prostitutes, allegedly only Russian women locally referred to as *matushkas* or puppets, offered their services in houses near the bars and at the outskirts of the town. Later, at the beginning of the Pahlavi reign, these 60-70 women were forced to take up residence in a newly created quarter outside the town, which was known as *Shahr-e Now*. 'Aziz Tavili, *Tarikh-e Jame'-ye Bandar-e Enzeli* 2 vols. (Tehran, 1370/1991), vol. 1, pp. 610, 618

newcomers settling there. The quarter has two broad streets (see map below) which were both without an outlet and were crossed by a number of smaller streets. All streets were unpaved and not graded. To a certain extent the quarter was self-sufficient with shops to cater to the daily needs of its population (such as grocers, bakers, butchers, barbers, tailors). There were two theaters, whose actors and actresses worked in the quarter, and which had shows all day till well into the night. The entrance fee was 5 and 10 riyals.[375] The old-fashioned houses in the quarter, with a tiled court-yard and pond, all had at least four and up to twelve rooms in which the prostitutes received their visitors and where they lived. On entering the quarter a visitor was immediately accosted by an old woman or *sar-dasteh*, usually a former prostitute, who offered her service as a guide to bring him to the best woman or *shagerd* (meaning apprentice) as the working girls were called. When the visitor had made his choice, he paid the *ma-man* as she was called by the prostitutes, and she gave him a leather token. There were also male procurers (*vaseteh*), who sat in a habitual joint (*patogh*), and acted as guides. Having taken the visitor to the woman of his choice they received an appropriate tip. Further, there were bouncers (*dar baz-kon*), who acted as jack-of-all trades in the house in the service of the *sar-dasteh*. In the past both had much more say in the affairs of the quarter, but due to effective police control this was no longer the case in the 1960s.

(2). The second milieu was that of the streetwalkers (*zan-e valgerd* or *zan-e khiyabani*), who in the evening took up positions at fixed street locations. Favorite spots, e.g., were on the Karaj Road, Pahlavi Avenue and Vanak. They were smartly dressed and wore a short *chador*. Most of their clients came by car, as they still do, and, to avoid police interference, it was a quick stop and get away even before the price had been agreed. Once the price had been agreed the car usually went to places on the outskirts of the city. The car usually had more than

---

375. About their popularity, in particular of the singer Mahvash, see H.E. Chehabi, "Voices Unveiled: Women Singer in Iran," in Rudi Matthee and Beth Baron eds. *Iran and Beyond* (Costa Mesa, 2000), pp. 151-66.

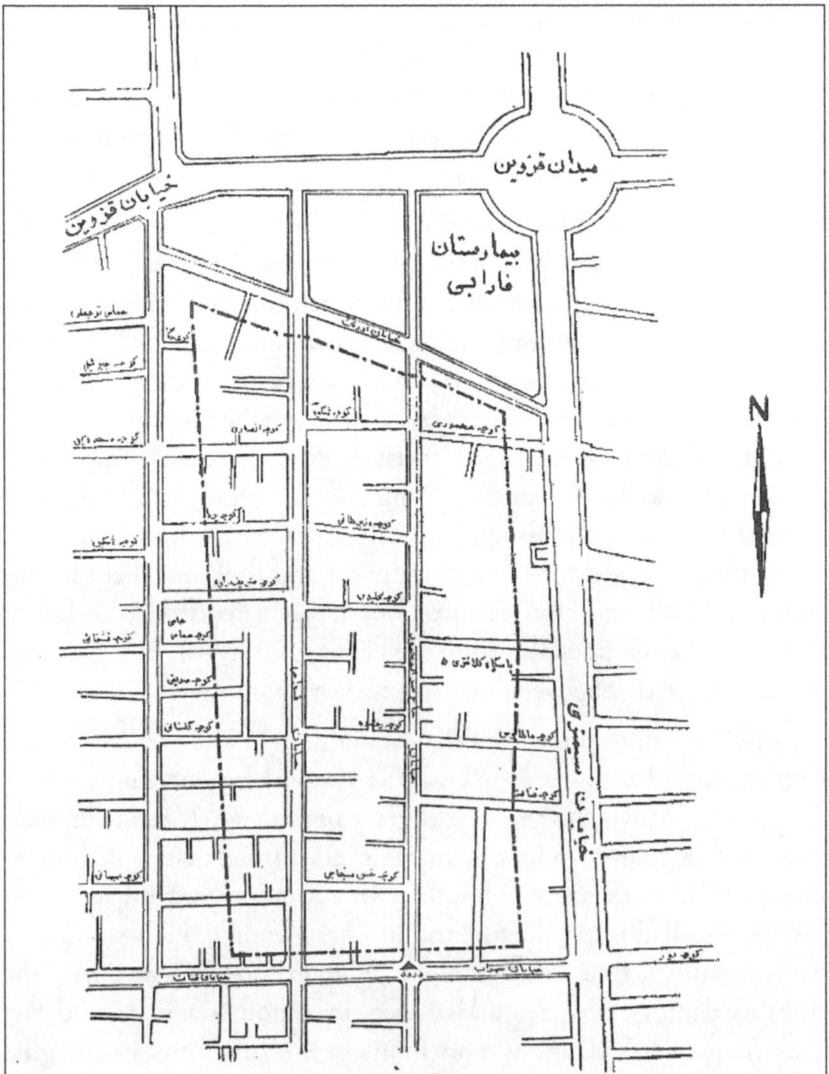

Figure 3.2: Plan of *Shahr-e Now* – the situation in 1970 (Farmanfarma'iyan)

one male occupant, who would all take turns. It sometimes happened that these women were taken advantage of by their clients, when, having taken their pleasure, they refused to pay and did not return the woman to the city. Because of police pressure and safety concerns some of these women had bought small cars and cruised the streets looking for clients, whose car she would follow after an agreement had been reached. Other women had contacts with taxi drivers who took them to clients. Given the risk involved, some of these women had (strong men) pimps (*chaqu-kesh*).

(3). The third milieu consisted of closed homes, complete with pimps (*pa-andaz*) and procurers (*vaseteh*), for a better clientele, because the women were younger and better educated. These homes were in the more salubrious parts of town and secluded; often, in part of the house a family would actually reside. The women arranged for the majority of their visitors by telephone. The procurers were to be found in their habitual spots in Islambul and Manuchehri streets, across from the British embassy, Amir Akram cross-roads, Shah Reza street at the Lalehzar crossing, and Ramsar street. Clients approached them, they arranged for the appointment and took the client to the woman's house and the procurer would get a fee from the house (10%), and sometimes also from the client (300 riyals). The price per visit usually varied between one and two thousand riyals.

(4). The fourth milieu was that of night-clubs and bars, where the women worked as hostesses to create an atmosphere where men would drink more, of which they would get a percentage. If the men were interested in a closer and more intimate encounter, that could also be arranged, either in his own house or in a location near-by, in which case he also had to pay for the room. These women often worked in bars from lunch-time to late at night. Women also performed in night clubs as dancers, actresses and singers in various stages of undress. They frequently had gigs in more than one club and thus, each night, they moved from one to the other. Often at the site of their last performance they, or a pimp, arranged for an intimate get-together with a client.

(5). The fifth and last milieu was that of the Holes (*gowdha*) in the south of Tehran, situated near Meydan-e Shush. A Hole, the result of excavation of soil for the brick-making industry, usually measured

3 ha in surface area and 10 meters deep.[376] Many families lived on the strips separating these Holes as well as in caves dug into their sides, while many coffee-houses were found there; it was the stamping grounds of drug smugglers, thieves and other criminals. The Holes were the dumping grounds for the very poor, often migrants, where women offered their sexual services, usually without making use of pimps, although several women had a male friend. Many of these women used a *maman* or procuress, who would get 50 percent of the payment received.

The 1969 study also provided a sociological profile of the surveyed prostitutes. It showed that most Tehran prostitutes came from the central province and had grown up in an urban environment (75%), mostly with both or one of their parents (81%). In 34 percent of the families, crime played a role, while poverty and familial problems resulted in the girls leaving home, nevertheless almost 70 percent said that they had had a happy youth. Given the early age of the 'flight from home' conditions had become difficult if not traumatic, for no less than 35 percent of the prostitutes had left home before and up to 12 years of age and 47 percent between the age of 13 and 16. Most of the women (88%) were illiterate, the majority of whom worked in *Shahr-e Now* and the Holes. The streetwalkers were the best educated. Most women were unattached; only some 5 percent had a husband and some 12 percent a 'male friend'. The women claimed that the main reason they became prostitutes was that they had been deceived and/or lured into prostitution (37%), while some 27 percent stated that they were sold to a brothel, while 20 percent were forced by economic necessity.

These working women served some 16,000 men each day; most of them regulars. Each woman had up to 15 men per day, although some had more. Most women (55%) charged less than 50 riyals for a visit, with an average price of 27 riyals. The price depended on the beauty,

---

376. On the living and working conditions of the brick-workers see Willem Floor, "The brick-workers of south Tehran: a striking record (1953-1979)," in *International Review of Social History* 48 (2003), pp. 427-55.

age and reputation of the woman as well as location. Streetwalkers made more than those in *Shahr-e Now*, who made more than those in the Holes. The average daily income of 55 percent of all prostitutes was between 100-600 riyals. The average figure for the streetwalkers was 1,440, for *Shahr-e Now* 743 and for the Holes 397 riyals/per day. Most of the women (71%) had a monthly expenditure between 5,000 and 20,000 riyals, while 21 percent of the women spent less than 5,000 per month. The majority (84%) had no savings, while some 62 percent had debts. The women had to work hard for their money, typically (72%) working between 3 to 12 hours per day, although some worked 18-hour days. The average workweek lasted 59 hours. One third of the women had a *sar-dasteh*. The women also had health, nutritional and drug addiction problems. They led a rather isolated life, for on average only 20 percent of their contacts were with people outside the world of prostitution. Only 25 percent used birth-control (condom, pill) measures, although they all had received medical counsel in this area, hence there were many children born out-of-wedlock.[377]

Neither the Hejazi study nor that by Farmanfarma'iyan suggests temporary marriage as a (partial) solution, or even as a preventive measure for prostitution. In fact, neither author even mentions the existence of temporary marriage, and through its application, the possibility of legalization of the sexual services offered by the prostitutes. This may have been, because marriage, temporary or covenanted, did not really constitute a viable socio-economic alternative for prostitutes, as most of them had already been married before, sometimes more than once, and with the wrong kind of man.

Because of the growing problem of prostitution, in particular in Tehran, the government was forced to take action other than just

---

377. Sattareh Farmanfarma'iyan, *Peyramun-e ruspigari dar shahr-e Tehran* (Tehran, 1349/1970). A short summary of this study was also published in the newspaper *Ettela'at* (February 19, 1972); Echo of Iran, *Iran Almanac* 1972, p. 517. Prostitution was not only the subject of literature and academic studies, but also of early Iranian films, see, e.g. Gönül Dönmez-Colin, *Women, Islam and Cinema* (London, 2004), pp. 37-38.

arrest prostitutes. The same Criminal Code that forced it to do so, also gave it other options. Article 273 of the then Criminal Code defined those that had no employment as vagrants and required that the government provided works for them. To that end the government established a number of vocational training centers for vagrants as of 1960, which aimed at enabling trainees to return to society as useful citizens. In the mid-1960s (4th Development Plan) the government decided to extend the same service to prostitutes. However, this did not work, because the women abandoned the red-light district and went to work in Tehran itself. By 1968, it was found that some 2,000 prostitutes were active in Tehran that the government knew about. Most of them (34%) were divorcees and another group (14%) had been led astray, i.e. had been taken advantage of by disreputable men. For them a house for "lonely mothers" was established.[378] As a result of various policies and trends, in 1972 the government claimed that prostitution was decreasing, because of the crack-down of pimps, the centralization of prostitutes in *Shahr-e Now*, where they were under the control of the police and health officials, better education, a rise in the standard of living, which made it easier for people to marry, literacy campaigns and vocational training among prostitutes.[379]

Islamic Republic of Iran (1979–to date)

After the Islamic Revolution of 1979, the authorities demolished *Shahr-e Now*, the red light district of Teheran, and jailed many and even executed some of its inhabitants. Many other women were taken to North Tehran for rehabilitation and purification. The slogan was "productive labor makes free" and even better if they would become *sigheh* to the revolutionary guards who were their prison wardens. This

---

378. Presumably 'single mothers' is meant. Echo of Iran, *Iran Almanac 1969*, pp. 480-81. However, there were prostitutes working outside *Shahr-e Now*. Daneshgah-e Tehran, *Sokhanraniha va Gozareshha dar nakhostin seminar-e bar-rasi-ye masa'el-e ejtema'i-ye shahr-e Tehran* (Tehran, 1343/1964), pp. 329, 354.

379. Echo of Iran, *Iran Almanac 1972*, p. 517.

had to be done on a rotation basis due to the fact that the guards were called up to fight at the front.[380]

Now, prostitution is strictly illegal in Iran and subject to harsh punishments under the new law. The new Penal Code prohibits procurement for the purpose of fornication (article 135). Punishment of a convicted man is 75 lashes and exile for a period of 3 months to a year from the location where the offense was committed. Punishment of a convicted woman is 75 lashes, but no exile (article 138). The code penalizes any person who promotes or facilitates immorality or prostitution (article 639). Establishing or managing a place of immorality or prostitution is a criminal act (article 639), subject to imprisonment from 1 to 10 years. The relevant premises may be closed by a court order. The code further prohibits living on income derived from prostitution and encouraging or protecting persons in prostitution. Facilitating the travel abroad by a woman for purposes of prostitution likewise is prohibited (article 213). The consent of such a woman is immaterial; punishment is imprisonment from 1 to 3 years. If the woman is under the age of 18, the penalty for facilitating her transport is enhanced. On 3 July 1980, two women accused of prostitution were buried up to their necks and then stoned to death. In 1997, in a similar case, three women were stoned to death in public after a court found them guilty of adultery and prostitution under Iran's Islamic law.[381] Despite such harsh punishments, prostitution is thriving as is detailed in what follows.

Prostitution has been recognized as major social problem both by the Iranian authorities and society. Social research carried out among a random sample of 147 prostitutes nationwide in 1999/2000 shows that almost 50 percent of the prostitutes began as teenagers (See Table 3-2).

---

380. Haeri, *Law*, pp. 99-100. For a discussion of the activities of the Bureau of Combating Corruption, which aimed to purify Iran of all form of corruption (prostitution, adultery, homosexuality, drug trafficking etc.), which was due to Western agents, and societal reactions to it see Paidar, *Women and the Political Process*, pp. 345-47.

381. ["Iran Stones Six to Death," Associated Press, 26 October 1997.]

Table 3.2: Age at which girls become prostitutes in Iran (2000)

Age/ Frequency	9-12 yrs	13-16 yrs	17-20 yrs	21-24 yrs	25-28 yrs	>29 yrs	Total
Total number	3	38	53	33	17	3	147
Percentage	2	26	36	22	12	2	100

Source: Zand, " 'Avamel," p. 25.

As in Western countries, they mostly come from dysfunctional families, where they have problems, especially their mother, and also have a low-level of self-esteem. At least 22 percent of the women surveyed had been the victim of sexual abuse by close family members (father, brother, uncle)[382] or friends of the family or neighbors during their youth, which stands in sharp contrast to the control group of non-prostitute women where this percentage was less than one. Many of the women had fled their paternal home (26%) or married (70%), which was also a means to flee home. However, these marriages were no real solution, because most of the men (80%) were petty criminals

---

382. This is not the first time that incest is reported to occur in Iran, but it is very rare. A famous case was reported by Hasan Sabah, who wrote to Malekshah, the Seljuq king, about Harun Rashid, whom he accused of having an incestuous relationship with his younger sister, while his son Amin, after his father's death, had a similar relationship with his aunt, whom he believed to be a virgin. Nasrollah Falsafi, *Chand Maqaleh-ye Tarikhi va Adabi* (Tehran, 1342), p. 423 ; for other examples see Gmelin, *Travels*, pp. 32, 159-60. The story related by Gmelin is reminiscent of the tale reported by several European travelers that Shah Jahan had an incestuous relationship with his daughter Jahanara Begum. The European traveler Francois Bernier, *Travels in the Mogul Empire AD 1656-1668* ed. Vincent A. Smith (Delhi, 1994), p. 11, wrote, "*Begum-Saheb*, the elder daughter of *Chah-Jehan* was very handsome. ... Rumour has it that his attachment reached a point which it is difficult to believe, the justification of which he rested on the decision of the *Mullahs*, or doctors of their law. According to them, it would have been unjust to deny the King the privilege of gathering fruit from the tree he had himself planted." Joannes de Laet was the first European to write about this rumor. Peter Mundy and Jean Baptiste Tavernier also wrote about the same allegations and Valentyn literally repeated Bernier.

(69%) and pimps (11%) and thus, did not provide them with the kind of environment that would give them a stable home and a socially more acceptable future. Even with marriage most of the women (94%) became prostitutes within 48 hours after they had fled the paternal home, because they had nobody to turn to and no income. Such steps were facilitated by the fact that 24 percent of the women were already drug addicts before they became prostitutes, while 44 percent became drug addict after they had started a prostitute's life, thus forcing them to stay in this life to feed their addiction. In short, a picture that is little different from what drives and characterized prostitution in Western countries.[383] Other groups such as gypsy women, who traditionally had offered their sexual services to men, are still active, driven by poverty caused by unemployment and family problems (divorce, etc.).[384]

ABUSE

Another contributing cause to prostitution is physical abuse of women and children by men. Using a random sampling cross sectional method, research was carried out in 2001 on married women to study the prevalence of wife abuse and its related factors. The researchers concluded that the level of wife abuse did not differ from that of Western countries, i.e. 42 percent. They determined that abuse of the highest frequency was due to the following: (i) negligence 63 percent; (ii)

---

383. Shahin 'Oliya Zand, "'Avamel-e zamineh-saz tan dadan-e zanan beh ruspigari," in Hamayesh-e melli-ye asibha-ye ejetam'i dar Iran, *Maqalat-e Avvalin Hamayesh-e Melli-ye Asibha-ye Ejtema'i dar Iran, Khordad 1381* 5 vols. (Tehran, 1386, 2007), vol. 5, pp. 17-39. See also Reza Khashayar, *'Elal-e ruspigari dar Iran* (Tehran, 1359/1380). For the psychiatric dimension of prostitution in Iran see Mahdis Kamkar et al. "Ruspigari va bi-mobalati-ye jensi, tafavot va tashaboh," in Hamayesh, *Maqalat*, vol. 5, pp. 41-60. For a psychological analysis of one the major reasons why girls flee their paternal home (relationship with parents) see Ma'sumeh Rostamkhani, "Barrasi-ye ta'thir-e naqsh-e valedin dar farar dokhtaran," in Hamayesh, *Maqalat*, pp. 171-90.

384. Sa'id Kharratha, "Ruspigari dar mahalleh-ye Ghorbat," in Hamayesh, *Maqalat*, vol. 5, pp. 61, 75-76.

contempt and reproach, 38 percent and (iii) abuse and insult 30 percent, which indicates the spread of psychological forms of wife abuse in society.[385] Other studies, although with different data, confirm the extent and nature of the problem and, moreover, note that social tolerance not only facilitates domestic violence, but also encourages it. Again, the husband's age, use of drugs or alcohol, smoking, income and number of children were all associated with wife abuse.[386] It is a telling instance that in a folk story of the Boir Ahmad tribe "an ideal husband is described [as] one who would not hurt her too much when he beats her up."[387]

A related problem is that of proven child rape. In the year ending March 2004, some 1,000 were reported. The director-general of the State Welfare Organization's (SWO) Center for Preventing Social Disorders, Sayyed Hadi Motamedi, told a ceremony to inaugurate the social emergency hotline, "Ever since 2002, when the seven-digit number to prevent child abuse was launched, we have been witnessing a rapid increase in the cases of child abuse, wife abuse/assault and domestic violence. Last year, some 8,000 cases of family violence were reported, a number of which pertained to abuse of juveniles." According to Motamedi, there was an urgent need for action due to the large number of abuse cases and the absence of supportive laws. "With the inauguration of the hotline 123, SWO social workers will provide counseling to young people who feel distressed. The first phase of

385. Mohammad Ali Seif Rabiee, Fahimeh Ramezani Tehrani, Zinat Nadiya Hatmi, "Wife Abuse and Related Factors," *Pazhuhesh-e Zanan, A Quarterly Journal of The Center for Women's Studies*, 1/4 (2002). These figures seem to be on the high side. For the 1980s see Paidar, *Women and the Political Process*, p. 353.

386. Hassan Shams Esfandabad, Suzan Emamipour , "Prevalence of Wife Abuse,"*Pazhuhesh-e Zanan, A Quarterly Journal of The Center for Women's Studies*, 1/1 (2004); M. Mousavi and A. Eshagian, "Wife abuse in Esfahan, Islamic Republic of Iran, 2002," 11/5 & 6 (September, 2005) *Eastern Mediterranean Health Journal*, pp. 860-69; see also two other articles on the same subject in the same journal [http://www.emro.who.int/Publications/EMHJ/1105_6/Artical1.htm]; Shahla E'zazi, *Khoshunat-e khvanevadegi: Zanan-e kotak-khvordeh* (Tehran: Sali, 1380).

387. Friedl, "Women in Contemporary Persian Folk Tales," p. 645.

the project cost 30 billion rials in credits. Another 10 billion rials are required to make the service nationwide," he stated. He further noted that 93 percent of complaints about child abuse can be resolved with the help of social workers and another 7 percent are in need of judicial intervention.[388]

Female sex workers are often forced to work underground and away from their local communities. Because they are treated as a distinct section of the community, combined with social rejection and isolation, this has serious repercussions on the health provisions for them and on their willingness to seek medical care. In some countries including Iran, the existence of prostitution and sexually transmitted diseases (STDs) has been systematically denied, being considered taboo by the government and the majority of society, although this is changing. In consequence, Iran's sex workers suffer from non-availability of medical services and knowledge about sexually transmitted diseases. Social stigmatization also stops these resource-deprived women from seeking proper medical care and treatment.[389]

What the above data from 2000 show is that the current problems are very similar to those of the 1960s. The main difference is that they have become more serious, particularly in size, both as to the number of persons involved as well as those addicted to drugs. Moreover, a further dimension to the latter problem is that AIDS/HIV has been added, which makes public health intervention even more mandatory than before. Like elsewhere in the world, the government does not know how to effectively address the problem. A law and order approach, therefore, is often a substitute for a public health policy. Police and Islamic militia raids on brothels are frequently reported. According to official figures, at least 300,000 prostitutes work in the Islamic republic, of which 45,000 are in Tehran.[390] In July 2001, authorities in

---

388. Iran Daily (15/02/2005), p. 1.

389. M. R. Mohebbi, "Female sex workers and fear of stigmatization," *Sexually Transmitted Infections* 81 (2005), pp. 180-181.

390. *Nowrooz*. Publication banned September 17, 2001:14; *Agence France Presse* (May 4, 2003).

the town of Mashhad rounded up 500 persons to shield them from the ongoing serial murders of prostitutes. Those murders had claimed 19 victims so far. Rumor has it that extremist groups who want to stop the spread of prostitution and corruption commit such crimes. Documented evidence corroborates the strangulation of 26 persons in prostitution between 1999 and 2001 in the northeastern province of Khorasan alone.[391]

Nevertheless, prostitution is thriving and only increases rather than decreases. Between 1995 and 2003, Tehran, Western Iran, North-Eastern Iran (Mashhad), Caspian provinces (Resht and Enzeli, Babol and Sari), Qom, Shiraz, Khuzestan (Ahvaz, Abadan), Arak, Kerman are mentioned in newspaper reports as places were police uncovered prostitution rings, girl-trafficking networks, brothels, and other schemes to offer sexual favors. The occasional police raids has led to closure of brothels, arrest of pimps and madams as well as girls, including minors. In fact, pimping of children has become a major market niche. Criminal gangs prey on the many boys and girls that flee their homes and try to find shelter. In Tehran alone every day some 90 children abandon their parental home due to poverty and abuse. One girl said that twice she had been given lashings by the police, but found them more bearable than the way she was treated at home.[392]

---

391. "Prostitution Returns to Iran," *Agence France Presse* (17 April 2001). "500 Prostitutes Roundup to Stop Serial Murder," *Agence France Presse* (26 July 2001), accessed through: [http://www.irna.com/newshtm/eng/02235523.htm].

392. [http://www.uri.edu/artsci/wms/hughes/refs_iran.htm]. According to a UN report, "The sale and trafficking of children is a criminal offence in Iran under the Civil Code. Child prostitution and child pornography are criminal offences in Iran and children involved who are under 18 years of age and who are mature according to Islamic jurisprudence will be tried in the Juvenile Court according to the criminal procedure. For other children, article 49 of the Islamic Criminal Code stipulates that if a child commits a crime he/she will not be held criminally liable. Such children are sent to correction and rehabilitation centers affiliated to the judiciary, which will study and consider their cases and provide appropriate assistance. According to data and information received from Judiciary Complex for Children, 1,339 cases of child prostitution were reported during 2000 and 2001." [http://www.hri.ca/fortherecord2003/documentation/commission/e-cn4-2003-79.htm]. On 31 July 2007, the Majles voted in favor of

If there is one major change from the 1960s, it is the enormous increase in the number of street children. According to a newspaper report (*Resalat*), there were 20,000 street children in Iran in 1999. Most of these, mainly teenagers, but also younger, are to be found in Tehran, but they are not absent either from religious cities such as Mashhad and Qom, which towns in fact rank immediately after Tehran in terms of their number. Most of these children (65% in Tehran) are not Iranian, but children of immigrants (legal or illegal), and many of them have medical problem due to malnutrition, sexually transmitted diseases, among which is AIDS. This problem is aggravated by the lack of an adequate and effective social service to take care of such children, who are being preyed upon. Since 1996 the so-called Center of Green House (*markaz-e khaneh-ye sabz*) is in operation to gather and take care of the street children and try to put them on a path to a useful life, but its funds and capacity are as yet insufficient. The national budget for 2001 had earmarked 19 billion *riyals* (US$ 2 million) to achieve this objective, although everybody concerned realizes that it will take time before this and other measures take effect.[393]

It seems that this social vacuum is filled by criminal elements. Some women who offer shelter to run-away girls have forced them into prostitution.[394] Girls are also lured by offers of well-paid employment abroad, are married to allegedly well-off foreign Moslem men, or are just shanghaied, and then smuggled across the border either to

---

a bill on Iran's accession to the United Nations' Optional Protocol on the sale of children, child prostitution and child pornography.

393. Tahmineh Shavardi, "Negahi beh vaz'iyat-e kudakan-e khiyabani dar Iran; 'elal va 'avamel-an," in Hamayesh, *Maqalat*, vol. 5, p. 102, 107-09, 112-13 (causes for abandoning home) [101-17]; Mostafa Janqoli, "Barrasi-ye vaziyat-e kudakan-e khiyabani," in Hamayesh, *Maqalat*, vol. 5, p. 121 (this article has more detailed data on the functioning of the system of the green house center and the taking care of street children). [119-41]; see also 'Ali Reza Saleh, "Moqayeseh-ye kudakan-e khiyabani va shabanehruziha-ye Tehran," in Hamayesh, *Maqalat*, pp. 143-70.

394. Shavardi, "Negahi," pp. 109-14; Chris De Bellaigue, "City Life: "Tehran -The Teenage Runaways of Gangland Tehran," *Independent*, (13 November 2000); Elaine Sciolino, "Runaway Youths a Thorn in Iran's Chaste Side," *New York Times* (4 November 2000).

the UAE or Pakistan where they are sold to brothels or individuals. Many of the parents of these boys and girls allegedly are addicts, and in one case a mother even sold her own daughter. In addition to these young boys and girls, there are many women (divorced, widowed, or otherwise) who are forced by economic circumstances into prostitution. So far, authorities in dealing with the problem have only applied the law rather loosely as to the existence of prostitution within the Iranian borders. However, girls who are expelled from the UAE because of prostitution are refused an Iranian passport and thus, cannot return. Although prostitutes are one of the major sources of sexually transmitted diseases such as AIDS, syphillis and gonorrhea they have no adequate access to health care and thus they infect an increasing number of men and women. Recently, the newspaper *Entekhab* reported that two sisters, ages 16 and 17, had infected 1,100 people with AIDS/HIV.[395]

A conservative newspaper, *Afarinesh*, said that two government agencies, which were not identified, had proposed legalizing brothels, under the name of "chastity houses", as a way of providing safe sex for the men of the city. Predictably "the government denied that such a plan was in the works." In her *New York Times* article Nazila Fathi quotes Ayatollah Mohammad Musavi Bojnordi in the journal *E'temad*. "I would not have supported chastity houses had it not been for the urgency of the situation in our society. If we want to be realistic and clear the city of such women, we must use the path that Islam offers us." The path proposed is "the practice of temporary marriage. It is especially recommended for widows who need financial support." The objection to these proposed 'chastity houses' by women's groups in Iran is not that temporary marriages are wrong for young people who need to be able to enjoy sex together, but that they legalize the practice of women earning a living by prostitution.[396] Meanwhile,

---

395. [http://www.uri.edu/artsci/wms/hughes/refs_iran.htm].

396. Nazila Fathi, "To Regulate Prostitution, Iran Ponders Brothels," *New York Times* (28 August 2002). The journal *Zanan*, which has just been closed down, has been vocal in drawing people's attention to the plight of girls and

poor women, who are often also single mothers and drug addicts, continue to sell their bodies to men to make ends meet, for as yet there seems to be no other solution in sight.[397]

DISCUSSION

From the above it is clear that female prostitution is indeed one of the oldest, if not the oldest profession in history and has no borders. It also is an indication and confirmation of effective male domination over women, who were and are forced by men, or by male-created circumstances, into selling their bodies to men, excluding the fact that some women may have actually chosen this employment because they like sex.

Despite rejection by religious and secular authorities, and hence by their own family and communities, prostitution cannot be blamed on the mostly poor and defenseless girls and women. Given the fact that they were and are raised in a patriarchal society where the father, or if he is not there, her other male relatives, are in legal and effective charge of her life. It is the failure of these males and the male authorities, who make and fail to enforce the laws that ban prostitution, that young girls are forced into a life of prostitution and that they are not respected as persons in their own right. At the same time, it is also these same males, who have created an environment in which girls

---

children, who are forced into prostitution, and strongly opposed the idea of the establishment of the houses of chastity. Throughout its existence it has argued for the need to radically reform gender relations, sexual mores and women's rights.

397. For a 2007 movie "Prostitution behind the veil," about prostitutes in Iran see [http://www.iranian.com/main/2007/prostitution-behind-veil-1].

and women are taken advantage off. It is not a way of life that they choose, because they like it. In this connection it is of interest to note that in 1890, when Ernst Höltzer enumerated occupations that were typically female, he also listed the occupation of *fahesheh*, which he did not translate as prostitute, the usual meaning, but rather as "abandoned woman."[398] In the past, women had no choice, especially when enslavement was a normal phenomenon. However, even when this was not the case, they often were abandoned and abused by their male relatives and/or husbands as well as in many cases sold by them to brothels. How could it be that a weak female, a *za'ifeh*, on her own volition would choose a life as a prostitute rather than that of a respected housewife? Recent sociological studies clearly points the finger at the self-appointed masters of the universe who failed, abandoned, cheated and/or sold their daughter, sister, or niece. The suggestion that marriage, temporary or covenanted, is a solution for prostitutes to lead a normal and respectable life, ignores the fact that most prostitutes were married, often more than once, or are still married, and this proves beyond a doubt that so-called technical marital solutions do not correct a social ill. In short, rather than hiding behind religious and social injunctions and putting the blame on the victims, the perpetrators of the crime should take their responsibility. As two Ilkhan kings realized in the 1300s, prostitutes could not be blamed for their lot, but rather the forces that had compelled them to enter that life. Therefore, women should be allowed to become full and equal members of society, in all respects, so that they can not only provide for themselves and be economically independent rather than rely on the good-will of males, but also so that they can make their own mistakes and then be really

---

398. Höltzer, *Persien vor 113 Jahren*, p. 22.

responsible for them. Even if such a societal change were successful it would not eradicate prostitution, because there always will be abusive parents of children as well as weak men and women who cannot cope without help and thus may end up in the vicious circle of prostitution and drugs; if society continues to ignore these problems and needs the vicious cycle will continue.[399]

---

399. For a discussion of abused children, who end up as prostitutes, drug addicts and victims of a judicial system that does not understand their problems as well as the efforts of the *Omid* (Hope) Foundation to help such girls abandoned by society to start a new productive life, see: [http://news.bbc.co.uk/1/hi/programmes/crossing_continents/default.stm"\o "blocked::http://news.bbc.co.uk/1/hi/programmes/crossing_continents/default.stm].

CHAPTER FOUR

HOMOSEXUAL RELATIONS: A COMMON AFFAIR

HOMOSEXUAL RELATIONS:
A COMMON AFFAIR

Buggery; a love that dares not show its face
Oscar Wilde

In this chapter I discuss the prevalence of homosexual behavior in Iran, Zoroastrian and Islamic religious tenets regarding homo-sexuality, the kind of homosexual behavior, the measures, if any, taken to regulate or ban it, and the current state of affairs. Other forms of sexual behavior are only briefly mentioned for completeness' sake.

The relationship between two males or two females is generally referred to as being homosexual in nature, either by sexual attraction and/or of sexual behavior. Usually, in the case of males, a further distinction is made between pedophilia (a sexual relationship with a pre-pubescent child, who is not yet sexually mature and an adult male), pederasty (a sexual relationship with pubescent boys or youths and an adult male) and sodomy (anal penetration of 'males'). It seems that a similar distinction is not made for female homosexuality or lesbianism. When homosexual behavior is mentioned in Persian writings, anal intercourse or sodomy is meant. Although the alluring gait of a boy was highly appreciated by their lovers, it was considered humiliating for an adult man to be branded as effeminate or unmanly because of his style of dress, and submissive behavior during sex. Thus, with few exceptions, homosexuals in Iran did not develop a lifestyle such as is currently the case in many Western countries.

IMPERIAL IRAN

ACHAEMENID–PARTHIAN–SASANIAN PERIOD (559 BCE–653 CE)

In the Avesta, homosexual behavior is not mentioned, but in later Zoroastrian literature it is. And when it is, it only concerns males, not women, boys or youths. And it is condemned. As later in Islamic times, anal intercourse (only) between men is meant; this is considered the creation of the Evil Spirit to plague Ahura Mazda's creation. Having intercourse with a man rather than with a woman, meant wasting seed and not creating new life, and thus in doing so one aided and abetted the Evil Spirit. Punishment for willing partners, therefore, is death, while the unwilling party only gets 800 lashes with a horse whip on the back or feet, the same as for killing a sheep-dog. If caught *flagrante delicto* one is allowed to kill the culprits, without permission from the authorities.[1]

Sirus Shamisa ascribes the practice of sodomy as having been introduced to Iran by the Greeks, in the form of Platonic love, and later by the Turks, in the form of sexual behavior, implying that it did not exist among the Persians before then.[2] This seems quite unlikely, despite the fact that Herodotus wrote: "Pleasures, too, of all sorts they [the Persians] are quick to indulge in when they get to know about them—a notable instance is pederasty, which they learned from the Greeks."[3] However, Plutarch rightly challenges Herodotus on this issue, writing: "Our historian persists in this sort of thing when he says

---

1. Prods Oktor Skjærvø, "Homosexuality," *Encyclopedia Iranica*; Ibid., "Middle Eastern Literature: Persian," in C. J. Summers, ed., *The Gay and Lesbian Literary Heritage*, New York, 1995, pp. 485-86.

2. Sirus Shamisa, *Shahed-bazi dar adabiyat-e farsi* (Tehran, 1381/2002), p. 15f.

3. Herodotus, *Histories*, I.135.

that the Persians learned from the Greeks to have sex with boys. Yet how could the Persians have taken lessons from the Greeks in this kind of debauchery when almost everybody agrees that the Persians castrated boys long before they ever saw the Greek sea?"[4] The Achaemenid court only received part of its supply of eunuchs from outside Persia proper. Babylonia alone was obliged to supply the Persian king for these purposes an annual tribute of 500 eunuch boys, while a specific number of slaves, in particular eunuchs, were purchased by Persians in the slave markets of Sardis and Epheses as well. It also happened that the most beautiful boys in areas that had been conquered after a rebellion, were selected for castration.[5] Herodotus's statement also runs counter to the fact that the Zoroastrian injunction against homosexual behavior predates the arrival of the Greeks, while modern research finds it to be a universal phenomenon that occurred and still occurs in all societies throughout history for which written sources are available and that it may even be genetically determined.

Whatever the truth, little is known about the actual prevalence of homosexuality in Achaemenid Iran, but of course, there are clear indications that it occurred. Apart from the observations by Herodotus and Plutarch, Quintius Curtius reported that the eunuchs who attended the king's gyneceaum (women's quarters) were "accustomed to prostitute themselves." One such eunuch was Tiridates, who was described as the most attractive man in Asia. He was Cyrus the Younger's favorite companion, who left him, however, for Ataxerxes II after the battle of Cunaxa (401 BCE). When Tiridates died some time thereafter, Ataxerxes II (r. 404-359 BCE), who loved him dearly, "lamented bitterly and was in great distress; there was public mourning throughout Asia as a gesture to the king from his subjects." He was greatly moved by the sympathy shown by his concubine Aspasia. He told her to wait in his bedroom and when he returned "he put the eunuch's cloak over Aspasia's black dress. Somehow, the young man's dress suited her and

---

4. Plutarch, *De Malignitate Herodoti*, translated into English by Anthony Bowen as *The Malice of Herodotus* (Warminster, 1992), xiii.II.

5. Herodotus, *Histories*, III.92; VI. 32; VIII. 105; see further Briant. *From Cyrus*, p. 273.

her beauty struck her lover even more powerfully. Overcome by this sight, he asked her to visit him in this attire until the severity of his grief waned." Darius III (r. 336-330 BCE) was in love with the eunuch Bagoas, who was beautiful and in the flower of boyhood and later he was loved by Alexander the Great.[6]

In Middle-Persian literature, anal intercourse is referred to as *kunmarz*, literally 'buttock-rubbing.' Here as well as in later Zoroastrian literature, anal intercourse continues to be equated with assisting the Evil Spirit and deserves death as punishment. Religiously speaking, the future does not look very bright for the deviant sinners, because snakes will devour them. However, in case of tearful and bodily repentance they can be saved and forgiven.[7] This terrible fate that awaited the sinners must have had an impact in the Sasanian period, if Ammianus Marcellinus is to be believed, according to whom the Persians did not practice pederasty.[8] This is not only very unlikely, but also, it is reported that it, in fact, did occur, although not everywhere was homosexual behavior accepted. For, according to the Essenes, "In the remoter parts of the East, if a boy be treated unnaturally, when it is discovered, he is killed by his brothers, or his parents, or any of his relations, and is left unburied."[9] The occurrence of intercourse with under-age boys is also mentioned in the later Pahlavi *rivayat*s, but this was considered 15 times less of a sin than doing so with an adult (i.e. 15 years and older), which was punishable by death.[10]

---

6. Briant, *From Cyrus*, pp. 269-70.

7. Skjærvø, "Homosexuality," *Encyclopedia Iranica*; Ibid., "Middle Eastern Literature: Persian," pp. 485-86; Gignoux, *Le Livre d'Arda Viraz*, p. 86 (para 71.3).

8. Ammianus Marcellinus 23.6, translated by J. Rolfe as Ammianus Marcellinus, *History* (Cambridge MA, Harvard University Press, 1963).

9. Clement, *Book of Recognitions*, Chapter XXIII.-Manners of the Susidae.

10. Skjærvø, "Homosexuality," *Encyclopedia Iranica*.

ISLAMIC PERIOD

ISLAMIC LAW AND HOMOSEXUALITY

The overthrow of the Sasanian empire by the Arabs brought much change, but not in sexual practices. During the Caliphate, sodomy was widespread, continuing existing practice, despite the fact that Moslem law considers the activity a sin, in consequence of the Koranic verse:

> We also (sent) Lut: He said to his people: 'Do ye commit lewdness such as no people in creation (ever) committed before you? For ye practise your lusts on men in preference to women: ye are indeed a people transgressing beyond bounds.' And his people gave no answer but this: they said, 'Drive them out of your city: these are indeed men who want to be clean and pure!' But we saved him and his family, except his wife: she was of those who legged behind. And we rained down on them a shower (of brimstone): Then see what was the end of those who indulged in sin and crime! (Koran, 7:80-84; see also 26:159-175; 27: 55, and 29: 28-29).[11]

Moslem jurists, whether Sunni or Shi'ite, explained this text, supported by much more explicit Traditions of suspect authenticity, as a prohibition of anal intercourse between bisexual males, but not of homosexuality. The qualifier bisexual has been added, because the problem of homosexuality in Islam is not entirely straightforward. True, Islamic law makes it clear that men cannot have a sexual relationship with men and neither can women with women. However, is the situation really that clear cut?

The Koran forbids the acts of Lot, which is interpreted as being that of sodomy between men.[12] The situation of anal sex with a woman is less clear. There are scholars who argue that it is lawful,[13]

---

11. For Koran translations see[http://www.usc.edu/dept/MSA/reference/reference.html]

12. See, e.g., El-Rouyaheb, *Before Homosexuality*, pp. 118-28.

13. Bukhari, *Sahih*, 6.60; *Tafsir al- 'Ayyashi* (al-Matba'ah al-'Ilmiyeh, Qom,

some that it is permissible, with the consent of the wife (though undesirable), while others state that it is forbidden.[14] Each side selects those
Traditions that support their view, of course.

At the same time, both the Koran and the Traditions acknowl-
edge the existence of eunuchs (*khasiy*; either natural or man-made),
although nothing is said about their sexuality, i.e. their sexual orientation and needs. Moreover, in the Traditions a third gender is explictly
recognized, viz. that of the *mokhannath* or an effiminate but seemingly
male person, a passive homosexual, a she-male. Although these passive homosexuals are not mentioned in the Koran, the latter (Koran
24:31) probably includes them in the category of those persons "who
are without [sexual] urgings."

Sodomy occurred during the prophet Mohammad's own lifetime,
as is clear from the many references to it in the Koran, as well as according to a Tradition:

> [Narrated by ibn Mas'ud:] "We used to fight in the holy
> battles in the company of the Prophet and we had no
> wives with us. So we said, "O Allah's Apostle! Shall we get
> castrated? [i.e. shall we use each other as eunuchs]" The
> Prophet forbade us to do so."[15]

Another version in Bukhari states that rather than let the companions "treat [some] as eunuchs" in the absence of their wives, the
Prophet "allowed them to marry corrupted women" from the vicinity,
and he recited to them from the Koran: "O ye who believe! Make not

---

1380H/1960), vol.1, p. 157; Mohammad Baqer b. Mohammad Taqi Majlesi, *Bihar al-Anwar* 44 vols. (Beyruth, 2001), vol. 21, p. 98; Arno Schmitt, "Different Approaches to Male-Male Sexuality/Eroticism from Morocco to Usbekistan," in Arno Schmit and Jehoeda Sofer eds., *Sexuality and Eroticism Among males in Moslem Societies* (London-New York, 1992), pp. 14-18; Maghen, *Virtues of the flesh*, p. 28.

14. See, for example, the Koran Tafsir of Ibn Kathir, [http://www.qtafsir.com/index.php?option=com_content&task=view&id=189&Itemid=36]. Shi'ites hold that any homosexual activity is forbidden. Avazeh, *Qanun-e Qovveh-ye Bah*, pp. 87-90.

15. Bukhari, *Sahih*, 62.9.

unlawful the good things which Allah has made lawful for you, but commit no transgression."[16] These Traditions and the various Koran verses support the conclusion that sodomy was quite common in Arabia, while members of early Moslem society, including the prophet Mohammad, were quite aware of the fact that people used, *inter alia*, eunuchs and each other for their sexual gratification. As is clear from the Traditions quoted above, the prophet forbade anal sex between what were clearly bisexual men, who obviously had been engaged in sodomy before as a normal and familiar method to find sexual gratification when no women were available. However, neither the Koran nor the prophet has addressed the question of a sexual relationship between persons who are neither heterosexual nor bisexual, who, in fact, it could be argued, are neither men nor women.

As mentioned above, the Koran and the Traditions explicitly mention the existence of a gender that is neither heterosexual nor bisexual, viz., the *mokhannath* or the she-male, the passive effeminate homosexual. Their special position is clear from the fact that they had access to places and situations where non-related men *(na-maharem)* were banned. Men not related to a woman cannot see her, let alone in undress. However, the prophet Mohammad allowed persons identified as *mokhannath* to have free and unlimited access to his own women's quarters.

> 'A'isha reported that a eunuch[17] [*mokhannath*] used to come to the wives of Allah's Apostle (may peace be upon him) and they did not find anything objectionable in his visit, considering him to be a male without any sexual desire. Allah's Apostle (may peace be upon him) one day came as he was sitting with some of his wives and he was busy in describing the bodily characteristics of a lady and

16. Bukhari, *Sahih*, 62.13.

17. The translation of the term *mokhannath* as 'eunuch obviously is wrong, because eunuchs have no sexual interest in women, having been castrated, either by nature or man, whereas the *mokhannath* is referred to as a male. Therefore, the term should be translated as passive effeminate passive homosexual or she-male.

saying: As she comes in front four folds appear on her
front side and as she turns her back eight folds appear on
the back side. Thereupon Allah's Apostle (may peace be
upon him) said: I see that he knows these things; do not,
therefore, allow him to enter. She ('A'isha) said: Then they
began to observe veil from him.[18]

From this and other similar Traditions,[19] it is clear that the prophet
and his women allowed this *mokhannath* in their most private sphere,
because they and 'A'ishah, the prophet's youngest wife, explicitly refers to the Koranic verse 24:31, because they considered him to be
"without [sexual] urging." The fact that he was a *mokhannath* or a
she-male, made it lawful for him to enter the women's quarters, like
any other woman or eunuch, but unlike any other man. The prophet
clearly held the same opinion, and it was only when he thought that
this particular *mokhannath* might be a bisexual man, because he had
expressed an appreciation for a woman as a sexual object of desire,
that he banned that particular person, but not other she-males from
entering his women's quarters.

No discussions on the sexual rights of eunuchs and she-males
have been found, both of whom are recognized as being neither man
nor woman, or in the words of the Koran, a man "who is without
[sexual] urging." Since their sexual nature is not of their own making, but divine in origin, one would assume that they have the right
to sexual gratification, which is a human urge explicitly recognized in
Islamic law. Therefore, simply forbidding anal sex to these persons,
because it is forbidden between men, begs the question, for neither
the eunuch nor the *mokhannath* is a hetero- or a bisexual man. As
anal sex with one's wife is permitted by some scholars it would seem
that a case could be made that it would be allowed to the eunuch and
the she-male.

---

18. Muslim, *Sahih*, 26.5416.

19. Muslim, *Sahih*, 26, 5414-5413; Bukhari, *Sahih*, 62, 162.

There is further evidence that supports the notion that pedophilia and pederasty are not necessarily unlawful. Bukhari mentions a Tradition that Abu Ja'far (not the prophet) stated that a pedophile is prohibited from marrying the mother of the boy in question, if there is penetration:

> As for whom(ever) plays with a boy: if he caused him to enter him, then he shall not marry his mother.[20]

What are the implications of this Tradition? First, the pedophile can marry the boy's mother as long as no penetration has occurred during the sexual encounter. Second, pedophilia does not seem to be an unlawful activity. The only punishment is that you cannot marry the boy's mother, if you have penetrated him. This is totally unlike the punishments of stoning, hell and damnation that are applicable, if anal intercourse takes place between men, so that the ban to marry the boy's mother comes rather as an anti-climax. Moreover, it is rather unlikely that a pedophile wants to marry a boy's mother, unless he wants to have unrestricted access to the boy, which perhaps is what this Tradition is all about. This Tradition makes clear that Islamic scholars did not condemn homosexuality per se, but only sodomy. To atone for the latter a special purification (*ghosl-e janabat*) needed to be carried out as well penitence (fasting) done and alms to be given to the poor.[21] The permissibility of pedophilia with boys is in complete harmony with the permissibility of pedophilia between a man and a pre-pubescent girl, who has not yet menstruated, as discussed in chapter one. That such cases really occurred is implied by a report by the royal physician

---

20. Bukhari, *Sahih*, 62.25 [http://hadith.al-islam.com/Display/Display.asp?Doc=0&Rec=7607]. He also cannot marry the sister or the daughter of that boy. If however he had sodomized the boy after he had married the boy's mother, sister, or daughter and he had consummated that marriage then these women were not unlawful to him. Khomeyni, *Towzih*, p. 505-06 (no. 2282, 2283), 519 (no. 2356).

21. Khomeyni, *Towzih*, pp. 81-83 (nos. 344-354); Ibid, *Tahrir*, vol. 1, pp. 33-38.

Polak, who, in the 1850s, determined that children between eight and ten years had been infected with syphilis.[22]

Do Some of the Traditions Allow Homosexuality?

Various people have tried to argue that in addition to the permissibility of pedophilia, there are Traditions and Koran verses whose interpretation implies that Islam allows the possibility for anal sex between men in certain cases. According to these advocates, the Traditions address this issue indirectly in a number of cases. One of them, quoted in what follows, infers that sodomy was permitted in the case of eunuchs, if we consider the implications of the following tradition that concerns Abu Hurayra, one of the Prophet's companions, in fact his servant. He went to the Prophet, saying that he was a "young male" who "feared torment for his soul," but that he "did not find the wherewithal to marry a woman". The Prophet remained silent, even after Abu Hurayra repeated his statement three times. Finally after the fourth time, Mohammad said: "O Abu Hurayra, the pen is dry regarding what is befitting for you. So be a eunuch for that reason or leave it alone."[23]

From Abu Hurayra's statement it is clear that he was afraid of committing a sin, more precisely of unlawful sexual intercourse. He cannot have meant that this referred to sexual intercourse with women, or else his reference to his inability to marry a woman makes no sense. For, if he wanted to marry, but had no means for the dowry, or if he wanted to commit adultery, the prophet would have either offered him to help with the dowry, as he had done with some of his companions or would have counseled him to act in accordance with Sura 24:33, i.e., that he had to fast and exercise patience. The prophet

---

22. J. E. Polak, "Ueber den Gebrauch des Quecksilbers In Persien," *Wiener Medizinische Wochenschrift* 10 (1860), p. 547. He also reports a similar case of a child of 1 years old. Ibid., Prostitution," p. 629. See also Sirjani, *Vaqaye'*, pp. 609, 638, 707, 714 for sodomy of boys between four to seven years.

23. Bukhari, *Sahih*, 62.8.

offered neither, and logically this means that Abu Hurayra referred to his desire to have homosexual intercourse, either actively or passively, because if he was impotent he could not have feared committing adultery either. In this light the prophet's answer makes sense. He first told Abu Hurayra that the Creator had determined the nature of his gender ("the pen is dry") and that, therefore, he had to come to grips with what he was, a male or a natural eunuch, and "So be a eunuch for that reason or leave it alone." This means that if he decided to be a man then he had to live accordingly and marry. If, however, he chose to be a eunuch, it is not clear what he then could do, i.e. could he have anal sex with men? Whatever the answer to this question, this tradition does not constitute an endorsement of homosexual behavior.

Finally, these same advocates of homosexual behavior also draw attention to the fact that the Koran promises for those that enter paradise that they will have the pleasure of boys and thus condones rather than condemns homosexual behavior.

> They will recline (with ease) on Thrones (of dignity) arranged in ranks; and We shall join them to Companions, with beautiful big and lustrous eyes. They shall there exchange, one with another, a (loving) cup free of frivolity, free of all taint of ill. ... Round about them will serve, (devoted) to them, young male servants (handsome) as Pearls well-guarded. (Koran 52:20-29).

> And round about them will (serve) youths of perpetual (freshness): If thou seest them, thou wouldst think them scattered Pearls. (Koran 76:19)

According to these same advocates, this means that innumerable boys are available to all and sundry, who are like hidden pearls (virgins), and with whom one can commit no sin, ergo have anal intercourse. This seems to be the correct inference that may be drawn from this text. However, if anal intercourse would be allowed in paradise this does not necessarily mean that it is allowed in the here and now. For, according to Islamic law, in paradise there are no religious obligations (*taklif*) and hence the rules that apply to the 'hereafter' do not apply to the 'here and now.' It is not only 'the other world,' but also a totally different world, that is why presumably it is paradise. 'Obeyd-e Zakani also makes this clear in his own tongue in cheek way when he wrote:

> Enjoy sleeping with handsome boys because it is a joy
> that you will not find in heaven.[24]

The homosexual overtones of these Koran verses were "generally ignored by the exegetes [interpreters], although certainly entertained from an early date by the wider society; and the Hanafi jurists, at least, were willing to discuss, if nevertheless ultimately to dismiss the idea that homosexual intercourse, like wine, was a pleasure forbidden in this world but offered to the male elect in the next."[25] However, in Iran and elsewhere in the Moslem world, "in popular thought there is no question of metaphor: paradise is sex and the believer prays to God to reserve him the promised huris."[26]

In short, it would seem that advocates for homosexual behavior have not been able to find any real religious justification for the practising of homosexual behavior in Islamic law. In fact, whether you agree with it or not, Islamic law is quite clear that homosexual behavior is an anathema to God and anyone who facilitates, knowingly consorts with, and aids and abets such behavior is equally guilty. As one guide to the true believer states:

> It is related in the Traditions that the curse of God and
> the angels will be upon that man whom God created

---

24. Obeyd-e Zakani, *The Ethics*, p. 80.

25. E.K. Rowson, "Homosexuality in Islamic Law," *Encyclopedia Iranica*.

26. Vieille, "Iranian Women," p. 461; El-Rouyaheb, *Before Homosexuality*, pp. 118-28. One of the most important Moslem jurists argued that Paradise held out the promise of sex. al-Ghazzali, *On the Treatment of the Lust of the Stomach and the Sexual Organs* translated by Muhammad Nur Abdus Saam (Chicago, 2002), p. 23 stated that "the appetite for sexual intercourse has been made dominant over a person that he spread his seed ... and also as a foretaste of the pleasure of Paradise." See also Ibid., *On Marriage*, p. 12.

a man but who makes himself like women and is a
catamite, and upon the woman who makes herself like a
man, that is, who lies down and rises with a woman. ...
God said, 'Seven persons are accursed: He who performs
the act of the tribe of Lot, or copulates with beasts, or
cohabits with a woman and her daughter.'[27]

As is clear from the quotation the same interdiction also applies to
lesbianism. However, the Koran does not mention female homosexual
behavior at all[28] and only some of the Traditions mention lesbianism.
It is referred to as an aside in legal texts and it plays a minor role in ribald stories, mostly about harem scandals. Lesbianism (*sihaka*, meaning 'rubbing')[29] is usually negatively linked to sodomy, but the term
is sometimes used to mean masturbation. Male authors feel uncom-
fortable with the subject matter, because they lack knowledge about
lesbian practices, and thus, it is an alien subject. Usually, they argue
in favor of 'converting' these women to normal male-oriented heterosexual behavior and the use of judicial discretion (*ta'zir*) rather than
the recommended death penalty.[30] The poet Rumi in his *Mathnavi*
takes a more humanistic and modern view of the nature of lesbian
women when he wrote:

As God endowed women with the nature of man
He gave them a craving for women like a lesbian.[31]

However, he was the exception to the rule. Various Traditions and
jurists' opinions are unequivocal in that homosexual behavior should

---

27. Meisami, *Sea*, pp. 325-26.

28. Only the Mu'tazilite Abu Moslem Esfahani (d. 934), understood two highly
ambiguous Koran verses (4:15-16) as referring to, respectively, female and
male homosexual behavior (with permanent house arrest prescribed for the
former and simple chastisement for the latter). Fakhir-al-din Razi, *al-Tafsir al-
kabir* (Cairo, 1934-1962), vol. 9, pp. 229-36. However, the orthodox consensus
is that the two verses concern heterosexual fornication.

29. In Persian texts, the term for tribadism also used is *tabaq zadan* or 'rubbing'
the vulva.

30. G. H. A. Juynboll, "Sihka," in *Encyclopedia of Islam2*.

31. *Loghat-nameh-ye Dehkhoda*, q.v. *sa'tari*.

not be tolerated, because Hell and Damnation will be the perpetrators' lot. The prophet is reported to have said that he who commits
sodomy should be burnt and stoned. Even kissing a slave boy lustfully
means 1,000 years imprisonment in Hell, while simply embracing
him means that there is no hope for paradise.[32] Sodomy and lying with
a woman for money who is unlawful to him are sins for which your
faith is taken back from man, according to Imam Shafi'i.[33] For those
that still are not convinced they should heed the prophet's words,
who, allegedly, has said that a city where fornication prevails should be
destroyed.[34] Believers have a responsibility to avoid indirectly aiding
and abetting homosexual behavior. For example, "It is unlawful to sell
a male slave to someone so that he may commit sodomy with him."[35]
In fact, believers were exhorted to take a pro-active stance against homosexual behavior. "If a master is seen committing sodomy with his
slave he should be prevented; if he does not heed, so that he is killed,
no talion is required"[36] Some Maliki jurists interpreted Koran 9:120
as authorizing the sodomy of non-Moslems youths or when traveling without a wife. Others concluded that the Traditions reserving
the legal shedding of Moslem blood for three offences only -adultery,
homicide and denial of faith - precluded any corporal punishment for
homosexuality.[37]

---

32. Meisami, *Sea*, p. 103, with more examples of frightening statements.

33. Meisami, *Sea*, p. 100; see also al-Mawardi, *The Ordinances of Government*, p. 243.

34. Meisami, *Sea*, p. 104.

35. Meisami, *Sea*, p. 140. The fact that this source mentions this indicates that it was common practice to buy slaves for the purpose of using them for sodomy. It was also a practice that drew Obeyd-e Zakani's attention when he wrote : «Buy Turkish slave boys at any price when they have no beard, and sell them at any price when their beards begin to grow.» Obeyd-e Zakani, *Ethics of Aristocrats*, p. 78.

36. Meisami, *Sea*, p. 132, for other similar statements see Ibid., pp. 126, 130-31.

37. Schmitt and Sofer, *Sexuality*, p. 22, n. 7. However, most Maliki scholars also held that sodomy was unlawful. Shamisa, *Shahed-bazi*, pp. 114-16; Ravandi, *Tarikh*, vol. 7, pp. 376-77; El-Rouyaheb, *Before Homosexuality*, pp. 126-28.

Despite the certainty portrayed and the pro-active attitude advocated in the above sayings there are no actual references to homosexuality in the canonical *hadith* collections of Bukhari and Muslim. There are no Traditions in these collections either that state that the prophet said or did anything about such situations, beyond saying "Turn them out of your houses." Moreover, it is further reported that in those cases the second Caliph 'Omar "turned out such-and-such woman."[38] Other less reputed collections of Traditions allege that the prophet in all cases of homosexual behavior decreed to kill both homosexual partners caught in the act. Most Sunni jurists, however, agree that sodomy (i.e. anal penetration), all other non-penetrative acts (e.g. intercourse between the thighs) as well as all sexual behavior between two women were not subject to execution, but subject to the discretion (*ta'zir*) of the judge. However, Shi'a jurists held that in both cases the homosexual parties had to be executed, the manner of execution is left to the judge. Over time the view developed that those, whether male or female, engaged in non-penetrative acts were to be punished with 100 lashes only.[39]

WHAT IS IN A NAME?

So far for the theory; let's now observe reality and see how Moslems heeded divine rules in this respect. But before doing so let's have a look by what terms pederasts and sodomists were known, because that provides an indication of how society viewed this practice and its practioners. In Islamic Iran the practice of homosexual behavior, i.e. sodomy, meaning anal intercourse, is known under a large variety of terms such as: *shahed-bazi, nazar-bazi, jamal-parasti, lavat, lavateh, eghlam, kar,* and *bachcheh-bazi*. Different terms were used for those who acted as the *agens* or the active (*fa'el*) partner or who acted as the *cinaedus*, i.e., the passive (*maf'ul*) partner during homosexual activity. The passive partner was called: beloved (*ma'shuq*), the beardless

---

38. Bukhari, *Sahih*, 72. 774.

39. Camilla Adang, "Ibn Hazm on Homosexuality. A Case-Study of Zahiri Legal Methodology," *Al-Qantara* 24 (2003), pp. 5-31.

one (*amrad*), catamite (*ma'bun*), beautiful young man (*shahed*), beloved, adored one (*manzur*), the passive one (*maful*), child (*kudak*), she-male (*mokhannath*), a youth, whose beard hairs are just appearing (*now-khatt*), the beardless one (*bi-rish*), child, son (*pesar*), beardless, smooth-faced boy (*sadeh*), beardless (*sadeh zanakh*), and catamite, also the name of a disease (*obneh'i*), fuckee, catamite (*gong-e sheikh*), catamite (*kuni*), and male whore (*sharmut, malut*). The active partner was referred to as boy-lover (*gholam-bareh, sheikh gong*), old pederast (*kaka*), adorer of beauty (*jamal-parast*), adorer of faces (*surat-parast*), pederast, sodomite (*bachcheh-baz*), graceful [in motion] (*mowzun*), sodomite (*luti*) and the like.[40]

Some of these terms need explanation, whilst the meaning and implication of some others is self-evident. It is clear that the appelation of the passive partner gives evidence of the great preference for pubescent youths, who still did not yet have beard hairs or it was just starting to grow, or even younger boys.[41] Also, that the beloved object was beautiful is everywhere implied,[42] while the term *mokhannath* is somewhat of an exception. It focuses more on the position of the passive partner, literally the term means 'he who bends', which is clear from Rumi's juxtaposition of a man and a she-male.

> In men, their passion is directed to their anterior, in
> *mokhannath* to their posterior[43]

The term *mokhannath* often generally meant an older partner, for in the case of a young men the other relevant terms were used.[44]

40. Shamisa, *Shahed-bazi*, pp. 13-14; 'Obeyd-e Zakani, *Resaleh-ye Delgosha*, pp. 156, 217, 248-49.

41. Kai Ka'us b. Iskandar, *Qabus Nama*, p. 74 (ch. XIV); the king sent a beautiful slave away, gave him land and a wife to marry, with instruction only to return to court when he had grown a beard.

42. One of the earliest Persian poets, Abu Sho'eyb Herati, wrote a lyric poem describing the beauty of his male lover. Lazard, *Les premiers poètes*, p. 127.

43. Quoted by Najmabadi, *Women with Mustaches*, p. 16.

44. 'Obeyd-e Zakani, *Resaleh-ye Delgosha*, p. 248.

The two terms that indicate a disease need further explanation. The term *obneh* is used to refer to the illness that allegedly has afflicted effiminate men with the desire to be penetraded by male partners, while the term *ma'bun* indicates the individual who is affected by this illness.[45] According to al-Razi, the affliction of *obneh* is due to the father's weak male sperm, which makes the male child effeminate, thus implying this was not a sin, because it had a natural, genetic cause, and, moreover, that it was a disease that could and should be treated. "Mostly he will have small and wrinkled testicles … as well as a small penis." Al-Razi concluded from his analysis of this affliction that:

> If it is in its beginning stages and the person affected by
> it is not obviously effeminate and not strongly inclined
> to pleasure but rather ashamed (of it) and would like to
> be free from it, it is possible for him to be treated. The
> best treatment consists of frequently massaging penis
> and testicles and drawing them downward. Maids and
> slaves with nice faces and much practice (mufritat) in this
> matter should be put in charge of the patient, in order
> to rub and massage that place and apply themselves to it
> and kiss it and fondle it. This should be done as much as
> possible. At other times, his treatment should consist of
> the application to the pubic region, penis, and testicles of
> ben oil to which borax, euphorbia, and musk are added.
> At times, some asafetida may be added to the oil. The
> penis is massaged with it, and drops of it are put into the
> urethra. When this treatment is applied, he should sit in
> hot water, and the penis and testicles are massaged while
> he is in the bath tub. … It is clear that there is nothing
> more harmful for someone affected by this disease than
> having passive intercourse, as there is nothing more useful

---

45. It was therefore also known as the *obneh* indisposition (*nakhoshi-ye obneh*) or the dervish disease (*'ellat-e mashayekh*). Joh. L. Schlimmer, *Terminologie Médico-Pharmaceutique: Française - Persane* (Tehran, 1874 [Tehran: Daneshgah, 1970]), q.v. 'sodomie' ; 'Obeyd-e Zakani, *Resaleh-ye Delgosha*, pp. 181, 208.

for him than practicing active intercourse or attempting
to practice such intercourse as much as possible.[46]

Another treatment was the taking of enemas. Ibn Sina, however, totally disagreed with al-Razi. He completely rejected the idea
that *obneh* was a disease and argued that they were "people of a vile
psychological *(suqut an-nafs)* and bad physical disposition who have
accustomed themselves to non-virtuous ways *(radā'at al-'adah)* and
feminine behavior." Ibn Sina further argued that "Any other theory
is wrong. He who wishes to treat them is the most stupid of men.
Their disease is one of the imagination, not a physical one. Things
that break the desire, such as worries, hunger, vigils, detention, and
beatings, constitute useful treatment."[47]

Similarly, the appelations for the active partner are clear, although
the terms *shahed* and *nazar* require explanation. In the ninth century
CE a practice came into being in Sufi circles known as 'gazing of the
unbearded youth', which meant that Sufi males would gaze *(nazar)* at
attractive pubescent boys as a sign, or 'witness' *(shahed)* of the beauty
of God. As such the practice also became known as *shahed-bazi* (the
witness game). The meditating sufis might be overcome by ecstacy
during the spiritual concert *(sama')* so that they rent the shirt of the
youth and danced with him breast to breast, which, as it was alleged,
led to more intimate contact. As a result, opponents of Sufism considered the Sufi convents to be dens of iniquity, where instead of God,
pederasty was venerated. To what extent such accusations were true is

---

46. Al-Razi (864 - 930 CE) Treatise on the cause and treatment of passive
homosexual desire *Risalah fi'l-Ubnah*, translated by Franz Rosenthal, *Bulletin
of the History of Medicine* 52 (1978): 45-60. [http://www.well.com/user/
aquarius/ubnah.htm]. According to Imam Sadeq, when a man is dyeing his hair
and sleeps with his wife the child born from that will be a *mokhannath* or she-
male, while, according to the prophet, thinking of another woman during sex
with your wife may result in a child that is an *obneh*. Avazeh, *Qanun-e Qovveh-ye
Bah*, pp. 35, 37.

47. [http://www.macalester.edu/~cuffel/ar-razi2.htm] For an entertaining story
concerning a *ma'bun* see 'Obeyd-e Zakani, *Resaleh-ye Delgosha*, p.172. The
term continued to be used in medical science to refer to "swoln Piles of several
forms, by them called *Obne.*" Fryer, *A New Account*, vol. 3, p. 99.

difficult to assess, although there is no doubt that sex was also experienced as being divine by many Sufis.[48] Sa'di had some wise words to say about this problem.

> One of the ullemma had been asked that, supposing one sits with a moon-faced beauty in a private apartment, the doors being closed, companions asleep, passion inflamed, and lust raging, as the Arab says, the date is ripe and its guardian not forbidding, whether he thought the power of abstinence would cause the man to remain in safety. He replied: 'If he remains in safety from the moon-faced one, he will not remain safe from evil speakers.'
>
> If a man escapes from his own bad lust
> He will not escape from the bad suspicions of accusers.
> It is proper to sit down to one's own work
> But it is impossible to bind the tongues of men.[49]

Leading religious scholars, such as Mohammad al-Ghazzali (1058-1111), allowed staring at boys as long as it was like staring at flowers, thus clinical in nature without any sensual thoughts. However, his brother and a famous Sufi, Ahmad al-Ghazzali (d. 1126), who engaged in the practice of *shahed-bazi* himself, defended it as a legitimate method to witness God as did other Sufis such as Owhad al-Din Kermani.[50] Ruzbehan-e Baqli (d. 1209) is reported to have had extraordinary visions, "such as dancing with God, or having his tongue

48. For more details see Peter Lamborn Wilson, "Contemplation of the Unbearded. The Rubaiyyat of Awhadoddin Kermani," *Paidika* V 3-4 (1995), pp. 13-26; Shamisa, *Shahed-bazi*, pp. 95-141, who also discusses the opinion of famous Sufis who were opposed to *shahed-bazi*. El-Rouayheb, *Before Homosexuality*, pp. 111-17.

49. The poem is from Sa'di's *Golestan*, chapter 5, story 12 in the translation by Richard Burton [http://www.enel.ucalgary.ca/People/far/hobbies/iran/Golestan/].

50. Shamisa, *Shahed-bazi*, pp. 101-05, 120; Helmut Ritter, *das Meer der Seele; Mensch, Welt und Gott in den Geschichten des Farid uddin 'Attar* (Leiden, 1955), chapter 26; Wafer, "Vision and Passion," pp. 118-19.

sucked by angels and the Prophet."[51] Ibn Taymiyya, a fourteenth-century arch-conservative enemy of Sufism, charged that kissing and embracing were also a part of these ceremonies. "One sufi, accused by Ibn Taymiyya of such sexual immorality, replied, 'And so what if I did?'" As a result of these accusations as well as the involvement of Sufis with boys for sexual relations outside the 'witness game', the term *shahed-bazi* and *nazar*, became synonyms for sodomy and catamite respectively.[52]

The term *gholam-bareh* once again indicates that the object of homosexual love was a pubescent boy (*gholam*) as does the term pederast or child-molester (*bachcheh-baz*), likewise the terms that are used to refer to homosexual behavior in general. The terms do not distinguish between pedophilia and pederasty, because like in ancient Greece and Rome the position taken, active or passive, was the important determinent irrespective of the gender of the partners. The terms all imply that the active partner, often the owner or the paying client of the passive partner, was a lover of handsome boys with their rose-faced beardless cheeks as is evidenced in so many Persian poems, such as the following by the eleven century poet Manuchehri.

> The slave boy and the ewer of wine I love
> Its no reason to reproach and reprove
> I know well that both shouldn't be done
> But that's why it is so much fun.

CAN THERE BE ONLY ACTIVE HOMOSEXUALS?

From the terms used it is clear that rather than homosexuality they refer to pedophilia, because the focus is on beardless boys, although some more generic names are also used (*obneh*, *mokhannath*), which refer exclusively to the passive, and in this case, older partner. This rather one-sided nomenclature, highlighting the rigid active-passive roles, requires an explanation. Until the mid-twentieth century

---

51. Wafer, "Vision and Passion," p. 122.
52. Wilson, "Contemplation," p. 20.

there was no term in Persian for homosexual, which was invented to translate this international term, which itself only dates from the mid-nineteenth century. This new term, *ham-jens bazi* as well as *ham-jens gara*, meaning respectively same-sex lover and having a same-sex orientation, tried to capture the full array of homosexual behavior rather than of sodomy alone. For this reason many have argued that same-sex orientation in Iran (and the Middle East) differs from that in Europe and America, because at present there is nothing in Iran that looks like a Western-style gay culture, which in itself is of recent origin. Quite a few studies, therefore, have pointed out that although same-sex relationships have been and still are quite common in Iran as well as in the Middle-East in general, the notion of having a gay culture, where partners change roles, have affection if not love for one another and are equals, is entirely foreign to Iranians and Middle-Easteners. These studies argue that in the Middle-East, throughout the Islamic period, a sexual relationship is one where dominance counts and where the act of penetration is done by (free) men to social inferiors, i.e. women, boys, slaves (male and female), prostitutes (male and female) and animals. Sexual intercourse is part of social hierarchies of age, class and status. Thus, for a man to admit that he actually likes, i.e. derives pleasure from, being the passive partner, in other words, to be penetrated, was "inexplicable, and could only be atributed to pathology."[53] It is for this reason that the synonyms (in particular the Arabic ones) used for 'to sodomize' all tend to have abusive, derogatory and violent connotations. There is no sense at all for reciprocity, tenderness or love.[54]

It was alright for unbearded youths to be on the receiving end, for they were not as yet (bearded) men and thus could loose neither

---

53. See, e.g., among many others Evereth K. Rowson, "The Categorization of Gender and Sexual Irregularity in Medieval Arabic Vice Lists," in Julia Epstein and Kristina Straub eds. *Body Guards: The Cultural Politics of Ambiguity* (New York-London, 1991), p. 73; see also Stephen O. Murray and Will Roscoe, *Islamic homosexualities: culture, history, and literature* (New York, 1997), p. 17. 'Obeyd-e Zakani, *Resaleh-ye Delgosha*, p. 228.

54. Schmitt, "Different Approaches," pp. 8-14.

status nor manliness. However, adult free men submitting willingly to penetration means loss of face, honor, and respectability, worse they are perverts. Contrariwise, men who are engaged in sodomy are not considered homosexuals, but rather as macho-guys, who show off their virility and masculinity by 'giving it to them' and by 'ramming the message home'. It does not matter who the 'them' are as long as they are penetrated.[55] Having the passive, the underlying role was a sign of weakness, of femininity and thus shameful for a real man. If therefore you wanted to humiliate somebody, in particular an enemy, you ascribed to him such feminine a role.[56] For example, in the very popular seventeenth century tale of *Hoseyn the Kurd*, the hero of the tale not only goes on a sexual romp and sexually abuses and kills the enemy's women, but also, after having raped the Uzbeg's ruler 'Abd al-Mo'men's wife, he sodomizes the ruler himself as a sign of the latter's utter degradation and humiliation. This was partly a pay-back for the fact that when the hero had been captured by the Uzbegs, he had been kept imprisoned in the women's quarters to show how little respect they had for him as an alleged effeminate Iranian.[57]

However, for these males to commit sodomy others have to play the passive role. It is hard to believe that this role was only played by beardless youths, who, moreover, in most cases had to be paid and money is what most people did not have. Thus, such men not having access to boys had to find other same-age willing passive partners. Often, Moslem men therefore sought non-Moslem men for that role

---

55. Several popular songs from the Qajar period indicate that to the males concerned it was indifferent whether they had sex with a male or a female. Phillot, "Some Lullabies," pp. 47, 52.

56. See, e.g. the Shirazi song cited by Phillot, "Some Lullabies," p. 53:
Farmanfarma with his little felt hat
Farted his way to Shiraz; and he was so dumb
He thought Kerman was where he'd come
No, no, we replied, our answer was quick,
'There is the arse hole, here is the prick.' The translation is by Dick Davis.

57. Rosemary Stanfield-Johnson, "Yuzbashi-ye Kurd and 'Abd al-Mu'min the Uzbek: A Tale of Revenge in the *Dastan* of Husayn-e Kurd," in Soussie Rastegar & Anna Vanzan eds. *Muraqqa'e Sharqi. Studies in Honor of Peter Chelkowski* (San Marino, 2007), pp. 175-78.

as they still do in modern times, an option facilitated by tourism.[58] Because there were not enough adult passive homosexuals (*mokhannath, obneh*), perforce other adult men had to assume the passive role as well. Because being manly was and is the male ideal, of course, nobody would tell that he had assumed that unmanly role, let alone that he preferred it. The ribald poets, who usually wrote about their or other males' prowess to penetrate boys, did not of course laud the pleasure of being the passive partner, because that was not something to boast about. Some poets like Rumi, who opposed pederasty, pointed out that some young boys were afraid of being sodomized.

> A boy alone was found by a big man
> The boy paled fearing the man's plan
> The man said: 'Don't be scared my belle
> You'd like to be on top of me as well
> If I'm frightening, know me as a homosexual
> And sit on me and ride me a like a camel.' [59]

Although rare, sometimes a historical text makes mention of a homosexual or gay couple, more or less co-habiting. And here no reference is made to the stylized love between two males such as between Soltan Mahmud and Ayaz. We also learn that even manly soldiers sometimes did not mind to be sodomized and fellatioed. And most telling, in Gulf Arab society, the passive partner par excellence, the *mokhannath*, was not an outcaste or a stigmatized member of society. True, there is no gay scene in Iran, characterized by gay bars and clubs and dressing up, which did not even exist in the 1970s in Tehran, but that does not mean that there was and is only sodomy in Iran and that other forms of homosexual behavior did not and does not exist.

Persian, and Arab poetry and romance for that matter, gave expression to the positive evaluation of male homoerotic (and, specifically,

---

58. M. Glünz, "The Sword, the Pen and the Phallus: Metaphors and Metonymies of Male Power and Creativity in Medieval Persian Poetry," *Edebiyat* 6 (1995), pp. 237-38.

59. Shamisa, *Shahed-bazi*, p. 125.

pederastic) feelings, although over time, some poets tended to blur the gender of the beloved (God, boy, girl). In fact, Shamisa submitted that Persian literature is nothing but homosexual literature.[60] It has, however, also been argued that the love expressed for in particular Turkish boys in poetry is not really homosexual in nature.[61] Beardless boys, like young girls, are physically very much alike after all. They lack body hair, are soft-skinned and slender, and like women are subordinate to men. However, because in Persian the same pronoun is used for 'he', 'she' and 'it', while words such as 'beloved', 'friend', 'gazing' (*nazar*), and 'witness' [of beauty] (*shahed*) are also genderless. This then explains why in these poems seemingly no difference is made between boys and girls, unless reference is made to her rising breast or his first signs of a beard.[62] Many men, therefore, considered having sex with pubescent boys as acceptable, because like natural eunuchs they also lacked 'the urge' of sexual potency with women. Furthermore, pedophilia or love for boys was different from homosexual love between two mature males, which was considered to be despicable. It is true that the homoerotic element in the above-mentioned genre of poems can be more symbolic and spiritual than real, and, therefore, it is often

60. Shamisa, *Shahed-bazi*, p. 10. See also S. O. Murray, "Corporealizing Medieval Persian and Turkish Tropes," in S.O. Murray and W. Roscoe, eds., *Islamic Homosexualities. Culture, History, and Literature* (New York and London, 1997), p. 136, who argues that the rose mentioned in this poetry cannot be God, "Lying, ogling, and promiscuously giving favors to rivals are not plausible attributes of an omnipotent, omniscient God. In much other poetry I am not convinced that the rose ... is 'really' God and not a boy's anus". In the poetry of the Turkish Mehmed Ghazali, the anus is explicitly compared to a rose or rosebud. Ch. J. Summers, ed., *The Gay and Lesbian Literary Heritage. A Reader's Companion to the Writers and Their Works, From Antiquity to the Present* (New York, 1995), p. 324.

61. See, e.g., Wheeler T.M. Thackston Jr. and Hossein Ziai in their introduction to their translation of Arifi, *The Ball and Polo Stick or the Book of Estacy* (Costa Mesa, 1999).

62. J. T. P. de Bruijn, "Beloved," *Encyclopedia Iranica*, p. 129; Ehsan Yarshater, *She'r-e farsi dar 'ahd-e Shahrokh (nimeh-ye avval-e qarn-e nohom) ya aghaz-e enhetat-e she'r-e farsi* (Tehran, 1324/1955), pp. 153-60; Wafer, "Vision and Passion," p. 121, points out that Arberry uses capital letters in his translations such as 'He' rather than 'he', thus opting for only one possible reading of these poems.

difficult to separate the symbolic from reality in many of these poems. However, the fact is, as is clear from this chapter, that men really had sex with boys, and with each other, and they wrote about it and that there was nothing symbolic about it. Men who took pleasure in the passive role kept this to themselves and a secret, because such an attitude was scorned and vilified. On the other hand, to play an active penetrating sexual role was entirely normal, no matter who or what was being penetrated.

CALIPHATE PERIOD (651–1258)

Despite the Koranic injuctions, the human sex drive overrode the religious one, because pederastic behavior was widespread in Iran during the Caliphate.[63] It was also done openly and widely referred to in letters and poetry. In Iran, the wave of homoerotic poetry really started in the eighth century and lasted until the beginning of the twentieth century. Its appearance was such an abrupt break with the pattern of the past that contemporaries wondered what could be the cause of this phenomenon. The famous literary scholar al-Jahez (d. 869) blamed the Iranian troops led by Abu Moslem, who had come from Khorasan to help establish the Abbasids as Caliphs. Because the soldiers had not been allowed to bring women they had sought sexual relief between the thighs of their pages, thus establishing a new lifestyle.[64] This seems really far-fetched, because it presumes that homosexual behavior was incidental before that time. This is hard to believe and, moreover, it does not explain why, in this respect, there was no difference in homosexual behavior between the Eastern and the Western lands of the Caliphate, where the Abbasids did not attain power?

Whatever the truth, the fact is that it became fashionable to write frankly about sexual matters and call a spade a spade, and not

---

63. Ahmad b. Yahya Baladhuri, *Liber expugnationis regionum* ed. M.J. de Goeje (Leiden, 1866), p. 403; Muqadassi, *Kitab ahsan*, p. 281 (10th century).

64. The treatise *Mufakharat al-jawari wal-ghilman* (Boasting Match over Maids and Youths), has been translated into English by William H. Hutchins in al-Jahiz, *Nine Essays of al-Jahiz* (New York, 1989).

necessarily only in poetry. The Abbasid prince Ibn al-Muʿtazz (d. 909) always wrote his reply on the back of the love letters he received, so that "my writing commits pederasty with your writing."[65] A visiting vizier from Rey, who was offended that his colleague of Baghdad did not receive him immediately wrote: "I am powerless before 'the gate' like an eunuch while others go in and out like a penis."[66] Sodomy was not done on the sly, in fact it was performed quite openly. One poet even boasted that that he had seduced many boys in the mosque of Basra, while he further counseled that with regard to those boys who were unwilling:

> Go to them with the coined dirham, then he will come
>   to you
> For the dirham brings down that what's in the air and
>   catches what lives in the desert.[67]

The Caliph al-Amin (r. 809-813) inordenately loved eunuchs, in particular the black eunuch Kawthar. His mother Zeynab was worried about his behavior and tried to divert his passion for eunuchs by surrounding him with slave girls, who were beautiful of face and of slender built, and dressed and made up as boys, with moustaches painted on their face, which group of boy-looking girls was referred to as *gholamiyat*.[68] Under one of his successors, al-Motavakkel (r. 847-861) free reign was given to a libertine lifestyle. He employed passive homosexuals (*mokhannath*) as musicians and jesters. This unbridled hedonism led to the composition of a stream of bawdy homoerotic poetry with titles such as 'Lesbians and passive homo-sexuals', or, 'the superiority of the rectum over the mouth,' and 'rare anecdotes about

---

65. Mez, *Die Renaissance*, p. 344.

66. Mez, *Die Renaissance*, p. 344.

67. Mez, *Die Renaissance*, p. 344.

68. Mir Khvand, *Rowzat al-Safa*, vol. 3, p. 512. In his *Khosrow and Shirin*, Nezami used the term *gholamiyat* to indicate women dressed in men's clothes, when they joined a hunting party, which he states was the custom at that time. Shamisa, *Shahed-bazi*, p. 260.

eunuchs.' None of these works have survived, but later Arabic erotic works have extensive quotations from them.[69]

The caliphal court was a behavioral trend setter for provincial courts and it is therefore not surprising to find that many of the rulers of Iran were engaged in sodomy, while their male lovers were known by name to the public at large.[70] Sodomy was quite widespread among the highest officials of the Buyid state, which held sway over most of Iran and Eastern Iraq between 934 and 1055. Both Subuktegin, the army commander as well as Abu'l-Fazl, the king's vizier had catamites. When the latter through a ruse lured away a beautiful boy from the former this led to their deadly enmity. The vizier dressed this catamite so richly that he was better dressed than all the others of Subuktegin's boys.[71] The same observation held for their rulers, both members of the Buyid dynasty. In 977 at the battle at Ahvaz between the cousins, Bakhtiyar and 'Azud al-Dowleh (r. 978-983), a Turkish slave named Beytegin was made captive. Athough he was not even very beautiful and previously, Bakhtiyar had not particularly favored him, he now became so disconsolate[72] that he did not eat, drink, receive anybody, or even sit on the throne. He only wanted to cry, and if he received people to discuss important matters he had to tell them his whole miserable story. People started talking, the army became restless and even asked Ibn Baqiyeh, Bakhtiyar's vizier, to take the reins of govern-

69. Everett K. Rowson, "Gender Irregularity as Entertainment: Institutionalized Transvestism at the Caliphal Court in Medieval Baghdad," in *Gender and Difference in the Middle Ages*, eds. Sharon Farmer and Carol Braun Pasternack (Minneapolis, 2003), pp. 45-72; Abu al-Faraj Muhammad b. Ishaq b. Muhammad b. Ishaq al-Nadim, *Kitab al- Fihrist*, translated into English by Bayard Dodge as *The Fihrist of al-Nadim: A Tenth-Century Survey of Muslim Culture* (New York, 1970), pp. 334-36.

70. Aruzi Nezami, *Chahar Maqaleh* ed. Mirza Mohammad Qazvini (London, 1927), pp. 39-41 (Mahmud of Ghazna); Abu'l-Fath Bundari, *Zubdat al-nusrah va nukhbat al-usrah* ed. M. Th. Houtsma (Leiden, 1889), pp. 271-74 (Sanjar); Mez, *Die Renaissance*, p. 337, n. 6.

71. Bürgel, *Die Hofkorrespondenz*, p. 35, n.1.

72. For a similar case see Kai Ka'us b. Iskandar, *Qabus Nama*, p. 75, which mentions that Soltan Mas'ud also had totally kept hidden his love for a slave-boy whom he previously had not paid any attention to.

ment in his hands. Bakhtiyar finally wrote his cousin begging him to return Beytegin, promising two specially trained female lute players, whom Abu Taghlib in vain had tried to buy for 100,000 dinars. The exchange was made and Bakhtiyar on learning this became extatic so that it seemed as if "he was certain of being the recipient of the blessings of this and the next world." However, it could not prevent his downfall.[73]

Soltan Mahmud of Ghazna's (r. 998-1030) love for his slave Ayaz became proverbial in Persian literature as symbol of mystical purity, while his son and successor Soltan Mas'ud (r. 1031-1041) also had male lovers.[74] Soltan Jalal al-Din Mankubarti loved one of his slaves, named Qalaj, very much. When this slave died, the Soltan ordered his soldiers to line the road to Tabriz past which his bier came, a distance of a few miles, and he himself walked behind the bier on foot part of the way, until at the insistence of his emirs he mounted up. On arrival at Tabriz, he ordered the population to pay their respects to the bier and cry. He did not bury the boy, but wherever he went he took the corpse with him, for he continued to lament his lover's death.[75]

'Attar used the roles of the catamite and of homosexual love as ingredients for many of his moral stories. In fact, the love story of Soltan Mahmud and his black slave Ayaz occurs more frequently in his *Ilahi-nameh* than all other love stories, including the epitome of heterosexual love stories, that of Leyla and Majnun. His description of the moon-faced beautiful boys clearly speak to the imagination and many a reader of and listener to his stories must have sighed in regret and/or empathy.[76] Not everybody was that tolerant. The Christians in Iran excommunicated the metropolite (bishop) of Merv because of his homosexual activities, who then immediately converted to Islam,

---

73. Bürgel, *Die Hofkorrespondenz*, pp. 102-04.

74. Beyhaqi. *Tarikh*, pp. 252, 417-18, 672; Nezami 'Aruzi, *Chahar Maqaleh*, pp. 39-41.

75. 'Abbas Eqbal Ashtiyani, *Tarikh-e Moghul* (Tehran, 1347/1968), pp. 140-41.

76. 'Attar, *Ilahi-nama*, pp. 60-61, 74-75, 77, 100, 127, 146, 166, 185. Nezami Aruzi, *Chahar Maqaleh*, pp. 39-41 states, of course, that their loved was unrequited and Platonic.

where his homosexual behavior apparently posed no problem, and he then vilified the Christians.[77]

A recurring theme in poetry is that of the cup bearer, who was, however, more than the poet's artistic prop. 'Attar implied that cup bearers did more than bear cups.

> Now Sanjar had a slave as a cupbearer, who was perfect
> in his beauty.
> And to that beauty he united charm. The king had his
> enjoyment of both qualities.[78]

The twelve century poet Suzani is even more explicit leaving no doubt about the function if a cup bearer:

> And many golden boys while serving wine
> I've hoisted upon this bugle of mine.[79]

The amorous role of the cupbearer is implied by the *Qabus-nameh*, where advice is given to the king's boon companion: "When the cupbearer passes the goblet to you, do not gaze into his face but keep your head bent forward as you accept the wine. While you are drinking it and when you return the goblet to him you must not stare at him nor give your patron cause to conceive any suspicious fancies."[80] The same warnings were given by the jurists, for the danger of master and novice becoming enamored by casting even a fleeting glance should not be underestimated. To avoid sleeping with a woman, fasting usually helped and if not, there was also the option to marry one. However,

---

77. Spuler, *Iran*, p. 144, n. 3

78. 'Attar, *Ilahi-nama*, p. 219. Mo'ezz al-Din Ahmad Sanjar was the Soltan of the Seljuqs (r. 1118-1153).

79. Sprachman, *Suppressed*, p. 23.

80. Kai Ka'us b. Iskandar, *Qabus Nama*, p. 199, ch. xxxviii. This also reflected religious sentiments, which hold that "it is sin to look at beardless boys." Meisami, *Sea*, p. 188.

there was no such lawful option to satisfy lust for a boy, and thus prevention was better than expiation.[81]

The reverse side of these admonitions was that Persian satirical literature identified the lifestyle of an ascetic or dervish with that of a pederast and made fun of their dilemma, how to harmonize love for God with that for a boy? [82] Hence the popular saying that being sodomized is an 'ailment of the sheikhs.' To avoid temptation, many scholars refused to allow beardless boys to attend their classes, who therefore were obliged to attach artificial beards to their chins so that their teacher would not fall in love with them.[83]

The practice of sodomy before the fall of the Abbasid caliphate in 1258 is hardly worth mentioning, because it was such a normal practice. Similarly, the use of obscene words to describe (homo)-sexual activity, either for erotic reasons or as satire became a normal way of communication and lampooning.[84] However, sodomy was not without its critics, such as Sana'i. The poet mocks the pederastic practices of his time, embodied in the doings of the Khvajeh of Herat, who takes his catamite into the mosque for a quick tryst:

> Not finding shelter he became perturbed,
> The mosque, he reasoned, would be undisturbed.

But he is discovered by a devout man, who, in his blame, echoes a traditional attack on same-sex relations:

> 'These sinful ways of yours,'—that was his shout—
> Have ruined all the crops and caused the drought!

---

81. See e.g., al-Ghazzali, *On the Treatment*, pp. 23-25.

82. For a specimen of such satire see Sprachman, *Suppressed*, pp. 40-42.

83. Mehdi Adhar, "Qalamru-ye Sa'di," *Rahnama-ye Ketab* Tir (1339/1960), p. 224.

84. For more information on this kind of literature see Sprachman, *Suppressed*; Abdel Wahab Boudhiba, *La sexualité en Islam* (Paris, 1975); El-Rouayheb. *Before Homosexuality*.

Sana'i drives the irony home by having the devout man, after the Khvajeh makes his embarrassed escape, mount the boy and complete the act.

> The crops now grow all over earth again,
> And people have the strength to live again.

The poet makes a final admonition to the reader to be sure that they draw the right lesson from all this:

> If all the world's *zahed*s are like this bloke
> You can expect no more from other folk.[85]

Another author, this time a Shi'ite, was Naser-e Khosrow, who ridiculed the four Sunni schools for allowing the playing of chess, drinking of wine, consuming of opium, and sodomy, respectively.

> Shafe'i said: 'Playing chess is not unlawful.
> Do not cheat for the Imam has ordered you to be
>   truthful.'
> But Hanifeh has even a better idea on wine:
> 'If it's boiled, drink it, for it is not unlawful.'
> The Hanbalites say: 'If stricken with grief
> Take bhang and stroll gaily!'
> If you follow the fourth jurist, Malek,
> He will prescribe for you cohabitation with a young boy!
> Take bhang, drink wine, lie with fair ones and gamble,
> Truly Islam has been perfected by these four Imams![86]

---

85. Sprachman, *Suppressed*, pp. 10-12; Paul Sprachman, "Le beau garçon sans merci: The Homoerotic Tale in Arabic and Persian" in *Homoeroticism in Classical Arabic Literature*, ed. J. Wright and K. Rowson, New York, 1997, p.199. [192-209]. Obeyd-e Zakani, *Ethics of The Aristocrats*, p. 61 has a similar story where a poet rebukes a man for sodomizing a boy in a mosque. Later that man sees the poet doing the same thing and asks him to explain himself. The poet answered: "Have you not heard of poetic license?"

86. The poem is from Naser Khosrow's *Divan* and the translation is by Hasan Javadi, *Satire in Persian Literature* (Cranbury, 1988), pp. 70-71. The poem explicitly refers to the opinon of Malikite scholars that sodomy was allowed under certain conditions (see above).

Whereas Sana'i and Naser-e Khosrow used irony and satire to expose the sinful homosexual behavior, the author of the twelfth-century *Fava'ed al-Bahr* reminds his readers with barely hidden anger at the affront, that no less than "the Greek infidels report that Moslem kings allow fornication and sodomy."[87] The implied lesson here is that not only don't Moslems heed the divine rules, but also Christians had to remind them, and jeeringly, of their shame and total neglect. And indeed, Kai Ka'us, the Gilani ruler, did not make a fuss about sodomy, it was no big deal. In fact, he only mentioned it to his son to ensure that he understood that he should not be ruled by passion, and, therefore, had to take his pleasure where he could, but in a measured and thoughtful manner. The *Qabusnameh* therefore counsels: "As between women and youths, do not confine your inclinations to either sex, thus you may find enjoyment from both kinds without either of the two becoming inimical to you." It further advises that: "During the summer let your desires incline towards youths and during the winter towards women."[88] Because it was also quite normal to make use of the boys that were available in the bath-houses. Kai Ka'us counseled his son as follows: "When men took baths they also would, if desire so dictated, engage in homosexual behavior," something he advised against, especially if it would take place in the hot chamber.[89]

Other authors take a somewhat moralizing tone without condemning the practice outright. 'Awfi tells the story of the shopkeeper who had fallen in love with a beautiful boy, who bilked him of his money with the help of a pimp. He then fell into the hands of the police for improper behavior, and then into the hands of a greedy governor so that, having lost all his money, ended up in prison where he died.[90] The author thus depicts the authorities as dishonest and

---

87. Meisami, *Sea*, p. 96.

88. Kai Ka'us b. Iskandar, *Qabus Nama*, pp. 77-78 (ch. XV).

89. Kai Ka'us b. Iskandar, *Qabus Nama*, p. 78 (ch. XVI). It is for this reason that 'Obeyd-e Zakani, *Resaleh-ye Delgosha*, p. 216 described the bath-house keeper (*hammami*) as the tax-collector of coitus (*tamghachi-ye jema'*); see also Ibid., p. 258.

90. 'Awfi, *Javame' al-Hekayat*, p. 255.

unjust, and the main character as being the victim of his own vice. Such misfortune not only might befall the lover, but also the beloved, for these boys often started out as well-behaved, proper and pious. When Baha al-Din Valad asked such a boy, who had become a bad boy, 'what did you do,' the boy replied, 'I did nothing, I only kept bad company.'[91] And bad company could be very exalted company. Sheikh Abu Zakariya Yahya b. 'Ali aka Khatib Tabrizi was the treasurer of the Nezamiyeh College at Baghdad. Each night he drank alcohol and engaged in sodomizing boys. When he was found out he rued his lifestyle and repented.[92] He clearly did not have the presence of mind of Mowlana Qotb al-Din, a famous scientist and physician, who also used his school to sodomize youths. "Suddenly someone put his hand on the door of the room and opened it. Mowlana said, 'What do you want?' He said, 'I want somewhere to sit down and say my prayers.' Mowlana replied, 'Are you blind? Don't you see that this place is so small that people have to pile on top of each other?'"[93]

Repentance seems to have been an exception, a reason why it had to be held up as an example to an otherwise sinning society. In fact, sinning occurred at the highest levels of intellectual society. The poet Sa'di left no doubt that he preferred boys to women any time.[94] One day when the Shi'ite polymath (scientist, philosopher, theologian) Naser al-Din Tusi (1201-1274) was riding on a dusty road with his student, who was very handsome with beautiful tresses, he saw that the dust settled on the student's tresses. Overcome by this phenomenon Naser al-Din Tusi recited an appropriate Koran verse (74.40), to wit: 'O! would that I were dust!', referring to his lust that he hoped could be transformed into dust that had mixed with the tresses of his student.[95]

---

91. Ravandi, *Tarikh*, vol. 7, p. 485.

92. Mojtaba Minovi, *Naqd-e Hal* (Tehran, 1351/1972), p. 222.

93. Obeyd-e Zakani, *Ethics of Aristocrats*, p. 120-21.

94. Minoo S. Southgate, "Men, Women, and Boys: Love and Sex in the Works of Sa'di," *Iranian Studies* 17/4 (1984), pp. 413-52; Shamisa, *Shahed-bazi*, pp. 143-65.

95. Ravandi, *Tarikh*, vol. 7, p. 411.

MONGOL-ILKHANID-TIMURID-TURKMEN PERIOD (1258-1500)

Pederasty was quite common under the Mongols, so much so that Jaghatay intervened to ban the practice.[96] However, Geykhatu (r. 1291-1295) was so enamored of boys that it contributed to his unpopularity among the Mongols and his downfall.[97] In 1385, Shah Ahmad, the governor of Baghdad, was so besotted with a beautiful Mongol boy that the qazi of Baghdad took offence and went to Tokhtamesh Khan (d. 1406), who had just conquered Tabriz, to complain, who then ordered his emirs to arrest the governor.[98]

Homosexual behavior, however, was not limited to that between an older male and a young boy; there was a similar behavior between two adult males. Such unions are seldom mentioned, because unlike a relationship with a boy, those with men of one's own age were socially unacceptable. In fact the passive man would be derided and ridiculed. 'Ala' al-Din Mohammad III, the ruler of Alamut, had a servant Hasan Mazandarani whom he loved passionately. He gave him his mistress as a wife, but also continued to sleep with her, while Hasan would not sleep with her unless he got Ala' al-Din's leave. The latter had "eyes for no one else and preferred him to beardless boys and such loves," even when there were signs of grey in his hair. Hasan Mazandarani also had a great influence in court politics.[99]

The prevalence of homosexual behavior between adult men is implied in the remarks of a local official Naser al-Din Monshi-ye Kermani, who felt that he had been mistreated. To highlight the extent of the disrespect shown he compared himself with a passive homosexual (*mokhannath*) when he felt insulted.[100] This type of relationship is also

---

96. Mir Khvand, *Rowzat al-Safa*, vol. 5, p. 43.

97. Mir Khvand, *Rowzat al-Safa*, vol. 5, p. 43; Ahmad b. 'Ali Maqrizi, *Histoire des sultans mamlouks de l'Egypte* 2 vols. in 4 ed. Etienne Quatremère (Paris, 1837-45), vol. 2/1, p. 40.

98. Samarqandi, *Matla'-ye Sa'deyn*, vol. 1, p. 574.

99. Juvaini, *History*, vol. 2, p. 710.

100. Naser al-Din Monshi-ye Kermani, *Semt al-Ola lel-Hezrat al-'Oliya dar*

satirized by 'Obeyd-e Zakani, indicating that such relationships were perhaps more common than is generally thought. In his satire of the *Shahnameh*, Iran's national epos, he has Rostam, Iran's quintessential hero and one of his opponents, Human, lay down their arms and attack one another with the swords that nature has endowed them with. The fight becomes an amorous bout, each taking turns to assume the active and passive role.

> When Rostam had undone his drawers
> He knelt down, the hero of many wars
> As Gudarz had taught him at night
> Houman made his pillar upright
> He rammed into Rostam in such a way
> That he thought his back will give away.
> Then was Houmans's turn to lie down
> And Rostam like a lion mounted on him
> Harder and harder into him he launched
> That Houmans's back was badly marred.

'Obeyd-e Zakani concludes this reciprocal sexual encounter with the advice:

> Eternal happiness lies in the game of lovemaking;
> Give in and you will win; the prize is for the taking.[101]

The Atabek ruler of Yazd, Hajji Shah, was so besotted with a boy that through his ignominious behavior the Atabeks lost Yazd.[102] Madrak b. 'Ali Sheybani, poet and teacher, lost his heart to a beautiful Christian boy, 'Amru, who did not respond positively to his advances. He did not return to the class room and Madrak became so despondent that he could not teach anymore and started to become crazy. He asked friends who came to visit him to seek 'Amru so that

---

Tarikh-e Qarakhati'iyan-e Kerman 'Abbas Eqbal ed. (Tehran, 1328/1949), p. 100.

101. 'Obeyd-e Zakani, *Ethics of the Aristocrats*, p. 43

102. Zarrinkub, *Az Kucheh-ye Rendan*, p. 85.

he might find healing. The friends found the student who, at their request, came to the house of Madrak and took his hand and asked after
his health. Madrak then read him some love poems and at the end
uttered a cry and passed away.[103] It was also quite normal that soldiers
passing through a village would take women and boys for their own
pleasure, reason why, if there was time, villagers fled on learning that
soldiers were nearby.[104]

Lest people would think that only the high and mighty were homosexuals, 'Obeyd-e Zakani, the great satirist (ca. 1300-1372) wants
us to believe that practically everybody were "catamites." He could
have meant this as a *double entendre*, or maybe he was just flippant,
but in some verses he makes quite clear that homosexual behavior was
the key to success in life:

> In your childhood, do not withhold the favor of your
> arse from friend or foe, relative or stranger, those near
> or remote, so that in your adulthood you can reach the
> rank of shaykh, preacher, world-champion, and chief of
> protocol.[105]

In other stories, 'Obeyd-e Zakani was even more explicit, singling
out specific towns.

> A preacher in Kashan says that on the Day of Judgment,
> 'Ali, the cousin of the Prophet, will be in charge of the
> heavenly well of Kowthar and will give its water to the
> person who has not slept with a homosexual. A man
> from Kashan gets up and leaving the mosque says: "O my

---

103. Mehdi Adhar, "Qalamru-ye Sa'di," *Rahnama-ye Ketab* Tir 1339 (1960),
p. 225. Usually, lover boys were more mercenary. 'Obeyd-e Zakani makes
various remarks about that. He also noted that they could not be bothered with
fasting and were ecumenical in their relations. "In the month of Ramazan a
homosexual boy was asked if the market was sluggish. He said, "Yes. But may
God keep Christians and Jews for us!". Obeyd-e Zakani, *Ethics of Aristocrats*, p.
80, 81, 92.

104. Ardabili, *Safvat al-Safa*, pp. 339, 1158.

105. Sprachmann, *Suppressed*, p. 46.

friend, surely he has to put back the water in the pitcher and drink it all himself!"

Even the inhabitants of the holy city of Qom are not spared by 'Obeyd.

> Two old gay men from the town, after making love at the top of a minaret, of all places, are talking. One says: "This city of ours is full of corruption."
>
> The other answers: "What do you expect from a city whose blessed old men are like us?"[106]

The ruler of Baghdad, Soltan Ahmad Jalayer (r. 1382-1410), made it a habit to drink excessively and take his pleasure with children.[107] Hence 'Obeyd-e Zakani commented: "Take advantage of the money and the bodies of slaves, so that you may be regarded as a perfectly law-abiding man."[108]

During the Timurids, the social scene changed little and homosexual behavior remained an integral part of partying and drinking. Often one of the party-goers would bring a catamite (*nazar*), who, if his master became incapacitated by drunkenness could then be serviced by other members of the group.[109] Babur provides many instances of the homoerotic environment of the Timurid period. "The Hisaris [in the Ferghana valley] and in particular the followers of Khusrau Shah engaged themselves unceasingly with wine and fornication. ... Another thing was that the young sons of the townsmen and shopkeepers, nay! even of the Turks and soldiers could not go out from their houses

---

106. 'Obeyd-e Zakani, *Ethics of The Aristocrats*, p. 102.

107. Samarqandi, *Matla'-ye Sa'deyn*, vol. 2, p. 85. For a discussion of Hafez's homoerotic poems see Shamisa, *Shahed-bazi*, pp. 165-70.

108. 'Obeyd-e Zakani, *Ethics of Aristocrats*, p. 78.

109. Vasefi, *Badaye' al-Vaqaye'*, vol. 2, p. 1047; for other stories involving homosexual love and behavior see Ibid., vol. 2, pp. 578, 1222.

for fear of being taken for catamites."[110] They were not the only ones. Mahmud Mirza, the third son of Abu Sa'id Mirza

> He drank wine continually. He kept a lot of catamites, and in his realm wherever there was a comely, beardless youth, he did everything he could to turn him into a catamite. He turned his beg's sons and his sons' begs and kükäldashes' [milk-brother] sons.[26] During his time this shameful vice was so widespread that there was no one at all who did not have catamites. To keep them was considered a virtue, and to not to keep them a fault.... Around him he had buffoons and clowns who performed lewd, indecent acts during his divan, right out in front of people.[111]

Beysanghor Mirza had a favorite *beyg* 'Abdollah Barlas, "his sons were such confidants and ichkis [insiders] that they were as close as lovers and beloveds. The Tarkhan begs and some of the Samarkand begs were offended by this…"[112] The governor of Herat, Mohammad Vali Beyg had a retainer called Khvajeh Mohammad Chenar, whom he loved dearly. He called him his son and made him the *darugheh* or police chief of the city. He committed every wicked act under the sun and people were so afraid of him that if they had handsome sons they did not allow them to leave the house, but nobody dared to tell the governor about his *darugheh*'s behavior.[113] No wonder that the poet Jami wrote a few lines as a warning to young men:

> To avoid that you have to wear a burkah over your head
> Don't leave the house to go into the street and the
>   market.[114]

---

110. Babur, *Babur-Nama*, p. 42.

111. *The Baburnama: Memoirs of Babur, Prince and Emperor*, translated, edited, and annotated by Wheeler M. Thackston (Washington, DC, 1996), pp. 60–61.

112. *The Baburnama*, pp. 72.

113. Vasefi, *Badaye' al-Vaqaye'*, vol. 1, p. 414.

114. Ravandi, *Tarikh*, vol. 7, p. 389.

One of the poet Jami's (1414-1492) contemporaries, the scholar Amir Sa'id Hoseyn Abivardi, had different ideas. When he traveled through Iran and Turkey he was accompanied by a beautiful youth to slake his passion, although he still had a roving eye and was aroused by the sight of a beautiful infidel boy in Istanbul.[115]

Even Babur (1483-1530) himself, who considered sodomy a vile and unlawful act, one day found himself in love for the first time in his life and greatly surprised that this love was for a boy, when, moreover, he had just married, also for the first time (in 1500 when he was 17 years old), although he barely visited his wife (eventually his mother forced him to visit her once every 40 days). As his description of his feelings is so unique in Middle-Eastern literature it is quoted here in full so that one may get an appreciation for Babur's mixed feelings and confusion about this unexpected sentiment.

> During this time [75b] there was a boy from the camp market named Baburi. Even his name was amazingly appropriate.
>
>> I developed a strange inclination for him—
>> rather I made myself miserable over him.
>
> Before this experience I had never felt desire for anyone, nor did I listen to talk of love and affection or speak of such things. At that time I used to compose single lines and couplets of Persian. I composed the following lines there:
>
>> May no one be so distraught and devastated
>> by love as I; May no beloved be so pitiless and
>> careless as you
>
> Occasionally Baburi came to me, but I was so bashful that I could not look him in the face, much less converse with him. In my excitement and agitation I could not thank him for coming, much less complain of his leaving.

---

115. Amir Sa'id Hoseyn Abivardi, "Anis al-'Asheqin," ed. Iraj Afshar, *Farhang-e Iran Zamin*, vol. 15 (Tehran, 1354/1975), p. 86f.

Who could bear to demand the ceremonies of fealty? One day, during this time of infatuation, a group was accompanying me down a lane, and all at once I found myself face to face with the boy. I was so ashamed I almost went to pieces. There was no possibility of looking straight at him or of speaking coherently. [76] With a hundred embarrassments and difficulties I got past him. These lines by Muhammad Salih came to my mind:

> I am embarrassed every time I see my beloved.
> My companions are looking at me, but my gaze is
> elsewhere.

It is amazing how appropriate this verse was. In the throes of love, in the foment of youth and madness, I wandered bareheaded and barefoot around the lanes and streets and through the gardens and orchards, paying no attention to acquaintances or strangers, oblivious to self and others.

> When I fell in love I became mad and crazed. I
> knew not this to be part of loving beauties.

Sometimes I went out alone like a madman to the hills and wilderness, sometimes I roamed through the orchards and lanes of town, neither walking nor sitting within my own volition, restless in going and staying.

> I have no strength to go, no power to stay. You
> have snared us in this state, my heart.[116]

But Babur was not the only one with such feelings; others had them too and acted upon them. This was the case with the sons, soldiers and the town (Herat) of Soltan Hoseyn Mirza Beyqara (r. 1469-1506), who all "were addicted to drink and lived with inordinate revelry and debauchery."[117]

There were poets who sang of homosexual love and one of them, Helali, much to the dismay of Babur, wrote a *mathnavi*, 'The Shah and the Dervish', about the subject. What upset Babur was not so

---

116. *The Baburnama*, pp. 112–113.
117. *The Baburnama*, p. 206.

much the homosexual behavior described in the poem, but that of the king's behavior, i.e., that the king was depicted as the passive partner, which implied weakness, a lack of virility and manliness, which was so unlike the ideal of how a king should behave and that image, he feared, reflected badly on the kings in the real world and the respect that they could command. The poet,

> made a dervish the lover and a king the beloved, a
> shameless strumpet in fact. It is really an affront that, in
> the interests of his poem, he describes a young man—and
> a king at that—as a brazen woman and prostitute.[118]

Some of the drinking parties at the Timurid court or those organized by their officials were real debaucheries, and even Babur, who did not drink wine until he was 30, at times was almost inclined to do so. "Later on when, with the young man's lusts and at the prompting of sensual passion, desire for wine arose." The drinking was heavy and drugs were taken as well, although it seems the alcoholics and the drug addicts preferred to carouse separately. The parties sometimes were rough and rude, but, when the atmosphere was warm and congenial, music was played and some of the men danced and poetry was recited and some coarse acts were performed for the amusement of the company. "Two slaves of the Mirza's, known as Big-moon and Little-moon, did offensive, drunken tricks in the drunken time."[119] The goings-on in the rest of Iran that was ruled by the Aq-Qoyunlu and later by the Qara-Qoyunlu dynasty were not dissimilar to those of the Timurid realm. A few persons in the entourage of Soltan Ya'qub (r. 1474-1490) were pederasts[120] and they must have been the tips of several icebergs.

---

118. *The Baburnama*, p. 225. His contemporary Sam Mirza, *Tadhkereh*, pp. 152-60, brother of Shah Tahmasp I, does not share this negative opinion about this work.

119. Babur, *Babur-Nama*, pp. 302-04, 386-88, 423.

120. Sam Mirza, *Tadhkereh*, pp. 47, 186, 349-50.

LESBIANISM

The practice of lesbianism is rarely referred to, but it existed as is clear from the following poem from the *Javame' al-Hekayat* (ca. 1220)

> I saw two courtesans fooling around, what a sight,
> They were 'bumping fur' and did not sleep all night.
> It is most strange to say, but both were 'catchers',
> But how can they score without 'pitchers'?[121]

Some texts refer to the use of a leathered dildo, called *machachang*, by lesbians, where one of the women would assume the male role. This word is attested already in the ninth century and it is likely that its use reflects pre-Islamic practice, because the use of the dildo was already known to the Greeks under the name of *olisbos*. Women who used such an artificial penis were referred to as *sa'tari* and the practice itself as *sa'tari-bazi*.[122] In Ottoman Turkey, according to a well-known miniature, the dildo allegedly was even allowed in the qazi's court as evidence of a man's impotence, which constitutes grounds for divorce (see figure 4.1). Cross-dressing women were still found at court, presumably to provide entertainment. Abu Sa'id's (r. 1316-1335) wife, Baghdad Khatun sent her greetings to Sheikh Safi al-Din Ardabili by way of "two persons from Yarmuk, i.e. girls who are like men."[123]

121. Mohammad Qazvini, *Yaddashtha-ye Qazvini*, Iraj Afshar ed. 8 vols. (Tehran, 1339/1960), vol. 5, pp. 98-99 (q.v. *sa'tari*).

122. Sprachman, "Le beau garçon," p. 198; Asadi Tusi, *Lughat al-Furs*, ed. Mohammad Dabir-Siyaqi (Tehran, 1336/1957), p. 113; Dehkhoda, *Loghat-nameh*, q.v. *sa'tari*. The use of the dildo, usually a wooden one, was well-known in Ottoman Turkey where it was referred to as *zibik*. It was the subject of many a saucy tale. Sema Nilgün Erdoğan, *Sexual Life in Ottoman Society* (Istanbul. 2001), pp. 86, 129.

123. Ardabili, *Safvat al-Sava*, p. 792.

Figure 4.1: Unhappy wife shows dildo to the Qazi as proof of her husband's impotence (from Hamse-i Atai)

SAFAVIDS (1501-1736)

Again, under the Safavids, homosexual behavior was an accepted and well-established practice. Shah Esma'il I, the founder of the state and the man who made Twelver Shi'ism the state religion in Iran, himself was actively engaged in sodomy. To inaugurate his reign, forced

himself upon twelve of the most beautiful youths of Tabriz, thus set-
ting an example for everybody. After he had no more use for them, he
passed them on to his courtiers.[124] Most of his courtiers were alcoholics and sexual debauchees. Of Qazi-zadeh Laheji, a protegé of Sheykh
Najm Zargar, the regent of Iran (1509-10), it was said that he "drank
so much that he could not any longer tell the difference between
morning and evening."[125] Mowlana Jarubi Heravi was an oddity in
his sexual taste. For him not just the *amrad*—the beardless youth with
the beautiful face—but anyone of high rank became the object of his
love. While in Qandahar he fell in love with Babur, who was then in
his thirties and had an old wizened face, and when he went to Herat
he fell in love with its governor, Durmish Khan, and thereafter with
whoever became governor there.[126] Sayyed Sharif Jorjani, the *sadr*—
chief of the religious establishment, the highest religious dignitary of
Iran—continued to have affairs with numerous men.[127] Habibollah
Saveji, the vizier of Khorasan, surrounded himself with catamites.[128]
The grand vizier, Mirza Shah Hoseyn (1514-24), who had led a rather
dissolute life in his youth,[129] became Esma'il I's boon companion during his last years, and given the shah's beauty and the fact that they
were of the same age suggests that they had more than a passing interest in each other.[130] No wonder that the Ottoman soldiers jeeringly
yelled at the Qezelbash, the pejorative term for Shah Esma'il's troops,
"Your Shah is Ali the sodomite."[131] Shah Esma'il was sodomized by

---

124. Barbaro, *Travels*, vol. 2, p. 207; Romano, "Viaggio d'un mercante che fu
nella Persia," in Giovanni Battista Ramusio, *Navigazioni e Viaggi* ed. Marica
Milanesi (Turin, 1978) vol. 3, p. 478.

125. Sam Mirza, *Tadhkereh*, p. 109.

126. Sam Mirza, *Tadhkereh*, p. 311.

127. 'Ali Shir Nava'l-Hakim Qazvini, *Majales al-Nafa'es* ed. 'Ali Asghar Hekmat
(Tehran, 1334/1945), pp. 384, 386, 400.

128. Qomi, *Kholasat*, vol. 1, p. 168.

129. Sam Mirza, *Tadhkereh*, p. 89.

130. Aubin. "L'Avènement ," p. 54.

131. *Hans Dernschwam's Tagebuch einer Reise nach Konstantinopel und
Kleinasien*, ed. F. Babinger (Munich-Leipzig, 1923), p. 210, quoted by Aubin.
"L'Avènement," p. 54.

Mani Shirazi, when he was 13 years old. Once, when Mani Shirazi was sent for by the shah and was allowed to make the foot kiss he instead kissed the shah's leg. The courtiers were aghast and urged the shah to sentence him to death, which he did. Mani Shirazi's friends then interceded and his life was spared, but the pardon arrived just after the execution.[132]

It was, therefore, no surprise that Italian travelers reported, with revulsion, that "In this city [of Tabriz] there is a public place and a school of Sodomy, where likewise they pay according to their beauty."[133] Not only in Tabriz, but also elsewhere, homosexual activities flourished. In Hormuz, men wore make-up,[134] jewelry and trinkets. Male prostitution thrived on the island, which was only to be expected in a cosmopolitan sea port.[135] Sodomy was indeed common, according to Pires. He reported that male prostitutes "are beardless and go about dressed like women, and the Moors laugh at us when we point out to them the turpitude of this sin." In 1515, a group of women lodged a complaint with Afonso d'Albuquerque, the governor of India, who was at that time in Hormuz, because their husbands were homosexuals. He had them arrested and "expelled from city and island with an arrow run through the nostrils."[136] There was a public place for male prostitutes in the city. Albuquerque had them also banished from the kingdom.[137] Kaempfer quoted a Persian verse that alludes to these homosexual practices.[138]

---

132. Nasrollah Falsafi, *Zendegani-ye Shah 'Abbas-e Avval* 5 vols. (Tehran, 1332/1951), vol. 2, p. 69.

133. Barbaro, *Travels*, vol. 2, p. 171.

134. Iarric, *L'histoire*, p. 363; Góis, *Crónica*, II/32, p. 108; Tenreiro, *Itinerários*, p. 5. On what constituted make-up at that time see Soudavar-Farmanfarmaian, "Haft Qalam Arayish," pp. 285-326.

135. Wicki, *Documenta Indica*, vol. 4, p. 202.

136. Pires, *The Suma Oriental*, vol. 1, p. 23; Barbosa, *The Book*, vol. 1, pp. 97, 104; Castenheda, *História*, III/142, p. 343; Correia, *Lendas da India*, vol. 2, pp. 441-42; Albuquerque, *Commentaries*, vol. 4/38, p. 169; Wicki, *Documenta Indica*, vol. 2, p. 250 (16/12/1551).

137. Pires, *Suma*, vol. 1, p. 23; Albuquerque, *Commentaries*, vol. 4/38, p. 169.

138. Engelbert Kaempfer, *Amoenitatum Exoticarum. Fasciculi V, Variae*

Hormuz of bitter water and blacks with unwashed bums
Do not reproach it for this brings rejoicing to Hell's
    slums.

The situation remained unchanged when the function of Hormuz was assumed by Bandar 'Abbas after 1622. Boys were still available, who, according to Della Valle, were dressed as a male from the waist-band upwards and as a female downwards; they offered their services in its streets by performing lewd and lascivious songs and gestures. Because some were black and ugly he did not believe that they were native Persians.[139]

Esma'il I was not the only Safavid king who loved boys, for so did his son Tahmasp I, who, before he found religion, had led a dissolute life committing not only adultery, but the entire range of all forbidden acts (*manahi*).[140] His eldest son Shah Esma'il II, was an active homosexual, although he also sired a child. However, his main object of affection was "Hasan Beg Halvachi-oghlu, with whom he had a close and affectionate relationship, and who was his boon companion night and day."[141] Likewise, Hamzeh Mirza, the heir-apparent of Shah Mohammad Khodabandeh, had a penchant for boys; in fact he was killed by a confidante, who allegedly resented the fact that the prince had a secret liaison with a boy whom he loved himself.[142] It was said that Shah Safi I had a liking for boys. In 1634, he gave the son of Da'ud Khan, a rebel, to the grooms for their sexual gratification, but the son of another rebel, who was very beautiful he kept for himself.[143]

Relationes, Observationes & Descriptiones Rerum Persicarum (Lemgo 1712 [1976]), p. 760.

139. Della Valle, *Voyages*, vol. 3, p. 641.

140. Shah Esma'il Safavi, *Tadhkereh*. ed. 'Abdol-Shokur (Berlin 1343/1925), p. 30.

141. Roger M. Savory, *The History of Shah 'Abbas the Great* 2 vols. (Boulder, 1978), vol. 1, p. 325.

142. Savory, *History*, vol. 1, p. 486 (this was a motive for the murder that was suggested at the time).

143. Olearius, *Vermehrte*, p. 593, 661.

Love for Boys sometimes Led to
Passion and Violence

The love for boys occurred, of course, in all layers of society. Mir San'i Nishapuri, a poet, "became enamored of the late Mirza 'Abd al-Husayn, nephew of Mir Rasti, *muhtasib*. In this love he reached the stage of burning passion. Like a madman he wandered in Tabriz and like a moth he was consumed in the fire of his love for the young man. Within a short time the bird of his soul flew a way and flitted to another world."[144] Another case of of unrequited love is that of Mowlana Abdali, a herbalist in Isfahan, who, having his love thwarted by his paramour, set fire to his stall and became an itinerant dervish (*qalandar*). He ended up in Tabriz where he frequented Armenian taverns.[145]

Sometimes, pederastic passion could result in rebellion or personal violence, especially when that passion was not appreciated. When Shahverdi Beyg Kachal was governor of Astarabad, representatives of the Turkmen tribes came to bring him presents. Among the emissaries was a beautiful boy, called Aba, with whom the governor fell in love. Aba did not respond favorably to his advances and realizing that he either had to give in or save himself, he fled. The Turkmen chiefs on hearing Aba's story killed the official that the governor had set over them and rebelled.[146] Another case was the love that Boraq Khan had for his tutor's son. One night, when he was drunk he wanted to take the boy by force. The boy lashed out and stabbed him five times from which he later died.[147] Indeed, you had to be careful which man you

---

144. Vladimir Minorsky, *Calligraphers and Painters. A treatise by Qazi Ahmad, Son of Mir-Munshi (circa A.H. 1015/A.D. 1606)* (Washington, 1959), pp. 149-50.

144. Vladimir Minorsky, *Calligraphers and Painters. A treatise by Qazi Ahmad, Son of Mir-Munshi (circa A.H. 1015/A.D. 1606)* (Washington, 1959), pp. 149-50.

145. Sam Mirza, *Tadhkereh*, pp. 212-13. Christian boys frequently occur in homoerotic poems as paramours, just as Christian girls do in heterosexual ones (see Najmabadi, *Women*, pp. 42-52; Sprachman, "Le beau," pp. 194-205). One of the places to find such boys was in the taverns, which were operated by non-Moslems (Christians, Jews, and Zoroastrians).

146. Qomi, *Kholasat*, vol. 1, p. 346.

147. Qomi, *Kholasat*, vol. 1, p. 387.

kissed and when, as Malek Qasem Kamancheh found out. He had left the royal palace, where he had played in the orchestra and was drunk. When he was behind the scene of the playing area he ran into the sleeping figure of Mohammad Zaman Cheraghchi, whom he kissed. The latter then stabbed the violin player and took out his eyes.[148] A similar case happened about 1609 to the nobleman Hoseynqoli Beyg Qajar, who was stabbed in his sleep by a youth from Gilan, one of his servants, because the boy feared that his master wanted to make advances. The boy was, of course, executed.[149] In 1620, the *darugheh* or governor of Isfahan, Mir 'Abdol-'Azim, was making life difficult for the town's Armenians, because he was jealous of his Armenian counterpart in Jolfa, who had slept with a boy from a coffee-house, who had totally bewitched Mir 'Abdol-'Azim.[150] In the 1640s, a confidante of the Lord High Justice, on mission near Shiraz, invited a newly wed young man to his camp. He was enamored and suggested that he sleep with him. When the young man refused the official became so angry that he killed him. His relatives demanded the official's blood and refused a considerable amount in blood money. The Lord High Justice who did not want to lose his confidante recused himself and told the relatives that they had to get justice from the shah. The latter, hearing the case, decided in favor of the relatives. The official was immediately led into the town square where first his widow, followed by his mother and sister, struck and killed him with a knife.[151]

Many soldiers were engaged in homosexual activities; they often grabbed young children during their march through the country to serve their needs. When Othman Pasha took Tabriz in 1585, "there was nothing but slaughter, pillings [sic], ravishing, spoiling, and murdering; virgins deflowered, men-children defiled with unspeakable and horrible sodomitry."[152] The Safavid soldiery was involved in similar

---

148. Molla Jalal, *Ruznameh*, p. 275.

149. Monshi, *Tarikh*, vol. 2, p. 804; Savory, *History*, vol. 2, p. 1007.

150. Della Valle, *Voyages*, vol. 3, p. 205.

151. Tavernier, *Voyages*, pp. 251-52.

152. Cartwright, *Preacher's Travels*, p. 728.

activities. After the capture of Herat in 1598 by 'Abbas I a big victory party was given. After the many hundreds of young beardless cupbearers (*saqiyan-e sadeh*), who were also drunk, had aroused the officers with their alluring gait, seductive glances, and giggling they committed sodomy and fellatio with the Qezelbash officers. The fact that the soldiers assumed a passive, non-virile role was not injurious to their reputation, as the cupbearers were but youths, and not mature men.[153] It is therefore, somewhat out of character to learn that Shah 'Abbas I punished a man with homosexual orientation. A certain Pirqoli Beyg, a kinsman of the shah, had fallen in love with one of the shah's *gholam*s, whom he promised much money if he would succumb to his desires. The boy refused and told the shah. The latter sent for Pirqoli Beyg and gave the boy a sword and told him to cut off the head of his would-be lover.[154] Therefore, it can only be concluded that Pirqoli Beyg was hunting on 'royal preserves', which were out-of-bounds.

PEDERASTS AND DENS OF INIQUITY

Dedicated sodomists (*'asheq-pisheh*[*gi*]) sought pleasure and love in taverns, and places that provided the cover of darkness such as cemeteries, where they sought boys for hire (*pesaran-e sahl al-bey*). Many of them, in their allegedly mindless and licentious pursuit of pleasure (*la-abali*), used drugs, alcohol and sex to achieve their goals, while seeking the company of all kinds of low-class life (*owbash, luti*s), such that they were branded with the same label of *lavand-e moshreb* or drunken dissolute, hedonist, sexual deviant. A few of these debauchees were poets, some of whom expressed themselves in an agressive (*hajv*) and bawdy (*hazl*) humoristic style of poetry, while not eschewing obscene language. Of one of them, Khvajeh Mirom Siyah, it was said that he preferred wine to religion. These dissolute hedonists came mainly from the middle and upper class of Safavid society. Some were

---

153. Siyaqi-Nezam, *Fotuhat-e Homayun (Les Victoires augustes, 1007/1598)*, edited and translated by Chahryar Adle, unpublished thesis (Paris, 1976), pp. 222, 722-23.

154. Falsafi, *Zendegani*, vol. 3, pp. 55-63.

dervishes and sayyeds or descendants of the prophet, and above all artisans and traders, were to be found among them.[155]

Apart from visiting brothels and picking up street walkers, those with a homosexual orientation frequented coffee-houses and taverns. They went there not only for the beverages and the ambiance, but also for the music and above all for the alluring and daringly dressed young 10-14 year old dancing boys with tresses (*pesaran-e zolfdar*), who were dressed in female clothing and wore make-up. They not only danced in a seducing, voluptuous and lewd fashion to divert and above all excite the customers, but were offered to patrons for their sexual gratification (*'eshq-bazi*). After this display, those customers who became so excited that they could not contain themselves, could, for a price, take one of the boys to a side-alley or directly to a brothel.[156] Herbert described the performance of the dancing boys in 1629 as follows:

> The Ganymedes with incanting voices and distorted
> bodies sympathizing, and poesy, mirth, and wine raising
> the sport commonly to admiration. But were this all,
> 'twere excusable; for though persons of quality here
> have their several seraglios, these dancers seldom go
> without their wages; and in a higher degree of baseness,
> the pederasts affect those painted antic-robed youths or
> catamites, a vice so detestable, so damnable, so unnatural
> as forces Hell to show its ugliness before its season.[157]

---

155. Sam Mirza, *Tadhkereh*, pp. 51-52, 71, 126, 176, 182, 237, 242, 258, 265, 267, 270, 279, 280-82, 292, 298, 308, 316, 354-55, 362. For a good introduction to, with excellent translated poems of this nature see Sprachman, *Suppressed*.

156. Mirza Mohammad Taher Nasrabadi, *Tadhkereh-ye Nasrabadi*. ed. Vahid Dastgerdi (Tehran, 1361/1982), p. 164; Olearius, *Vemehrte*, p. 558; see also description of *qahveh-khaneh* and the young boys in F.A. Kotov, *Khozhenie kuptsa Fedota Kotova* ed. N.A. Kuznetsova (Moscow 1958), p. 67 translated by P.M. Kemp, as *Russian Travellers to India and Persia [1624-1798] Kotov-Yefremov-Danibegov* (Delhi 1959), pp. 19-20; Della Valle, *Voyage*, vol. 3, p. 31; Silva y Figueroa, *Comentarios*, vol. 1, pp. 289, 295.

157. Herbert, *Travels*, p. 248.

At the same time, there were also groups of entertainers (dancers, musicians, actors) composed of adult cross-dressers and passive-homosexuals (*mokhannath*), who performed for the public in general and the mighty and wealthy in particular.[158]

OCCASIONAL BANS OF HOMOSEXUAL BEHAVIOR HAD LITTLE IMPACT

Sometimes action was taken against homosexual behavior. The general ban on brothels and the like issued in 1532 by Tahmasp I included the prostitution of boys and the penalty of not obeying the ban was death.[159] Tahmasp I also banned beardless youths and women, of any age, from being present or near public performances of entertainers, while the latter were not allowed to have boys older than twelve with them.[160] Shortly after the ban, Mir 'Enayatollah Khuzani Esfahani, who had been grand vizier for a short period, was:

> accused of carrying on a love affair with a young man
> named Baseliq Beg, one of the Shah's servants, and thus
> incurred the Shah's wrath. Together with Mozaffar Soltan
> [a rebel] .... Mir Enayatollah was suspended in an iron
> cage slung between the minarets of the mosque Hasan
> Padeshah ... and was burned."[161]

Mir 'Enayatollah Khuzani Esfahani was not punished because he loved a boy, but because the boy was one of the shah's servants. This is also clear from the fact that the shah did not interfere with other pederasts among his entourage such as the 90-year old court poet Qazi Sanjani, who had become totally obsessed with love for a beautiful boy.

---

158. Rumlu, *Ahsan*, p. 356.

159. Brosset, *Collection d'Historiens Armeniens*, vol. 1, p. 554; vol. 2, p. 8.

160. Mohammad Taqi Daneshpazhuh, "A'in-e Shah Tahmasp," *Barrasiha-ye Tarikhi* 7/1 (1351/1972), p. 137 (art. 64).

161. Monshi, *Tarikh*, vol. 1, p. 160; Savory, *History*, vol. 1, p. 252.

Qazi, from loving boys, you've become totally senile,
Tell me, old man, what was the secret of making love?

Sometimes it was not the shah, but concerned people, who took action. Nur al-Din Ahmad Esfahani, who was the tax receiver of Herat, went to the bathhouse one day, and while he was reclining, a beardless boy gave him a massage. Some people, who were opponents of pederastic behavior, were looking through the small windows on top of the bathhouse building, which they then broke and threw rocks wounding him.[162]

Around 1620, Saru Taqi, the famous grand-vizier (1634-1645), then vizier of Qarabagh, was accused of having sodomized a boy. When the boy's parents lodged a complaint with Shah 'Abbas I, he ordered him to be castrated, although later it became clear that Saru Taqi had been falsely accused.[163] This particular story of castration, as a means of punishment, seems somewhat out of character given the fact that 'Abbas I took a rather relaxed and *laissez-faire* attitude towards any kind of fornication. He forgave Mullah Baqer for the errors of his way on the religious path (he was a Noqtavi, who otherwise were immediately executed by the shah), because he had done so for the love of a beardless boy.[164] Ironically, Saru Taqi, the grand vizier, who himself had been castrated because of alleged sodomy, banned male and female prostitution, but its effect was nil. His successor, Khalifeh Soltan (1645-1652) did the same and he had a few pimps

---

162. Qomi, *Kholasat*, vol. 1, p. 249. Bembo, *The Travels*, p. 301 alludes to homosexual practices when he reports that "the employees of the bathhouse wash one in a very improper way. They climb on one and rub the whole body indiscreetly; as a result, during the whole time I was in Persia, I did not want to go into their baths anymore."

163. For a discussion of this case see Willem Floor, "The Rise and Fall of Mirza Taqi, the Eunuch Grand Vizier (1043-55/1633-45)," *Studia Iranica* 26 (1997), p. 242. Mirza Taqi later ordered a servant in his employ to be castrated as a punishment for the rape of a woman. Della Valle, *Voyages*, vol. 2, p. 610.

164. Mahmud b. Hedayatollah Ashofteh'i Natanzi, *Naqavat al-Athar* ed. Ehsan Eshraqi (Tehran, 1350/1971), pp. 526-27.

impaled, because they prostituted boys.[165] In the 1670s, punishment
for sodomy was much lighter, viz. the bastinado.[166]

However, it is known from the accounts of Chardin and others
that homosexual behavior flourished in the decades after the 1640s
ban. The large number of slave boys that continued to fill the markets
from the Caucasus became a major supply of catamites for the Persian
cognoscenti, many of whom were put to work in brothels.[167] In the
1630s, the Dutch reported that "there also are many boys here [in
Isfahan] with whom they commit sodomy. This horrible sin is not
deemed to be so and thus is not punished."[168] Thirty years later nothing had changed, for young boys, properly seductively dressed were
paraded by their pimps in the streets of Isfahan.[169] Fryer wrote, referring to the 1670s, that the Persians, "covet Boys as much as Women; ...
these poor Children thus abused are sad Spectacles, looking diseased,
and are not long liv'd." Such was the fear of wealthy parents that their
young sons might be seduced by a pederast that they never left the
house "without a Train of Eunuchs and Servants, for fear of Sodomy,
so much practised among the pestilent Sect of Mahometans."[170] The
seventeenth Persian philosopher Sadr al-Din al-Shirazi asserted that:

> We do not find anyone of those who have a refined heart
> and a delicate character . . . to be void of this love at one
> time or another in their life, but we find all coarse souls,
> harsh hearts and dry characters . . . devoid of this type of
> love, most of them restricting themselves to the love of
> men for women and the love of women for men with the

---

165. Chardin, *Voyages*, vol. 2, p. 216.

166. Ange de Saint-Joseph, *Souvenirs*, pp. 84-85.

167. De Silva y Figueroa, *Comentarios*, pp. 50-51, 380. Olearius, *Vermehrte*, p.
445, relates that in Shamakhi, when the Russian envoy, Alexi, wanted to buy a
handsome boy for 6 *tumans*, the slave trader, jeeringly replied, while slapping
the boy on his buttocks, "You surely can afford to enjoy and use this part of his
body [at a] higher [price]."

168. Leupe, " Beschrijvinge," p. 205.

169. Chardin, *Voyages*, vol. 2, p. 216.

170. Fryer, *A New Account*, vol. 3, pp. 66, 131.

aim of mating and cohabitation, as is in the nature of all
animals [...] [171]

The same author argued that it was necessary that men who frequented and cared for boys to ensure that "the arts and sciences of
civilization would be transferred from generation to generation." El-
Rouayheb points out that this was not a new idea, but one that also
was advocated by the Brethren of Purity (*Ikhvan al-Safa*) in the tenth
century. Moreover, that this idea echoes similar concepts propounded
by Plato.[172]

If we may believe the *Rostam al-Tavarikh*, the Ottoman ambassador, who came to seek audience with Shah Soltan Hoseyn in 1717,
was sodomized by the shah's entourage to humiliate him.[173] This seems
doubtful, because the ambassador himself does not report this. However unlikely that would have been, other ambassadors, who were at
the Safavid court at that time (the Russian ambassador Volinsky; the
Dutch ambassador Ketelaar), did not report anything about it.[174] The
last reigning Safavid, Shah Tahmasp II (r. 1723-1732), "loved beautiful beardless boys so much, that he preferred one, when he looked
like Joseph, to one-thousand girls even when they were as beautiful
as Zoleykha, shaped like Leyla or alluring like Shirin. In acting the
cock (*khorus-bazi*) he was peerless." During the banquet that Tahmasp Khan (the later Nader Shah) organized for Shah Tahmasp II
in early 1732 the latter became so drunk that he took off his clothes
and told his beardless boys to do likewise. They all went down on
their knees with their bottoms up, while one of them, "the *lo'abchi*

---

171. El-Rouayheb, *Before Homosexuality*, pp. 57-58.

172. El-Rouayheb, *Before Homosexuality*, p. 35.

173. Asaf, *Rostam al-Tavarikh*, p. 114.

174. No mention of this alleged event is made in the accounts left respectively
by Volinsky, the ambassador and Bell, a member of the mission. P. P. Bushev,
Posol'stvo Artemiya Volinskogo v Iran v 1715-1718 gg. (Moscow 1978); John
Bell of Antermony, *Travels from St. Petersburg in Russia* 2 vols. (Edinburgh,
1788); or by the Dutch ambassador Ketelaar, see Willem Floor, *Commercial
Conflict between Persia and the Netherlands 1712-1718*, University of Durham
Occasional Paper Series no. 37 (1988).

(the lubricator), had a golden pot with lubricant, which he applied to their bottoms. The drunken [shah] then graciously serviced each one of them." Nader and his emirs were watching from behind a screen and he rhetorically asked them: 'do we have to follow such a king?' He then deposed Tahmasp II. This did not mean, however, that homosexual behavior also came to an end.[175]

Not much information is available for the Afsharid and Zand period, but, of course, boys continued to be loved as much as before. Sodomy among boys in the Koran schools *(maktab)* in the eighteenth century is mentioned.[176] Important men kept boys in their establishment for, among other things, sexual purposes. In 1770, Hedayat Khan of Rasht, had "an entire band of Georgian boys, and each year he adds to them."[177] In fact, some men loved some of the youths indiscreetly, because some Zand courtiers carried on affairs with members of the inner royal court, which was considered to be inappropriate. As a result they were sentenced to death and executed.[178] Love for beautiful youths *(nazar)* ensured that the poet Aqa Yadgar Hajat, who reached the age of more than seventy, remained a bachelor for his entire life.[179]

LESBIANISM

Lesbianism also existed, of course, during this period, but given the paucity of data little is know about it. In a *hajj-nameh* or an account of a pilgrimage, the author, the widow of a high Safavid official, expresses in homoerotic terms her longing for her female friend, from whose company she had been forcibly separated, because of rumors that their

---

175. Asaf, *Rostam al-Tavarikh*, pp. 147, 200-01.

176. Asaf, *Rostam al-Tavarikh*, p. 19. Pederasts were also laying in wait near Koran school to accost young boys. Shamisa, *Shahed-bazi*, p. 263.

177. Gmelin, *Travels*, p. 100.

178. Ghaffari, *Golshan*, pp. 131-34.

179. Ghaffari, *Golshan*, p. 404; for another poet's yearning for rose-faced youths see Ibid., p. 460.

relationship was a lesbian one.[180] Such friendships between women seem to have been common. It was not uncommon for married women to make a kind of sisterhood vow (*sigheh-ye khvahar khvandegi*) for life, which had to be performed at a shrine (*emamzadeh*) on the day of *'Eyd-e Ghadir* in the presence of a mullah. The same custom was still practiced in the early twentieth century. The husbands often did not want their wives to conclude such a pact as they suspected that it was a cover for a lesbian relationship. It was known or alleged that these adopted sisters made use of a leather dildo (*charmineh; machachang*) as part of their erotic relationship. Therefore, some men divorced their wives if they found out that they had an such adopted sister. However, even so, the sisters did not abandon one another as the bond was said to transcend earthly life.[181] Men also practiced the same ceremony (*sigheh-ye baradar khvandegi*), which probably dates back to the early Islamic period if not before that time. However, it is not clear whether it had homoerotic implications as in the case of women. Qodsi, referring to early nineteenth century, wrote that it was a very strong relationship between two men, like that with a cousin (*pesar-e 'amu*).[182]

Qajar Period (1794–1925)

There are no statistical data on the prevalence of homosexual behavior in nineteenth century Iran, but there was basically no change from

---

180. Kathryn Babayan, "Safavid Iran: 16th to mid-18th Century," in Joseph Suad ed. *Encyclopedia of Women & Islamic Cultures* 6 vols. (Leiden, 2003), vol. 1, pp. 91-92.

181. Aqa Jamal Khvansari, *Resaleh-ye 'Aqayed al-Nesa' mashhur beh Kolthum Naneh* ed. Mahmud Katira'i (Tehran, 1349/1970), pp. 35-38, 62-64; Massé, *Croyances*, vol. 1, pp. 137-39; Babayan, "Safavid Iran," vol. 1, pp. 91-92; Ibid., "The 'Aqa'id al-nisa. A glimpse at Safavid women in local Isfahani culture," in G. Hambly ed. *Women in the medieval Islamic world: power, patronage, and piety* (New York, 1998), pp. 349-81. For an artistic representation in Mughal art, see Murray and Roscoe, *Islamic Homosexualities*, p. 101.

182. Hasan A'zam Qodsi, *Ketab-e Khaterat-e Man* 2 vols. (Tehran, 1342/1963), vol. 1, p. 19. It was stil practiced in the 1930s, see Massé, *Croyances*, vol. 1, p. 138. For the Safavid period see Ibid., vol. 1, pp. 137-38, and for the medieval period see *Sokhan* 19/1 (1348/1969), pp. 4-22 and the *Samak-e 'Ayyar*.

the situation in the preceding periods, i.e. there was a relaxed attitude about homosexual activities. Fath 'Ali Shah, who had 158 wives and sired 260 children, also liked boys and sodomized them.[183] It was, therefore, no surprise that others followed his example and sodomy thrived in Iran. Southgate, an American Presbyterian missionary, with great revulsion, reported on

> The awful prevalence of the sin alluded to by St. Paul, Rom, I.27. among men of rank it is well nigh universal, and it is practised among all classes without restraint. It is spoken of, and the evidences of it are exhibited, without shame. Facts which I have upon record, prove indubitably that there are very few in Persia who are altogether free from the vice. The same sin prevails in Turkey, especially in the capital and in the army, to a most flagrant extent, though far less than in Persia. The same is true of Egypt, and in all these countries the crime is more or less patronized and practised by Franks. In Persia alone, however, it is a prominent feature of the national character. The disclosures that were there made to me were shocking beyond description. The scene of moral pollution which they presented, filled me with horror and dismay, and made me almost ready to abandon this modern Sodom to the fires of Heaven.[184]

Richard Burton, reporting on homosexuality in Iran in the 1840s, which he referred to as the Persian vice, also claims that it was a very widespread phenomenon.

---

183. Ahmad b. Fath 'Ali 'Azud al-Dowleh, *Tarikh-e 'Azudi* ed. 'Abdol-Hoseyn Nava'i (Tehran, 2535, 1976), pp. 70-72; Fath 'Ali Khan Saba, *Divan-e Ash'ar* ed. Mohammad 'Ali Nejai (Tehran, 1341/1962), p.156.

184. Southgate, *Narrative*, vol. 2, p. 39. George Keppel, *Personal Narrative of a Journey from India to England* 2 vols. (London, 1827), vol. 2, pp. 58-59, 69, mentions the *molla-bashi* or tutor of one of the princes as the instigator and participator in "every species of debauchery" and whom he saw "with two or three effeminate-looking boys, stealing down one of the avenues."

The corruption is now bred in the bone. It begins in boyhood and many Persians account for it by paternal severity. Youths arrived at puberty find none of the facilities with which Europe supplies fornication. Onanism [masturbation] is to a certain extent discouraged by circumcision, and meddling with the father's slave-girls and concubines would be risking cruel punishment if not death. Hence they use each other by turns, a 'puerile practice' known as Alish-Takish, the Lat. *facere vicibus* or *mutuum facere*.[185]

He further wrote that "Later in life, after marrying and begetting children, 'Paterfamilias returns to the Ganymede.'" For this somewhat older generation, who preferred young boys rather than the equally aged members of their own age group with whom they had cavorted when they were young, there were establishments that offered peder-asts relief, for "houses of male prostitution are common in Persia and the boys are prepared with extreme care by diet, baths, depilation, unguents and a host of artists in cosmetics. Le Vice is looked upon at most as a peccadillo and its mention crops up in every jest-book."[186]

Buckingham had a slightly different impression of the mat-ter, although he implied that homosexual behavior was widespread. However, "for while the Jelabs or public boys of Turkey and Persia are as much despised and shunned in those countries, as abandoned women are with us, or even more so, the youths who are the avowed favourites or beloved of particular individuals, are as much respected, and thought as honourably of, as any virtuous girl."[187] Buckingham's

---

185. Sir Richard Burton, "Terminal Essay" to his English translation of *The Arabian Nights* 10 vols. (London, 1885), [http://www.fordham.edu/halsall/pwh/burton-te.html]. *Alish-takish* is a word play on the Azeri expression *alish-varish* or 'give and take.' In this case *alish-takish* means 'give and put in'; both Latin terms mean 'taking turns'.

186. Burton, "Terminal."

187. Buckingham, *Travels*, vol. 1, pp. 94-95. Armenian priests not only pimped girls but also boys. "I must say that the Armenian priesthood around Tabreez and Khoy, together with those priests of the Chaldean nation who have been converted to Romanism..., are most depraved and generally perform the office

description is borne out by Polak for the 1850s, who reports that, although officially banned, pederasty was almost universal, and was not only tolerated, but also flaunted without problems. The boys were groomed, expensively dressed up and let their hair grow in long ringlets and tresses.[188] The ban that Polak refers to came about in 1848, when the famous grand vizier Amir Kabir (1848-1851) took action against the fact that "the public baths of Tehran had been allowed to become the scene of open debauchery." He punished all those who profited from these goings-on.[189] At the same time, Polak reports that it was customary in Tabriz for men to have sex with their wives only on Fridays, to satisfy religious requirements, while on the other days of the week they were engaged in pederasty.[190] The situation described by Polak is confirmed by Persian sources, which record that there were rich people who kept a number of boys for their own wicked purpose. Moreover, Qazvini considered that "the beardless youths (amrad) of Tehran are even a worse evil. Government magnates had at least two to four of them."[191] Bassett, referring to the situation in the 1880s, opined that "the prevalence of sodomy is notorious. ... a common

---

of a Ruffiani to Europeans who are of a gay disposition. I gave that Armenian priest something for the permission to depart with his Neophyte." Joseph Wolfe, *Narrative of a Mission to Bokhara in the years 1843-1845* (New York, 1845), pp. 331-32.

188. Polak, "Die Prostitution," pp. 627-29; Brugsch, *Reise*, vol. 1, p. 240, vol. 2, p. 103.

189. Watson, *History*, p. 372. Morier, *Second*, p. 59 reported in 1812 or thereabouts, "we were told of some of the detestable scenes that are practised in these baths." According to Polak, "Die Prostitution," p. 628 n. 8, the situation was really bad, for young boys were not even safe in their homes during the reign of Mohammad Shah (r. 1834-1848)

190. Polak, "Die Prostitution," p. 627; see also Brugsch, *Reise*, vol. 1, p. 240.

191. Qazvini, *Qanun*, p. 122; Polak, "Die Prostitution," p. 628. See also Momtahen al-Dowleh, *Khaterat*, p. 239; "Raportha," *Yaghma*, Ordibehesht (1339/1960), p. 96. Mohammad Hasan Khan Sani' al-Dowleh (E'temad al-Saltaneh), *Safarnameh-ye Sani' al-Dowleh* Mohammad Golbon ed. (Tehran, 2536/1977), p. 23 observed that on his return from Europe in 1873, when he was in Tiflis, that his servants had bought some boys. His main worry was not they they had bought them, or the purpose for which they would be used, but whether his servants would be allowed to 'export' them.

vice of the men."[192] It occurred in particular among soldiers, who were not allowed to take women with them while campaigning.[193]

It seems it was not always easy to find a boy when a pederast needed one. Bibi Khanom relates the following story, which also shows that women were very familiar with the practice of sodomy.

> A man had a very beautiful wife, in whom he was not
> interested. Every day he would find a new fault with her
> and would leave in anger the women's quarters and sleep
> elsewhere in the house. One night, in the middle of the
> night he ordered a servant go and find a boy for him.
> The poor servant looking for the boy went and searched
> everywhere, but could not find one. He finally went to
> the house of a prostitute who had a handsome, shapely
> brother and asked for him. The sister said: "My brother
> has gone on a journey, but I am ready to go in his place."
> The poor servant said: "my master is a pederast and will
> not want you." The woman said: "I will dress like a boy
> and behave like one, so that he will not notice it and
> he will take me and will reward you well." The servant
> agreed, because he had no choice and he was greedy. The
> woman dressed as a boy and came to the house of the
> master.
>
> The master, as soon as he heard the door, came
> running on bare feet and embraced the boy-look-alike

192. Bassett, *Persia*, pp. 56-57. Nineteenth century Persian authors who had become aware of European opinion about the culture of pederasty in Iran reacted by pointing out that it was true that such things existed and happened in Iran, like in all countries in the world, including those in Europe where they had brothels of youths and committed their own evil acts. These European men also propositioned total strangers, as Sahhaf-bashi personally experienced. Mirza Fattah Khan Garmrudi, *Safarnameh-ye Mirza Fattah Khan Garmrudi beh Orupa* Fath al-Din Fattahi ed. (Tehran, 1348/1969), pp. 962-64; Ebrahim Sahhaf-bashi, *Safarnameh-ye Ebrahim Sahhaf-bashi* Mohammad Moshiri ed. (Tehran, 1357/1978), pp. 50-52, 57-58.

193. Polak, "Die Prostitution," p. 629. When the shah went hunting and traveling nobody but the shah was allowed to bring women with him. As a result, the men who accompanied the shah brought boys, because it was considered unnatural not to have sex at all. Ibid., p. 628.

woman, as if he were a boy from paradise. In his passion and excitement he didn't even take her clothes off, but threw her onto the bed face down. Since the woman was not accustomed to anal sex, her passage was tight and the man ordered her to be lubricated. The woman, to confuse matters, used lubrication as an excuse to hold onto his private parts. The master was pressing so hard that it made the servant, watching through a key-hole, die with envy. During the ups and downs of sexual intercourse the master started to search for the boy's penis. After much effort, he realized that she was a woman and that the entrance was from the front and not from the back. His penis became flaccid and his sexual drive went away. He got angry and shouted: "You deceitful servant, what is this? Who is this person you've brought here?" The servant became flustered and said, "You can do it both ways, do not become frustrated. There is no need for violence and anger." "But this is a woman!" shouted the master. The servant replied, "Whatever the boy has she also has." "She has no penis," said the master. The servant replied: "What do you want a penis for at such a time?" "When I enter from behind I want play with the penis," said the master. The servant replied "The anus is the anus and the penis is the penis. Enter her from behind and play with my penis." The master started laughing so hard that he fell off the bed, which was under a tree. His penis caught on a nail on the bed and a branch from the tree tore his arse. He cried out and fainted.

The prostitute and the poor servant had no choice but to flee. They took whatever was valuable in the house with them. A boy-servant came and saw the master in that situation and ran back shouting to inform the lady of the house. Seeing her husband in that condition, she tore at her dress and wept bitterly. The neighbors came with a surgeon, and a physician and brought the master to his senses. The poor master was very remorseful of what he had done and with all these trials and tribulations could not stay in his country any longer. He chose to go on a long journey.

This is the fate of most pederasts, womanizers,
gamblers, and alchemists because they treat their
women and their wives in this way. O people of
intelligence take heed![194]

HUNTING FOR BOYS

Some lifelong pederasts were believed to hunt for boys, because Eʿtezad
al-Saltaneh mentions that boys steered clear from Mirza ʿAbbas Fo-
rughi, a poet at Mohammad Shah's court, because they feared for their
reputation by being seen in his company.[195] The blind poet, Monʿam,
continued to pursue beautiful youths in his old age and claimed that
the brilliance of beauty of the face of the youths helped him overcome
his disability.[196] A sayyed and panegyrist, who was part of the governor
of Kermanshah's court, kept a seminarian as his bum-boy.[197] The so-
called *gholam-bachchehha*, pages of eleven to fifteen years of age, often
of very good families, who were placed in the homes of influential
Persians, also constituted a reservoir of beardless youths. "These boys
often serve the master in another capacity, and even sometimes the
ladies, which leads to the stories of the darkest and most scandalous
part of the harem life."[198] Wealthy families therefore guarded their
sons well when they went out into the streets, and just going out
alone might earn them a bad reputation. It was necessary to be on
guard because the risk of becoming the target of pederasts was great.
Violence was even used to get beautiful boys. Prime-minister Mirza
Nurollah Khan Nuri (1851-1858) felt that he was unable to protect
his young nephew in Tehran against such unwanted attention and,
therefore, sent him home to Mazandaran, where, presumably, he was

---

194. Bibi Khanom, "Maʿayeb al-Rejal," pp. 136-38.

195. ʿAli Qoli Mirza Eʿtezad al-Saltaneh, *Eksir al-Tavarikh* ed. Jamshid Kiyanfar
(Tehran, 1370/1991), p. 562.

196. Mirza Mahmud, *Safinat al-Mahmud* ʿAbdol-Rasul Khayampur ed. (Tabriz,
1347/1968), p. 543.

197. Momtahen al-Dowleh, *Khaterat [...]* ed. Hoseyn Qoli Khanshaqaqi (Tehran,
1353/1974), p. 239.

198. Ponafidine, *Life*, p. 317; Eʿtemad al-Saltaneh, *Ruznameh*, p. 73.

safer.[199] That such a move was necessary is clear from the fact that some pederasts were really brazen. The poet Akhtar, for example, had a relationship with a youth from Soleyman Khan Qajar's inner circle and thus overstepped social boundaries. As a result the poet lost his tongue.[200] Even wealthy families could use money, for Polak reported that in the 1850s such a family made one of their young sons available for one night against a payment of 200 ducats, which was a considerable amount of money.[201] Other eminent families, such as a number of Qajar princely households with many children, prostituted their sons, and some were also accused of incest.[202] Such pederastic liaisons, however, could be beneficial to one's career as is clear from the fact that youths from elite families, who had been the beloved of Mirza Hoseyn Khan Sepahsalar, Na'eb al-Saltaneh and Amin al-Soltan, later became important men themselves.[203]

It would seem that as long as the sexual relationship between an older man and a youth was consensual (which, in the case of a slave was not necessary) such a liaison was not frowned upon. On the contrary, it was considered proper. However, in case a man forced himself on a boy then the authorities intervened, if the case could be proven, and punishment was meted out.[204] Those who did not have the means

199. Polak, "Die Prostitution," p. 628, n. 6; Ibid., *Persien*, vol. 1, p. 271. Sometimes, boys were just kidnapped by government officials, "for purposes familiar to the Persians." Stack, *Six Months*, vol. 1, p. 49.

200. Mahmud Mirza, *Safinat al-Mahmud* ed. 'Abdol-Rasul Khayyampur (Tabriz, 1347/1968), p. 159. This author disapproved of the lifestyle of the poet 'Ali Naqi Hasrat, whose behavior was outrageous.

201. Polak, "Die Prostitution," p. 628, note 3.

202. Polak, "Die Prostitution," p. 628.

203. E'temad al-Saltaneh, *Ruznameh*, pp. 103-04, 118, 657-58, 671, 723-24, 726, 728, 730-32, 763, 822, 875, 1003, 1046, 1053, 1081, 1107-08, 1150; see also Mirza 'Ali Khan Amin al-Dowleh, *Khaterat-e Siyasi* ed. Hafez Farmanfarmaiyan (Tehran, 1341/1962), pp. 117-18, 238; Ehtesham al-Saltaneh, *Khaterat*, pp. 209-10; Polak, "Die Prostitution," p. 628.

204. If the person was too highly placed no action was undertaken. Polak, "Die Prostitution," p. 628 ascribes the lack of success of the *Dar al-Fonun*, Iran's first school of higher learning, to the fact that parents withheld or withdrew their sons from the school because of the immoral behavior of its director 'Ali Qoli

to have their own catamites, or to pay for them in a brothel, sometimes tried to have consensual or forced sex with young handsome
beardless youths, whom they accosted in the streets of Tehran. Often,
it involved alcohol, *lutis*—rowdies—and more than one man. The
locations where these activities took place varied from alleys, to gardens and even a *madraseh*, where the seminary students (*tollab*), who
found the fornicators beat them, but, after payment of five thousand
dinars, let them go.[205] Punishment by the authorities usually consisted
in the bastinado, and, although rarely, the cutting off of an ear and
being paraded around the bazaar. The worst punishment—flogging,
ears cut, parade though bazaar, four fingers cut plus 50 *tumans* fine—
was given to a man who had raped a five-year old boy, although a
sayyed who had done the same was less severely punished.[206] What
was frowned upon was that a youth, once he had become an adult
with beard continued to serve his earlier older male adult admirers,
because this indicated that he was interested in anal sex per se, which
was socially unacceptable.[207]

Anal Sex as a Cure

It was also quite normal that Iranian physicians prescribed anal sex
as a remedy against certain ailments. Polak, who personally saw them
prescribe this remedy, also recounts that the court physicians of Mohammad Shah (1834–1848) prescribed anal sex so that he might be
cured of his gout. However, the shah was too pious to follow their

---

Mirza, the shah's uncle.

205. Reza'i and Azari, *Gozarehsha-e Nazmiyeh*, vol. 1, pp. 16, 103, 241, 321;
vol. 2, pp. 426, 428, 433, 511, 527, 573, 585.

206. Sirjani, *Vaqaye'-ye Ettefaqiyeh*, pp. 95, 218, 276, 424, 609, 638, 707, 714.
According to Polak, "Die Prostitution," p. 629, the penalty for rape of young boys
was castration.

207. Mahmud Mirza, *Safinat*, p. 177. Polak, "Die Prostitution," p. 629, mentions
that he only knew three old individuals who liked passive anal sex. One of them,
a servant in the service of the governor of Isfahan, was given the bastinado
a few times, but refused to give up his habit. The practice was universally
despised as were the individuals engaged in it, who were derisively called *gav*
or cow.

advice. As a consequence, the physicians blamed the worsening of the shah's situation on his refusal to listen to them.[208]

Homosexuals in the Royal Court, and Handsome Men from the West

Burton also reported that the European traveler, if he were handsome, had to be on his guard, for hospitable Persian hosts might take advantage of the alluring guest. The tale of the beautiful young lieutenant Strachey, who was a member of Malcolm's embassy, is an indication thereof. The Persians, including Fath 'Ali Shah, who saw him were dumbstruck with his beauty and could barely leave him alone. Such was the ardor felt for him that the Shah even ordered to have his effigy depicted on the wall of various palaces. Nobody, at least as far as I know, got to know him better, but the missionary Martyn was less fortunate. The prince-governor of Shiraz fed-up with his incessant preaching wanted to teach him a lesson for this intrusion into his peace and quiet. Burton tells the story, as usual, with much gusto.

> I once asked a Shirazi how penetration was possible if the patient resisted with all the force of the sphincter muscle: he smiled and said, 'Ah, we Persians know a trick to get over that; we apply a sharpened tent-peg to the crupper-bone (*os coccygis*) and knock till he opens.' A well-known missionary to the East during the last generation was subjected to this gross insult by one of the Persian Prince-governors, whom he had infuriated by his conversion-mania: in his memoirs he alludes to it by mentioning his 'dishonoured person;' but English readers cannot comprehend the full significance of the confession.[209]

The use of the tent peg occurred in cases of punishment, to drive a message home (no pun intended) and the sexual act was meant to degrade Martyn. Not so in other cases, where Europeans were sought

---

208. Polak, "Die Prostitution," p. 628 n. 8.
209. Burton, "Terminal."

after for purely sexual gratification even when that initially was unbeknownst to them.

> About the same time [as Martyn's case] Skaykh Nasr,
> Governor of Bushire, a man famed for facetious
> blackguardism, used to invite European youngsters
> serving in the Bombay Marine and ply them with liquor
> till they were insensible. Next morning the middies
> mostly complained that the champagne had caused a
> curious irritation and soreness in la parte-poste.[210]

At the parties given by debauched persons such as Sheikh Naser (r. 1832-50) usually wine flowed, drugs were consumed, boys danced and merriment was general. The conversation was ribald and sensual, which was part of the build-up and excitement for those not so easily aroused. Like in earlier periods coarse acts were also performed to entertain the guests and to create the appropriate atmosphere of sensuality and license.

> The same Eastern 'Scrogin' [Sheikh Naser] would ask his
> guests if they had ever seen a man cannon (Adami-top);
> and, on their replying in the negative, a greybeard slave
> was dragged in blaspheming and struggling with all his
> strength. He was presently placed on all fours and firmly
> held by the extremities; his bag-trousers were let down
> and a dozen peppercorns were inserted *ano suo*: the target
> was a sheet of paper held at a reasonable distance; the
> match was applied by a pinch of cayenne in the nostrils;
> the sneeze started the grapeshot and the number of hits
> on the butt decided the bets.[211]

Naturally, homosexual behavior was found in court circles. E'temad al-Saltaneh reported that a woman named Golin was a pimp (*qavvadi*), who had a stable of 14 boys and five girls ready for her clients. Her husband, a former coachman, had trained some of the

---

210. Burton, Terminal.
211. Burton, "Terminal."

beardless boys, whom he regularly supplied to courtiers who wanted to have an evening of fun.[212] For there was a steady demand for
such services, such as by Mirza Hedayat, the 68-year pay-master of
the army, who continued to seek the company of youths,[213] while
E'temad al-Saltaneh during the 1870-1880s and 'Eyn al-Saltaneh
in the 1890s and early 1900s mention a number of very important
courtiers, whose sexual inclination leaned strongly towards beautiful
young boys rather than women.[214] Naser al-Din Shah kept a number
of closely guarded dancing-boys and as 'play mates', because this was
expected of him.[215]

Shoja' al-Saltaneh, the husband of Taj al-Saltaneh, Mozaffar al-
Din Shah's sister, loved boys inordinately,

> There was a dancer named Tayhu, almost twenty years
> old; my husband was beside himself, enthralled by this
> dancer, on whom he spent a fortune.[216]

He did not limit himself to boys, for he also loved girls and had a
liaison with Katy, a Russian circus girl, and he did not forget to do his
spousal duties either, dutifully producing children. However, when
some beautiful youth came within his field of vision passion would
overtake him. He apparently made use of a certain Soleyman Khan
Dallal, who was a procurer of boys.[217] One particular boy he loved
inordinately:

---

212. E'temad al-Saltaneh, *Ruznameh*, p. 947. Polak, "Die Prostitution," p. 627
reports that to his knowledge there were no European sodomists in Iran with
the exception of a few Napolitaneans and Malthesians.

213. Mohammad Khan Majd al-Molk, *Kashf al-Ghara'eb mashur beh Resaleh-
ye Majdiyeh* ed. Fazlollah Gorgani (Tehran, 1358/1979), p. 61. Majd al-Molk
added that he closely shaved his beard, unlike other bureaucrats.

214. E'temad al-Saltaneh, *Ruznameh*, pp. 73, 96; 'Eyn al-Saltaneh, *Ruznameh*,
vol. 1, p. 793, 916; vol. 2, pp. 1026, 1051; vol. 4, p. 3136.

215. Polak, "Die Prostitution," p. 628. At that time the shah had no interest in
boys Polak reports.

216. Taj al-Saltaneh, *Crowning*, p. 270.

217. Hakim-Olahi, *Ba man*, vol. 2, p. 35.

> Everything he owned, everything he could snatch away
> from people through force or oppression, went into
> satisfying the young boy's whims and caprices.[218]

Mozaffar al-Din Shah also was very much interested in beautiful youths and, therefore, had several of such lovers.[219]

Love for a boy could be as passionate as that for a girl. The poet Mirza Qorban ʿAli Borhan swooned whenever he saw a beautiful youth, while another poet, Mohammad ʿAli Mahjur pined away as a young man and died for the love of a boy.[220] A seminarian shot himself when his lover ended the liaison.[221] In another case, a butcher killed a rival adult male, because the latter had seduced his young lover.[222] These altercations even occurred in court circles such as when in the 1850s, the major-domus of the royal palace, ʿEyn al-Molk fought with the ambassador, ʿAbbas Qoli Khan, because they wanted the same boy.[223]

Singing and dancing boys also excited the men (and probably the women as well) with their lewd and alluring movements. European observers (who probably frequented dens of iniquity of their own in Europe) generally expressed their disgust concerning their lewd and lascivious movements and innuendos.[224] They also performed certain

---

218. Taj al-Saltaneh, *Crowning*, p. 272.

219. ʿAbdol-Hoseyn Khan Sepehr, *Mer'at al-Vaqaye'-ye Mozaffari va Yaddahstha-ye Malek al-Mo'arrekhin* 2 vols. in one. ed. ʿAbdol-Hoseyn Nava'i (Tehran, 1368/1989), vol. 2, pp. 28, 84, 108-09, 120, 129.

220. Mahmud Mirza, *Safinat*, pp. 184, 306.

221. Sirjani, *Vaqaye'*, p. 152.

222. Sepehr, *Vaqaye'*, vol. 1, pp. 241-42.

223. Polak, "Die Prostitution," p. 628, note 4.

224. For example, J.M. Tancoigne, *A Narrative of a Journey into Persia* (London: William Wright, 1820), p. 67; George Keppel, *Personal Narrative of a Journey from India to England* 2 vols. (London, 1827), vol. 2, pp. 47-48; Gaspard Drouville, *Voyage en Perse pendant les années 1812 et 1813*. 2 vols. (Paris, 1819 [Tehran: Imp. Org. f. Social Services, 1976), pp. 212-13; von Kotzebue, *Narrative of a Journey*, p. 103.

ribald plays in which anal sex was enacted, usually with a qazi or mullah. To that end the actors wore an artificial penis. Until about 1860 it was normal that such shows were performed, amongst others, during the official New Year's audience with the shah.[225]

Figure 4.2: Persian performer with artificial penis
(from a contemporary Persian postcard)

---

225. Polak, "Die Prostitution," p. 628. These plays continued to be performed in public until the beginning of the twentieth century, see Willem Floor, *The History of Theater in Iran* (Washington DC, 2006), pp. 49ff.

Browne described such a dancing boy, 11-years old, as wearing the usual raiment of an acrobat (presumably a tight-fitting dress), "with the addition of a small close-fitting cap, from beneath which his black hair streamed in long locks, a tunic reaching half way to the knees, and a mass of trinkets which jingled at every movement."[226] It seems that by the turn of the twentieth century, Persians did not invite Europeans to parties where such dancers performed, or at least less so than before. "At dinners given to Europeans, however, the 'singing boy' was not *en evidence*. His posturing and antics, as the Persians realized, were often not palatable to those from the Western world," Neville piously remarks.[227] This may have been under the influence of a trend among elite Iranians to deny homoeroticism, because of, among other things, European criticism of the culture of pederasty, and who thus made an effort to present a society that looked and acted more heteroerotic.[228] In November 1905 (during the month of Ramazan), for example, the governor of Tehran had Asadollah Khan bastinadoed. Asadollah Khan was one of the most beautiful youths of Tehran and a well-known catamite (*malut*), who had many lovers.[229] Although the traditional open homoeroticism in art and literature disappeared as a result of this politically-correct-attitude and was replaced by one that abhorred it, this did not change anything in people's behavior, because many men still loved boys to distraction.

The late Qajar poet, Iraj Mirza, blamed the penchant of many men for boys on the segregation of the sexes in Iran. Having no access to girls, who, moreover were veiled, society left them no choice but to love and sodomize boys, which was a common vice among the

226. E. G. Browne, *A Year Amongst the Persians* (London, 1970), p. 320. In Abadan such dancers were known as *gheytoss* or *gheytass*, who were homosexual and perhaps transsexuals. [http://www.obudan.com/abadani_dictionary.htm]

227. Nevill, *Unconventional*, p. 147.

228. For a detailed discussion of this development see Najmabadi, *Women with Mustaches*; see also Ibid. "Remembering *Amrads* and *Amradnumas*: Reinventing the (Sedgwickian) Wheel," in Franklin Lewis and Sunil Sharma eds. *The Necklace of the Pleiades* (Amsterdam-West Lafayette, 2007), pp. 295-307.

229. Sepehr, *Vaqaye'*, vol. 2, p. 268.

high- and low-born. In his satirical poetic work entitled 'Arefnameh he attacks the occurrence of pederasty as follows:

> O Lord, what thing is this pedomania
> That plagues Aref and greater Tehrania?
> Why is it only in this commonwealth
> Does sodomy take place with little stealth?
> The European with his lofty bearing
> Knows not the ins and outs of *garçon*-tearing.
> Since Iran's haven to every donkey buck
> Who else are these asses going to fuck?[230]

SISTERHOOD CEREMONY

Lesbianism also occurred, of course, although there are not many data about its prevalence during this period. According to Polak, it was less common than pederasty. As in previous centuries, women held a sisterhood ceremony (*khvahar khvandegi*) in certain mosques on the last Wednesday before New Year (*Nowruz*), which was solemnized in the presence of a mullah and which unions were said to be lesbian in nature.[231] In a letter to a Persian newspaper, a Persian mother wrote: "Many women, on account of these evil [debauchery] practices of their husbands, give themselves up also to wicked ways."[232] This could, of course, refer to adultery as well.

In consequence, he argued in favor of unveiling. Apart from the fact that such a man could always marry or have sexual intercourse

---

230. Paul Sprachman, "The Poetics of Hijab in the Satire of Iraj Mirza," in Kambiz Islam ed. *Iran and Iranian Studies* (Princeton, 1998), p. 349; see also Najmabadi, *Women with Mustaches*, p. 240.

231. Polak, "Die Prostitution", p. 629; Häntzsche, «Haram,» p. 424 ; Khvansari, *Resaleh-ye 'Aqayed al-Nesa'*, pp. 63-64; Loghat-nameh-ye Dehkhoda, q.v. *khvahar khandegi*. The leathern dildo (*charmineh* ; *machachang*) was still in use, see Mohammad Sadeq b. Hoseyn Adib al-Mamalek Farahani, *Divan-e Kamel*. Vahid Dastgerdi ed. (Tehran, 1354/1975), p. 740; Fowq al-Din Ahmad Yazdi Tafti, *Divan-e Hazaliyat*. Modarres Gilani ed. (Tehran 1342/1963), p. 28, who, with much exaggeration and poetic license, writes that it was four fingers bigger than a donkey's penis.

232. Van Sommer and Zwemer, *Our Moslem Sisters*, p. 218.

with a woman, if he really wanted that, the unveiling and the freer interaction between men and women in the years after 1932 proved Iraj Mirza wrong, of course.[233]

PAHLAVI PERIOD (1925–1979)

It would seem that nothing much changed for sodomists under the Pahlavis and people continued to do what they did in the past. Of course, there were still brothels *('azab-khaneh)*, which provided services on a varying price scale. The latter were among the cleanest and the nicest places in Tehran, according to Shahri.[234] Apart from brothels and people's homes, lovers also went to public gardens. In Tehran, the garden surrounding the Imamzadeh-ye Da'ud was a meeting point for all lovers for various trysts.[235] In the 1920s, the pick-up place for boys was at the beginning of the Qazvin road in the *Shahr-e Now* quarter.[236] As a result, Norden observed that:

> Even in these days when homosexuality, flaunted in every large city of the world, has become a thing of common knowledge and discussion, the extent of its practice in Persia is amazing. There is not the perversion of the ultra-artistic, the experiment in sensation and emotion that it is in the West, but apparently a common practice with all sorts of and conditions of men.[237]

LESBIANISM

What seems to be new, but perhaps because such a phenomenon was not reported previously, was that,

233. Sprachman, *Suppressed*, p. 77; F. Shirazi, *The Veil Unveiled: The Hijab in Modern Culture* (Gainsville, Fl., 2001), p. 179; Najmabadi, *Women with Mustaches*, pp. 148-50. Bassett, *Persia*, p. 56 agreed with Iraj Mirza.

234. Shahri, *Tarikh*, vol. 1, p. 470; vol. 3, p. 400.

235. Shahri, *Tehran-e qadim*, vol. 3, p. 429.

236. Shahri, *Tarikh*, vol. 1, pp. 468-9; Ibid, *Tehran-e Qadim*, vol. 1, p. 28, vol. 3, pp. 394-96.

237. Hermann Norden, *Under Persian Skies* (Philadelphia, [1928]), p. 196.

At Shiraz there were prostitutes for women, as lesbianism is probably as common as homosexuality (with men and boys) among men. But these forms of perversion are becoming less as greater opportunities are allowed for the sexes to meet; this is interesting, as exactly the opposite is occurring in the West.[238]

As in the case of prostitutes, upper-class women were available in the homosexual market for sexual and/or financial reasons. "Generally the sexual life of the polygamous marriage is not satisfactory for the women, so lesbianism is common and lovers not uncommon. Some of the richer women even receive money, as their husbands, in their search after the other woman, do not give them enough to keep up their social position. I met a woman in Ispahan whose husband had taken away her car and who depended upon what she could earn to pay for her hired carriage."[239] Not only were upper class women involved in lesbian activities, but also it pervaded society at large, just as in the rest of the world. The sisterhood ceremony (*khvahar khvandegi*) was still performed in the 1930s and Sadeq Hedayat in his novel the 'Blind Owl' writes that some of these adopted sisters engaged in lesbian activities. Apart from tribadism (rubbing) and the like they also used the dildo, which in the 1930s was sold in rubber form at apothecary Garnik in Tehran.[240] In 1948, an Iranian journalist wrote about lesbian activities of lower class women that he secretly observed in Bandar 'Abbas.[241] The Jews in Shiraz claimed that there was no homosexuality among females, but Loeb observed "a great deal of fondling and other physical contact among teenage girls, perhaps to compensate for the lack of premarital heterosexual interaction."[242] A similar behavior among Moslems teenage girls must also have occurred.

---

238. Merritt-Hawkes, *Persia*, p. 289.

239. Merritt-Hawkes, *Persia*, p. 288.

240. Khvansari, *Resaleh-ye 'Aqayed al-Nesa'*, pp. 63-64; Massé, *Croyances*, vol. 1, pp. 138-39.

241. Daneshvar, *Didaniha*, vol. 1, pp. 206-07.

242. Loeb, *Outcaste*, p. 71.

New Law Criminalizing Homosexuality
Has Little Impact

Under the Pahlavis, both the government and society took a laid-back approach towards homosexuality, despite the fact that the new penal code made sodomy a crime. Article 207 the Iranian Penal Code, approved in 1925, treats sodomy in the same category as rape. Sodomy as well as rape of the opposite sex, is punishable with 3 to 10 years of prison. Seven aggravating factors require the imposition of the maximum sentence if the victim is: (i) a minor (<18 years), (ii) a married woman; (iii) a virgin girl; (iv) mentally ill and for sodomy was: (v) by force; (vi) done by a teacher or servant of the victim, or who works for someone who is superior to the victim; (vii) done by a married man. If the offender had a first degree relation by marriage or third degree blood relationship with the victim, life imprisonment would apply. The penal code also addressed consensual sexual acts between people of different sex. When the female side is above 15 but below 18 years, the punishment is 3 to 7 years in prison. The same aggravating factors as for forced sex require the imposition of the maximum punishment of 7 years. For sexual relations with females below 15 years of age, the punishment is 3 to 10 years of imprisonment.

Thus, there was no direct reference to homosexuality in the first penal code of Iran, which element only appeared in the new 1995 penal code of the Islamic Republic of Iran. This indicates that homosexual behavior was not seen as a major social problem, which is also reflected in other media. Occasionally a newspaper article would report on certain homosexual activities as an oddity, without upsetting anybody. For example, in 1947 there was an article on the prevalence of homosexual 'marriage' in the provinces, where, according to the reporter, "One also still sees followers of Sheikh Rahl [?] there, i.e. they marry boys instead of girls."[243] This was no surprise, as sodomy was not a rare occurrence. In Shushtar, in 1946, pederasty was very widespread and each class and trade had a den of iniquity, locally was

---

243. Anonymous, "Dar Khuzestan," p. 10.

known as a *kot*, where adult men spent their evenings with young boys who were passed around from one to the other.[244] At that time, dervishes were still believed to be engaged, among other things, in pederastic relations with young boys that they allegedly had stolen from their parents.[245]

One foreign homosexual who lived in Iran in the 1970s wrote:

> "Iran was for me, and for others like me, a sexual
> paradise. In terms of both quantity and quality, it was the
> most exciting experience."

Sex with other men could be had anywhere,

> "in alleys, parks, theaters, moving and parked vehicles,
> construction sites, etc."

And the best place to pick up men was the street. In the Pahlavi days there was also just one real gay bar in Tehran, "the Chelsea Pub atop the Bel Air Hotel." Public baths offered a venue for homosexuals, in particular the Versailles Hotel Bath and the Vila Bath, where masseurs were available to act as studs. Furthermore, there were pimps (*kunkesh*) who arranged contacts with boys.

As was the case with female prostitutes, Iranian men sometimes had religious scruples, for example, not engaging in sodomy during Ramazan, or asking that an object with the name of Allah on it in the room where the sex took place be turned around during sodomy. Of course, there were also many Iranian men who did not engage in sodomy, because they considered it a mortal sin and/or, of course, because they had no homosexual inclinations.

---

244. Daneshvar, *Didaniha*, vol. 1, p. 44. See also the ribald verse about political parties, amongst which the sodomists' party (*hezb-e bachchehbazha*) and the womanizers' party (*hezb-e khanom-bazi*) by Mahvash, *Asrar-e Magu* (Tehran, n.d.), p. 16.

245. Daneshvar, *Didaniha*, vol. 2, p. 174.

Western Homosexuals Did Not Find a Gay Scene in Iran

Having male anal sex, according to the experience of foreign homosexuals, was quite normal for Iranian men, in particular before they were married. Lower class men thought nothing of it, considering it business-as-usual, while upper class men were more hypocritical about their practice of sodomy. Anal sex was such a matter-of-fact occurrence that many Iranian males told their Western partners that having anal sex for them was not different from having sex with their wife. However, these foreign observers and participants were struck by the fact that the number of real 'gays' was very small in Iran and they considered the Iranians with whom they had sex as bisexuals rather than as homosexuals. With few exceptions, all of these Iranian men wanted to be the active partner. Fellatio, although enjoyed, was mistakenly considered by many Iranian men a Western perversion. Iranian men often remarked, as a *double entendre*, "'American men like to take it in the ass.' Note the semantic subtlety; Iranian men fuck, and act that preserves their macho self-image; they say American men like to *get* fucked, so they are unmanly, effeminate, queer. And certainly not worthy of respect."[246]

This conviction that being the stud is normal for a man was and is universal in Iran and throughout the greater Middle-East, according to homosexual practitioners. Because of this attitude it does not matter whether you have sex with a woman, man, or animal, it is the same stud act, the manly thing par excellence. It confirms one's virility, having the upper hand, and being in charge and on top, in short the strong man's role. It also confirms the strict distinction between the active (*fa'el*) and passive (*maf'ul*) partner. At the same time,

---

246. This section is based on Jerry Zarit, "Intimate Look of the Iranian Male," in Arno Schmitt and Jehoeda Sofer eds. *Sexuality and Eroticism Among Males in Moslem Societies* (New York, London, 1992), pp. 55-60 and David Reed, "The Persian Boy Today," in Schmitt and Sofer, *Sexuality*, pp. 61-66, who was less positive about the nature of the homosexual banquet offered in Iran than Zarit, although he confirmed its availability. Polak, "Die Prostitution", p. 517 reports that fellatio, irrumation and cunninglingus were unknown in his time in Iran.

nothing is more scathing or painful for an Iranian male, even for those who like being engaged in passive homosexual behavior, to be called a gay, a nancy, a pansy (*eva-khahar* in Tehran; *kham-posht* in Shiraz, or generically, a *kuni* or a *sharmut*), because such a label carries overtones of being an unmanly weakling, if not a pervert. For the active partner there was and is no such social stigma, because the manner of intercourse is the same with man or woman; he is in charge, he is the stud, while the other is the underlying (no pun intended) and thus weaker partner. Such effeminate men, therefore, try to avoid looking and behaving feminine out of fear of social derision and the shame that is brought on their family. This anti-effeminate attitude is part of the male macho culture and is reinforced by religion as is highlighted by the following tradition.

> Narrated Ibn 'Abbas:
>
> The Prophet cursed effeminate men (those men who are in the similitude or assume the manners of women) and those women who assume the manners of men, and he said, 'Turn them out of your houses.' The Prophet turned out such-and-such man, and 'Umar turned out such-and-such woman.[247]

It is of interest to note that the prophet Mohammad did not order to stone or kill them, which has become the religious prescribed punishment. As discussed above, such punishment is based on rather suspect non-canonical traditions. It is therefore of some interest to note that on the island of Qeshm, and probably in other parts of the Iranian littoral areas, the phenomenon of the *mokhannath*, i.e. of she-male, was totally accepted. These she-males dressed and behaved like women were employed in female jobs and were totally accepted in society. In 1948, the governor (*bakhshdar*) of the island even employed a servant who was a *mokhannath*, who kept his house, prepared his food and looked after his children.[248] Mahvash, the very popular Iranian

---

247. Bukhari, *Sahih*, 72, 774.
248. Daneshvar, *Didaniha*, vol. 1, pp. 196-205. Perhaps the social acceptance

singer-dancer and comedienne of the 1950s, made fun of pederasts, because of their universal presence by including the party of pederasts among her satire of a number of similar fictitious political parties.[249]

Men in Iran always claim that they are the active partner, for admitting in public that you are the passive partner comes at a serious social cost, for other men will always deride you as a sissy. However, given the fact that sodomy is widely practiced in Iran, at times, some (if not most) men have to act as the passive partner with the possible loss of face and honor, both for themselves and their family, if this became known, which often resulted in suicide.[250] This risk of possible stigma is partly offset by the fact that passive partners look for anonymous contacts with complete strangers. Thus, when being sodomized by a stranger, in particular a foreigner, who does not even speak Persian, anonymity is guaranteed and thus the danger of being exposed as being the submissive, effeminate partner is rather low. Those who liked to be sodomized as well as those weaker, in particular younger, males were taken advantage of by stronger types (such as in the army), who fancied themselves as studs, were, of course, taken advantage of.

Islamic Republic of Iran (1979–to date)

Nowadays, the older terms indicating homosexual activity are still used, but homosexuals are more often called *hamjens-baz*, which means same-sex lover, while homosexual orientation is referred to as *hamjens-gara*. The fact that less derogatory terms are used does not

---

of the *mokhannath* was a peculiarity of the culture prevailing in the Persian Gulf at large. See also the easy and traditional acceptance of the so-called *khanith* in Omani society. Unni Wikan, *Behind the Veil in Arabia: Women in Oman* (Chicago, 1991), chapter 9.

249. Mahvash, *Asrar-e magu*, p. 16.

250. See, e.g., J. T. Monroe, "The Striptease that was Blamed on Abu Bakr's Naughty Son...," in J. W. Wright Jr., and E. K. Rowson, eds., *Homoeroticism in Classical Arabic Literature* (New York, 1997), pp. 119-20, comparing Mediterranean and Moslem machismo; on suicide see Reza Barahani, *The Crowned Cannibals. Writings on Repression in Iran* (New York, 1977), pp. 58-60.

mean that official policy towards homosexual behavior has softened. Nothing could be farther from the truth, for the Islamic Republic of Iran wants to make the 'Islamic' in the official name of the country a reality. Because, according to Islamic law, homosexual behavior of any kind is unlawful, the policy and action taken by the revolutionary Islamic authorities as well as the new laws reflect this determination. Immediately after the establishment of the Islamic Republic of Iran in 1979, hundreds of political opponents were executed on the grounds of having engaged in sodomy.[251] It was therefore no surprise that in 1991, Iran's Islamic penal law proclaimed that "sodomy is a crime, for which both partners are punished." Further, "non-Moslem and Moslem alike are subject to punishment," which punishment is much harsher than in the period before 1979.

Articles 108 to 126 of the new Penal Code define the crime and provisions for the punishment of sodomy. According to article 108, sodomy is sexual intercourse between men, while article 110 stipulates that the penalty for sodomy is death, the means and the provision to be determined by the judge. Proof has to be provided by four males, or by confession (articles 114-118). Testimony of a woman alone or together with a man does not prove sodomy (article 119). A judge may also proceed based on his own knowledge obtained through normal judicial methods (article 120). Articles 109 and 111 stipulate that the law applies to both the active and passive partner, provided that they are mature, sane and have committed the act with free will. Article 112 sets 74 strikes of the lash for a passive party being a minor, while the active adult will be killed. If both parties are minors, they both will be punished with 74 lashes (article 113). The law then goes on to define the punishment for putting the penis between the thighs or buttocks (*tafkhidh*) and the like, without intercourse having taken place. Article 121 sets the punishment for *tafkhidh* at 100 strikes of the lash. If this occurs four times then the fourth time the penalty is death (art. 122). Article 123 stipulates that if two unrelated men be

251. Khalid Duran, "Homosexuality in Islam." Homosexuality and World Religions. (Valley Forge, Pennsylvania: Trinity P International, 1993), p. 194.

seen naked under the same roof with no good reason, they will each be punished with 99 strikes of the lash. Kissing in a sensual manner will be sentenced with 60 lashes (art. 124). Only if the person concerned confesses before the witnesses testify, will the penalty be suppressed (art. 125). In case of a confession and the perpetrator repents, the judge may ask the Leader for a pardon (art. 126).

There is a separate section in the Penal Code for lesbianism (*mosaheqeh*), which is defined as homosexual relations between women (art. 125), without further description. The requirements of proof are the same as for sodomy, while only those who have maturity, sanity, free will, and intention may be punished and then with 100 lashes (art. 130). If it happens the fourth time the punishment is death (art. 131). Only if the person concerned confesses, before the witnesses testify, will the penalty be suppressed (art. 132). In case of confession and the perpetrator repents, the judge may ask the Leader for a pardon (art. 133). If two unrelated women are seen naked under the same roof with no good reason, each will be punished with less than 100 strikes of the lash, but for repeating the act three times punishment is 100 lashes (art. 134).[252]

An interesting development in this context is that the Iranian authorities offer another way out for homosexuals, transvestites and other people who find it difficult to adhere to the sexual behavior laws. This alternative - a sex change - is being offered as a solution to their problem, according to many persons who were caught *flagrante delicto*. This became possible after Fereydun, now Maryam Khatun Molkara, then a 33-year old man, submitted his problem in 1978 to the late Ayatollah Ruhollah Khomeyni. The latter found merit in the request for a sex change and he issued a statement in which he declared that sex-change surgery was permitted since it is not mentioned as forbidden in the Koran. Still, it took until the mid-1980s before actual operations took place. In certain cases, the considerable cost of the operation appears to have been borne by the state, or loans have

---

252. Penal Code of the IRI; see also Eghtedari, *Islamic Republic*. [http://www.eghtedari.com/vome/hr/DP_Paper.pdf%22%20/t%20%22_blank]

been provided by a religious foundation, for in most cases the persons concerned have to pay for the operation themselves. Allegedly hundreds of such operations have been carried, and one surgeon says that he has performed 320 of them in 12 years. No study has been carried out to assess their total number and to evaluate the impact of such operations on the persons affected most, including their immediate family. For the changed men or women still have to face many problems in a society that finds it difficult to accept sex change, despite the fact that the new identity card shows their new, not their old, gender. But even that does not provide enough protection, for "people talk." A woman who had a sex change in 2002, "was about to get married [in 2005] when the parents of his bride found out he had been born a woman. They were horrified and refused to allow their daughter to marry what they considered to be another woman."[253]

Not only is it unlawful to be engaged in homosexual activities, but also to have relations with people who are known to be engaged in or propagate unlawful sexual behavior. A very recent case makes this very clear. On Saturday, 4 August 2007, *Sharq*, a leading moderate daily in Tehran, published a full-page interview with Saghi Ghahreman, an expatriate Iranian poetess who lives in Canada, under the headline 'Feminine Language.' On 6 August 2007 the authorities shut down *Sharq*. Mehdi Rahmaniyan, *Sharq*'s licence-holder and managing director, told AFP that "We had an article which was an interview with an expatriate writer. They [the Ministry of Islamic Guidance] said she had moral problems, they say she is homosexual and promotes that in her weblog."[254]

---

253. [http://news.bbc.co.uk/2/hi/programmes/newsnight/4115535.stm]; [http://ai.eecs.umich.edu/people/conway/TSsuccesses/Maryam/Maryam.html]

254. ["http://isna.ir/Main/NewsView.aspx?ID=News-973828&Lang=P"]. On 19 March 2008, Iranian authorities have closed down nine mostly lifestyle magazines this week for publishing photos of "immoral" Western celebrities and reporting about their private lives, while thirteen others were given warnings. [http://www.rferl.org/featuresarticle/2008/03/801c5706-52be-409d-a952-b8449d124f0b.html].

Although the government has a very strict ban in place against any kind of homosexual behavior, in actual practice the policy seems to be one of 'do not tell and do not ask'. Homosexual orientation itself is neither pursued nor punished, only that of proven public homosexual behavior. It is not known how many people have been executed for homosexual behavior since 1979, but given the high prevalence of sodomy and the draconian laws that the IRI has in place the number seems rather small. Table 4.1 gives the number of executions of homosexuals in the IRI since 1994.

Table 4.1: Number of executions of homosexuals in Iran (by year)

Year	1994	1995	1996	1997	1998	1999	2000
No.	139	47	110	143	n/a	165	75

Year	2001	2002	2003	2004	2005	2006
No.	139	113	108	159	94	177

Source: Amnesty International Yearbooks.

Amnesty International qualifies the data in Table 4.1 by stating that they represent "at least" the reported number of persons that were executed, and that "their number may have been considerably higher." This is, among other things, because the reasons for execution are not often clearly stated by the Iranian authorities. Usually, the information provided does not allow identification of the nature of the crime by individuals. For example, on May 13, 2003 Agence France Press quoted a judiciary official as stating: "An Iranian was beheaded in public and eight others hanged for offences ranging from rape and murder to kidnapping women and girls, homosexual acts, sodomy and fornication." But even if somebody is executed for homosexual behavior he usually is also accused of other crimes that are punishable by death. In April 1992, Dr. ʿAli Mozaffarian, a Sunni Moslem leader in Fars province, was executed in Shiraz. He was convicted on charges of espionage, adultery and sodomy. Nevertheless, it would seem that the total number of annually reported executions seem to have decreased considerably since 1988, the year with highest number (3,200) reported by Amnesty International. Moreover, most of these executions concerned persons who were not engaged in homosexual behavior. According to Amnesty International, death sentences were imposed for a variety of crimes including drug smuggling, armed robbery, murder, political violence and sexual offences. Execution is by stoning, beheading, or hanging, or other means, for, as stated above, the law leaves the method of execution to the judge.[255] However, there are cases where those who repent and promise to sin no more are allowed to resume their now heterosexual life. Nevertheless, it still means that the law is in contradiction to the international Human Rights Convention, but that does not bother the IRI, because it knows that God is on its side.

BESTIALITY

For completeness' sake mention is made of the occurrence of bestial sexuality about which there is the occasional report. Bestiality occurred, of course, in Iran just like in any other society. In his 'Indecencies' (*Khabithat*), the poet Sa'di (1184-1283) advises those who have no wife to:

> Find a donkey with round white flanks, sharp-eared, full-buttocked, round-rumped, and long-tailed, and do what scholars have described as follows: One may place three bricks under one's feet, but if one cannot do that, one may tie a board to the two knees of the donkey, place one's feet upon that, and screw the donkey, holding a bunch of green so that if at the time of ejaculation one wishes some kisses of her lips like lump-sugar, one holds the green before her so that when she turns her head, one can give her a kiss on her sugar-like muzzle...[256]

---

255. Amnesty International, *Annual Reports* 1988-2007.

256. John D. Yohannan, *The Poet Sa'di. A Persian Humanist* (Lanham MD, 1987), p. 113. The 'Indecencies' were written for a princely patron, with the excuse that 'scurrility in discourse is like salt in food." Ibid., p. 110.

This was but a shocking story to enliven the atmosphere of a party, but bestiality occurred in real life and apparently was not only practiced by men. The well-known poet Rumi wrote a very provocative story in his *Mathnavi* with the title 'the Maidservant and the Ass' (*kanizak o khar*):

> A passionate, pleasure-loving maidservant had trained an ass to perform the sexual functions of a man. The crafty woman had a gourd which answered the measurement of the male, so that at the time of intercourse only half of it could penetrate. Had the whole member gone into her, her womb and intestines would have been in utter ruin.
>
> The story is allowed to proceed. The ass was becoming lean, and his mistress was worried, but no ailment could be discerned in him. She began to investigate in earnest until one day, through a crack in the door, 'she saw the little narcissus sleeping under the ass.' The ass was treating the maidservant exactly in the same manner as a man takes a women.
>
> The mistress became envious and said: 'Since this is possible, then I have the best right, for the ass is my property.' The ass had been perfectly trained and instructed and the mistress decided to take advantage of him. [After the mistress sent her maid on an errand] she closed the door behind her and said (to herself): 'Now I can shout my thanks! Now I am free of all my worries.' Out of pleasure her vagina (was singing like) a nightingale. She was impatient for the flame of passion.
>
> The woman closed the door and dragged the ass and undoubtedly she enjoyed herself. Slowly she pulled him into the house and slept below the big ass. In order to achieve her end she stood on the same chair as she had seen the maidservant use. She raised her legs and the ass penetrated her. From his member he set her on fire. The ass politely pressed the lady up to his testicles until she was dead. [...] Such a bad end, O reader; have you ever seen a martyr to the member of an ass!

Rumi used this story to make the point that you should not sacrifice your life in a shameful cause, for "if you die in egoism in the way of the fleshly soul, know for certain that you are like that woman."[257]

In the 1670s, Fryer reported that the Persians "to speak an horrid Truth, are too guilty of Buggering other Creatures".[258] In the nineteenth century, because sodomy was so widespread among soldiers, they were advised to follow Sa'di's advise and use a she-donkey for their sexual gratification.[259] Taj al-Saltaneh reported that a photograph was sent to Naser al-Din Shah showing her brother, the heir-apparent, copulating with a mare. However, she believed that the photo had been fabricated out of malice, but he could have just been following doctor's orders.[260] For bestiality also had a non-sexual use, to wit: as a remedy against gonorrhea, to which end it was prescribed by Iranian physicians.[261] Despite the fact that Islamic jurists condemned the practice it continued to take place. There are even illustrations of such goings-on, such as in the sixteenth century manuscript *Haft Awrang*, where against the background of an encampment a debauchee is depicted mounting a camel. It has been suggested that this depiction "is intended not as a morality, but as a joke,"[262] which suggests that many people had a rather relaxed attitude about this form of sexual gratification and that it occurred frequently. The same is suggested by the fact that Islamic scholars tried to make sure that believers not only knew that bestiality was unlawful, but also how to purify themselves

257. Afzal Iqbal, *The Life and Work of Rumi* (London: Octagon, 1956), pp. 295–299

258. Fryer, *A New Account*, vol. 3, p. 131.

259. Polak, Die Prostitution," p. 629.

260. Taj al-Saltaneh, *Crowning*, p. 235. Anal sex with animals seems to have been allowed as a medical remedy. Häntzsche, "Haram," p. 378.

261. Polak, Die Prostitution," p. 629.

262. J.M. Rogers in his review of Marianna Shreve Simpson, 'Haft Awrang". A princely manuscript from sixteenth-century Iran, in *The Burlington Magazine* vol. 141, no. 1157 (August 1999), p. 483.

properly so as to be able to perform their obligatory daily religious ritual.[263]

Discussion

From the foregoing it is clear that homosexual relations existed in Iran for as long as there is recorded history. In the case of men, it mostly took the form of pedophilia and pederasty and the technique most used was sodomy. Given the male-centered nature of the sources, very little information is available on lesbianism in Iran. In imperial Iran sodomy was as commonly practiced as it was in contemporary Greece. The prevalence of sodomy did not change in Islamic Iran. Although Islamic law forbids sex between people of the same gender it did and does not stop anybody from doing so. Many of the caliphs and kings set the example by allowing and being actively engaged in pederasty, gratefully followed by the rest of Islamic society. Poetry extolled the virtue of love for boys, even more so than that for a girl. Same gender sex, like any other form of sex, knows no boundaries, religious or otherwise, and thus the establisher of the Shi'ite religion in Iran, Shah Esma'il I, by being actively and passively engaged as a homosexual set an excellent precedent to his followers, who enthusiastically followed his example. And thus, throughout the centuries, sodomy remained a way of life in Iran that upset nobody. Men who could not afford to keep one or more boys had recourse to dedicated brothels to serve their needs or sought out like-minded men. Women also engaged in homosexual practices, including making use of a dildo. They were often driven to lesbianism because of neglect by their husbands, either due to polygyny, pederasty, or male sexual inadequacy, in addition to a preference for sex with their own gender in a small percentage of the female population.

However, with rare instances, there does not seem to have been a homosexual way of life, i.e. a long-term partnership between men based on equality and love. The prevailing culture was and is that sexual

---

263. Khomeyni, *Towzih*, p. 81 (no. 345). For the penalties see al-Mawardi, *The Ordinances of Government*, p. 243.

relationship is one based on dominance of one partner of the other. The act of penetration is the male act *par excellence*, done by (free) men to social inferiors, i.e. women, boys, slaves (male and female) and prostitutes (male and female). Sexual intercourse is not just an act between individuals, it takes place within the context of clearly circumscribed social hierarchies of age, class and status. Thus, a man would not lose status by penetrating boys, but adult free men submitting willingly to penetration means loss of face, honor, and respectability, worse they are considered to be perverts. Contrariwise, men who are engaged in sodomy are not considered homosexuals, but rather as macho-guys, who show off their virility and masculinity by 'giving it to them'. It does not matter who the 'them' are as long as they are penetrated, i.e. dominated. Having the passive, the underlying role was a sign of weakness, of femininity and thus shameful for a real man.

As the Islamic Republic of Iran tries to give meaning to the pronoun Islamic, its laws ban the practice of same gender sex, and in case of four strikes you are out—death awaits the sinner. Despite the public floggings and hangings the number of such cases is dwarfed by the widespread practice of sodomy and lesbianism, which take place behind closed doors just like the equally banned other forms of fornication—premarital sex, adultery, and so on.

CHAPTER FIVE

VENEREAL DISEASES IN IRAN (1500-2008): A PUBLIC AFFAIR

VENEREAL DISEASES IN IRAN:
A PUBLIC AFFAIR

Sexual misbehavior not only has consequences for access to the afterlife, but also in this life. In this chapter I show that in Iran (i) until recent times, venereal diseases (VD) were one of the major endemic diseases; (ii) in the nineteenth century and early twentieth century carriers of this class of disease were not socially stigmatized as in Europe; (iii) hence information on what to do about VD was discussed among people in social gatherings as well as publicly in print, which was available to the educated class; (iv) openness about this disease changed once it be-came generally known that VD was caused by sexual encounters that, generally, were adulterous in nature and hence immoral, according to Islam; (v) however, sexual behavior did not change significantly in that sexual intercourse outside marriage, in other words fornication, remains prominent, for prostitution and male-on-male sodomy continues to be a major dimension of social and sexual life. However, after the 1960s, the prevalence of VD was reduced due to access to modern curative rem-edies, and condoms started to be used on a limited scale; (vi) govern-ment and societal responses to VD were based on male sexuality and assumptions about male sexual behavior; and (vii) government and societal reactions with regard to HIV/AIDS have not yet learned from the past; and sexual behavior has not adjusted to reflect the high risk involved in unsafe sex.

What Is VD?

Venereal disease (VD) or *amraz-e moqarebati* or *amraz-e amizeshi* is a term used to refer to a class of infections acquired mainly through sexual contact. Under the term VD people traditionally referred to five diseases: gonorrhea, syphilis, and the less common *Granuloma inguinale*, *Lymphogranuloma venereum*, and chancroid (*Hemophilus ducreyi*). In the 1960s some 20 other diseases, such as genital herpes and *Chlamydia trachomatis*, were recognized as being transmitted by sexual contact. It was then that the term "sexually transmitted disease" (STD) or *bimari-ye jensi* was coined. Later HIV-AIDS was added to this list of STDs. I will not discuss discus VD in detail, but briefly mention the main characteristics of syphilis and gonorrhea, which are the most well-known of these diseases.

Syphilis is commonly called the 'great imitator', because it imitates many other diseases and therefore it can be difficult to diagnose. The syphilis bacteria are passed by sexual contact with a sore (chancre). The sores are found in the genitals, vagina, anus, rectum, lips, and inside the mouth. Pregnant women with syphilis can also spread it to their child *in utero*, a condition known as congenital syphilis. Syphilis is characterized by four stages of development: primary syphilis, secondary syphilis, latency and tertiary syphilis.

> PRIMARY SYPHILIS: ulcers of chancre appear usually at the genitals, but it can be anywhere on the body. Chancre may be painless and small and thus may go unnoticed. If not infected, the ulcers will heal after 1-2 months without treatment. At this stage the disease is highly contagious to others. Primary syphilis lasts 10 days to three months.

> SECONDARY SYPHILIS: while the chancre is healing, skin rash with brown spots develops (6 weeks to 6 months from infection). The rash may resemble measles, chicken pox, or any number of skin eruptions, though occasionally it is so mild as to go unnoticed. The rash usually affects the palms of the hands and feet soles, but may cover the entire body. Other symptoms include:

mild fever, tiredness, headache, sore throat, hair loss, muscle pains, weight loss, and swollen glands through the body. These signs can come and go for up to two years. At this stage, it is still highly contagious to others.

LATENCY: no symptoms show at this stage, even without treatment. If a person is treated, no other complications will occur. But, if a person is not treated for syphilis, the disease will continue to develop silently for up to 30 years, without the person knowing he or she still has it. The disease will move into internal organs throughout the body, affecting the brain, heart, liver, bones, joints, eyes, nerves, blood vessels, or almost every body part. At this stage, the disease is no longer contagious.

TERTIARY SYPHILIS: this stage is also called 'late syphilis.' It is the most acute and destructive stage of the disease. At this stage, syphilis causes mental illness, blindness, neurological problems, heart disease, dementia and even death.

Gonorrhea (*Neisseria gonorrhoeae*) is a bacterial infection that often co-exists with Chlamydia (an infection that inflames the urethra and cervix) and mainly affects the mucous membranes of the genitourinary tract. Symptoms can occur within 7 to 21 days of contact with an infected person, but they are usually so mild that they are ignored. In women, gonorrhea often presents no symptoms until the disease has progressed. It may occasionally spread to membranes in other parts of the body, especially those of the joints and the eyes. In the latter case it is called gonorrheal conjunctivitis, which was once a prominent cause of blindness in the newborn, the infection being transmitted during delivery. Application of a silver nitrate solution in the eyes of every infant at birth has largely overcome this problem. If untreated, gonorrhea causes pelvic inflammatory disease, ectopic pregnancy and infertility in women and testicular and prostate infections in men.

What Did Iranian Physicians Know about VD?

Mohammad Baha al-Dowleh, an Iranian physician (d. 1507), wrote *Kholasat al-Tajareb* (The Quintessence of Experience), a work based on his clinical medical experience, which contained the first known description of whooping cough as well as accounts of chicken pox and German measles. His manuscript also details the earliest description of syphilis or *atishak* in the Middle East. He wrote that wine was useful in the treatment of syphilis for which 'Emad al-Din Mas'ud Shirazi criticized him. In 1569, the latter wrote the earliest Islamic treatise on syphilis. He probably had access to Europeans, because he recommended for its treatment the use of China root *(chub-e chini)*, the rhizome of Smilax found in eastern Asia, which treatment was also advocated in Europe.[1] By that time syphilis was a well-known disease. Babur, who was one of the first to mention the disease, wrote in his memoirs about the chief justice Khvajeh 'Abdollah Marvarid, who by 1505, had become "the captive of a sinful disease through his vicious excesses, outlived his hands and feet, tasted the agonies of varied torture for several years, and departed from the world under that affliction."[2] Sam Mirza mentions several poets who died of the disease in the sixteenth century.[3] VD indeed had become a growing problem in the major urban areas, such that about 1680 the French friar Raphael Du Mans wrote that the youth of Isfahan lost its innocence in the brothels and as a result half of the population of that city had contracted venereal or the Frankish pox *(atesh-e ferangi)*.[4] Educated

---

1. Cyril Elgood, *Safavid Medical Practice* (London, 1970), xii, 21-23, 40; Ibid., "Translation of a Persian monograph on syphilis," *Annals of Medical History* 3/5 (1931), pp. 465-486.

2. Babur, *Babur-Nama*, pp. 278-79.

3. Sam Mirza, *Tadhkereh*, pp. 319, 325.

4. Richard, *Du Mans*, vol. 2, pp. 371-75. Labrosse, a contemporary and colleague of Du Mans, wrote: "I do not know why the Turks and the Persians call syphilis (*atishak* the Frankish pox (*abeleh-ye Ferangi*), because it is obvious that one may call it rather the Turkish or Persian pox, because among one thousand persons there is not one who has not contracted this disease." He further states that the disease was treated with a concoction made from radix China, dieting for one month, including not eating any young fowl and all sweets. Ange

Iranians also knew about the danger of contracting VD if they frequented prostitutes for sexual intercourse, but it is doubtful that the mass of uneducated people knew. Ghayath al-Din Mansur Dashtaki Esfahani (b. 1541) was so afraid of contracting VD (*ateshak*) that he, therefore, refused to have contact with other people lest he contracted the feared disease.[5] Tavernier reports that because of the dry climate, Persians were less prone to contract VD, but, moreover, Persian men never slept with the same woman a second time before they had thoroughly washed themselves, and thus the contracted venom was evacuated via transpiration, or so he believed.[6] At that time, Iranian physicians did not know the difference between the various forms of VD, but neither did European doctors until the end of the nineteenth century. At this time, through training in modern Western medical science, both in Iran and Europe, Iranian physicians learnt how to diagnose the various forms of VD and the current, and changing, ideas about their treatment.

What Was the Prevalence of VD in the Nineteenth Century?

In nineteenth century Iran, "Skin diseases are not often met with, and are generally of syphilitic origin," according to Baker,[7] writing in the 1880s. This was rather an understatement. In fact, venereal

---

de Saint Joseph, *Souvenirs de la Perse safavide et autres lieux de l'Orient (1664-1678)*, translated by Michel Bastiaensen (Brussels, 1985), pp. 122-23 (item 153).

5. Dhabihollah Safa, *Tarikh-e Adabiyat-e Iran* 5 vols. (Tehran, 1371/1992), vol. 5/1, p. 100; see also Nasrabadi, *Tadhkereh*, pp. 182, 382. Straußens, *Sehr schwere*, p. 181 reports that people in Isfahan when they had their hair shorn off head they would bring their own razor, if the could afford it, out of fear of getting "Kefchi or the Frankish [disease]."

6. Tavernier, *Voyages*, p. 276. The washing after having had intercourse was a religious required activity, not a medically prescribed one.

7. James E. Baker, "A few remarks on the most prevalent Diseases and the Climate of the North of Persia," appendix to Mr. Herbert, Report on the present State of Persia and her Mineral Resources, in Government of Great Britain, *Accounts & Papers* 67 (1886), pp. 323-26.

disease (*bimariha-ye jeldi*) was rampant in Iranian cities.[8] It was estimated that 20-40 percent of the entire population of Tehran, for
example, was affected. It may have been less prevalent in rural areas.
Ivanov observed regarding Khorasan's peasant population that, "it is
remarkable that very few traces of small-pox are seen or cases of sore
eyes and signs of venereal disease."[9] According to Landor, "Siphylitic
tonsillitis is almost the only throat complaint noticeable in Sistan, but
inflammation of the palate is not rare, and there are but very few lung
affections."[10] However, Forbes-Leith, who had medical training and
spent a few years in Latgah (Hamadan district) around 1920 as an
estate manager and a doctor-by-necessity, observed that, in the rural
districts, "cases of venereal disease existed in huge numbers."[11]

In contrast to Europe, the tertiary stage of the syphilis rarely manifested itself in Iran, probably because the form of syphilis in Iran
was more benign than in Europe, according to European physicians.
However, the secondary symptoms (*ateshak, kuft-e jeldi*) would be
manifested soon after the first stage, in 6-8 weeks. European physicians considered the Iranian variety of syphilis (*sifilis, maraz-e mashhur,
kuft, akaleh*) much more benign than the European one.[12] In harmony
with the prevalence of syphilis, gonorrhea (*suzanak, harqat al-bowl,
komsuzak*, and in Isfahani idiom, *suzak*) was widespread and the cause

---

8. Government of Great Britain, *The Persian Gulf Trade Reports, Report on the
    Trade of Bushire ... 1920-21* 2 vols. (Gerrards Cross: Archive Editions, 1987),
    1-2 ("venereal disease is rampant" in Bushire); Landor, *Across*, vol. 2, p. 181
    ("Venereal complaints are almost as common."); Rice, *Persian Women*, p. 256;
    Hommaire de Hell, *Voyage*, vol. 2, p. 17.

9. W. Ivanov, "Notes on the Ethnology of Khurasan," *Geographic Journal* (1926),
    p. 148, note *

10. Landor, *Across*, vol. 2, p. 181. In the 1960s, syphilis, locally known as *azar*,
    was a hereditary disease and very common. Iraj Afshar, "Kerman va Seystan,"
    in *Savad va Bayaz* Iraj Afshar ed. 2 vols. (Tehran: Dehkhoda, 1349/1970), vol.
    1, p. 313.

11. Forbes-Leith, *Checkmate*, 88.

12. Polak, *Persien*, vol.. 2, p. 308; Schlimmer, *Terminologie*, p. 527; Nilofar
    Jozani, *La Beauté Menacée* (Paris-Tehran: IFRI, 1994), pp. 214-16; A. R.
    Neligan, "Public Health in Persia. 1914-24," *The Lancet* Part II, 27 March 1926,
    p. 693.

of much infertility. The term *suzanak* also referred to other mucous membrane infections. If not interfered with, and the patient is kept to the prescribed regime, syphilis heals (or so it was claimed), otherwise it became chronic and a long-term disorder.[13] Finally shanker (*kufti, taqereh-y solb-e kufti, akaleh*) also occurred, which was treated with a sulphuric arsenic powder.[14]

Although venereal diseases were widespread in Iran, European sources do not report much about the actual treatment given for VD. Häntzsche reports that in case of gonorrhea, Persian physicians prescribed anal sex with a black she-ass.[15] In Iranian medical lore, both formal and folk medicine, treatment ranged from a glass of wine to China root and literally anything in between. Because medicines were mostly herbal in nature, some of the herb sellers were even specialized in certain diseases such as VD.[16]

The earliest chemical treatment of syphilitic sores was mercury applied both topically and orally as early as 1496. Mercury remained the treatment of choice for more than three centuries in Europe until the late 1800s. At the same time, other miracle remedies were offered to VD sufferers. The development and use of potassium iodide in the 1840s was an important advancement in the treatment of syphilis. First, because it was effective even in the late stages of the disease (mercury was not), and second, because it paved the way to the discovery of more effective treatments. Mercury, which kills the syphilis

---

13. John Gilmour, *Rapport sur la situation sanitaire de la Perse* (Geneva, League of Nations, 1924), p. 49; Polak, *Persien*, vol. 2, pp. 308-09; Ibid., "Ueber die Syphilis in Persien," *Zeitschrift der Gesellschaft der Aertzte in Wien* (1857); Schlimmer, *Terminologie*, p. 79 (in case of women, syphilis was known as *suzanak-e mozmen-e gheyr-e mosri-ye anath*), p. 527; Jozani, *La beauté*, pp. 217-18; Neligan, "Public Health," part II, p. 693.

14. Schlimmer, *Terminologie*, p. 123 (q.v. chancre).

15. Häntzsche, "Haram," p. 378. For the treatment according to Persian sources see, for example, Jozani, *La beauté*, pp. 216-17.

16. Shahri, *Tarikh*, vol. 4, pp. 327-31 (with a description of some of the remedies). E'tesam al-Molk, *Safarnameh*, pp. 115-17, 133, 139, 142-43, 145, 148. For other treatments prescribed or dissuaded by Iranian physicians see Jozani, *La beauté*, pp. 218-19 and Shahri, *Tarikh*, vol. 2, pp. 696-97.

bacterium, became a treatment of choice in Iran in the nineteenth century to cure the sores and lesions from syphilis, but it also often had a lethal impact on the patient.[17] Landor reported that, "The most terrible form of syphilis, curiously enough, being treated even by Iranian doctors with mercury—a treatment called the *Kalyan Shingrif*—but administered in such quantities that its effects are often worse than the ailment itself."[18] As soon as newer treatments were developed in Europe and the USA these became available in the Iran. Old women who specialized in syphilis treatment used "Calomel fumigations, but since the introduction of salvarsan less has been seen of their results."[19]

WHAT FACILITATED THE SPREAD OF VD?

Mainly, VD was spread by the promiscuous behavior of men through frequenting male and/or female prostitutes, the contracting of temporary wives (*sigheh*) principally in the major pilgrimage and trading towns, and/or sodomy between males. Occasionally, it was spread through lesbian relationships. The prevalence of sodomy, in streets, back alleys, parks, cemeteries, cabarets and coffeehouses or in people's homes through the hiring of musicians and their dancing boys (*geda*s) and/or others also contributed to the transmission of VD.[20]

WHAT WAS THE REACTION OF PEOPLE TO VD?

In the nineteenth and early twentieth century, Iranians did not consider syphilis as being infectious and it was not something to be ashamed of. In fact, the disease was discussed in polite society, even in the pres-

---

17. Floor, *Public Health*, p.121. The side effects of mercury treatments include tooth loss; mouth, throat, and skin ulcerations; neurological damage; and death.

18. Landor, *Across*, vol. 2, p. 181.

19. Neligan, "Public Health," part III, p. 742.

20. See chapter four.

ence of women and children.[21] This was quite understandable for two reasons. One, medical science until the 1890s did not know that VD was a sexually transmitted class of diseases. Two, because syphilis imitates many other diseases and was difficult to diagnose, people had no idea that they had VD. They just had a painful disease, of which they often had more than one. Of course, you would discuss it with others, if only to find out if they knew a cure based on their own experiences. Given its high prevalence this was, in fact, an understandable and even a sensible approach.

However, it was considered shameful, even repulsive, to discuss diseases that affected the lower body orifices (genitals, anus). Occasionally, when it was discussed, it was done in hyperbolic language, without referring to the problem areas by their proper names, or it was the subject of bawdy jokes. In short, nobody called a spade a spade, because it was and is too embarrassing. Some non-infectious diseases are and were not discussed either, such as hemorrhoids, because there is a popular belief that this affliction is caused by anal intercourse, in this case in the passive, thus effeminate partner, a fact that a man wanted to hide at all cost. Various Iranian maxims explicitly refer to this type of activity and its consequences, while the activity (and its effect) is discussed in treatises of traditional medicine. Sodomy was not only engaged in by men, but was, and maybe still is, practiced as a form of birth control (or to have sex during the woman's menstruation), which is another reason, why people are loath to talk about it. The same repulsion and shame was felt, of course, once it eventually became known that VD was a STD.[22]

---

21. Polak, *Persien*, vol. 2, p. 308; Schlimmer, *Terminologie*, p. 527; Jozani, *La beauté*, pp. 214-16; Neligan, "Public Health," part II, p. 693.

22. Jozani, *La Beauté*, pp. 204-06, 211-14; Mahvash, *Asrar-e Magu*, p. 91 (*magar bavasir*), 104 (*suzaki*). However, according to A. Bricteux, *Les comédies de Malkom Khan* (Liège, 1933), p. 61, n. 89 people felt no shame to discuss gonorrhea, even at the end of the Qajar period. This is also borne out by Javadi et al., *Do Ruyaru'i*, p. 58, where the author has an exasperated mother curse her disobedient child as follows: "May you be struck with syphilis, may you get gonorrhea".

WHAT CHANGED IN EUROPE?

In the 1870s medical science was able to make the distinction between gonorrhea and syphilis. By 1890 physicians began to understand the pathology of the disease, i.e. that it was sexually transmitted. This resulted in policies in Europe and its colonies that focused on prostitutes as the source of infection and regulation to control them and thus, hopefully, stop the spread of vd. At the same time, in Europe syphilis also became associated with sin and sex outside of marriage. In 1905, German researchers discovered the etiological agent of syphilis, *Treponema pallidum*, which is a type of bacterium called a spirochete. One year later another team of German researchers developed the Wassermann test, which even today is the main test for syphilis detection. In 1909, Paul Ehrlich and his colleague, Sahachiro Hata, found that *arsephenamine* destroyed *Treponema pallidum*. Ehrlich called the compound *salvarsan* and touted it as the "magic bullet," because he and his adherents considered it the miracle cure for syphilis. However, it soon became apparent that *salvarsan* was neither miraculous nor a cure and the same held for its derivative, *neosalvarsan*. Through extensive trials with the drugs, physicians concluded that treatment with *salvarsan* and *neosalvarsan* had to be supplemented with applications of mercury or bismuth ointments. Even this new combination of drugs did not produce a complete healing. In 1928, Alexander Fleming discovered penicillin. However, it was only in 1942 that the drug was used on a large scale, in this case on the battlefront to prevent and cure infections in wounded American troops. It was only in 1945 that penicillin became widely available and accepted as the preferred treatment for syphilis, although it took another 15 years before the doses were finally standardized.

WHAT CHANGED IN IRAN?

In Iran, the government was totally impotent to counter the havoc that vd wrought, because it neither had the infrastructure nor the funds to take decisive action, even if it had wanted to. The newspapers and journals preceded the government's hesitant steps in trying to change people's minds and attitudes and promote the development of the necessary modern medical infrastructure of Iran with a view to improve public health in the country. They did this with articles on the importance of hygiene, information about diseases and advances in medical science. The first privately owned newspaper in Iran, *Tarbiyat*, occasionally paid attention to the problem of VD in its pages. For example, the first time it did so (February 1898), there was a small article reporting that Hakim Olahi had recounted that a relative of his had been infected with syphilis. Nothing helped until someone found a remedy that was effective against the disease. He recommended it to all his 'brothers'; it helped in 20 days.[23] There was a similar article, but with more 'credibility'. It was reported that a physician, Mirza Hasan Khan Sa'id al-Atteba, had just returned from France. He mentioned that there were many new treatments available, amongst which one was one for *suzanak*. The new remedy had only been discovered 5-6 months before and he had brought it from Paris. It healed the sores in 3 days to one week. For a long time, syphilis was not treatable. Now Dr. Fournier had found a new remedy that healed the disease in 15-30 days.[24] Sa'id al-Atteba apparently had found VD a remunerative line of business, for, two years later, he discussed in the newspaper *Tarbiyat* eye problems due to syphilis.[25] Thereafter, for some time, the sheen of science was abandoned and its place was taken by an advertisement for Dr. Duwayyan's *stafilaz* [?] that helped against all kinds of ailments, including boils due to VD. Sa'id al-Atteba also discussed the problem of anemia and recommended a certain remedy that allegedly was effective against syphilis.[26] In particular, VD, in addition to many

23. *Tarbiyat* 3 vols. (Tehran, Ketabkhaneh-ye Melli, 1377/1998), vol. 1, p. 239 (11 Ramazan 1315/3 February 1898). Around that time Dr. Kermanshahi also published his *Amraz-e Moqarebati* (venereal diseases), but its use was limited to medical students. Floor, *Public Health*, p. 243.

24. *Tarbiyat*, vol. 2, pp. 1139-40 (16 Safar 1321/4 May 1903), 1303 (13 Ramazan 1321/3 December 1903).

25. *Tarbiyat*, vol. 3, p. 1828 (4 Rabi' II 1323/8 June 1905).

26. *Tarbiyat*, vol. 3, p. 1835 (11 Rabi' II/15 June 1905). The same ad as in Ibid., vol. 3, pp. 1828, 1883 (23 Jomadi I 1323/27 July 1905). The same ad

other diseases and public health issues, was a subject that received more attention around 1900. For example, both the general and the feminist press made the occurrence of venereal disease a main public health concern in their publications.[27] They also treated many other factors that contributed to a less optimal public health situation, including prostitution.[28]

Advertisements that informed the small group of educated people about the latest new remedies for VD continued to appear regularly in the major newspapers. The range of remedies offered to the syphilitic public was growing and must have bewildered those infected. For example, in 1924, Dr. Koplovich, former head of the medical staff of the Austrian Red Cross, advertised a treatment using an electric machine of the latest German design that was effective, amongst other things, against syphilis.[29] The use of *Sulfersenol* (Sel de sodium de l'ether sulfereux acide du methyle olaminoarsenophol) was advertised as being effective against syphilis "in particular in cases of young children who were afflicted with hereditary [congenital] syphilis (*ektesabi*) it is the first remedy that has cured thousands."[30] In another advertisement the use of the so-called Albert pills was strongly recommended. On the same page, *Metarsan* was advertised as being the latest and best remedy against syphilis. It was promised that its healing effect would occur shortly after four doses, while not having the negative effect of *Usalvarsan*.[31] Another product, *No Varsenobenzol*, was advertised as

concerning *kuft* in Ibid., vol. 3, p. 2297 (26 Shavval 1324/13 December 1906) pleads for clean and hygienic bath-houses as they are a source of infection for VD. Ibid., vol. 3, p. 2371 (15 Moharram 1325/27 February 1907).

27. *Shekufeh beh enzemam-e Danesh. Nakhostin nashriyehha-ye zanan-e Iran* (Tehran: Ketabkhaneh-ye Melli, 1377/1998), part 2, no. 20, 7 Dhu'l-Qa'deh 1332/September 21, 1914, 147; *'Alam-e Nesvan* 3/1 (September 1922), pp. 36-42.

28. *'Alam-e Nesvan* 3/1 (September 1922), pp. 29-34; *Shekufeh*, Index q.v., for example, Otrish, Orupa (*zanan-e badkar*). Prostitution was a theme that resounded very much in contemporary fiction as well; see chapter three.

29. *Setareh-ye Jahan* IX, no. 172, 20 April 1924, also nos. 174 and 189.

30. *Setareh-ye Jahan* IX, no. 177, 30 April 1924.

31. *Setareh-ye Jahan* X, no. 15, 20 August 1924.

a "gift" to those afflicted with gonorrhea. It was sold in capsules that gave complete healing (*'alaj-e qat'i*). It was to be taken during one entire month and only at a physician's instruction.[32] *Nuri Sirop* was to be taken by those with inherited (congenital) syphilis in the third stage.[33] The Modern Pharmacy (Naseriyeh) advertised two remedies called *Gonovaccin Merz* and *Bismogenol* that were supposedly effective against chronic gonorrhea and syphilis respectively.[34] Dr. Yahya Khan Karubiyan advertised an effective and cheap treatment of chronic gonorrhea (*amraz-e mozammaneh-ye suzanak*), which had been certi-fied by the Pasteur Institute.[35] Further, there was an advertisement for so-called *Kaveol* capsules, which killed the microbes that caused syphilis; 8 capsules had to be taken per day and complete healing was guaranteed.[36] In the 1928-29 issues of the newspaper *Nahid*, for example, there were advertisements for remedies against VD such as *aleh ade'ul, kapsul-e kanukur* (also *kunkur*) and *vadrul* against gonor-rhea and *diyantil* against VD in general.[37] It is an indication of the high prevalence of VD, that in addition to advertising the various remedies, most doctors found it remunerative to include their expertise in treat-ing VD when listing their specialties.

During the late Qajar and early Pahlavi period, the government's and public's approach to the problem of VD changed little. Only in the 1920s were there the first government activities in this field (mainly medical in nature), which was through the establishment of the Pas-teur Institute (1921). In 1922, with the reorganization of the munici-pality of Tehran, a medical service was established. Several treatment

32. *Setareh-ye Jahan* X, no. 290, 11 September 1924, & nos. 70, 74, 76, 78, 80, 82, 84, 86, 88.

33. *Setareh-e Jahan* X, no. 50, 2 February 1925, also nos. 53, 56, 59, 61, 65, 70.

34. *Setareh-ye Jahan* X, no. 96, 30 April 1925, also nos. 98, 100, 102, 103, 104.

35. *Setareh-e Jahan* I, no. 2, 9 January 1929, also nos. 3, 4, and 7.

36. *Kushesh* VIII, no. 310, 3 October 1930, also nos, 311, 312, 314, 315, 316, 318.

37. *Nahid* VIII, 1307 Shamsi/1928 AD, nos. 1-10, 63-65, 73, 87 and & 1308 Shamsi/1929 AD), nos. 9-10.

service centers for the poor were opened: "Six for general diseases, one for women's diseases, one for venereal diseases, and a dental clinic."[38] Sexual behavior does not seem have undergone any significant change (see preceding chapters).

Although books and articles that focused on both personal and public hygiene were published,[39] both by the government and the private sector, very few seem to have been published on the issue of VD, at least, I have only come across one. This was an article published in a *Salnameh* or Yearbook for the year 1930, which was aimed at an educated audience. The article drew attention to the fact that syphilis was a terrible disease and caused among other things sterility. It further pointed out that syphilitic people could infect healthy people by kissing them or when the latter used personal items such as pipes or combs belonging to a syphilitic person. One major cause of infection was through the breasts of a syphilitic wet nurse who might infect a healthy child. Therefore, the article recommended having a doctor first examine such a wet nurse before engaging her. It is of interest to note that sexual intercourse was not mentioned as the major cause of infection. It was different in the case of gonorrhea of which the article explicitly stated that sexual intercourse was the major cause of infection. It further pointed out that the mother might infect her child, which could cause blindness. Because prostitutes were not controlled, the prevalence of VD was on the increase. Therefore, those men and women who choose to have illegal sexual relations could be sure that 80 percent of the time they would get VD. Due to the immoral behavior of the husbands prior to the permanent marriage the wives would

---

38. Government of Great Britain, *Geographical Handbook*, p. 409; Gilmour, *Rapport*, pp. 57-61. Bricteux, *Les comédies*, p. 61 n. 89 suggests that being infected with syphilis still did not imply social stigma at the end of the Qajar period and the subject of gonorrhea was not a taboo subject in polite conversation.

39. Ali Nowruzeh, "Essai de bibliographie persane," *Revue du Monde Musulmane* 60 (1925), pp. 29-34. See, for example, Amir Jahed, *Salnameh-ye Pars* (Tehran, 1926-41). The possibility of infection by using e. g. a pipe etc. that another infected person had held in his mouth was already published in the 1882 journal *Danesh* no. 9, 30 Moharram 1299 AH/15 October 1882 AD, p. 3.

be infected. Therefore, the article argued in favor of a health certificate before the conclusion of a permanent marriage without which, this should not be permissible. Men and women might have been infected due to ignorance, but in the interest of everybody concerned that should be taken care of. The article therefore describes in some detail the symptoms of syphilis and gonorrhea, for both men and women. It continues stressing the importance of prevention and that those who are infected should not marry, but first have themselves healed by a competent physician. Those having gonorrhea should wash their hands with soap before shaking hands with other people. The article finally describes, in some detail, how to treat both diseases from which it is clear that those infected had a long period of treatment ahead of them.[40]

In later issues of the *Salnameh*, VD did not receive any further attention, although other medical subjects are dealt with. The impression is given that this was a conscious decision based on the conviction that even discussing such a sensitive subject in a publication was indelicate. This despite the fact that Dr. Yahya Khan Puya, the director of the laboratory of the Municipal Hospital in Tehran published some articles in the newspaper *Ettela'at* in 1932, discussing the danger and symptoms of VD. He urged those infected to contact government treatment centers. In other articles in the same newspaper between 1929 and 1932 it is argued that VD is a disease that is prevalent among the middle and lower class, who cannot afford the medical cost of treatment. Furthermore, it states, that prostitutes were the vectors of the VD, which infected seven out of every ten young men.[41] However, after 1932 this type of article is rarely seen in journals, newspapers or magazines. I have also noted that advertisements recommending a

---

40. Amir Jahed, *Salnameh-ye Rasmi-ye Mamlekat* (Tehran, 1309/1930), pp. 98-105; Ibid., *Salnameh-ye Pars* (Tehran, 1308/1929), pp. 80, 19-21 (description of treatment).

41. See Mohammad Faghfoory, "The Impact of Modernization on the Ulama in Iran, 1925-1941," *Iranian Studies* 26 (1993), pp. 302-03 citing *Ettela'at* 19 Mehr 1311/9 October 1932); 30 Bahman 1311/11 February 1933; 18-16 Aban 1311/ 9-17 November 1932; 29 Mordad 1308/ 20 August 1929; 28 Mehr 1309/ 20 October 1930) and several issues in Tir 1310/July 1931.

range of remedies against VD were no longer frequently published in newspapers after 1931. Thus, measures to prevent the spread of VD left much to be desired, in particular, measures taken by the government, which were totally inadequate to the task in hand.

PREVALENCE OF VD INCREASED DURING THE 1930S

Despite these fledgling activities to inform the public, the prevalence of VD did not drop. Of course, this was to be expected given the dissemination instrument chosen: the written word. At best 5 percent of the population and less than 1 percent of women could read. Most villages and even large towns, or city quarters in large cities, were very isolated and had no ready access to such information. Also, the information was not packaged in such a way that the bulk of the population could absorb the message that the government and others wanted to pass to them. Even if they might have understood the message it failed to give them the means to act upon it. For the remedies available were too expensive and visits to the few hospitals in, for example, Tehran shows that the number of patients was rather limited in relation to the size of the problem. Therefore, people did not change their sexual behavior and as a result VD thrived. In 1929, the Pasteur Institute in Tehran undertook 3,498 tests of which 1,525 were positive (43 %) and the study concluded that the disease was increasing daily.[42] The municipality published figures that summarized the dangers of syphilis and gonorrhea (Table 5.1). Even if more people had been literate and able to understand the published table it would have been of little use. For then, as now, this particular publication is so rare that even many scholars have not seen it even if they knew of its existence.

---

42. Baladiyeh-ye Tehran, *Dovvomin Salnameh-ye Ehsa'iyeh-ye Tehran* (Tehran: Baladiyeh, 1310/1931), pp. 55, 89.

Table 5.1: Effects of syphilis and gonorrhea

Syphilis	Gonorrhea
Kills the seed	Results in abortion
Is a real social disease	Is one of the most widespread contagious diseases
In the large towns 10% are affected	All prostitutes are afflicted
80% of the public women are afflicted	In each age group somebody is infected
It is the cause of half of the abortions and incomplete pregnancies	Main cause of blindness in newborns
Cause of handicapped (na-layeq) progeny	Cause of 75% of cases of female surgery
Cause of various kinds of paralysis	50% of women become barren
Infects the fetus	50% of the men also become infertile
Decreases of life expectancy by one-third	Important cause of population decrease
It is the cause of various serious diseases such as of the heart, liver, kidney, nervous system, etc.	It is the cause of serious chronic diseases that results in invalidity

Source: Baladiyeh-ye Tehran, *Dovvomin Salnameh-ye Ehsa'iyeh-ye Tehran* (Tehran, 1310/1931), 95.

Public health publications on the subject of VD ceased. At least from the late 1930s and the 1940s none could be traced. That did not mean that the government ignored the importance of VD. However, it would seem that rather than taking a national, broad-based, results-oriented public health approach to eradicate VD, the government retreated into the policing of morals; and even that was more in word than deed. There were still newspaper ads touting remedies for VD, but it seems that their number was less than before, although the problem of VD was just as pressing.[43]

STDs such as syphilis and gonorrhea were seen as a danger not only to public health but to the institution of marriage. The new Civil Code of 1932 (section 1040) therefore stipulated that "either of the parties to a promised marriage can demand the other party to produce a certificate from an authorized physician stating that the party is free from all major contagious diseases, such as syphilis, gonorrhea, and tuberculosis."[44]

In Tehran an attempt was made to keep a register of the prostitutes in *Shahr-e Now*, the red-light district in South Tehran. It was reported that "In October 1933 a law was passed, but not signed by the Shah, making it illegal to keep a brothel and that by the end of December all would be closed. A further clause ordered the arrest of any officer found with a prostitute, but it is open to doubt that this order was obeyed."[45] Protecting the health of the armed forces had been the initial impetus behind contagious disease legislation in Europe and it would seem that Iran followed suit. "New regulations required that every prostitute must be registered, carry a card with her photograph and a statement of the date when she was last admitted to, and discharged from, the hospital. There had been a rumour in the town that every sick woman was to be compelled to wear iron bracelets."[46] Shortly thereafter the order was revoked, much to the chagrin of public health officials. "Many doctors wish to revive compulsory examination of prostitutes, as they recognize the gravity of venereal disease. It is alleged that the majority of men contract venereal disease sooner or

---

43. Rosalie Slaughter Morton, *A Doctor's Holiday* (New York, 1941), pp. 219-20 ("a menace to the nation.").

44. Ali Reza Naqvi, "The Marriage Laws of Iran (II)," *Islamic Studies* 7/2 (1968), pp. 129, 161 see also the issues 7/3 and 7/4.

45. Merritt-Hawkes, *Persia*, p. 289.

46. Merritt-Hawkes, *Persia*, p. 114.

later. Several women said they did not mind the examination, as it was free and taught them how to keep healthy."[47]

The policing of prostitutes in Europe, which became widespread in the late nineteenth century, was a strategy related to quarantine responses to infection control. However, in Qajar Iran and even before that time, the physical separation and policing of prostitutes was a morality issue so as not to corrupt the rest of society. It was also controlled for fiscal purposes, because concentration of this activity facilitated the collection of revenues. It was only under Reza Shah, ironically at a time that in many countries in Europe (but not France) such controls were relaxed or were strongly criticized, that infection control of prostitutes became part of the policing function. The medical officials who insisted on basically copying the French model of controlling prostitutes were the same men who "blamed Europe for having brought venereal disease to Persia."[48]

Legal support for other preventives measures was also established. In 1941, the *Majles* approved a Law concerning "Prevention of Venereal and Contagious Diseases" to provide safeguards, in particular to children, for whom syphilis often had disastrous consequences. Article 10 of the Law stipulates that a syphilitic woman who is aware of her disease or suspects that her disease is contagious and infectious, and with that knowledge breast-feeds a healthy child belonging to someone else, shall be deemed guilty and sentenced to prison or pay a cash penalty. Should such a child be infected by the disease as a result of being breast-fed, the woman shall be deemed guilty and on conviction thereof, a more severe punishment shall be meted out. The same punishment shall be applied to the person who knowingly gives a child infected by syphilis to a healthy woman to breast-feed if the woman is afflicted by the disease as a consequence. Article 11 stipulates that any person who wishes to engage the services of a wet nurse is required to secure the opinion of a physician, through a medical examination, as regard the health of both the child and the wet nurse to ensure

47. Merritt-Hawkes, *Persia*, p. 289.
48. Merritt-Hawkes, *Persia*, p. 114.

that neither is affected by syphilis. In case of a violation, the guilty party shall be punished. The law also provided the legal framework to mount an active anti-VD campaign, but lack of funds, trained people and infrastructure made at least this part of the law a dead letter.[49]

The prevalence of VD still seems to have been very high in the 1940s. Precise data are not available, although VD was believed to be more prevalent in towns than in rural districts. To put the problem of VD in perspective, Hedayatollah Hakim-Olahi an investigative reporter, who based his findings on the data from hospitals, reported that some 300,000 or 40 percent of the 750,000 inhabitants of Tehran had VD in 1946.[50] Another journalist rang the alarm bell and warned that the future generation of Isfahan was at stake where 80 percent of young males had gonorrhea and 8 percent were syphilitic; and the number was on the increase.[51] Yet another Iranian journalist wrote that about one-third of the total urban population in Iran had VD and that the number of VD doctors was three times that of elementary schools teachers and two times that of bakers.[52] By that time, condoms were available in Iranian pharmacies.[53] However, both their price (for all but high-income males) and its association with immoral sexual behavior and prostitution constrained their use. It was shameful to buy them, for in the public mind its only use was for illicit sex. One public health official reported that in his (unnamed) city 50 percent of people were syphilitic, while in many villages the percentage was believed to be even higher. In particular, the prevalence of congenital

---

49. Overseas Consultants, *Report*, vol. 2, p. 61.

50. Hakim-Olahi, *Ba man*, vol. 2, p. ii.

51. Anonymous, "Suzak va sifilis nasl-e ayandeh-ye Esfahanra fana mikonad," *Khvandaniha* 7/72 (1326/1947), p. 10.

52. Anonymous, "'Ettela'at-i geranbaha-ye ejtema'i darbareh-ye Iran," *Khvandaniha* 8/33 (1326/1947), p. 14.

53. Condom or *kaput* (from the French *capote*) was a term so familiar that Mahvash used it in her jokes without the need to explain it. Mahvash, *Asrar-e Magu*, pp. 19 (*bachcheh va barani*), 99 (*kaput-e siyah*). The fact that in Persian the word is derived from the French indicates that it must have been introduced before World War II, when there was a large influx of English-speaking major users of condoms.

syphilis seems to have been high. However, the prevalence of syphilis seems to have been rare in remote villages and among the migratory tribal population.

Gonorrhea was widespread and the cause of much sterility, while *chanchroid, Granumola inguinale* and *Lymphogranuloma venereum* were not widespread in the cities. Despite the seriousness of the problem public health officials were not properly trained in VD control. There were no public educational programs. Treatment programs were available in cities and some large villages, but the approach was curative and not preventive. For syphilis traditional methods were used. Although penicillin was widely used for gonorrhea in the large cities, elsewhere traditional methods were still used. Although prostitution existed in all urban areas, often in restricted districts, these had no prophylactic stations. Only in *Shahr-e Now* a volunteer organization had established a treatment clinic. Although the army had a reasonably efficient medical corps, soldiers constituted a major source of infection in rural areas due to returning recruits who had been infected while doing military service. There was no educational or even a curative program in the army to ensure that the recruits returned healthy to their village. In Tehran there was a "Society for the Prevention of Venereal Disease" with a budget of 15,000 *riyals*/month. It also tried to collect private voluntary donations and some 5,000 *riyals* per month were collected in 1948. The society provided information and training of public health officials. It operated a treatment clinic, but not a prophylactic one, which was much needed. Finally, it provided drugs to some government clinics. There was a private clinic in Tehran that had half of its 60 beds available for VD patients. "Infected prostitutes [were] isolated in a 14-bed ward."[54]

Despite the enormity of the problem there was no real public discussion about VD and its treatment. In 1945, the newspaper *Mard-e Emruz* published a number of articles on prostitution, arguing that women were driven to become sexual workers out of economic need.

---

54. Overseas Consultants, *Report*, vol. 2, pp. 8-9, 29, 36, 41-42. See also Government of Great-Britain, *Persia. Geographic Handbook*, p.420.

The paper further argued that Iran should follow the Turkish example of putting prostitutes under police control for public health reasons. It proposed allowing both prostitution and temporary marriage as a sexual outlet, for males, of course.[55] One further attempt was made by Hakim-Olahi in 1946, whose book *Ba man beh Shahr-e Now beya'id* was reprinted at least three times. Hakim-Olahi's aim was to prod and shame the government into action as is clear from the "Foreword" to his book, which was addressed to the shah. He outlined the size and danger of the problem and the need to obtain reliable objective data. He cited an unnamed foreign source that had stated that it would be a surprise if one found a person in Tehran who did not have syphilis. The shock therapy may have had some effect in that the "Society for the Prevention of Venereal Disease" received its monthly budget from the Imperial Social Service Organization.

Hakim-Olahi recommended that *Shahr-e Now* be relocated away from South Tehran and normal decent people, and reopened in a red-light district under strict control of public health officials. If relocation of the district was impossible, then the existing district had to be walled, with a door for ingress and egress, which would allow everybody passing through to be checked for VD by public health officials at the cost of a few *riyals*. This would prevent the spread of the disease. The income generated should be used for the unfortunate women who had to sell their sexual favors. Because he believed that it was impossible to eradicate prostitution, Hakim-Olahi recommended that the women plying this trade as well as their house be examined every day and that they keep their health card with them. He was convinced that in this manner it would no longer happen that many new syphilis cases would be added daily. Further, he suggested cutting the high salaries of the management of the "Red Lion and Sun Society" and using those savings to help prostitutes to start a new life.[56] Despite his efforts

---

55. Amin, *The Making*, quoting *Mard-e Emruz* of 10 August /1945; 10 December 1945, and 3 November 1944.

56. Hakim-Olahi, *Ba man*, vol. 2, pp. ii-iv. His figure of 15,000 new syphilis cases per day is, of course, ridiculous. It is interesting to note that he did not mention boys in his Foreword, who also were available in *Shahr-e Now*

and that of others, the prevalence of VD seemed to have abated little in the next 20 years. In 1963 it was reported that "venereal diseases pose a serious problem, although the exact incidence is unknown. In some rural areas it is said to be as high as 80 percent."[57]

One of the main sources of infection remained prostitutes. In 1949, it was estimated that there were 4,000 prostitutes in *Shahr-e Now* plus an unknown number in the rest of Tehran. These were supposed to be examined every fortnight, but the laboratory made only 40 smears a day and that number included all patients. Wasserman tests were only done when the presence of VD was suspected based on examination of the throat and skin. From this it is clear that few prostitutes reported for examination and that the authorities did not enforce the law requiring prostitutes to be checked for VD.[58] In the intervening years, access to medical services for sex workers was rather limited. In 1966, one researcher reported that in Malayer, prostitutes were not medically examined at all; neither were they controlled by the police, and no data were collected on the prevalence of STDs.[59] Things were no better in Tehran, for a medical study carried out in 1975 in Tehran's red-light district (Shahr-e Now) showed that of 921 women examined, 112, or 12 percent, had gonorrhea. These results were compatible with the results of a similar but larger study

---

(e.g. Ibid., vol. 2, p. 1) as well as in the various brothels in Tehran nowadays. The journal *Khvandaniha*, which published parts of Hakim-Olahi's book, also occasionally addressed the issue of VD, but as a side issue to other social issues such as prostitution.

57. US Army, *Area Handbook for Iran* (Washington DC, 1963), p. 147. In this connection it is interesting to note that one study on rural health does not mention the occurrence of VD at all. Angela Petrosian, Kazem Shayan, K.W. Bash, and Bruce Jessup. *The Health and related characteristics of four selected villages and tribal communities in Fars Ostan, Iran* (Shiraz, April 1964). But it is clear that the study avoided the subject, even in the literature that it quoted, which provided information on VD in Iran. The same holds for Loeb's study on the Jews in Fars, where VD is not listed either among the diseases that existed among this group. Loeb, *Outcaste*, p. 7.

58. Overseas Consultants, *Report*, vol. 2, p. 42.

59. Zahereddini, *Medizinische Topographie*, p. 31. There was no police control in Shiraz either. Loeb, *Outcaste*, p. 72.

reported in the USA.[60] This high prevalence of gonorrhea came about despite the fact that prostitutes were supposed to be subject to regular monthly health checks. Failure to do so resulted in fines and even arrest. Given the study's result, it is doubtful that this regulation was consistently applied.[61]

After the Islamic Revolution in 1979, prostitution was banned and officially eradicated from social life in the Islamic Republic of Iran (IRI). Also, strict Islamic behavior was required from all citizens, which meant the discontinuance of loose sexual behavior. One author actually claims that the incidence of syphilis in the IRI has declined because of these measures.[62] It is certainly true that social control in Iran, both before and after 1979, had a dampening effect on immoral behavior. This was further reinforced because VD is still considered to be a shameful affliction for several reasons. It has less to do with the official establishment of Islamic rule, for Moslem precepts were respected prior to 1979 by most people. What does strict Islamic behavior (apart from abstinence for the unmarried and no adultery by married men/women) imply in this context? It means that if somebody had been engaged in sexual intercourse, he or she had first to take the required ablutions, if he/she wanted to pray or be engaged in other religious rituals. Not praying would be an indication that there was a problem (of impurity due to e.g. illicit sexual intercourse), while doing the required ablution (*ghosl* or *vozu*) signaled that the person concerned had become ritually unclean (e.g. through sexual intercourse). The persons concerned either had to go to the public bath or to the 'bathing facility' in one's house. In either case everyone in the house knew the person had taken his or her ablution. For contrary to the situation nowadays, where taking a shower or a bath tends to blur

60. T. Zirak-Zadah, H. Delavarian, M.A. Bahavar, V. Majidi, R. Yaminifar, and P. Masoumi, "Penicillin-resistant strains of Neisseria gonorrhoeae in Shahre-Now." *Tropical Doctor* 7/2 (1977), pp. 57-58.

61. Haeri, *Law*, p. 181.

62. N. Simforoosh, "A decrease in incidence of syphilis in Iran and the effect of Islamic rules in controlling sexually transmitted diseases," *Medical Journal of the Islamic Republic of Iran* 12 (1998), p. 283.

the hygienic activity (*tamiz*) with that of purifying (*pak*), the opposite was the case in the past. Then, bathing was for ritual not hygienic purposes, the latter is done because a person is dirty (*kathif*); the former because a person is religiously unclean (*najes*). However, with the growing availability of showers in many homes that are used daily for hygienic rather than religious purposes as well as more nuclear families living in their own house rather than with their extended family, the performance of the necessary ablution after sex has become less the object of familial scrutiny than before.[63]

Despite the fact that prostitution (both offering sexual services and using them) is illegal, the Islamic Republic has had as little success in suppressing it as did the secular Pahlavi regime. As prostitution (involving sexual intercourse between two persons who are not married to each other or involving unmarried persons) implies adultery and fornication, both of which require stoning to death, one is surprised at the prevalence of sinning and the high number of 'sinners' in the IRI. For, despite the crackdown on prostitution under the IRI, it has come back with a vengeance, as shown by the spread of HIV/AIDS, about which later.

Although no published studies have been carried out it is reported that there are now some 300,000 prostitutes in Iran, including 45,000 in Tehran. Prostitutes and possibly the majority of *sigheh* wives provide sexual services for financial reasons. Being mostly uneducated, these sex workers easily accept risky sexual behavior. Therefore, these two groups constitute a major source of infection. The very high rate of persistent infection despite standard treatments is disturbing. However, medical care and education for sex workers as needy patients in a

---

63. For a detailed discussion of this issue see Papoli-Yazdi, *Khaterat*, p. 43; see also Alberts, *Social Structure*, vol. 1, p. 217. Similar sexual controls existed among Iranian Jews. Loeb, *Outcaste*, pp. 49, 120-22, 221-22. This control went so far that to avoid masturbation a Jewish boy when old enough to ejaculate was taken to a Moslem prostitute or "In the past he would be married off to avoid the problem." Ibid., p. 72.

safe and unprejudiced environment is unavailable, because it does not yet fit the IRI's moral code.[64]

The result of this official denial of reality is discouraging. In 1983 a study was published on the prevalence of chlamydial genital infection (one of the major STDs) in 177 prostitutes—100 in Teheran and 77 in the port of Bandar Abbas. The results indicate that these women were commonly infected with *C. trachomatis* and probably were a major reservoir of chlamydial genital infection.[65] In a study carried out among 1,500 people who came to the laboratories for STDs examination between 1998 and 2000 at Mashhad University it was found that the prevalence of STD in this population was nearly 5 percent for syphilis and 6 percent for gonorrhea. Furthermore, the data indicated that the prevalence was significantly more evident in patients with low socio-economic status.[66] From these two studies it is clear that despite the official denial of prostitution, STD persists among sex workers, (who refuse to go away), and is also prevalent among the general public.[67] In another study light is shed on how males may have contracted gonorrhea.

> From 1997 through 2000, for a mean of 18 months (range 8–42 months), 100 male gonorrhea patients were followed in Kermanshah. The results of the study showed that 4% of patients became infected by girlfriends, 24% by temporary wives (sigheh), and 64% by prostitutes; the remaining 8% denied having had intercourse with sex

---

64. J. Zargooshi, "Characteristics of gonorrhoea in Kermanshah, Iran," *Sexually Transmitted Infections* 78 (2002), pp. 460-461; M. R. Mohebbi, "Female sex workers and fear of stigmatization," *Sexually Transmitted Infections* 81 (2005), pp. 180-181.

65. S. Darougar, B. Aramesh, J. A. Gibson, J. D. Treharne, B. R. Jones, "Chlamydial genital infection in prostitutes in Iran." *British Journal of Venereal Diseases* 59/1 (1983), pp. 53-55.

66. J. Ghanaat, A. Sadeghian, K. Ghazvini, M. R. Nassiri, "Prevalence and risk factors for hepatitis B virus infections among STD patients in northeast region of Iran." *Medical Science Monitor* 9/2 (2003): CR91-4.

67. For a theoretical extrapolation of the prevalence of syphilis in Iran and other countries see [http://www.wrongdiagnosis.com/s/syphilis/stats-country.htm]

workers. Of 38 married cases, 31 reported unprotected intercourse with permanent wives while infected and only four of 38 gave prescribed drugs to their wives. 89% of contacts with prostitutes were unprotected. Most of the prostitutes and professional sigheh wives were practicing survival sex. Fear of stigmatization and presumed severe penalties prevented prostitutes from seeking medical care, and 26% of the patrons reported self medication.[68]

Of course, sex workers are not the only source of infection. Their clients display irresponsible behavior such as having unprotected sex and having sexual relations with healthy persons, even when infected. Partly, this is the result of ineffective and incomplete information about how to have safe sex. How did/do people get information on this subject? In one ethnographic study in the village of Davarabad, the informants said that around 1940, "A boy and a girl knew practically nothing until instructed by their attendants." The latter, the best man and the maid of honor of the groom and bride, were relatives and/or friends of a similar age group and already married. By 1960, this had become merely a custom, but in the majority of the cases the bride and groom had "Little beyond theoretical knowledge of human sex biology."[69] It is quite likely that the situation was little different in urban areas, although young men may have had pre-marital sexual intercourse with prostitutes.[70] For the educated public, and for those

68. Zargooshi, "Characteristics of gonorrhoea," pp. 460-461.

69. Alberts, *Social Structure*, vol. 2, p. 656; see also Borhanian, *Die Gemeinde Hamidieh*, p. 145.

70. Zahereddini, *Medizinische Topographie*, p. 31; Loeb, *Outcaste*, p. 73; Borhanian, *Die Gemeinde Hamidieh*, p. 145. A stuy carried out in 2002 yielded the following results concerning "their most important source of information and their preferred source of information on sex, respondents most often cited peers (34% and 21%, respectively) or teachers (21% and 15%, respectively). Books and magazines were the preferred source of 15% of the respondents. Relatively few adolescents cited their parents as their most important (16%) or preferred (12%) source of information on sex." Mohammad Reza Mohammadi, Kazem Mohammad, Farideh K.A. Farahani, Siamak Alikhani, Mohammad Zare, Fahimeh R. Tehrani, Ali Ramezankhani and Farshid Alaeddini. "Reproductive Knowledge, Attitudes and Behavior Among Adolescent Males in Tehran, Iran," *International Family Planning Perspectives* 32/1 (2006), pp. 40-42

who read, information was available. For example, in 1951, there appeared an article in *Khvandaniha*, a popular weekly, about the mechanics of meiosis, or egg and sperm production and why 30 percent of married women are barren. One of the causes of barrenness mentioned in the article was gonorrhea.[71] In the same journal there was also an ad announcing the publication of "A Guide to Love" (*Rahbar-e 'Eshq*). It was described as the first book of its kind in Persian and as an encyclopedia of sexual problems highlighting scientific, psychological and sexual aspects.[72] I have not found many references to similar publications in Persian for the subsequent decades, but undoubtedly there are such ones.[73] In the 1970s, information on human reproduction was given as part of biology class in the second year of high school. This component was discontinued under the IRI.

Another formal source of information was and is religious instruction in schools, where students are taught basic Islamic rituals (five daily prayers, the rules of purity, etc.). They are made aware what activities make a Moslem unclean (including menstruation, childbirth, ejaculation, and penetration, both human and animal) and what ablutions are necessary in those cases to restore religious purity for prayer to be valid. In this way students acquire some measure of knowledge of the reproductive organs and sexual practices. This type of information is made available via the television, mosques, local prayer meetings and individual advice from mullahs. However, it should not be mistaken for safe sex education; it is education about ritual purity

---

71. Anonymous, "Chera 'addeh'i az khanomha namitavanand owlad beyavarand va darman-e an chist?" *Khvandaniha* 11/81 (1330/1951), p. 21.

72. Anonymous, "Rahbar-e 'Eshq," *Khvandaniha* 7/2 (1325/1946), p. 13 (the price of the book was 50 *riyals*).

73. One book that qualifies is by A. Keyhan-niya, *Zan-e emruz, Mard-e diruz! Tahlili bar ekhelafat-e zanashavin* (Tehran, 1376/1997). This kind of popular psychological guide for spouses how to behave towards one another, to be aware of each other's needs (including sexual ones) and how to avoid discord. Originally published in 1996 it soon was reprinted three times, indicating that there is a demand for such a kind of 'guide.' A much earlier and very shallow publication is that by Mahvash, *Raz-e kamyabi-ye jensi* (Tehran, 1336/1957), which allegedly was ghost-written by the journalist Ahmad Sorush.

and Islamic morality with the emphasis on abstinence for unmarried persons.[74]

Yet another possible source of formal information is that from family planning. Before the widespread distribution of condoms, coitus interruptus (*azal; jelow-giri*) was the main male-initiated form of contraception and it still is (See Table 5.2).[75] Under the Pahlavi regime, as of 1967, a beginning was made with a national program of family planning. One problem was that its message was mainly aimed at women rather than men, which meant that fewer men were reached than was desirable. The family planning services were suspended after 1980, although they were still made available to those who wanted them, even the continuation of the free dispense of condoms and the birth-control pill.[76] After the end of the Iran-Iraq (1980-88) war, the country faced the prospect of a population explosion and, therefore, the government reversed its passive policy to a pro-active one. In 1989, it created a population council and reestablished Family Planning (FP) services. A mass media campaign promoted specific contraceptive methods (even tubal occlusion and vasectomy), a practice other Middle Eastern countries do not do. Condoms are made available at the FP centers and are openly sold in pharmacies and on many a street corner in towns. Services are provided in 400 centers, which emphasize sterilization and provide a range of contraceptive options including Norplant and injectables. Young couples are obliged to attend the clinic, and they cannot get married without the requisite certificate of attendance. In Seistan and Baluchistan, for example, they are given a blood test for thalassaemia (a common inherited disorder), but the test is not used to check for STDs. Table 5.2 gives the male share of contraceptive users in Iran from 1976 to-2000.

---

74. See, for example, Khomeyni, *Tahrir*, vol. 1, pp. 9-121; Ibid., *Towzih*, pp. 16-160. For the same reasons, a similar source of information existed among Iranian Jews. Loeb, *Outcaste*, pp. 222-23.

75. This was also the case for Iranian Jews, despite the fact that birth control is not permitted by Jewish religious law. Loeb, *Outcaste*, p. 222.

76. Amir Mehryar, F. Mostafavi, Homa Agha, "Men and Family Planning in Iran" [http://www.iussp.org/Brazil2001/s20/S22_P05_Mehryar.pdf]

Table 5.2: Share of Male Method Users of All Contraceptive Users
in Iran (1976-2000)

Year of Survey	Urban Areas	Rural Areas
1976	Percent	Percent
Condom	14.0	2
Withdrawal	31.7	15.5
Vasectomy	0	0
Total	45.7	17.5
1989		
Condom	12	8.3
Withdrawal	42	25
Vasectomy	0	0
Total	54	33.3
1992		
Condom	10.8	8.2
Withdrawal	36.4	20.2
Vasectomy	0	0
Total	46.4	28.4
1996		
Condom	12	6.4
Withdrawal	24.2	9.5
Vasectomy	4.3	1.8
Total	40.5	17.7
1997		
Condom	12	8.3
Withdrawal	42	25.0
Vasectomy	4.3	1.8
Total	58.3	35.1
2000		
Condom	9.3	5.3
Withdrawal	27.8	13.9
Vasectomy	4.4	1.8
Total	41.5	21

Source: Mehryar et al. "Men and Family Planning."

Data from the 1976-77 Iran Fertility Survey (IFS) and the 1992 Contraceptive Prevalence Survey (CPS) showed that 36 percent of all currently married women were using contraceptives; the corresponding CPS figure was 65 percent. This number increased to 75 percent in 1996 (81% urban and 71% rural) and remained at that level in 2000. The urban-rural gap in knowledge and use of contraception methods, which existed in 1976, also narrowed by 1992, but the popularity of certain methods varied by urban-rural residence. Important in this connection is the decline of male methods, apparently due to the revival of the family planning program and the increased availability of modern female contraceptive methods. However effective the program is (and it is, due to the support from the highest religious authorities), its focus is on the prevention of pregnancy not of STDs and, therefore, it does not really provide safe sex education. This is also clear from the fact that the use of condoms is decreasing rather than increasing (see Table 5.2), while production of condoms in Iran amounts to only 45 million per year.[77] Nevertheless, certain aspects of this program as well as other formal sources of information mentioned above have given the public (in particular the younger generation) the opportunity to better understand how sexual intercourse works and how infection with STDs can be avoided. The fact that the taboo of speaking and writing about condoms has been breached is in itself a helpful development.

---

77. A. Aghajanian, "A new direction in population policy and family planning in the Islamic Republic of Iran," *Asia Pacific Population Journal* 10 March 1995, pp. 3-20; Butta P. "Iran rebuilds family planning services," *AVSC News* (Association for Voluntary Surgical Contraception) 31 July 1993, pp. 3, 5; Mehryar et al, "Men and Family Planning." Condoms are imported from China, but these, although cheaper than the ones made in Iran, have the reputation of being unreliable (and wrong size). Also other factors play a role. A study carried out among 4,417 women in 1996 concluded: "Despite reluctance to conceive, >30% of couples do not use any method of contraception. Health concerns, side effects, failure of the method and some demographic issues such as education, age, residential region and the number of living children have a major effect on contraceptive use." F. Ramezani-Tehrani, F. Khalaj Abadi Farahani, and M.S. Hasemi, "Factors influencing contraceptive use in Tehran," *Family Practice* 18/2 (2001), pp. 204-08.

HIV/AIDS

In the Islamic Republic of Iran, public discussion of sex and related issues is largely taboo, as it was under the Pahlavis, because it deals with religiously unlawful activities.[78] Nevertheless, it would seem that the young have a different opinion about this. In a survey of university students in Qazvin, two-thirds of respondents said that they did not believe educating young people about unintended pregnancies and STDs would lead to sexual immorality.[79] Another survey conducted among male adolescents in Tehran in 2002 concluded that their limited knowledge regarding STDs and contraceptives put the sexual and reproductive health of their age-group at risk.[80] However, the Education Ministry refused to include an AIDS awareness program in schools, because it would promote corruption among young people. Although the government of Iran has been in denial for a long time, in April 2002 it publicly acknowledged that Iran faced a budding AIDS crisis. In 1999, the number of people having HIV/AIDS was only 1,800. More than half of those infected (65%), according to the Ministry of Health, were drug addicts who had used contaminated syringes. However, that argument does not hold, because about 50 percent of these drug users were married and thus must also have infected their wives. By January 2002, the official number had almost doubled to 3,340 HIV-positive cases. But experts estimate that there are about 31,000 people that carry HIV (Table 5.3). This higher figure is due to a lack of testing capacity and reluctance of infected people to seek

---

78. Zahereddini, *Medizinische Topographie*, p. 31.

79. A total of 1,111 students participated in the survey: 654 female students and 457 male students, with an average age of respectively 21.4 years and 22.7 years. Only 187 of the respondents were married. M. Simbar, F. Ramezani-Tehrani, and Z. Hashemi, "The Needs of Reproductive Health of University Students," *The Journal of Gazvin University of Medical Sciences*, no. 28, Autumn Supplement (2003) quoted by Jocelyn DeJong et al. "Young People's Sexual and Reproductive Health in the Middle East and North Africa," *Population Reference Bureau* [www.prb.org/pdf07/ MENAYouthReproductiveHealth.pdf].

80. Mohammad R. Mohammadi et al., "Reproductive Knowledge, Attitudes and Behavior Among Adolescent Males in Tehran, Iran," *International Family Planning Perspectives* 32, no. 1 (2006), pp. 35-44.

treatment, because of the social stigma attached to AIDS.[81] The trend of transmission has changed from intravenous drug users to high risk sexual behavior (12%), according Minoo Mohraz, a doctor and specialist in Iran's official AIDS Association, attached to the Ministry of Health. "People cannot afford to get married so young, and are getting married older. The gap is being filled by more prostitution," she said.[82] The newspaper *Entekhab* reported in 2002 that two sisters, ages 16 and 17, had infected 1,100 people with HIV.[83] The reason for this is not only ignorance. A study among sex workers in Kermanshah, found that most of them knew about condoms, "but only 50 percent had ever used one. Both sex workers and clients in Iran have cited high condom prices as the main reason for shirking their use."[84]

Table 5.3: Estimated number of HIV cases by age group (2003)

Figures	Number
Estimated number of total HIV cases	31,000
Adults (15-49 years)	31,000
Women (15-49 years)	3,800
Children	-.-
Estimated number of death due to AIDS	800
Estimated number of AIDS orphans	-.-

Source: UNDP/UNAIDS [http://www.youandaids.org/Asia%20Pacific%20 at%20a%20Glance/Iran/index.asp]

---

81. "Official Says AIDS Awareness in School Curriculum Is Iran's New Revolution," Associated Press (04.15.02) [http://www.cdcnpin.org/PrevNews/2002/apr02/ update041602.tx]. According to RFE/RL Iran Report, 8, no. 17, 25 April 2005, the government of Iran now estimates the number of HIV/AIDS persons at more than 10,000, while the WHO estimates it at more than 40,000.

82. [http://www.iranmania.com/News/ArticleView/Default.asp?NewsCode=274 89&NewsKind=Current%20Affairs]

83. [http://www.brow.on.ca/Articles/Fathi.htm]

84. [http://www.unaids.org/wad2004/EPIupdate2004_html_en/Epi04_11_ en.htm]

The realization of the seriousness of the looming problem, the government announced that Iranian children would be taught about AIDS and how to avoid it for the first time starting in September 2002. AIDS awareness materials are included in compulsory secondary school programs in the new academic year and later the subject will be included in textbooks. For younger students, AIDS will be described in the simplest way, such as a "bad disease that harms people." For high school students, the material describes how people can be infected, including through sexual intercourse. The materials for older students also mention condoms, but the emphasis is on respecting religious and family values and avoiding sex outside marriage. The material cautions against used hypodermic syringes.[85] The awareness campaign is not only limited to the educational system, but also includes other social sectors such as the corrections system as well as the public at large. In Iran, World AIDS Day has been marked with a fresh barrage of information being broadcast over the radio and television. Some officials have even gone on the air to call for the state to distribute condoms free of charge.[86] According to UNDP/UNAIDS, "about 1.2 million people are annually tested for HIV in Iran. Injecting drug users, STD patients and people who frequently travel abroad are among those who are tested. There are more than 154 sites for voluntary testing and counseling and more than 600 sites only for voluntary counseling." The government intends to target both the public at large as well high-risk groups such as street children, sex workers, drug users. It is also planning to reduce the social stigma for people living with and having AIDS through special targeted programs.[87]

---

85. "Official Says AIDS Awareness in School Curriculum Is Iran's New Revolution" Associated Press, 15 April 2002; [http://www.cdcnpin.org/PrevNews/2002/apr02/update041602.tx]

86. [http://www.iranmania.com/News/ArticleView/Default.asp?NewsCode=274 89&NewsKind=Current%20Affairs]

87. [http://www.youandaids.org/Asia%20Pacific%20at%20 a%20Glance/Iran/index.asp]. Also, [http://64.233.161.104/ search?q=cache:eTbLZ77d1AgJ:www.neshat.org/html_pages/a_country_ study_to_review_existi1.htm+&hl=en&start=1]

So far, the impact of the information campaign (including 700,000 posters and 200,000 brochures distributed to 3rd and 4th grade teachers as well as to lower and upper secondary schools) has had encouraging, albeit varying results. Through a cluster-sampling, 4,641 students from 52 high schools in Tehran were assessed by anonymous questionnaires in February 2002. The students identified television as their most important source of information about AIDS. Only a few students answered all the knowledge questions correctly, and there were many misconceptions about the routes of transmission. Mosquito bites (33%), public swimming pools (21%), and public toilets (20%) were incorrectly identified as routes of transmission. 46 percent believed that positive Human Immunodeficiency Virus (HIV positive) students should not attend ordinary schools. Most of the students wanted to know more about AIDS. The study concluded that although the knowledge level seems to be moderately high, misconceptions about the routes of transmission were common. There was a substantial intolerant attitude towards AIDS and HIV positive patients.[88] Researchers were somewhat more positive about the knowledge that prisoners in Kerman had regarding HIV/AIDS. Analysis of a sample survey of 350 prisoners showed that they had relatively high knowledge about HIV/AIDS and its modes of transmission. However, they had a lower level of knowledge about HIV/AIDS prevention. The overall knowledge of men about AIDS was significantly lower than women. Persons aged 46 years and older and illiterate inmates had the least knowledge about modes of transmission. In addition, the knowledge of illiterate prisoners about HIV/AIDS prevention was significantly lower than others.[89] While admitting that the information campaign on HIV/AIDS left much to be desired, another researcher submits that

88. A. Tavoosi, A. Zaferani, A. Enzevaei, P. Tajik, Z. Ahmadinezhad, "Knowledge and attitude towards HIV/AIDS among Iranian students." *BMC Public Health* 4 (2004), p. 17; see also *Indian Pediatrics* 41, no. 9 (2004), pp. 966-67; see also Ibid., pp. 7-13 regarding M.R. Mohebbi and R. Navipour, "Preventive education against HIV/AIDS in the schools of Iran."

89. F. H. Nakhaee, "Prisoners' knowledge of HIV/AIDS and its prevention in Kerman, Islamic Republic of Iran." *East Mediterranean Health Journal* 6, 8 November 2002, pp. 725-31.

the situation has greatly improved, because as of 2004 the Ministry of Education was engaged in training "13,000 in-service biology teachers and school physicians to provide preventive education in schools. A special course on HIV/AIDS has been designed as an appendix to biology books for first grade high school students."[90]

The somewhat positive view of what people know about AIDS, its transmission and its possible prevention, is not shared by Mahmud Reza Musavi, a psychologist working at one of Tehran's dedicated clinics. He stated to Agence France Presse in early December 2004 that "The general public is extremely ignorant. Some families lock the infected members in the cellar and cut off all contact with them." He warns that women in particular were reluctant to come forward for testing and support. His rather pessimistic view is shared by Dr. Mohraz (AIDS Association). She felt that Iran still has a long way to go in accepting that HIV/AIDS is not a problem that remains confined to the country's injecting heroin addicts. "Policy makers think that if you talk about something, it will encourage the activity," she said. "So public awareness and education is by no means consistent. They talk about it on TV for World AIDS Day and that's the end of it until next year."[91] The relatively high prevalence of sexual activity and the lack of knowledge regarding STDs and contraceptives among Iranian youths pose a significant threat to the sexual and reproductive health of adolescent males in Iran.

90. Mohammad Reza Mohebbi, "Preventive education against HIV/AIDS in Iran," [http://www.biomedcentral.com/1471-2458/4/17/comments/comments]. Also, R. Gheiratmand, R. Navipour, M. R. Mohebbi, K. M. Hosseini, M. Motaghian-Monazzam, A. K. Mallik et al. *A Country Study to Review Existing Capacity Building and Management of the Training of Teachers on Preventive Education against HIV/AIDS in the Schools in I.R. Iran.* Available from the official website of the Deputy of Physical Education and Health, Ministry of Education of the I.R. Iran: URL: http://www.neshat.org/html_pages/a_country_study_to_review_existi1.htm . Accessed July 28, 2004.

91. [http://www.iranmania.com/News/ArticleView/Default.asp?NewsCo de=27489&NewsKind=Current%20Affairs] This pessimistic view is borne out by the almost blank data sheet on the incidence of HIV/AIDS in Iran as produced by WHO, for most of the data requested by WHO are blank. [http://64.233.187.104/search?q=cache:akB_SVhCOj4J:www.childinfo.org/eddb/hiv_aids/factsheets/pdfs/Iran_en.pdf+syphilis+iran+incidence&hl=en].

Because of the outbreak of AIDS and the realization that now prostitution (not sexual intercourse in general!) has become a main cause of AIDS, the authorities are not only willing to talk about AIDS prevention, but also to transform prostitutes into legal sex workers. As mentioned previously, there were said to have been plans proposing the legalizing of brothels, under the name of 'chastity houses', as a way of providing safe sex for the men of the city. However, the government has denied the existence of such plans. The proposed alternative path is temporary marriage. Women's groups in Iran are not that enthusiastic about this as it would legalize female prostitution, in their view.[92] Of course, it is also an affirmation of a rather male-centered view of society.

Discussion

Putting the above discussion on the prevalence of VD into perspective four phases may be distinguished. The first phase was the one of ignorance. VD was widespread, but it just was one of the many other diseases that people in Iran had. Therefore, the practice of having unprotected sex with more than one partner was widespread, in particular in urban areas. Villagers probably were infected when they went on a pilgrimage or were in the army, during which period they had sex with sex workers (*sigheh* and/or prostitute) and their comrades. Because it was not known that the disease was sexually transmitted people did not feel the need to change their behavior. Therefore, they openly discussed the disease in social gatherings to share experience about remedies and the like. In the 1890s it became known in Europe and the USA that VD is a STD. Modern medical science was being introduced into Iran at that time, although its knowledge barely trickled down. The first efforts to draw attention to the danger of VD as well as to the existence of new remedies appeared in Iranian newspapers around 1900. However, unlike Europe where discussion about VD was taboo and those afflicted were socially stigmatized, in Iran VD could be discussed in a social context. Still most people had no idea that VD

92. [http://www.brow.on.ca/Articles/Fathi.htm]

was a STD, while it made little sense to stigmatize 40 percent of the population, because that seems to have been the level of prevalent level of infection. It was a different matter when the sores manifested themselves on the genitals, because speaking about such always had been a taboo subject. Despite the fact that VD was a STD people did not change their sexual behavior. In Iran this was facilitated by the fact that there were two classes of sex workers. One, the so-called temporary wives (*sigheh*), who legally exercised their profession and the other prostitutes,- who did so illegally. However, prostitution was and is rampant in the towns and cities due to the financial need of poor women and the demand for their services by men and thus, the prevalence of VD has increased.

The second phase was the one where discussion of VD became taboo in Iran as of the early 1930s, when the sexual nature of the disease finally hit home. Publications about the subject remained essentially limited to advertisements for remedies against VD. However, the audience for that information was the educated elite and the population at large remained just as ignorant about the nature of the disease. To stem the spread of the disease somewhat, the government made a proforma effort to bring prostitution under control following the French model. That meant monthly medical check-ups and health cards. This measure neither brought prostitution under control nor VD, because it was not really implemented; it only existed on paper. There was no program to inform the public at large about the need for prevention, while there was no change in sexual behavior. The high prevalence of prostitution and VD is an indication thereof. Nevertheless, there was a decrease in the incidence of VD after 1960, which was almost entirely due to the growing access to effective curative medical assistance, but hardly to a change in sexual mores. As to the latter, the only positive development was the increased use of condoms, which rose from hardly any around 1950 to 14 percent of the sexually actice population in 1976. However, like in the preceding period prostitution continued to be big business responding to a persistent demand.

The third phase started in 1980 when the IRI officially declared prostitution banned and eradicated. Prostitutes were either rehabilitated or transformed into *sigheh*s, apart from those that were executed. At that time, the authorities actively promoted the development of the institution of temporary marriage to prevent the re-occurrence of prostitution and thus VD. The policy was a failure, because it was based on false premises, both concerning human behavior and the vectors of VD. Victory was declared too soon. By 2000, prostitution was rampant again and STDs on the rise. Because of the significant success of the family planning program (since 1989) there was, however, a decrease in the use of condoms (from 14% in 1976 to 9% in 2000) indicating that still there was not an effective STD prevention program in place.

The fourth phase began with the outburst of AIDS, which cannot be ignored because it is no longer restricted to drug users, but is being spread through sexual intercourse (and not necessarily only with sex workers). The government has started an AIDS awareness campaign, but clearly it is still shying away from a persistent and consistent policy. For the public discussion, the cause of the spread of STDs and how to practice sexual intercourse in a safe manner is still taboo. Also, because prostitution is seen as the leading cause for AIDS some politicians and bureaucrats are suggesting transforming brothels into so-called 'chastity houses'. Thus, once again, the state is trying to transform illegal prostitution into legal temporary marriage. This assumes that, even if it works, this would stop the spread of STDs through risky sexual behavior, as if this sort of thing only took place with prostitutes. However, as long as the practice of safe sex is not the object of discussion, it is difficult to see how this transformation of prostitutes into *sigheh*s might actually be effective. The fact that Iranians have not changed their sexual practices combined with the reduction in the use of condoms means that the population is still at risk and that the incidence of STDs will rise.

Of further importance, people have only slowly 'adapted' their sexual behavior. Well into the 1960s VD was rampant, which implies unprotected sexual intercourse particularly outside marriage. This de-spite the fact the information was available to the infected persons, especially through a visit to a physician to obtain treatment. Also, the means to reduce infection (condoms) were widely available as of the 1940s, but were and are hardly used. Then and now people, includ-ing sex workers, consider them too expensive. Consequently condoms were and are not a major implement to have safer sex. In fact, the use of condoms is decreasing (See Table 5.2). Nevertheless, people must have adapted their sexual behavior somewhat in that the incidence of VD has decreased, for it cannot be explained only by curative practice. Although STDs are still high among sex workers the figures are current-ly lower than they were 40 years ago. As prostitution is still rampant, implying a great demand for its services, there is the danger of a rise in STDs. This is already the case with HIV/AIDS, which initially was treated as a disease that concerned only drug addicts, but now shows strong growth among non-drug users through the practice of unsafe sex.

Another dimension to the discussion is that when the course of events are observed during the last 150 years, one cannot escape the impression that Islamic Iran was little different from Christian Europe in that the victim of VD infection was the male. He became afflicted (*mobtala*); rarely the fact that women were also 'victimized' is raised. This is clear when the wave of advertisements with anti-VD remedies appeared in newspapers. At whom was all that information directed? And for whom were all the remedies meant to be? And this was only during the period when it was not known that VD was sexually trans-mitted. As in Europe, when this became known, it was the prostitutes who were targeted as the 'vectors of infection' although rather later (1930s). As of then, prostitutes formally needed to be controlled, to be checked, to be fined and if need be arrested, but not their male clients who were by implication only the 'innocent' victim of the wan-ton females who did not take proper care to prevent infection. At the same time these 'female vectors' were neither given information nor the means to prevent VD.

Emblematic of this male outlook of the problem is a certain in-digenous treatment to get rid of syphilis that was used in the past. The method is a well-known one in traditional medicine, viz. to transfer the disease from one person to another, thus healing the original sick person.[93] In this case, the syphilitic man marries a woman with whom he has sexual intercourse to purify himself (*pak kardan*) of the disease. This method was also used by married men to get children in case their first wife was infertile due to VD. No thought was given that the second wife he married (who presumably was healthy and not infected with VD) would now also become infected.[94] Even nowadays, condoms are mostly not used, and women cannot refuse men who want to have unprotected sex. This poses a protracted health threat. In fact, in Iran it would seem that the entire 'discussion', if there ever was such a thing on this subject and its resulting policies, was based on assumptions of male sexual behavior and that legal and police pre-ventive responses to VD were also based on these notions. Sex workers, excluding temporary wives, needed to be reformed and saved. Under the last shah this was to be achieved through honest productive work and under the IRI likewise. It is of interest to note that after 1980, in case of the interned prostitutes doing penance for their sin, offering oneself as a temporary wife was considered honest work. Although since the rise of the prevalence of AIDS the government has taken ac-tion to make people aware of what can and should be done to prevent being infected, it still has not really started a real discussion in society about sexual mores. Also, the policy pursued is still mainly based on male sexual behavior and the needs of women are still not receiv-ing full attention. As a result, despite the looming growing danger of STDs, sexual behavior and attitudes about it have not changed all that much over the past 2500 years.

---

93. For a discussion of this phenomenon of disease transfer see Floor, *Public Health*, pp. 98-99.

94. Jozani, *La Beauté*, p. 217.

AFTERWORD

I have not much to add to what has been said in the foregoing. I want to stress, however, that leaving aside the different cultural and religious context, what this study shows is that the nature, variety and problems of sexual relations in Iran over the ages did not and does not differ that much materially from that of countries in Europe, for example. This is good news, for it shows that Iranians, just like the rest of us, are trying to make the best of their lives, despite all the societal, cultural, historical and religious baggage that we all have to face and deal with.

Furthermore, this study shows that Iranians, as far as sexual relations are concerned, have behaved no differently after becoming Moslems for the past 1,200 years (nor any better than, say, Christians in Europe). This is a sobering thought, for apparently being an adherent to a self-proclaimed superior belief system does not necessarily translate into better behavior, whether from a parochial religious, ethical or a humanistic point of view.

Finally, the nature of sexual relational problems that Iranian society faces is not dissimilar to that of many other industrial nations— the challenge to the male claim to dominance over women, change in the age of marriage; premarital sex, rising divorce rate; rising promiscuity; prostitution, street children, homosexuality; and sexually transmitted diseases. However, whether the government of Iran will be able to tackle these problems in an effective way will very much depend on how pragmatic it will and can be, given its theological constraints. The future will tell.

BIBLIOGRAHY

ARCHIVES

KA 1057, f. 359-85, Dagh Register gehouden bij den oppercoopman
Leonard Winninx 'tsindert den 6 Julij anno 1645 dat uijt Gamron naer
Spahan vertreckt, tot den 24e November, daeraen volgende, als wanneer
in gemelte Gamron wederom gearriveert is.

VOC 1224

VOC 2253

VOC 2255

VOC 2269

VOC 2322

VOC 2323

VOC 2416

VOC 2511

VOC 2584

BOOKS AND ARTICLES

Abbott, K. E. "Geographical Notes taken during a Journey in Persia in 1849 and 1850" *JRGS* 25 (1855), pp. 1-78.

Abivardi, Amir Sa'id Hoseyn. "Anis al-'Asheqin," ed. Iraj Afshar, *Farhang-e Iran Zamin*, vol. 15 (Tehran, 1354/1975), pp. 86-160.

Adhar, Mehdi. "Qalamru-ye Sa'di," *Rahnama-ye Ketab* Tir (1339/1960), pp. 212-25.

Afary, Janet. *Iranian constitutional revolution, 1906-1911: grassroots democracy, social democracy & the origins of feminism* (New York, 1996).

Afshar, Iraj. "Bayaz-e Safar (Kerman va Seystan)," in *Savad va Bayaz* Iraj Afshar ed. 2 vols. (Tehran: Dehkhoda, 1349/1970), vol. 1, p. 299-328.

———. "Bist Shahr va Hazar Farsang," in Iraj Afshar ed. *Savad va Bayaz* 2 vols. (Tehran: Dehkhoda, 1349/1970), vol. 2, pp. 54-133.

Afzal al-Molk, Gholam Hoseyn Khan. *Safarnameh-ye Khorasan va Kerman* Qodratollah Rowshani Za'frananlu ed. (Tehran, n.d.).

Aghajanian, Akbar. "Living Arrangements of Widows in Shiraz, Iran," *Journal of Marriage and the Family* 47/3 (1971), pp. 781-784.

———. "Some Notes on Divorce in Iran," *Journal of Marriage and the Family* 48/4 (1986), pp. 749-55.

———. "A new direction in population policy and family planning in the Islamic Republic of Iran," *Asia Pacific Population Journal* 10 March 1995, pp. 3-20.

Aghajanian, A. and Mehryar, A.H. "Fertility transition in the Islamic Republic of Iran, 1976ñ1996," *Asia-Pacific Population Journal*, 14/1 (1999), pp. 21–42.

'Alam-e Nesvan (monthly).

Alberts, Robert Charles. *Social Structure and Culture Change in an Iranian Village* 2 vols. (Ph.D. dissertation University of Wisconsin, 1963).

Albuquerque, Afonso de. *Cartas de Afonso de Albuquerque, seguidas de documentos que as elucidam* 7 vols. eds. Raimundo António de Bulhão Pato and Henrique Lopes de Mendoça (Lisbon, 1884-1935).

——. *Comentários do grande Afonso de Albuquerque, capitão geral que foi das Indias orientais em tempo do muito poderoso Rey D. Manuel, o primeiro deste nome* 4 vols. , translated into English by Walter de Gray Birch as *The Commentaries of the Great Afonso DAlboquerque, second viceroy of India.* 4 vols. (London, 1875).

Alexander, James Edward. *Travels from India to England* (London, 1827 [New Delhi, 2000]).

Allemagne, Henri-Réné d'. *Du Khorasan au Pays de Bakhtyaris*, 4 vols. (Paris, 1911).

Alonso, Carlos. "Due lettere riguardanti i primi tempi delle missioni agostiniane in Persia," *Analecta Augustiniana* 24 (1961), pp. 152-201.

Amin, Camron Michael. *The Making of the Modern Iranian Woman* (Gainsville, Fl., 2002).

Amini, Ayatollah Ebrahim. *Entekhab-e Hamsar* (Tehran, 1374/1995).

——. *Ayin-e Hamsardari* (Tehran, 1378/1999) [http://www.hawzah. net/Per/K/Ain-Hams/Index.htm].

Ammianus Marcellinus, *Res Gestae Libri XXXI* translated by J. Rolfe as Ammianus Marcellinus, *History* (Cambridge MA, Harvard University Press, 1963).

Amnesty International, *Country and International Reports.*

Andrea, Bernadette. "Lady Sherley: The First Persian in England?" *The Muslim World* 95/2 (2005), 279ñ295.

Ange de Saint Joseph, *Souvenirs de la Perse safavide et autres lieux de l'Orient (1664-1678)*, translated by Michel Bastiaensen (Brussels, 1985).

Anonymous, "Die moderne Perserin," *Das Ausland* 1880, pp. 847-49.

Anonymous, "The Education of Wives" translated from the French by E. Powys Mathers, *Eastern Love* 3 vols. (London, New York, 1930), vol. 1, pp. 199-256.

Anonymous, *Tarikh-e Seystan* ed. Malek al-Sho'ara Bahar (Tehran, 1314/1935).

Anonymous, *A Chronicle of the Carmelites in Persia and the Papal Mission of the Seventeenth and Eighteenth Centuries*, 2 vols. (London, 1939).

Anonymous, "Rahbar-e 'Eshq," *Khvandaniha* 7/2 (1325/1946), p. 13.

Anonymous, "Suzak va sifilis nasl-e ayandeh-ye Esfahanra fana mikonad," *Khvandaniha* 7/72 (1326/1947), p. 10.

Anonymous, "Etella'at-e geranbaha-ye ejtema'i darbareh-ye Iran," *Khvandaniha* 8/33 (1326/1947), p. 15.

Anonymous, "Du dokhtar-e Shahr-e Now," *Khvandaniha* 8/34 (1326/1947), pp. 21-23.

Anonymous, "Chand amar-e tazeh va jaleb-e tavajjoh az zanan-e Iran," *Khvandaniha* 8/37 (1326/1947), pp. 14-15.

Anonymous, "Avval daf'eh shoharam Amir Khan mara beh Shahr-e Now bord," *Khvandaniha* 8/40 (1326/1947), pp. 21-23.

Anonymous, "Arzu-ye yek dokhtar-e Shahr-e Now," *Khvandaniha* 8/50 (1326/1947), pp. 19-20.

Anonymous, "Zanhara beshanasid," *Khvandaniha* 8/55 (1326/1947), pp. 18-20.

Anonymous, "Chera zanamra talaq dadam," *Khvandaniha* 8/56 (1326/1947), p. 17.

Anonymous, "Dar Khuzestan, Banader-e Jonub, Gorgan, Korasan va Baluchestan didam," *Khvandaniha* 8/62 (1326/1947), p. 10.

Anonymous, "Sar-anjam-e sigheh-ye mahramiyat," *Khvandaniha* 8/62 (1326/1947), p. 13.

Anonymous, "Fahesheh-ye Shesh-saleh," *Khvandaniha* 7/96 (12 Mordad 1327/1948), p. 16.

Anonymous, "Chera 'addeh'i az khanomha namitavanand owlad beyavarand va darman-e an chist?" *Khvandaniha* 11/81 (1330/1951), p. 21.

Anonymous, "Raportha," *Yaghma*, Ordidbehesht (1339/1960), pp. 93-97.

Anonymous, "Raportha," *Yaghma* Farvardin (1341/1962), pp. 47-48.

Anonymous, *Hadith-e Nader Shahi* ed. Reza Sha'bani (Tehran, 2536/1977).

Anonymous, *'Alamara-ye Shah Tahmasp* ed. Iraj Afshar (Tehran, 1370/1991).

'Abdol-Hoseyn Mas'ud Ansari, *Zendegani-ye Man* 4 vols. (Tehran, 1352/1973).

Arabshah, Ahmad ibn. *Tamerlane or Timur. The Great Amir* translated by J.C. Sanders (London, 1936).

Arak'el of Tabriz, *The History of Vardapet Arak'el of Tabriz* 2 vols. translated into English by George A. Bournoutian (Costa Mesa, 2005).

Arasteh, Reza and Arasteh, Josephine. *Man and society in Iran* (Leiden, 1964).

'Aref Qazvini, Abu'l-Qasem. *Kolliyat-e Divan* (Tehran, 1337/1958).

Arunova, M.R. and Ashrafiyan, K.Z. *Gosudarstvo Nadir-Shakha Afshara* (Moscow, 1958).

Asaf, Mohammad Hashem (Rostam al-Hokama). *Rostam al-Tavarikh* ed. Mohammad Moshiri (Tehran, 1348/1969).

Asaf al-Dowleh, *Asnad-e Mirza 'Abd al-Vahab Khan Asaf al-Dowleh* 3 vols. eds. 'Abdol-Hoseyn Nava'i and Nilufar Kasri (Tehran, 1377/1998).

Ashofteh'i Natanzi, Mahmud b. Hedayatollah *Naqavat al-Athar* ed. Ehsan Eshraqi (Tehran, 1350/1971).

'Attar, Farid al-Din. *The Ilahi-nama or Book of God* translated into English by John Andrew Boyle (Manchester, 1976).

Aubin, Eugène. *La Perse d'aujourd'hui* (Paris, 1907).

Aubin, Jean. "L'Avènement des Safavides reconsiderée" (Etudes Safavides III), *Moyen-Orient et Océan Indien*, 5 (1988), pp. 1-130.

Avazeh (Razavi), Mohammad Ebrahim. *Qanun-e Qovveh-ye Bah* (Qom, 1382/2003).

'Awfi, Mohammad. *Javame' al-Hekayat* ed. Mohammad Mo'in (Tehran, 1335/1956)

'Azud al-Dowleh, Ahmad b. Fath 'Ali. *Tarikh-e 'Azudi* ed. 'Abdol-Hoseyn Nava'i (Tehran, 2535, 1976).

Babayan, Kathryn. "The 'Aqa'id al-nisa. A glimpse at Safavid women in locals Isfahani culture," in G. Hambly ed. *Women in the medieval Islamic world: power, patronage, and piety* (New York, 1998), pp. 349-81.

―――. "Safavid Iran: 16th to mid-18th Century," in Joseph Suad ed. *Encyclopedia of Women & Islamic Cultures* 6 vols. (Leiden, 2003), vol. 1, pp. 89-94.

Babur, Zahiruddin Muhammad. *The Baburnama: Memoirs of Babur, Prince and Emperor* translated, edited and annotated by Wheeler M. Thackston (Washington, DC, 1996).

―――. *Babur-Nama (Memoires of Babur)* translated into English by A.S. Beveridge 2 vols. in one (Delhi, 1989).

Bafqi, Mohammad Mofid Mostowfi-ye. *Jame'-ye Mofidi*. 3 vols. ed. Iraj Afshar (Tehran 1340/1961).

Baker, James E. "A few remarks on the most prevalent Diseases and the Climate of the North of Persia," appendix to Mr. Herbert, Report on the present State of Persia and her Mineral Resources, in Government of Great Britain, *Accounts & Papers* 67 (1886), pp. 323-26.

Baladhuri, Ahmad b. Yahya. *Liber expugnationis regionum* ed. M.J. de Goeje (Leiden, 1866).

Baladiyeh-ye Tehran, *Dovvomin Salnameh-ye Ehsa'iyeh-ye Tehran* (Tehran: Baladiyeh, 1310/1931).

Barbaro, Josef et al., *Travels to Tana and Persia by Josef Barbaro and Ambrogio Contarini* 2 vols. translated into English by Lord Stanley (London, 1873).

Barbosa, Duarte. *The Book of Duarte Barbosa* translated by M. Longworth Dames, 2 vols. (London, 1918-21).

Bardesanes, *The book of the laws of the countries: dialogue on the date of Bardasein of Edessa* translated by H.J.W. Drijvers (Assen, 1954).

Bardsiri, Mir Mohammad Sa'id Moshiri. *Tadhkereh-ye Safavi*, ed. Ebrahim Bastani Parizi (Tehran, 1369/1990).

Barth, Fredrik. *Nomads of South Persia. The Baseri tribe of the Khamseh confederacy* (Boston, 1961).

Barthold, W. *Zwölf Vorlesungen über die Geschichte der Türken Mittelasiens* (Darmstadt, 1962).

―――. *Turkestan down to the Mongol Invasion* (Karachi, 1981).

Bartholomae, Christian. *Die Frau im sasanidischen Recht* (Heidelberg, 1924).

Bassett, James. *Persia, the Land of the Imams* (New York: Charles Scribner's Sons, 1886).

―――. *Persia: Eastern Mission. A Narrative of the founding and the fortunes of the Eastern Persia Mission* (Philadelphia, 1890).

―――. "Child Life in Persia," *Frank Lesley's Popular Monthly* 36 (August 1893), pp. 167-75.

Bastani-Parizi, Mohammad Ebrahim. *Khatun-e haft qal'eh: majma'-ye maqalat-e tarikhi* (Tehran, 1344/1965).

―――. *Haft Sang* (Tehran, 1346/1967).

―――. *Siyasat va Eqtesad-e 'Asr Safavi* (Tehran, 1348/1969).

Beck, Lois. *Nomad. A Year in the Life of an Qashqa'i Tribesman in Iran* (Berkeley, 1991).

Beck, Lois and Keddie, Nikki eds. *Women in the Muslim World* (Cambridge, 1978).

Bélanger, Charles. *Voyage aux Indes-Orientales.* 2 vols. (Paris: Arthus Bertrand, 1838).

Bell, John. *Travels from St. Petersburgh in Russia* etc. 2 vols. (Edinburgh, 1788).

Bembo, Ambrosio. *The Travels and Journal of Ambrosio Bembo.* Translated by Clara Barginelli (Berkeley, 2007).

Benjamin, S.G.W. *Persia and the Persians* (London, 1887).

Benson, Linda. "Islamic Marriage and Divorce in Xinjiang: The Case of Kashgar and Khotan," *Association for the Advancement of Central Asian Research* 5/2 (Fall 1992), pp. 5ñ8.

Beyhaqi, Abu Fazl Mohammad b. Hoseyn. *Tarikh-e Beyhaqi* eds. Ghani and Fayaz (Tehran, 1324/1945).

Bibi Khanom, "Ta'dib al-Rejal," in Hasan Javadi, Manjeh Mar'ashi and Simin Shakarlu eds. *Ruyaru'i-ye zan va mard dar 'asr-e Qajar. Du Resaleh. Ta'dib al-Nesvan va Ma'ayeb al-Rejal* (Washington DC, 1992), pp. 97-206.

Binder, Henry. *Au Kurdistan* (Paris, 1887).

Binning, R.B.M. *A Journal of Two Years' Travel in Persia, Ceylon, etc.* 2 vols. (London: Wm. H. Allen & Co, 1857).

al-Biruni, Mohammad b. Ahmad. *India,* translated into English by Edward C. Sachau (London, 1888).

Borhanian, Khosro. *Die Gemeinde Hamidieh in Khuzistan* (dissertation University of Cologne, 1960).

Bosworth, C. E. *The Ghaznavids, Their Empire in Afghanistan and Eastern Iran, 994-1040* (Edinburgh, 1963).

Boudhiba, Abdel Wahab. *La sexualité en islam* (Paris, 1975).

Briant, Pierre. *From Cyrus to Alexander. A History of the Persian Empire* (Winona Lake, 2002).

Bricteux, Auguste. *Au Pays du Lion et du Soleil* (Brussels, 1908).

———. *Les comédies de Malkom Khan* (Liège, 1933).

Brosius, Maria. *Women in Ancient Persia* (Oxford, 1996).

Brosset, M. F. *Collection d'Historiens Armeniens* 2 vols. (St. Petersburg, 1874-76).

Browne, E.G. *A Year Amongst the Persians* (London, 1970).

Brugsch, Heinrich. *Die Reise der K.K. Gesandtschaft nach Persien 1861-1862,* 2 vols. (Berlin: J.C. Hinrichs, 1863).

———. *Im Lande der Sonne ñ Wanderungen in Persien* (Berlin, 1886).

Brunschvig, R. "'Abd," *Encyclopedia of Islam* 2.

Buckingham, J. S. *Travels in Assyria, Media, and Persia* (Westmead, 1071).

Buhl, Frants. *Das Leben Muhammads* (Heidelberg, 1961).

Bukhari, *al-Sahih*. [http://www.usc.edu/dept/MSA/reference/ reference.html]; also [http://hadith.al-islam.com/Display/Display. asp?Doc=0&Rec=7607].

Bundari, Abu'l-Fath. *Zubdat al-nusrah va nukhbat al-usrah* ed. M. Th. Houtsma (Leiden, 1889).

Bürgel, J. Christoph. *Die Hofkorrespondenz Adud ad-Daulas* (Wiesbaden, 1965).

Burton, Richard. "Terminal Essay" to his English translation of *The Arabian Nights* 10 vols. (London, 1885), [http://www.fordham.edu/ halsall/pwh/burton-te.html].

Carré, Abbé. *The travels of Abbé Carré in India and the Near East (1672-74)*, 3 vols. (London: Hakluyt, 1947).

Cartwright, John. *The Preacher's Travels* (London, 1611).

Castanheda, Fernão Lopes. *História do descobrimento e conquista da India pelos Portugueses.* 2 vols. (Porto, 1979).

Castro, D. João de, *Obras Completas de D. João de Castro*, eds. Armando Cortesão e Luis de Albuquerque (Coimbra, Academia Internacional de Cultura Portuguesa, 1976).

Chardin, Jean. *Voyages*, ed. L. Langlès, 10 vols. (Paris 1811).

Chehabi, H. E. "Voices Unveiled: Women Singer in Iran," in Rudi Matthee and Beth Baron eds. *Iran and Beyond* (Costa Mesa, 2000), pp. 151-66.

Choksy, Jamsheed K. "Women during the Transition from Sasanian to Early Islamic Times," in Guity Nashat and Lois Beck eds. *Women in Iran. From the rise of Islam to 1800* (Chicago, 2003), pp. 48-67.

Clement, *Book of Recognitions* [http://www.essene.com/Recognitions/ Book9.htm]

Cocceianus, Cassius Dio. *Roman History.*

[http://penelope.uchicago.edu/Thayer/E/Roman/Texts/Cassius_Dio/ home.html].

Correia, Gaspar. *Lendas da India* ed. Rodrigo José de Lima Felner 4. vols. in 8 parts (Coimbra, 1860-66).

Curzon, George Nathaniel. *Persia and the Persian Question* 2 vols. (London, 1892).

Dandamayev, M. A. and Macuch, M. "Barda," *Encyclopedia Iranica.*

Daneshgah-e Tehran, *Sokhanraniha va Gozareshha dar nakhostin seminar-e bar-rasi-ye masa'el-e ejtema'i-ye shahr-e Tehran* (Tehran, 1343/1964).

Daneshpazhuh, Mohammad Taqi. "A'in-e Shah Tahmasp," *Barrasiha-ye Tarikhi* 7/1 (1351/1972), pp. 121-42.

Daneshvar, Mahmud. *Didaniha va Shenidaniha-ye Iran* 2 vols. (Tehran, 1327/1948).

Dankowitz, Aluma. "Pleasure Marriages in Sunni and Shi'ite Islam" (MEMRI, *Inquiry and Analysis Series - No. 291* (August 31, 2006). [http://memri.org/bin/articles.cgi?Page=archives&Area=ia&ID=IA29 106].

Darougar, S., Aramesh, B., Gibson, J. A., Treharne, J. D. and Jones, B. R. "Chlamydial genital infection in prostitutes in Iran." *British Journal of Venereal Diseases* 59/1 (1983), pp. 53-55.

Davis, Dick. "Women in the Shahnameh: exotics and natives, rebellious legends and dutiful histories," in *Women and Medieval Epic: gender, genre and the limits of epic masculanity,* ed. Sara S. Poor and Jana K. Schulman (New York, 2007), pp. 67-90.

———. *Vis and Ramin* (Washington DC: Mage, 2008).

Dehgan, Ebrahim ed., *Tarikh-e Safaviyan. Kholasat al-Tavarikh- Tarikh-e Molla Kamal* (Arak, 1334/1955).

Dehkhoda, 'Ali Akbar. *Loghat-nameh.*

Delavar M.A. and Hajian-Tilaki, K.O. "Age at menarche in girls born from 1985 to 1989 in Mazandaran, Islamic Republic of Iran," *Eastern Mediterranean Health Journal* 14/1 (2008) [http://www.emro.who.int/ Publications/EMHJ/1401/article9.htm].

Della Valle, Pietro. *Les Fameux Voyages* 4 vols. (Paris, 1663-64).

Dernschwam, *Hans Dernschwam's Tagebuch einer Reise nach Konstantinopel und Kleinasien,* ed. F. Babinger (Munich-Leipzig, 1923).

Dhahibi, Masih and Setudeh, Manuchehr. *Az Astara ta Astarabad* 10 vols. (Tehran, 1366/1987).

Dieulafoy, Jane. *La Perse ,la Chaldée et la Susiane* (Paris, 1887).

Djirsarai, Ali Akbar. *Das Dorf Ahar (Iran). Die bevölkerungs-, sozial-, und wirtschaftsgeographische Struktur und Entwicklung* (Bonn, 1970).

Donboli, 'Abdol-Razzaq Maftuni. *Tajrabat al-Ahrar va Tasliyeh al-Abrar* 2 vols. Hasan Qazi Tabataba'i ed. (Tehran, 1349/1970).

Don Juan of Persia, *A Shi'ah Catholic* translated into English by Guy Le Strange (New York-London, 1926).

Dönmez-Colin, Gönül. *Women, Islam and Cinema* (London, 2004).

Drew, P. E. "Iran," in R. T. Francoeur ed. *The International Encyclopedia of Sexuality* (New York, 2004).

Drouville, Gaspard. *Voyage en Perse pendant les années 1812 et 1813.* 2 vols. (Paris, 1819 [Tehran: Imp. Org. f. Social Services, 1976).

Dunlop, H. *Bronnen tot de geschiedenis der Oostindische Compagnie in Perzi'* (The Hague, 1930).

Dupré, A. *Voyage en Perse fait dans les années 1807, 1808, 1809,* 2 vols. (Paris, 1819).

Duran, Khalid. "Homosexuality in Islam." Homosexuality and World Religions. (Valley Forge, Pennsylvania: Trinity P International, 1993).

Duval, Rubens. *Les dialects néo-araméens de Salmas* (Paris, 1883).

Ebn Zarkub, *Shiraznameh* ed. I. Va'ez Javadi (Tehran, 1350/1971).

Echo of Iran, *Iran Almanac* 1964, 1965, 1969, 1972, 1976.

Eghtedari, Goudarz. *Islamic Republic of Iran and Execution for Adultery and Homosexuality.* [http://www.eghtedari.com/vome/hr/DP_Paper.pdf%22%20/t%20%22_blank]

Ehtesham al-Saltaneh, *Khaterat-e Ehtesham al-Saltaneh* (Tehran, 1366/1987).

Elgood, Cyril. *Safavid Medical Practice* (London, 1970).

———. "Translation of a Persian monograph on syphilis," *Annals of Medical History* 3/5 (1931), pp. 465-486.

Ende, Werner. "Ehe auf Zeit (*mut'ah*) in der innerislamischen Diskussion der gegenwart," *Die Welt des Islams* 20 (1980), pp. 1-43.

Eqbal Ashtiyani, 'Abbas. *Tarikh-e Moghul* (Tehran, 1347/1968).

Erdoğan, Sema Nilgün. *Sexual Life in Ottoman Society* (Istanbul. 2001).

Esfandabad, Hassan Shams and Emamipour, Suzan. "Prevalence of Wife Abuse,"*Pazhuhesh-e Zanan, A Quarterly Journal of The Center for Women's Studies*, 1/1 (2004).

Eshraqi, Ehsan. "Shah Soltan Hoseyn dar Tohfat al-'Alam," *Tarikh* 1/1 (2335/1976), pp. 90-91.

Esna-Ashari, Farah. "Differences in attitude towards premarital sex: The Impact of Some Demographic and Socio-Economic Factors in a Sample of Shiraz City Youth (Poster Session), 2005." [available via internet].

E'temad al-Saltaneh, Mirza Mohammad Hasan Khan. *Al-Ma'ather va'l-Athar* (Tehran, 1306/1889).

———. *Ruznameh-ye Khaterat-e E'temad al-Saltaneh* Iraj Afshar ed. (Tehran, 1345/1966).

———. *Khalsah*. ed. Mahmud Katira'i (Tehran, 1348/1969).

E'tesam al-Molk, *Safarnameh-ye Mirza Khanlar Khan E'tesam al-Molk*. ed. Manuchehr Mahmudi (Tehran, 1351/1972).

E'tezad al-Saltaneh, 'Ali Qoli Mirza. *Eksir al-Tavarikh* ed. Jamshid Kiyanfar (Tehran, 1370/1991).

'Eyn al-Saltaneh, Qahraman Mirza Salur. *Ruznameh-ye Khaterat-e 'Eyn al-Saltaneh* 9 vols. Iraj Afshar and Mas'ud Salur eds. (Tehran, 1374/1995).

E'zazi, Shahla. *Khoshunat-e khvanevadegi: Zanan-e kotak-khvordeh* (Tehran: Sali, 1380).

Faghfoory, Mohammad. "The Impact of Modernization on the Ulama in Iran, 1925-1941," *Iranian Studies* 26 (1993), pp. 277-312.

Falsafi, Nasrollah. *Zendegani-ye Shah 'Abbas-e Avval* 5 vols. (Tehran, 1332/1951).

———. *Chand Maqaleh-ye Tarikhi va Adabi* (Tehran, 1342).

Farid al-Molk, Mirza Mohammad 'Ali Khan. *Khaterat-e Farid* ed. Mas'ud Farid Qaragozlu (Tehran, 1353/1975).

Farmanfarma, 'Abdol-Hoseyn Mirza. *Siyaq-e ma'ishat dar 'ahd-e Qajar —Hokmrani va Molkdari* eds. Mansureh Ettehadiyeh and Sirus Sa'dvandiyan 2 vols. (Tehran, 1362/1983).

Farmanfarma'iyan, Sattareh. *Peyramun-e ruspigari dar shahr-e Tehran* (Tehran, 1349/1970).

Fasa' i, Hajj Mirza Hasan Hoseyni. *Farsnameh-ye Naseri.* 2 vols. ed. Mansur Rastgar Fasa'i (Tehran, 1378/1999).

Feuvrier, J.B. *Trois ans à la Cour de Perse* (Paris: F. Juven, 1900).

Fischer, Michael M. J. "On Changing the Concept and Position of Persian Women," in Lois Beck & Nikki Keddie eds. *Women in the Muslim World.* (Cambridge: Harvard University Press, 1979), pp. 189-215.

Fischer, Michael M.J. and Abedi, Mehdi. *Debating Muslims. Cultural Dialogues in Postmodernity and Tradition* (Madison, 1990).

Floor, Willem. "The office of muhtasib in Iran," *Iranian Studies*, vol. 18 (1985), pp. 53-74.

―――. "The Rise and Fall of Mirza Taqi, the Eunuch Grand Vizier (1043-55/1633-45)," *Studia Iranica* 26 (1997), pp. 237-66.

―――. *The Afghan Occupation of Safavid Persia 1721-1729* (Paris, 1998).

―――. *A Fiscal History of Iran in the Safavid and Qajar Periods 1500-1925* (New York, 1999).

―――. 'Art (*Naqqashi*) and Artists (*Naqqashan*) in Qajar Persia, *Muqarnas* 16 (1999), pp. 125-54.

―――. *The Economy of Safavid Persia* (Wiesbaden, 2000).

―――. *Safavid Government Institutions* (Costa Mesa, 2001).

―――. *Public Health in Qajar Iran* (Washington DC: Mage, 2004).

―――. "A Note on the Grand Vizierate in Seventeenth Century Persia," *ZDMG* 155 (2005), pp. 435-81.

Floor, Willem and Faghfoory, Mohammad. *Dastur al-Moluk, a Safavid State Manual* (Costa Mesa, 2007).

Forbes-Leith, A.C. *Checkmate and Fighting* (London, 1927).

Forsat Hoseyni Shirazi, *Ketab-e Athar-e 'Ajam* (Bombay, 1314 AH/1896-97).

Friedl, Erika. "Women in Contemporary Persian Folk Tales," in Lois Beck and Nikki Keddie eds. *Women in the Muslim World* (Cambridge, 1978), pp. 629-50.

————. "Women and the Division of Labor in an Iranian Village," *MERIP Reports* March/April, 95 (1981), pp. 12-18.

————. "Parents and children in a village in Iran," in A. Fathi, ed., *Women and the Family in Iran*. (Leiden, 1985), pp. 195-211.

————. *Women of Deh Koh* (Syracuse, 1989).

————. *Children of Deh Koh: young life in an Iranian village* (Syracuse, 1997).

Fryer, John. *A New Account of East India and Persia Being Nine Years' Travels, 1672-1681*, 3 vols. (London, 1909-15).

Garmrudi, Mirza Fattah Khan. *Safarnameh-ye Mirza Fattah Khan Garmrudi beh Orupa* ed. Fath al-Din Fattahi (Tehran, 1348/1969).

Gemelli Careri, Giovanni Francesco. *Giro del Mundo* 6 vols. (Naples, 1699).

Gignoux, Philippe. *Le Livre d'Arda Viraz*, transliteration and transcription of the Pahlavi text. Persian translation by Zhaleh Amouzegar (Paris-Tehran, 1984).

Ghaffari Kashani, Abu'l-Hasan. *Golshan-e Morad* ed. by Gholamreza Tabataba'i-Majd (Tehran, 1369/1990).

Ghaffari, Qazi Ahmad Qazvini. *Tarikh-e Jahanara* (Tehran 1343/1964).

Ghanaat, J., Sadeghian, A., Ghazvini, K. and Nassiri, M. R. "Prevalence and risk factors for hepatitis B virus infections among STD patients in northeast region of Iran." *Medical Science Monitor* 9/2 (2003), pp. 91-94.

al-Ghazzali, Abu Hamed Mohammad. *On Marriage.* translated by Muhammad Nur Abdus Salam (Chicago, 2002). [separately published chapter from al-Ghazzali's *Kimiya al-Sa'adat* or the Elixir of Happiness]

——. *On the Treatment of the Lust of the Stomach and the Sexual Organs.* translated by Muhammad Nur Abdus Salam (Chicago, 2002). [separately published chapter from al-Ghazzali's *Kimiya al-Sa'adat* or the Elixir of Happiness]

Gilmour, John. *Rapport sur la situation sanitaire de la Perse* (Geneva, League of Nations, 1924).

Givens, Benjamin P. and Hirschman, Charles. "Modernization and Consanguineous Marriage in Iran," *Journal of Marriage and the Family* 56 (1994), pp. 820-34.

Glünz, Michael. "The Sword, the Pen and the Phallus: Metaphors and the Metonymies of Male Power and Creativity in Medieval Persian Poetry," *Edebiyat* 6 (1995), pp. 223-43.

Gmelin, Samuel Gottlieb. *Travels through Northern Persia 1770-1774,* translated and annotated by Willem Floor (Washington DC, 2007).

Gobineau, A. de. *Trois Ans en Asie (de 1855 A 1858)* 2 vols. (Paris, 1923).

——. "Lettres Persanes," *Revue de la Littérature Comparée* (1952), p. 218.

Góis, Damião de. *Crónica de felicissimo rei D. Manuel.* 4 vols. (Coimbre, 1949-55).

Goldsmid, Sir Frederic J. et al. Eastern *Persia, An Account of the Journeys of the Persian Boundary Commission 1870-71-72,* 2 vols. (London, 1876).

Goodwin, J. *Price of Honor* (Boston, 1994).

Gouvea, António de. *Jornada do Arcebispo de Goa Dom Frey Aleixo de Meneses Primaz da India Oriental* (Coimbra, 1606).

Government of Great Britain, Naval Intelligence Division, *Persia. Geographic Handbook Series* (September, 1945).

——. *The Persian Gulf Trade Reports, Report on the Trade of Bushire ... 1920-21* 2 vols. (Gerrards Cross: Archive Editions, 1987).

Grenet, Frantz. *La geste d'Ardashir fils de Pabag* (Die, 2003).

Grothe, Hugo. *Wanderungen in Persien* (Berlin, 1910).

Gulbenkian, Roberto. *L'ambassade en Perse de Luis Pereira de Lacerda* (Lisbon, 1972).

Gulick J. and Gulick, M.E. "The domestic social environment of women and girls in Isfahan, Iran," in Lois Beck & Nikki Keddie eds. *Women in the Muslim World.* (Cambridge: Harvard University Press, 1979), pp. 501-557.

Gulick, J. *The Middle East: An Anthropological Perspective.* (Pacific Palisades, Calif., 1983).

Haberland, Detlef. *Von Lemgo nach Japan. Das ungewöhnliche Leben des Engelbert Kaempfer 1651 bis 1716* (Bielefeld, 1990).

Haeri, Shahla. *Law of Desire. Temporary Marriage in Shi'i Iran* (Syracuse, 1989).

Hakim-Olahi, Hedayatollah. *Ba man beh Shahr-e Now beya'id* 2 vols. (Tehran, 1326/1947).

Hamayesh-e melli-ye asibha-ye ejetam'i dar Iran, *Maqalat-e Avvalin Hamayesh-e Melli-ye Asibha-ye Ejtema'i dar Iran, Khordad 1381* 5 vols. (Tehran, 1386/2007), vol. 5.

Häntzsche, J.C. "Haram und Harem," *Zeitschrift für allgemeine Erdkunde* XIII (1862), pp. 375-434

———. "Spezialstatistik von Persien," *Zeitschrift der Gesellschaft für Erdkunde* 1869, pp. 429-50.

Hanway, Jonas. *An Historical Account of the British Trade over the Caspian Sea* (London, 1753).

Hedayat, Rezaqoli Khan. *Tarikh-e Rowzat al-Safa-ye Naseri* 10 vols. (Tehran, 1339/1960).

Heffening, W. "Mut'a," *Encyclopedia of Islam* 2.

Herbert, Thomas. *Travels in Persia, 1627-1629,* ed. W. Foster. (New York, 1929).

Herodotus, *Histories.*

Hendushah b. Sanjar al-Sahebi al-Kirani, *Tajareb al-Salaf dar Tarikh* ed. 'Abbas Eqbal (Tehran, 1344/1965).

Heytier, Adrienne Doris ed. *Les dépêches diplomatiques du comte de Gobineau en Perse* (Geneva, Paris, 1959).

Hejazi, Qodsiyeh. *Barrasi-ye jara'em-e zan dar Iran* (Tehran, 1341/1962; 2nd ed. 1357/1978).

Hojat, Mohammadreza; Shapurian, Reza; Nayerahmadi, Habib; Farzaneh, Mitra; Foroughi, Danesh; Parsi, Mohin and Azizi, Maryam. "Premarital Sexual, Child Rearing and Family Attitudes of Iranian Men and Women in the United States and in Iran," *Journal of Psychology* 133 (1999), pp. 19-31.

Höltzer, Ernst. *Persien vor 113 Jahren* (Tehran, 2535/1977).

Hommaire de Hell, X. *Voyage en Turquie et en Perse.* 2 vols. (Paris: P. Bertrand, 1856).

Honarfar, Lotfollah. *Ganjineh-ye Athar-e Tarikhi-ye Esfahan* (Esfahan, 1350).

Hotz, A. ed. *Reis van de gezant der O.I. Compagnie Joan Cunaeus naar Perzi' in 1651-1652* (Amsterdam, 1908).

Houssay, F. "La structure de sol et son influence sur la vie des hommes. Etudes sur la Perse méridionale 1885-6, " *Annales de Géographie* 3 (1894), p. 293.

Houtum-Schindler, A. "Notes on Persian Baluchistan. From the Persian of Mirza Mehdi Khan," *JRAS* 1876, pp. 147-154.

———. "Reisen in südlichen Persien 1879," *Zeitschrift der Gesellschaft für Erdkunde zu Berlin* 16 (1881), pp. 307-66.

Howard, I. K. A. "Mut'a marriage reconsidered in the context of the formal procedures for Islamic marriage," *Journal of Semitic Studies* 20/1 (1075), pp. 82-92.

Hume-Griffith, M.E. *Behind the Veil in Persia and Turkish Arabia* (Philadelphia, 1909).

Iarric Tolosain, P. Pierre du. *L'histoire des choses plus memorables advenues tant ez Indes Orientales, qu'autres pais de la descouverte des Portugais* 2 vols. (Bovrdeavs, 1610-14).

Ibn al-Athir, *Kamil f'il-Tarikh* 15 vols. ed. C. J. Tornberg (Leiden, 1885).

Ivanov, W. "Notes on the Ethnology of Khurasan," *Geographic Journal* (1926), pp. 143-58.

Izedpenah, Hamid. *Athar-e Bastani va Tarikhi-ye Lorestan* 2 vols. (Tehran, 1363).

Ja'fariyan, Rasul. "Amr beh ma'ruf va nahi az monkar dar dowreh-ye Safaviyeh" in Ibid., *Maqalat-e Tarikhi* 5 vols. (Qom, 1378/1999), vol. 5, pp. 19-26.

————. "Tarikh-e mas'aleh-ye ghana dar dowreh-ye Safaviyeh," in Ibid., *Safaviyeh dar 'arseh-ye din, farhang va siyasat* 3 vols. (Qom,1379/2000), vol. 2, pp. 697-722.

Ja'fariyan, Rasul ed., *Mirath-e Eslami-ye Iran* 10 vols. (Qom, 1373/1994).

Jahed, Amir. *Salnameh-ye Pars* (Tehran, 1926-41). Also with the title *Salnameh-ye Rasmi-ye Mamlekat.*

James, Lionel. *Side-Tracks & Bridle-Paths* (Edinburgh-London, 1909).

Janqoli, Mostafa. "Barrasi-ye vaziyat-e kudakan-e khiyabani," in *Maqalat,* vol. 5, pp. 119-41.

al-Jahiz, *Nine Essays of al-Jahiz* translated by William H. Hutchins (New York, 1989).

Javadi, Hasan. *Satire in Persian Literature* (Cranbury, NJ-London, 1988).

Javadi, Hasan and Selleé, Susan. *Another Birth. Selected Poems of Forugh Farrokhzad* (Emeryville, CA, 1981).

Javadi, Hasan; Mar'ashi, Manzheh and Shakarlu, Simin eds. *Ruyaru'i-ye zan va mard dar 'asr-e Qajar. Du resaleh. Ta'dib al-Nesvan va Ma'ayeb al-Rejal* (Bethesda, 1371/1992).

Jewett, Mary. *Reminiscences of My Life in Persia* (Cedar Rapids, 1909).

Jones-Brydges, Hardford ed., *The Dynasty of the Kajars* (London, 1833).

Josephus, Flavius. *Wars of the Jews.* [http://www.interhack.net/projects/library/wars-jews/b1c13.html]

————. *Judean Antiquities.* [http://classics.mit.edu/Josephus/j.aj.html]

Jozani, Niloufar. *La Beauté Menacée* (Paris-Tehran: IFRI, 1994).

Justinus, Marcus Junianus. *Epitome of the Philippic History of Pompeius Trogus*, translated, with notes, by the Rev. John Selby Watson. (London: Henry G. Bohn, 1853).

Juvaini, 'Ata Malik. *The History of the World Conquerer* translated by John Andrew Boyle 2 vols. (Manchester, 1958).

Juynboll, G. H. A. "Sihaka," in *EI²*.

Kaempfer, Engelbert. *Amoenitatum Exoticarum. Fasciculi V, Variae Relationes, Observationes & Descriptiones Rerum Persicarum* (Lemgo 1712 [1976]).

———. *Am Hofe des persischen Grosskönigs*, translated by Walther Hinz (Leipzig, 1940).

Kai Ka'us b. Iskandar, *A mirror for princes, the Qabus Nama*, translated into English by Reuben Levy (London, 1951).

Kamshad, H. *Modern Persian Prose Literature* (Cambridge, 1966).

Kazemi, Mortaza Shafaq. *Ruzegar va Andisheh* 3 vols. (Tehran, 1350/1971).

Kellermann, Bernard. *Auf Persiens Karawanen Strassen* (Berlin, 1928).

Keyhan-niya, A. *Zan-e emruz, Mard-e diruz! Tahlili bar ekhelafat-e zanashavin* (Tehran, 1376/1997).

Khaleghi-Motlagh, Djalal. "Erotic literature," *Encyclopaedia Iranica*.

Kharratha, Sa'id. "Ruspigari dar mahalleh-ye Ghorbat," in *Maqalat*, vol. 5, pp. 61-92.

Khashayar, Reza. *'Elal-e ruspigari dar Iran* (Tehran, 1359/1380).

Khomeyni, Ruhollah. *Tahrir al-Wasila* 2 vols. (Qom, 1404 hijri/1984).

———. *Towzih al-Masa'el* ed. Moslem Qolipur Gilani (Qom, 1385/2006).

Khosrovi, Khosrow. "Tahqiqi dar bareh-ye jorm-e zanan dar Tehran," *Masa'el-e Iran* 1/9 (1342/1963), pp. 343-47.

Khu'i, Amin al-Shar'. "Safarnameh-ye 'Atabat," ed. 'Ali Sadra'i Khu'i in Rasul Ja'fariyan ed. *Mirath-e Eslam dar Iran* 10 vols. (Qom, 1373-78/1994-99), vol. 7, pp. 489-530.

Khvandamir, Ghiyath al-Din. *Tarikh-e Habib al-Siyar* 4 vols. ed. Mohammad Dabir-Siyaqi (Tehran, 1362/1983).

Khvansari, Aqa Jamal. *Resaleh-ye 'Aqayed al-Nesa' mashhur beh Kolthum Naneh* ed. Mahmud Katira'i (Tehran, 1349/1970).

al-Kirani, Hendushah b. Sanjar al-Sahebi. *Tajareb al-Salaf dar Tarikh* ed. 'Abbas Eqbal (Tehran, 1344/1965).

Kotbi, Mahmud. *Tarikh-e Al-e Mozaffar* ed. 'Abdol-Hoseyn Nava'i (Tehran, 1364/1985).

Kotov, F.A. *Khozhenie kuptsa Fedota Kotova* ed. N.A. Kuznetsova (Moscow 1958), translated into English by P.M. Kemp, as *Russian Travellers to India and Persia [1624-1798] Kotov-Yefremov-Danibegov* (Delhi 1959).

Kuhan, Gu'el. *Tarikh-e sansur dar matbu'at-e Iran* 2 vols. (Tehran, 1362/1983).

Kushesh VIII (1930), nrs. 310, 311, 312, 314, 315, 316, 318. (newspaper).

Ladier-Fouladi, Marie. "The Fertility Transition in Iran," *Population: An English Selection* 9 (1997), pp. 191-213.

Lammens, P.H. *La cité arabe de Taif à la vieille de l'hégire* (Beyrouth, 1922).

———. *Le Mecque à la vieille de l'hégire* (Beyrouth, 1924).

Landor, E. Henry. *Across Coveted Lands* 2 vols. (New York: Scribners, 1903).

Layard, A. H. *Early Adventures in Persia, Susiana, and Babylonia* (London, 1894 [Westmead: Gregg Int., 1971]).

Lazard, Gilbert. *Les premiers poètes persanes* (Paris, 1964).

Le Bruyn, Cornelius. *Travels into Moscovy, Persia and part of the East-Indies*, 2 vols. (London, 1737).

L. Leupe ed., "Beschrijvinge van de coninclijcke stadt Spahan," in Ibid., "Stukken over den handel van Perzi' en de Golf van Bengalen, 1634," *Kronijk van het Historisch Genootschap gevestigd te Utrecht* X (1854), pp. 191-208.

Levy, Reuben. *The Sociology of Islam* (London, 1957).

Lindisfarne, Nancy. "Variant Masculinities, Variant Virginities: Rethinking 'Honour and Shame," in *Dislocating Masculinity: Comparative Ethnographies*, eds. Andrea Cornwall and Nancy Lindisfarne (London, 1994), pp. 82-96.

Lockyer, Charles. *An Account of British Trade in India* (London, 1711).

Loeb, Lawrence. *Outcaste - Jewish Life in Southern Iran* (New York, 1977).

Lorey, Eustace de and Sladen, Douglas. *Queer Things About Persia* (Philadelphia-London: J.B. Lippincot Co, 1907).

————. *The Moon of the Fourteenth Night: Being the Private Life of an Unmarried Diplomat in Persia during the Revolution* (London: Hurst & Blacket, 1910).

Lumsden, *A Journey from Meerut in India to London in the Years 1819 and 1820* (London, 1822).

Lycklama à Nijeholt, T. M. *Voyage en Russie, au Caucase et en Perse* 4 vols. (Paris-Amsterdam, 1872).

MacBean-Ross, Elizabeth N. *A Lady Doctor in Bakhtiari Land* (London, 1921).

Mafi, Hoseyn Qoli Khan Nezam al-Saltaneh. *Khaterat* [...] 2 vols. Ma'sumeh Nezam-Mafi, Mansureh Ettehadiyeh, Sirus Sa'dvandiyan and Hamid Ram-pisheh eds (Tehran, 1361/1982).

Maghen, Ze'ev. *Virtues of the flesh: passion and purity in early Islamic jurisprudence* (Leiden, 2005).

Mahdavi, Mo'ezz al-Din. *Dastanha'i az panjah sal* (Tehran, 1348/1969).

Mahmud Mirza, *Safinat al-Mahmud* ed. 'Abdol-Rasul Khayyampur (Tabriz, 1347/1968).

Mahvash, *Asrar-e Magu* (Tehran, n.d.).

————. *Raz-e kamyabi-ye jensi* (Tehran, 1336/1957).

Majd al-Molk, Mohammad Khan. *Kashf al-Ghara'eb mashur beh Resaleh-ye Majdiyeh* ed. Fazlollah Gorgani (Tehran, 1358/1979).

Majlesi, Mohammad Baqer b. Mohammad Taqi. *Bihar al-Anwar* 44 vols. (Beyruth, 2001).

Malcolm, John. *The History of Persia.* 2 vols. (London, 1820 [Tehran, 1976]).

Malcolm, Napier. *Five Years in a Persian Town* (London: John Murray, 1905).

Malekzadeh, Mehdi. *Tarikh-e Enqelab-e mashrutiyat-e Iran* 7 vols. (Tehran, 1328/1949).

Maqrizi, Ahmad b. 'Ali. *Histoire des sultans mamlouks de l'Egypte* 2 vols. in 4 ed. Etienne Quatremère (Paris, 1837-45).

Markwart, J. *Eranshahr nach der Geographie des ps. Moses Xorenacci* (Berlin, 1901).

Massé, Henri. *Croyances et Coutumes Persanes* 2 vols. (Paris: Maisonneuve, 1938).

al-Mawardi, *al-Ahkam al-Sultaniyya w'al-Wilayat al-Diniyya* translated into English by Wafaa H. Wahba as *The Ordinances of Government* (Reading, 2006).

Mehryar, Amir, Mostafavi, F., and Agha, Homa. "Men and Family Planning in Iran"

[http://www.iussp.org/Brazil2001/s20/S22_P05_Mehryar.pdf]

Meisami, Julie Scott. *The Sea of Virtues (Bahr al-Fava'id) A Medieval Islamic Mirror for Princes* (Salt Lake City: Utah UP, 1991).

———. "The Body as Garden; Nature and Sexuality in Persian Poetry," *Edebiyat* 6 (1995), pp. 245-74.

Merritt-Hawkes, O. A. *Persia. Romance & Reality* (London, 1935).

Mervi, Mohammad Kazem. *'Alamara-ye Naderi* 3 vols. ed. Mohammad Amin Riyahi (Tehran, 1369/1990).

Mez, Adam. *Die Renaissance des Islam* (Hildesheim, 1968).

Milani, Farzaneh. *Veils and Words. The emerging voices of Iranian women writers* (Syracuse, 1992).

Miller, Janet. *Camel-Bells of Baghdad* (Boston-New York, 1934).

Minorsky, Vladimir. *Hudud al-Alam, 'The Regions of the World': a Persian geography 372 [A.]H.-982 A.D.* (London, 1937).

————. "Vis u Ramin, a Parthian Romance," *Bulletin of the School of Oriental and African Studies, University of London* 11/4 (1946), pp. 741-763.

————. "The Aq-Qoyunlu and Land Reforms," *Bulletin of the School of Oriental and African Studies* 17/3 (1955), pp. 449-62.

————. *Calligraphers and Painters. A treatise by Qadi Ahmad, Son of Mir-Munshi (circa A.H. 1015/A.D. 1606)* (Washington, 1959).

————. "Vis and Ramin: A Parthian Romance," in Ibid., *Iranica. Twenty Articles* (Tehran, 1964), pp. 741-763.

————. *The Tadhkirat al-Muluk, A Manual of Safavid Administration.* (Cambridge, 1980).

Minovi, Mojtaba. *Naqd-e Hal* (Tehran, 1351/1972).

Mir-Hosseini, Ziba. *Marriage on trial: Islamic family law in Iran and Morocco* (London, 2000).

Mir Khvand, Mohammad b. Khavandshah. *Tarikh-e Rowzat al-Safa* 10 vols. (Tehran, 1339/1960).

Moghith al-Saltaneh, Yusof. *Namehha-ye Yusof Moghith al-Saltaneh* ed. by Ma'sumeh Mafi (Tehran, 1362/1983).

Mohammadi, Mohammad R. et al., "Reproductive Knowledge, Attitudes and Behavior Among Adolescent Males in Tehran, Iran," *International Family Planning Perspectives* 32, no. 1 (2006), pp. 35-44.

Mohebbi, M. R. "Female sex workers and fear of stigmatization," *Sexually Transmitted Infections 81 (*2005), pp. 180-181.

Mokhber al-Saltaneh, Mehdi Qoli Hedayat, *Khaterat va Khatarat* (Tehran, 1344/1965).

Momeni, Djamchid A. "The Difficulties of Changing the Age at Marriage in Iran," *Journal of Marriage & Family* 34/3 (1972), pp. 545-51.

————. "Polygyny in Iran," *Journal of Marriage and Family* May 1975, pp. 453-56.

Momtahen al Dowleh, Mirza Mehdi Khan. *Khaterat [...]* ed. Hoseyn Qoli Khanshaqaqi (Tehran, 1353/1974).

Monajjem, Molla Jalal al-Din. *Ruznameh-ye 'Abbasi ya Ruznameh-ye Molla Jalal*, ed. Seyfollah Vahidniya (Tehran, 1366/1967).

Monshi, Eskander Beyg. *Tarikh-e 'Alamara-ye 'Abbasi*. Iraj Afshar ed. 2 vols. (Tehran, 1350/1971).

Monshi-ye Kermani, Naser al-Din. *Semt al-Ola lel-Hezrat al-'Oliya dar Tarikh-e Qarakhati'iyan-e Kerman* ed. 'Abbas Eqbal (Tehran, 1328/1949).

Moosa, Matti. *Extreme Shiites. The Ghulat Sects* (Syracuse, 1988).

Momtahen al-Dowleh, *Khaterat-e Momtahen al-Dowleh* ed. Hoseynqoli Khan-Shaqaqi (Tehran, 1353/1974).

Morier, James. *A Second Journey through Persia, Armenia, and Asia Minor ... between the years 1810 and 1816* (London, 1818).

Morton, Rosalie Slaughter. *A Doctor's Holiday* (New York, 1941).

Moser, Henri. *A Travers l'Asie Centrale* (Paris, 1885).

Mostowfi, 'Abdollah. *Sharh-e Zendegani-ye Man* 3 vols. (Tehran, n.d.).

Mousavi, M. and Eshagian, A., "Wife abuse in Esfahan, Islamic Republic of Iran, 2002," 11/5 & 6 (September, 2005) *Eastern Mediterranean Health Journal*, pp. 860-69; [http://www.emro.who.int/Publications/EMHJ/1105_6/Artical1.htm]

Müller Max ed. *Sacred Books of the East* (New York, 1898).

al-Muqadassi, Muhammad b. Ahmad. *Kitab ahsan al-taqasim fi ma'rifat al-taqalim* ed. M.J. de Goeje (Leiden, 1906).

Murata, Sachiko. *Temporary Marriage in Islamic Law* (MA thesis Tehran University 1974); for the electronic version of this study see [http://www.al-islam.org/al-serat/muta/]).

Murray, Stephen O. and Roscoe, Will. *Islamic homosexualities: culture, history, and literature* (New York, 1997).

Musallam, B. F. *Sex and Society in Islam: Birth Control before the Nineteenth Century* (Cambridge, 1986).

Muslim, *Sahih*. [http://www.usc.edu/dept/MSA/reference/reference.html]

al-Nadim, Abu al-Faraj Muhammad b. Ishaq b. Muhammad b. Ishaq. *Kitab al- Fihrist*, translated into English by Bayard Dodge as *The Fihrist of al-Nadim: A Tenth-Century Survey of Muslim Culture* (New York, 1970).

Nahid VIII (newspaper. issues from 1928 and 1929).

Najm ol-Molk, 'Abdol-Ghaffar. *Safarnameh-ye Khuzestan*. ed. Mohammad Dabir-Siyaqi (Tehran, 1342/1963).

Nakhaee, F. H. "Prisoners' knowledge of HIV/AIDS and its prevention in Kerman, Islamic Republic of Iran." *East Mediterranean Health Journal* 6, 8 November 2002, pp. 725-31.

Nakhjavani, Hajj Hoseyn. "Masjed-e jame'-ye Tabriz va sharh-e katibehha-ye an," *Nashriyeh-ye Daneshkadeh-ye Adabiyat-e Tabriz* 6/1 (1333/1964), pp. 32-41.

Nakhjevani, Mohammad b. Hendushah. *Dastur al-katib fi ta'yin al-maratib* 2 vols. in 3 A.A. Ali-zadeh ed. (Moscow, 1964).

Naqvi, Ali Reza. "The Marriage Laws of Iran (II)," *Islamic Studies* 7/2-4 (1968).

Narshakhi, *The History of Bukhara* translated into English by Richard Frye (Cambridge, 1954).

Nashat, Guity and Beck, Lois eds. *Women in Iran. From the rise of Islam to 1800* (Chicago, 2003).

Nasiri, Mohammad Ebrahim b. Zeyn al-'Abedin. *Dastur-e Shahriyan*. ed. Mohammad Nader Nasiri Moqaddam (Tehran, 1373/1995).

Nasrabadi, Mirza Mohammad Taher. *Takhkereh-ye Nasrabadi*. ed. Vahid Dastgerdi (Tehran, 1361/1982).

Nassehi-Behnam, Vida. "Change and the Iranian Family," *Current Anthropology*, 26/5 (1985), pp. 557-62.

Nava'i, 'Abdol-Hoseyn ed. *Asnad va Makateb-e Tarikhi-ye Iran az Timur ta Shah Esma'il* (Tehran, 1341/1962).

———. *Asnad va Makateb-e Tarikhi-ye Iran az sal-e 1038 ta 1105* (Tehran, 1360).

Nava'i, 'Ali Shir - Hakim Qazvini, *Majales al-Nafa'es* ed. 'Ali Asghar Hekmat (Tehran, 1334/1945).

Nazem al-Eslam Kermani, *Tarikh-e Bidari-ye Iraniyan* 3 vols. Sa'id Sirjani ed. (Tehran, 1346/1967).

Neligan, A. R. "Public Health in Persia. 1914-24," *The Lancet* Part II, 27 March 1926, p. 690-94.

Neville, Ralph. *Unconventional Memories* (New York, 1923).

Nezami, Aruzi. *Chahar Maqaleh* ed. Mirza Mohammad Qazvini (London, 1927).

Nizam al-Mulk, *The Book of Government or Rules for Kings* translated into English by Herbert Darke (London, 1960).

Norden, Hermann. *Under Persian Skies* (Philadelphia, [1928]).

Nowruzeh, Ali. "Essai de bibliographie persane," *Revue du Monde Musulmane* 60 (1925), pp. 29-34.

Nystrom, P. *Fem År i Persien som gendarmofficer* (Stockholm, 1925).

Oberhelman, Steven M. "Hierarchies of Gender, ideology, and Power in Ancient and Medieval Greek and Arabic Dream Literature," in J.W. Wright Jr and Everett K. Rowson eds. *Homoeroticism in Classical Arabic Literature* (New York, 1997), pp. 55-93.

'Obeyd-e Zakani, *Resaleh-ye Delgosha* ed. 'Ali Asghar Halabi (Tehran, 1383/2004).

————. *The Ethics of Aristocrats and Other Satirical Stories*, translated into English by Hasan Javadi (Washington, DC, 2007).

Olearius, Adam. *Vermehrte newe Beschreibung der moscowitischen und persischen Reyse*, ed. D. Lohmeier (Schleswig, 1656 [Tübingen, 1971]).

Otter, Jean. *Voyage en Turquie et en Perse* (Paris, 1748) translated into Persian by 'Ali Eqbali as *Safarnameh-ye Zhan Uter* (Tehran, 1363/1984).

William Ouseley, *Travels in various countries of the East; more particularly Persia* 3 vols. (London, 1819).

Overseas Consultants, *Report on seven year development plan for the Plan Organization of the Imperial Government of Iran* 5 vols. (New York, 1949).

Paidar, Parvin. *Women and the Political process in Twnetienth century in Iran* (Cambridge, 1995).

Pakezegi, Behnaz. "Legal and Social Positions of Iranian Women," in Lois Beck and Nikki Keddie eds. *Women in the Muslim World* (Cambridge, 1978), pp. 216-26.

Papoli-Yazdi, Mohammad Hoseyn *Khaterat-e Shahzdah-e Hammam* (Mashhad, 1384/2005).

Perkins, Justin. *A Residence of Eight Years in Persia* (Andover, 1843).

Perry, John R. *Karim Khan Zand, A History of Iran, 1747-1779* (Chicago, 1979).

Petrosian, Angela; Shayan, Kazem; Bash, K.W. and Bruce Jessup. *The Health and related characteristics of four selected villages and tribal communities in Fars Ostan, Iran* (Shiraz, April 1964).

Pigulevskaia, N. *Les Villes de l'Etat Iranien aux epoques Parthe et Sassanide* (The Hague-Paris, 1963).

Pires, Tomé. *The Suma Oriental of Tomé Pires, an account of the East, from the Red Sea to Japan, written in Malacca and India in 1511-1515* translated and edited by Armando Cortesão 2 vols. (London, 1944).

Plutarch, *Life of Crassus* [on line edition].

———. *De Malignitate Herodoti,* translated into English by Anthony Bowen as *The Malice of Herodotus* (Warminster, 1992).

Polak, J.E. "Ueber die Syphilis in Persien," *Zeitschrift der Gesellschaft der Aertzte in Wien* (1857).

"Ueber den Gebrauch des Quecksilbers in Persien," *Wiener Medizinische Wochenschrift* 10 (1860), pp. 564-68.

———. "Die Prostitution in Persien", *Wiener Medicinische Wochenschrift* 32 (1861), pp. 516-17, 563-65, 627-29.

———. *Persien. Das Land und seine Bewohner* 2 vols. (Leipzig, 1865).

Ponafidine, Pierre. *Life in the Moslem East* (New York, 1911).

Porter, Robert Kerr. *Travels in Georgia, Persia, Armenia, Ancient Babylonia* 2 vols. (London, 1821).

Procopius *The Secret Histories*, translated by G.A. Williamson, (Harmondsworth, Penguin, 1981).

Qazvini, 'Ali Shir Nava'i-Hakim. *Majales al-Nafa'es* ed. 'Ali Asghar Hekmat (Tehran, 1334/1945).

Qazvini, Mohammad. *Yaddashtha-ye Qazvini*, Iraj Afshar ed. 8 vols. (Tehran, 1339/1960).

Qazvini, Mohammad Shafi'. *Qanun-i Qazvini*. ed. Iraj Afshar (Tehran, 1370/1991).

Qodsi, Hasan A'zam. *Ketab-e Khaterat-e Man* 2 vols. (Tehran, 1342/1963).

al-Qomi, Qazi Ahmad ibn Sharaf al-Din al-Hoseyn al-Hoseyni. *Kholasat al-Tavarikh*, 2 vols., ed. Ehsan Eshraqi. (Tehran, 1363/1984).

Querry, A. *Droit musulman. Receuil des lois concernant les musulmans-schyites* 2 vols. (Paris, 1871-72).

Seif Rabiee, Mohammad Ali, Tehrani, Fahimeh Ramezani and Hatmi, Zinat Nadiya. "Wife Abuse and Related Factors," *Pazhuhesh-e Zanan, A Quarterly Journal of The Center for Women's Studies*, 1/4 (2002).

Rabino, H. L. *Mazandaran and Astarabad* (London, 1928).

Raghib Esfahani, Abu'l-Qasem Hoseyn b. Mohammad. *Navader - Mohazarat al-Odaba va Mohavarat al-Sho'ara va'l-Bolagha*; translated into Persian by Mohammad Saleh b. Mohammad Baqer Qazvini edited by Ahmad Mojahed (Tehran, 1372/1993).

Ramezani-Tehrani, F., Khalaj Abadi Farahani, F. and Hasemi, M.S. "Factors influencing contraceptive use in Tehran," *Family Practice* 18/2 (2001), pp. 204-08.

Rashad, Hoda; Osman, Magued and Roudi-Fahimi, Farzaneh. *Marriage in the Arab World* (Washington, DC: Population Reference Bureau, 2005).

Rashid al-Din, *Jame' al-Tavarikh* 2 vols ed. Bahman Karimi (Tehran, 1362/1983).

————. *Geschichte Ghazan-Khan's* ed. Karl Jahn (London, 1940).

Rasokh, Shahpur. "Sokhani-ye chand dar bareh-ye hara'em-e zan," *Masa'el-e Iran* 3/4-5 (1344/1965), pp. 103-08.

Ravandi, Mohammad b. 'Ali. *Rahat al-Sodur fi Ayat al-Surur* ed. Mojtaba Minovi (London, 1921).

Ravandi, Morteza. *Tarikh-e Ejtema'i-ye Iran* 9 vols. (Tehran, 1368/1987).

Razi, Fakhir-al-din. *al-Tafsir al-kabir* 32 vols. (Cairo, 1934-1962).

————. "Treatise on the cause and treatment of passive homosexual desire *Risalah fi'l-Ubnah*," translated by Franz Rosenthal, *Bulletin of the History of Medicine* 52 (1978), pp. 45-60. For the electronic version see [http://www.well.com/user/aquarius/ubnah.htm].

Rebelo, N. Orta de. *Un voyageur portugais en Perse au début du XVII siècle* ed. J. Ver'ssimo Serrão (Lisbon, 1972).

Reed, David. "The Persian Boy Today," in Schmitt and Sofer, *Sexuality*, pp. 61-66.

Rego, António da Silva ed., *Documentação para a história das missões do padroado português do Oriente* 12 vols. (Lisbon, 1947-58).

Reza'i, Ensiyeh Sheykh and Azari, Shahla. *Gozareshha-ye Nazmiyeh az Mahallat-e Tehran* 2 vols. (Tehran 1377/1998).

Rice, Clara C. *Mary Bird in Persia* (London, 1916).

————. *Persian Women and Their Ways* (London, 1923).

Rich, Claudius James. *Narrative of a Residence in Koordistan* 2 vols. (London, 1836).

Richard, Francis ed., *Raphael du Mans, missionnaire en Perse au XVIIè s.* 2 vols. (Paris, 1995).

Ritter, Helmut. *Das Meer der Seele; Mensch, Welt und Gott in den Geschichten des Farid uddin 'Attar* (Leiden, 1955).

Rochechouart, Julien de. *Souvenirs d'un Voyage en Perse* (Paris, 1867).

Roemer, Hans Robert. *Staatsschreiben der Timuridenzeit* (Wiesbaden, 1952).

Röhrborn, Klaus-Michael. *Provinzen und Zentralgewalt Persiens im 16. und 17. Jahrhundert* (Berlin 1966).

Romano, "Viaggio d'un mercante che fu nella Persia," in Giovanni Battista Ramusio, *Navigazioni e Viaggi* ed. Marica Milanesi (Turin, 1978) vol. 3, pp. 425-79.

Roschan-Zamir, Mehdi. *Die Zand-Dynastie* (Hamburg, 1970).

El-Rouayheb, Khaled. *Before Homosexuality in the Arab-Islamic World, 1500–1800* (Chicago, 2005).

Rowson, Evereth. K. "Homosexuality in Islamic Law," *Encyclopedia Iranica*.

———. "The Categorization of Gender and Sexual Irregularity in Medieval Arabic Vice Lists," in Julia Epstein and Kristina Straub eds. *Body Guards: The Cultural Politics of Ambiguity* (New York-London, 1991), pp. 50-79.

———. "Gender Irregularity as Entertainment: Institutionalized Transvestism at the Caliphal Court in Medieval Baghdad," in *Gender and Difference in the Middle Ages*, eds. Sharon Farmer and Carol Braun Pasternack (Minneapolis, 2003), pp. 45-72.

Rumlu, Hasan. *Ahsan al-Tavarikh* ed. 'Abdol-Hoseyn Nava'i (Tehran, 1349/1970).

Rydelius, Ellen. *Pilgrim i Persien* (Stockholm, 1941).

Saad, Dr. "La frontiere turco-persane et les pelerins de Kerbela," *Journal asiatique* V (1885), pp. 532-47.

Saba, Fath 'Ali Khan. *Divan-e Ash'ar* ed. Mohammad 'Ali Nejati (Tehran, 1341/1962).

Sabir, 'Ali Akbar. *HopHop-Nameh* translated into Persian by Ahmad Shafa'i (Baku, 1962).

Sa'di, *Golestan*, in the translation by Richard Burton

[http://www.enel.ucalgary.ca/People/far/hobbies/iran/Golestan/]

Sadr, Mohsen. *Khaterat-e Sadr al-Ashraf* (Tehran, 1364/1985).

Sa'edi, Gholam-Hossein. *Dandil. Stories from Iranian Life* (New York, 1981).

Safa, Dhabihollah. *Tarikh-e Adabiyat-e Iran* 5 vols. (Tehran, 1371/1992).

Safa-Isfahani, Kaveh. "Female-Centered World Views in Iranian Culture: Symbolic Representations of Sexuality in Dramatic Games," *Signs* 6/1 (1980), pp. 33ñ53.

Safar, Baba. *Ardabil dar Godhargah-e Tarikh* 3 vols. (Tehran, 1350-62/1971-83).

Sahhaf-bashi, Ebrahim. *Safarnameh-ye Ebrahim Sahhaf-bashi* ed. Mohammad Moshiri (Tehran, 1357/1978).

Saleh, 'Ali Reza. "Moqayeseh-ye kudakan-e khiyabani va shabanehruzihaye Tehran," in *Maqalat*, pp. 143-70.

Samarqandi, Kamal al-Din 'Abdol-Razzaq. *Matla'-ye Sa'deyn va Majma'-ye Bahreyn* 2 vols. ed. 'Abdol-Hoseyn Nava'i (Tehran, 1353/1974).

Sam Mirza, *Tadhkereh-ye Tohfat-e Sami* ed. Rokn al-Din Homayunfarrokh (Tehran, n.d.).

Sanson, M. *The present state of Persia* (London, 1695).

Sayyah, Hajj. *Khaterat-e Hajj Sayyah ya Dowreh-ye Khowf va Vahshat* ed. Hamid Sayyah (Tehran, 1347/1968).

Schacht, J. "Nikah," *Encyclopedia of Islam*2.

Schlimmer, Joh. L. *Terminologie Médico-Pharmaceutique: Française - Persane* (Tehran, 1874 [Tehran: Daneshgah, 1970]).

Schmitt, Arno. "Different Approaches to Male-Male Sexuality/Eroticism from Morocco to Usbekistan," in Arno Schmit and Jehoeda Sofer eds., *Sexuality and Eroticism Among males in Moslem Societies* (London-New York, 1992), pp. 14-18.

Schneider, Irene. *The Petitioning System in Iran. State, Society and Power Relations in the Late 19th Century* (Wiesbaden, 2006).

Schwarz, Paul. *Iran im Mittelalter nach den arabischen Geographen* 7 vols. (Leipzig, 1929).

Schwartz, Benjamin ed., *Letters from Persia. Written by Charles and Edward Burgess 1828-1855* (New York, 1942).

Sedghi, Hamideh. *Women and Politics in Iran. Veiling, Unveiling, and Reveiling* (Cambridge, 2007).

Sepehr, 'Abdol-Hoseyn Khan. *Mer'at al-Vaqaye'-ye Mozaffari va Yaddahstha-ye Malek al-Mo'arrekhin* 2 vols. in one. ed. 'Abdol-Hoseyn Nava'i (Tehran, 1368/1989).

Sepehr, Mohammad Taqi Lesan al-Molk. *Nasekh al-Tavarikh-e Qajariyeh* 3 vols. in 2 ed. Jamshid Kiyanpur (Tehran, 1377/1998)

Serena, Carla. *Hommes et Choses en Perse* (Paris: G. Charpentier, 1883).

Setareh-ye Jahan (newspaper) various issues from 1925-1929.

Shahri, Ja'far. *Tarikh-e ejtema'i-ye Tehran dar qarn-e sizdahom,* 6 vols. (Tehran, 1368/1989).

———. *Tehran-e Qadim* 5 vols. (Tehran, 1371/1992).

Shah Esma'il Safavi, *Tadhkereh.* ed. 'Abdol-Shokur (Berlin 1343/1925).

Shaki, Mansour. "Divorce," *Encyclopedia Iranica.*

Shamisa, Sirus. *Shahed-bazi dar adabiyat-e farsi* (Tehran, 1381/2002).

Shapurian, Reza and Hojat, Mohammadreza. "Sexual and Premarital Attitudes of. Iranian College Students" *Psychological Reports,* 1985, pp. 67-74.

Shavardi, Tahmineh. "Negahi beh vaz'iyat-e kudakan-e khiyabani dar Iran; 'elal va 'avamel-an," in *Maqalat,* vol. 5, pp. 101-17.

Shay, Anthony. "*Bazi-ha-ye Namayeshi*: Iranan Women's Theatrical Plays," *Dance Research Journal* 27/2/ (1995), pp. 16-24.

Sheil, Lady. *Glimpses of Life and Manners in Persia* (London, 1856 [New York: Arno, 1973]).

Shekufeh beh enzemam-e Danesh. Nakhostin nashriyehha-ye zanan-e Iran (Tehran: Ketabkhaneh-ye Melli, 1377/1998). (newspaper)

Sherley, Anthony. *Anthony Sherley and His Persian Adventure,* ed. Sir E. Denison Ross (London 1933).

Shirazi, 'Abdi Beyg. *Takmeleh al-Akhbar,* ed. 'Abdol-Hoseyn Nava'i (Tehran, 1369/1990).

Shirazi, F. *The Veil Unveiled : The Hijab in Modern Culture* (Gainsville, Fl., 2001).

Shirazi, Mirza Saleh. *Majmu'eh-ye safarnamehha-ye Mirza Saleh Shirazi*, ed. Gholam Hoseyn Mirza Saleh (Tehran, 1364/1985).

Shirvani, Jamal al-Din Khalil. *Nozhat al-Majales* ed. Mohammad Amin Riyahi (Tehran, 1366/1987).

Silva y Figueroa, Don Garcia de. *Comentarios de la embajada que de parte del rey de España Don Felipe III hizo al rey Xa Abas de Persia* 2 vols. (Madrid, 1903).

Simforoosh, N. "A decrease in incidence of syphilis in Iran and the effect of Islamic rules in controlling sexually transmitted diseases," *Medical Journal of the Islamic Republic of Iran* 12 (1998), p. 283.

Sirjani, 'Ali Akbar Sa'idi. *Vaqaye'-ye Ettefaqiyeh* (Tehran, 1361/1982).

Siyaqi-Nezam, *Fotuhat-e Homayun (Les Victoires augustes, 1007/1598)*, edited and translation by Chahryar Adle, unpublished thesis (Paris, 1976).

Skjærvø, Prods Oktor. "Homosexuality," *Encyclopedia Iranica*.

———. "Middle Eastern Literature: Persian," in C. J. Summers, ed., *The Gay and Lesbian Literary Heritage*, New York, 1995, pp. 485-86.

Smith, E. & Dwight, H.G.O. *Researches of the Rev. E. Smith. & Rev. Dwight, H. G. O in Armenia* 2 vols. (Boston, 1833).

Smith, Ronald Bishop. *The First Age. Of the Portuguese Embassies, Navigations and Peregrinations in Persia (1507-1524)* (Bethesda, 1970).

Soudavar-Farmanfarmaian, Fatema. "Haft Qalam Arayish: Cosmetics in the Iranian World," *Iranian Studies* 33/3-4 (2000), pp. 285-326.

Southgate, Horatio. *A Tour Through Armenia and Mesopotamia*, 2 vols. (New York: D. Appleton & Co, 1840).

Southgate, Minoo S. "Men, Women, and Boys: Love and Sex in the Works of Sa'di," *Iranian Studies* 17/4 (1984), pp. 413-52.

Sprachman, Paul. *Suppressed Persian. An Anthology of Forbidden Literature* (Costa Mesa, 1995).

————. "Le beau garçon sans merci: The Homoerotic Tale in Arabic and Persian" in *Homoeroticism in Classical Arabic Literature,* ed. J. Wright and K. Rowson, New York, 1997, pp. 192-209.

————. "The Poetics of Hijab in the Satire of Iraj Mirza," in Kambiz Islam ed. *Iran and Iranian Studies* (Princeton, 1998), pp. 341-57.

Spuler, Berthold. *Iran in Früh-Islamischer Zeit* (Wiesbaden, 1952).

Stack, Edward. *Six Months in Persia* 2 vols. (New York, 1882).

Stanfield-Johnson, Rosemary. "Yuzbashi-ye Kurd and 'Abd al-Mu'min the Uzbek: A Tale of Revenge in the *Dastan* of Husayn-e Kurd," in Soussie Rastegar & Anna Vanzan eds. *Muraqqa'e Sharqi. Studies in Honor of Peter Chelkowski* (San Marino, 2007), pp. 167-81.

Stern, Henry A. *Dawnings in the East; with biblical, historical, and statistical notices of persons and places visited during a mission to the Jews in Persia, Coordistan, and Mesopotamia* (London, 1854).

Strauszens, Joh. Jansz. *Sehr schwere, wiederwärtige, und Denckwürdige Reysen* (Amsterdam, 1678).

Stuart, Emmeline M. *Doctors in Persia* (London, n.d. [1921?]).

Surieu, Robert. *Sarve Naz, essai sur les représentation érotiques et l'amour dans l'Iran d'autrefois* (Geneva, 1976).

Sykes, Ella. *Through Persia on a Side-saddle* (London, 1901).

————. "A Talk About Persia and Its Women," *National Geographic Magazine* 21/10 (1910), pp. 847-66.

Sykes, Percy M. *Ten Thousand Miles in Persia or Eight Years in Iran* (New York, 1902).

Tabataba'i, Sayyed Jamal Torabi ed., *Athar-e Bastani-ye Adharbayjan* 2 vols (Tehran, 1355).

Tabataba'i, 'Allamah Sayyid Muhammad Husayn. *Shi'ite Islam*, translated by Seyyed Hossein Nasr (Albany, 1975).

Tabataba'i, Modarresi. *Farmanha-ye Torkmanan-e Qara-Qoyunlu va Aq-Qoyunlu* (Qom, 1352/1973).

Tafsir al- 'Ayyashi (Qomm, 1380H/1960-61).

Tafsir of Ibn Kathir.

[http://www.qtafsir.com/index.php?option=com_content&task=view& id=189&Itemid=36].

Taj al-Saltaneh, *Crowning Anguish: memoirs of a Qajar princess from the harem to modernity 1884-1914*, translated into English by Anna Vanzan and Amin Neshati (Washington DC, 1993).

Tancoigne, J.M. *A Narrative of a Journey into Persia* (London: William Wright, 1820).

Tapper, Nancy. "The Women's Subsociety among the Shahsevan Nomads of Iran," in Lois Beck and Nikki Keddie eds. *Women in the Muslim World* (Cambridge, 1978), pp. 374-98.

Tarbiyat 3 vols. (Tehran, Ketabkhaneh-ye Melli, 1377/1998). (newspaper)

Tashakkori, Abbas, Thompson, Vaida D. and Mehryar, Amir H. "Iranian Adolescents' Intended Age of Marriage and Desired family Size," *Journal of Mariage and the Family* 49 (1989), pp. 917-27.

Tavernier, Jean-Baptiste. *Voyages en Perse et description de ce royaume* (Paris, 1930).

Tavoosi, A. Zaferani, A., Enzevaei, A., Tajik, P. and Ahmadinezhad, Z. "Knowledge and attitude towards HIV/AIDS among Iranian students." *BMC Public Health* 4 (2004), p. 17.

Teflisi, Habish b. Ebrahim b. Mohammad. *Bayan al-Sana'at* ed. Iraj Afshar, *Iran Farhang Zamin*, pp. 279-458.

Tenreiro, António. *Itinerários da India a Portugal por terra.* António Baião ed. (Coimbra, 1923).

Teymur, Ebrahim. *Qarardad-e 1890 rezhi-ye tahrim-e tanbaku* (Tehran, 1362/1983).

Thot, L. "Das persische Rechssystem," *Zeitschrift für vergleichende Rechtswisenschaft* 22 (1909), pp. 348-429.

Tucker, Judith. *Gender and Islamic History* (Washington DC, 1993).

Tusi, Asadi. *Lughat al-Furs*, ed. Mohammad Dabir-Siyaqi (Tehran, 1336/1957).

US Army, *Area Handbook for Iran* (Washington DC, 1963).

Vahid Qazvini, Mohammad Taher. *Tarikh-e Jahanara-ye 'Abbasi* ed. Sayyed Sa'id Mir Mohammad Sadeq (Tehran, 1383/2004).

Vahraman, Faraxvmart i. *The Book of a Thousand Judgements (A Sasanian Law-Book)*, transcribed and translated from Pahlavi into Russian by Anahit Perikhian; translated into English by Nina Garsoïan (Costa Mesa, 1997).

Vakil al-Dowleh, Hoseyn Qoli Maqsudlu. *Mokhabarat-e Astarabad* eds. Iraj Afshar and Mohammad Rasul Daryagasht 2 vols. (Tehran, 1363/1984).

Valeh Qazvini, Mohammad Yusef. *Iran dar Zaman-e Shah Safi va 'Abbas Dovvom.* ed. Mohammad Reza Nasiri (Tehran, 1380/2001).

Valentyn, François. *Oud en Nieuw Oost-Indien* 5 vols. (Dordrecht, 1726), vol. 5.

Vambery, Arminius. *Meine Wanderungen und Erlebnisse in Persien* (Pesth, 1867).

Van Sommer, Annie and Zwemer, Samuel. *Our Moslem Sisters* (New York, 1907).

Varjavand, Parviz. *Sima-ye Tarikh va Farhang-e Qazvin* 3 vols. (Tehran, 1377/1998).

Vasefi, Zeyn al-Din Mahmud. *Badaye' al-Vaqaye'*, 2 vols. ed. Aleksandar Baldruf (Tehran, 1350/1971).

Vendidad see [http://www.avesta.org/vendidad/vd_tc.htm].

Vieille, Paul. "Iranian Women in Family Alliance and Sexual Politics," in Lois Beck and Nikki Keddie eds. *Women in the Muslim World* (Cambridge, 1978), pp. 451-72.

Von Kotzebue, Moritz. *Narrative of a Journey into Persia in the suite of the Imperial Russian Embassy in the year 1817* (Philadelphia: Carey & Sons, 1820).

Von Poser, Heinrich. *Als Schlesischer Adliger in Iran und Indien.* ed. Helmhart Kanus-Credé (Allendorf a/d Eder: Antigone, 2003).

Von Rosen, Maud. *Persian Pilgrimage* (London, 1937).

Wafer, J. "Muhammad and Male Homosexuality," in Murray and Roscoe, eds., 1997, pp. 87-96.

————. "Persian Mystical Literature," in Murray and Roscoe, *Islamic Homosexualities*, pp. 117-31.

————. "Vision and Passion," in Murray and Roscoe, *Islamic Homosexualities*, pp. 107-31.

Wagner, M. *Travels in Persia, Georgia, and Koordistan.* 3 vols. (London, 1856 [Westmead, 1971]).

Waring, Edward Scott. *A Tour to Sheeraz* (London, 1807).

Warzeé, Dorothy de. *Peeps into Persia* (London, 1913).

Wicki, Joseph ed. *Documenta Indica* 16 vols. (Rome, 1948-84).

Wikan, Unni. *Behind the Veil in Arabia: Women in Oman* (Chicago, 1991).

Wills, C. J. *Persia as it is* (London 1886).

————. *In the Land of the Lion and the Sun* (London, 1893).

Wilson, A.T. *Southwest-Persia. Letters and Diary of a Young Political Officer 1907-1914* (Oxford, 1941).

Wilson, Peter Lamborn. "Contemplation of the Unbearded. The Rubaiyyat of Awhadoddin Kermani," *Paidika* V 3-4 (1995), pp. 13-26.

Wilson, S.G. *Persian Life and Customs* (New York, 1895).

Windt, Harry de. *A Ride to India across Persia and Baluchistan* (London, 1891).

Wishard, John G. *Twenty Years in Persia. A Narrative of Life under the Last Three Shahs* (New York: Fleming H. Revell, 1908).

Woods, John E. *The Timurid Dynasty, Papers on Inner Asia* no. 14 (Bloomington, Indiana 1990).

Woodsmall, Ruth Frances. *Moslem women enter a new world* (New York, 1936).

Wright, Denis. *The Persians Amongst the English* (London, 1985).

————. *The English Amongst the Persians* (London, 2001).

al-Ya'qubi, Abu'l-'Abbas Ahmad b. Abi Ya'qub. *Kitab al- Buldan* ed. M.J. de Goeje (Leiden, 1892), p. 298, translated into French by Gaston Wiet as *Les Pays* (Cairo, 1937).

Yaghma'i, Esma'il Honar. *Jandaq va Qumis dar avakher-e dowreh-ye Qajar*, ed. by 'Abdol-Karim Hekmat Yaghma'i (Tehran, 1363/1984).

Yakubovich, Ilya. "Marriage Contract," *Encyclopedia Iranica.*

Yamauchi, E.M. "Cultic Prostitution: A Case Study in Cultural Diffusion," in H.A. Hoffner ed. *Orient and Occident* (Kevelaer, 1973), pp. 213-22.

Yashts and Yasna, see James Darmesteter and L.H. Mills in Max Müller ed. *Sacred Books of the East* (New York, 1898), vols. 23 and 31.

Yassari, N. "Who is a child" in: Rutten ed., *Recht van de Islam* 22 Teksten van het op 18 juni 2004 te Leiden gehouden tweeentwintigste RIMO-symposium (Maastricht, 2005), pp. 17-30.

Zahedi, Ashraf. "State ideology and the status of Iranian war widows," *International Feminist Journal of Politics*, June 2006, pp. 267-86.

Zahereddini, Badri. *Medizinische Topographie der iranischen Stadt Malayer* (Eerlangen, 1966).

Zand, Shahin 'Oliya. "'Avamel-e zamineh-saz tan dadan-e zanan beh ruspigari," in *Maqalat-e Avvalin Hamayesh-e Melli-ye Asibha-ye Ejtema'i dar Iran, Khordad 1381* 5 vols. (Tehran, 1386, 2007), pp. 17-39.

Zargooshi, J. "Characteristics of gonorrhoea in Kermanshah, Iran," *Sexually Transmitted Infections* 78 (2002), pp. 460-461.

Zarit, Jerry. "Intimate Look of the Iranian Male," in Arno Schmitt and Jehoeda Sofer eds. *Sexuality and Eroticism Among Males in Moslem Societies* (New York, London, 1992), pp. 55-60.

Zarrinkub, 'Abdol-Hoseyn. *Az Kucheh-ye Rendan* (Tehran, 1364/1985).

Zirak-Zadah, T. Delavarian, H.; Bahavar, M.A.; Majidi, V.; Yaminifar, R. and P. Masoumi, "Penicillin-resistant strains of Neisseria gonorrhoeae in Shahre-Now." *Tropical Doctor* 7/2 (1977), pp. 57-58.

WEBSITES

[http://www.cais-soas.com/CAIS/Law/family_law.htm]

[http://www.cais-soas.com/CAIS/Women/women_ancient_iran.htm]

[http://www.qtafsir.com/index.php?option=com_content&task=view&
id=189&Itemid=36]. = Tafsir ibn Kathir.

[http://www.usc.edu/dept/MSA/reference/reference.html] Bukhari and
Muslim, Collection of Traditions

INDEX

www.ingramcontent.com/pod-product-compliance
Lightning Source LLC
Chambersburg PA
CBHW021842020426
42334CB00013B/154